PLATO'S *CHARMIDES*

The *Charmides* is a difficult and enigmatic dialogue traditionally considered one of Plato's Socratic dialogues. This book provides a close text commentary on the dialogue which tracks particular motifs throughout. These notably include the characterisation of Critias, Charmides, and Socrates; the historical context and subtext; literary features such as irony and foreshadowing; the philosophical context, especially how the dialogue looks back to more traditional Socratic dialogues and forward to dialogues traditionally placed in Plato's middle and late period; and, most importantly, the philosophical and logical details of the arguments and their dialectical function. A new translation of the dialogue is included in an Appendix. This will be essential reading for all scholars and students of Plato and of ancient philosophy. This title is also available as open access on Cambridge Core.

VOULA TSOUNA is a Professor in the Department of Philosophy at the University of California, Santa Barbara. Her other books include *Philodemus: On Choices and Avoidances* (1995), a critical edition and commentary on one of the Herculaneum papyri on Epicurean ethics, which received the Theodor Mommsen Award; *The Epistemology of the Cyrenaic School* (1998), recently translated into modern Greek (2019); *The Ethics of Philodemus* (2007); and a collection of essays on the Socratics and the Hellenistic schools (2012). She is currently preparing a monograph on the *Republic* Books 8 and 9 and another on *The Normativity of Nature in Hellenistic Philosophy*, to appear in the series Cambridge Elements in Ancient Philosophy, edited by James Warren.

PLATO'S *CHARMIDES*

An Interpretative Commentary

VOULA TSOUNA

University of California, Santa Barbara

CAMBRIDGE
UNIVERSITY PRESS

Shaftesbury Road, Cambridge CB2 8EA, United Kingdom

One Liberty Plaza, 20th Floor, New York, NY 10006, USA

477 Williamstown Road, Port Melbourne, VIC 3207, Australia

314–321, 3rd Floor, Plot 3, Splendor Forum, Jasola District Centre, New Delhi – 110025, India

103 Penang Road, #05–06/07, Visioncrest Commercial, Singapore 238467

Cambridge University Press is part of Cambridge University Press & Assessment, a department of the University of Cambridge.

We share the University's mission to contribute to society through the pursuit of education, learning and research at the highest international levels of excellence.

www.cambridge.org
Information on this title: www.cambridge.org/9781009364928

DOI: 10.1017/9781009036610

First published 2022
First paperback edition 2023

A catalogue record for this publication is available from the British Library

Library of Congress Cataloging-in-Publication data
NAMES: Tsouna, Voula, author.
TITLE: Plato's Charmides : an interpretative commentary / Voula Tsouna.
DESCRIPTION: Cambridge, United Kingdom ; New York, NY, USA : Cambridge University Press, 2022. | Includes bibliographical references and index.
IDENTIFIERS: LCCN 2021035319 (print) | LCCN 2021035320 (ebook) | ISBN 9781316511114 (hardback) | ISBN 9781009005319 (paperback) | ISBN 9781009036610 (ebook)
SUBJECTS: LCSH: Plato. Charmides. | Ethics – Early works to 1800. | Knowledge, Theory of – Early works to 1800. | BISAC: PHILOSOPHY / History & Surveys / Ancient & Classical
CLASSIFICATION: LCC B366 .T76 2022 (print) | LCC B366 (ebook) | DDC 184–dc23
LC record available at https://lccn.loc.gov/2021035319
LC ebook record available at https://lccn.loc.gov/2021035320

ISBN   978-1-316-51111-4   Hardback
ISBN   978-1-009-36492-8   Paperback

Contents

This title is part of the Cambridge University Press *Flip it Open* Open Access Books program and has been "flipped" from a traditional book to an Open Access book through the program.

Flip it Open sells books through regular channels, treating them at the outset in the same way as any other book; they are part of our library collections for Cambridge Core, and sell as hardbacks and ebooks. The one crucial difference is that we make an upfront commitment that when each of these books meets a set revenue threshold we make them available to everyone Open Access via Cambridge Core.

This paperback edition has been released as part of our Open Access commitment and we would like to use this as an opportunity to thank the libraries and other buyers who have helped us flip this and the other titles in the program to Open Access.

To see the full list of libraries that we know have contributed to *Flip it Open*, as well as the other titles in the program please visit www.cambridge.org/fio-acknowledgements

Preface and Acknowledgements

I have been intrigued by the *Charmides* ever since I first studied it as a graduate student at King's College, Cambridge. It seemed familiar in some ways but entirely unfamiliar in others, and although I worked through the argument as best I could, I eventually put the dialogue aside with a sense of unease and the determination to return to it at some future time. In fact, it proved impossible to switch focus altogether. I kept thinking about the *Charmides* even as I was working on other topics and acquired what might be described as an obsession with that work and the challenges that it poses.

The few articles that I published partly or wholly on the *Charmides* over a period of approximately two decades are indicative of the ways in which I gradually developed a distinctive approach to the work. It is appropriate therefore, first, to extend my thanks to the colleagues, students, editors, and referees whose comments led to substantial revisions and improvements of these papers before their publication. I wrote the first draft of 'Socrates' Attack on Intellectualism in the *Charmides*' (1998) during a lengthy stay in Cambridge and owe a debt of gratitude to Myles Burnyeat for extensive discussion of the paper and of the central argument of the dialogue. A later version of that paper was published in a special volume of *Apeiron* and benefited from the editors' comments. Two further articles, 'Interprétations socratiques de la connaissance de soi' (2000) and 'Interpretations of Socratic Self-Knowledge' (2004), were drafted in Cambridge and delivered in Paris, Athens, and Delphi. I am grateful for the input I received from these audiences, the referees of the relevant journals, the members of the B Caucus of the Cambridge Faculty of Classics, and, moreover, John Cooper, Michael Frede, and Michel Narcy. Later in time, well into the process of composing a full draft of the book and while holding a Senior Fellowship of the Onassis Foundation (2016), I wrote 'What Is the Subject of Plato's *Charmides*?' for the

Festschrift in honour of John Glucker. I thank the Onassis Foundation for its generous support and the editors of the Festschrift for their remarks.

A full draft of approximately two-thirds of the book was produced in the years 2015 and 2016. I had the privilege of holding a Beaufort Visiting Fellowship at St John's College, Cambridge in Lent term 2015. I wish to thank the College for its legendary hospitality and Malcolm Schofield for our almost daily conversations on the *Charmides* and much else. I returned to Cambridge in Lent term 2016 as Distinguished Visiting Scholar at Christ's College, Cambridge. I am grateful to Christ's College for providing ideal living conditions, to the college staff for their practical guidance, and to the Fellows and students for a uniquely stimulating intellectual environment. In particular, it is a pleasure to thank Gabor Betegh and David Sedley for many conversations about the *Charmides* and the different ways in which my own manuscript could take its final shape. I am also indebted to James Warren for his incisive remarks on the topic of the so-called craft analogy and to Matthew Duncombe for discussion of the logical behaviour of relatives. The basis for most of the chapters of this book lies in the lectures I gave on the *Charmides* at the University of Edinburgh in the capacity of the 2016 Centenary Fellow of the Scottish Philosophical Association. I thank the SPA for this honour, the University of Edinburgh for hosting the lectures, Ina Kupreeva for her kind hospitality, and the colleagues and students in the audience for their remarks. Sara Broadie's interventions were especially helpful and our correspondence in the aftermath of the lectures has influenced my interpretation of the opening scene of the *Charmides* and of 'the best method of enquiry' proposed by Socrates.

Moving on to the other side of the Atlantic, I extend my warm thanks to UC Santa Barbara for the generosity and flexibility it has shown over the last several years in order to facilitate my research and professional activities in the USA and overseas. In addition to two years of sabbatical leave (2009–10 and 2015–16), both the university and my own department have supported the project of this monograph by enabling me to arrange my teaching obligations, administrative duties, and academic resources in ways that were effective and compatible with the necessities of conducting research. I am grateful to the colleagues who recommended philosophical literature relevant to the topics treated in the *Charmides*. In particular, I thank Matthew Hanser for his suggestions regarding the subjects of shame and modesty and Tony Anderson for a crash course on reflexive relations and the logical problems that they give rise to.

My students, undergraduates as well as graduates, have been an inexhaustible source of learning and inspiration. My understanding of the *Charmides* gradually became richer and deeper by teaching Plato to the undergraduates and by running graduate seminars on Platonic dialogues traditionally classified as belonging to different periods of Plato's production. Especially important for my project have been two graduate seminars focused on the *Charmides* and taught several years apart from each other. I owe a debt to all the participants, and especially to Michael Augustin and Robert McIntyre, both of whom have subsequently earned their PhDs and joined the academic ranks.

I have had the opportunity to present material from the book in invited talks and express my gratitude to the institutions and colleagues that hosted these talks, as well as the audiences that attended them. Specifically, I thank the Philosophy and the Classics Departments of the University of Patras for inviting me and Panos Dimas (University of Oslo) to jointly give a three-day seminar on the *Charmides* in 2014. I am grateful to Mauro Bonazzi for the invitation to give a lengthy presentation of the Argument from Benefit at the University of Milan in the spring of 2017, and for his incisive and helpful comments. In that same year I was asked to give a talk on the use of the so-called craft analogy in the *Charmides* at the University of Leiden and received constructive and detailed comments from Frans de Haas and Jaap Mansfeld. These led me to revisit the debate between Socrates and Critias in respect of the craft analogy and rewrite the relevant chapter in the form of a talk that I gave at UC Berkeley in the winter of 2018. I am very grateful to the audience for the particularly enjoyable discussion, and to Tony Long and Sara Magrin for follow-up written comments. The penultimate version of that chapter was presented at UC San Diego at the invitation of Monte Johnson and the UCSD Philosophy Department. The discussion that followed gave me a new and illuminating perspective on certain aspects of Plato's argument.

Few people read the complete manuscript in the final stages of its preparation. Alexander Nehamas sent me extensive comments on Chapters 1 and 2 with the result that I made substantial changes to both. I thank him for his critical remarks, his kind words, and his unwavering support. Paul Kalligas has followed my thinking about this book since its inception, has debated with me virtually every bit of Plato's text, and has influenced my understanding of the drama as well as the argument of the *Charmides*. I would like to express my gratitude for everything that he has contributed to this project and for our ongoing dialogue on the philosophy of Plato for almost four decades.

I wish to extend my warmest thanks to the two referees chosen by CUP for the thoughtful, incisive, and detailed work that they did on the manuscript. All their comments have been taken into account and, I believe, led to improvements. My greatest debt of gratitude is to David Sedley. It is impossible to convey how much the book owes to him without getting into cumbersome detail. His comments touched on every aspect of the book and concerned form as well as content. They included substantive philosophical and literary issues, textual and philological points, matters of style, grammar, and punctuation, and a thorough overhaul of the translation in the Appendix. I am profoundly grateful to him for this massive undertaking and the time and effort that it must have cost him.

The book went into production in the early summer of 2021. Many thanks to Michael Sharp for his characteristic patience and courtesy and for his wise advice all along. Also, warm thanks to Sally Evans-Darby for her prompt copy-editing, to Judy Oliver for the Index, and to the Project Manager Akash Datchinamurthy as well as the staff of Cambridge University Press for an impeccable process of publication.

I wrote the book in two continents and three locations: UCSB, Cambridge, and Athens. All three are important to me in different ways and each of them is linked to a phase or aspect of my life, even though Athens is my birthplace and therefore has a special hold on my emotions and imagination. In all three places I have lived with my family for extended periods. I have tried to temper the hours of solitude devoted to intellectual work with time in the company of my husband, Richard McKirahan, our daughter, Eleni, and, for ten years, our dog, Spot. I am thankful for their affection and support and for the happiness that they have brought into my life. This book is for Richard, with all my love.

Athens, 29 August 2021

CHAPTER I

Introduction

The *Charmides* is a strangely attractive and unsettling work.[1] Narrated by Socrates to a 'noble friend' whose identity remains undisclosed, it unfolds as both a powerful drama of characters and a complex philosophical argument assessed in vastly different ways by interpreters of the dialogue. According, for instance, to T. Godfrey Tuckey, author of the first analytic monograph on the *Charmides*,

> no better introduction to Plato's thought could be devised. The *Charmides* forces the reader to study the historical background of the early dialogues. It shows us Plato's political and educational thought in formation. It helps us to see the origins of those logical and metaphysical theories which Plato later constructed to provide a framework for his ethical doctrine. Above all, it forces us to think hard and analyse meanings with care and precision, compelling clear thought by the form of its argument as well as advocating it by its content.[2]

Paul Shorey, however, provides a check to such enthusiasm: 'the dialogue involves so much metaphysical subtlety that some critics have pronounced it late, some spurious, and many feel the same distaste for it that they do for the subtlest parts of the *Theaetetus*'.[3] Both statements are outdated by over half a century and neither is entirely defensible. But, taken together, they convey an idea of the range of readings that the *Charmides* is susceptible to and also indicate what I take to be a peculiarity of this dialogue: perhaps more than any other Platonic composition, everything about the *Charmides* has been debated, all of it at once: not merely this or that aspect of the drama or the argument, but the nature and purpose of the work taken as a whole. The present monograph

---

[1] Gould 1955, 36, groups together the *Charmides*, *Hippias Minor*, and the first book of the *Republic* on the grounds that they have at least one thing in common: they may all be called Plato's 'problem plays' in the sense that they have all caused controversy regarding their real significance.
[2] Tuckey 1951, 105.   [3] Shorey 1933, 103.

is no exception. It has the form of a running commentary that closely follows Plato's text and gradually develops a new and integral reading of the dialogue. I hope to be able to defend that reading thoroughly and, as far as possible, convincingly. Nonetheless, I believe that the dialogue is deliberately open-ended and, at times, deliberately ambiguous. Partly for that reason it remains open to diverging approaches and multiple viewpoints. We may gain a preliminary understanding of why or how this happens by surveying the dialogue's salient features: the story, the characters, the subject, the argument, the interplay between the dramatic and the philosophical elements of the dialogue, the intertextual connections that it evokes, and its declared objectives.

1 An Interpretative Summary of the Dialogue

The *Charmides* is a narrated dialogue, artfully crafted and masterfully executed. Drama and philosophical argument are interwoven in a story whose external frame is drawn by Socrates as narrator at the beginning of the dialogue but not at its end. He is represented as relaying to an anonymous friend an encounter that he has had some time in the past with two fellow Athenians, the young Charmides and the guardian and relative of this latter, Critias. Socrates' narrative consists of the particulars of that encounter and exactly coincides with the dialogue's content.

In the unusually long prologue, Socrates relates that, upon his return to Athens from the battle of Potidaea, he went to the palaestra of Taureas where he found many of his acquaintances, including Chaerephon and Critias, son of Callaeschrus. In the ensuing narrative, after giving them news from the camp, he enquires about his own concerns, namely what is the present state of philosophy and whether there are any young men distinguished for wisdom or beauty or both. Critias answers that his cousin and ward, Charmides, is notable for both and, indeed, Charmides' entrance confirms that the young man has a splendid stature and appearance. Socrates proposes to examine whether his soul is just as perfect as his body and Critias volunteers to facilitate the undertaking by summoning Charmides on the pretext that Socrates has a cure for the morning headaches bothering the young man. Charmides' approach causes a stir in the male company and sexual arousal in Socrates who, however, shows himself capable of mastering himself. He answers affirmatively Charmides' question whether he knows the headache's remedy, claims that the remedy consists in a leaf and a charm, and appeals to the authority of Zalmoxis, a divinity of the Getae in Thrace, to convince the youth that the part cannot be treated independently of the whole and, therefore, Charmides' head and body cannot be cured unless his soul is first treated by means of charms consisting in 'beautiful words'. He stresses the paramount role of *sôphrosynê*, temperance,[4] as the cause of everything good for a person, and underscores the importance of finding out whether temperance is present in one's soul. For his own part, Charmides agrees to submit his soul to the charm before being given the remedy for the headache and, after a short speech in which Socrates traces Charmides' noble lineage, he agrees to investigate together with Socrates the question of whether or not he possesses *sôphrosynê*, temperance – a cardinal virtue of Greek culture, literally associated with the possession of a sound and healthy mind, widely believed to involve self-control and a sort of self-knowledge, and carrying civic and political connotations as well.[5]

Sôphrosynê, temperance, and the successive attempts to define it turn out to be the main subject of the conversation, first between Socrates and young Charmides, and then between Socrates and the mature and experienced Critias. According to Charmides' first definition, 'temperance is to do everything in an orderly and quiet way'; it is, in other words, a sort of quietness (159b2–5). Working from Charmides' own set of beliefs, Socrates brings counterexamples to show that, in fact, temperance is only contingently related to quietness and occasionally is more closely related to the opposite of quietness. Charmides then proposes a second definition, that temperance is modesty or a sense of shame (160e3–5), which is also refuted. Charmides owns himself convinced by the argument, at which point he proposes a third definition which he says he has heard from someone else, namely that temperance is 'doing one's own' (161b5–6). It becomes clear that the author of the definition is Critias who gets increasingly angry because Charmides accepts the naïve assumption that '*doing* one's own' is equivalent to '*making* one's own' and hence is unable to defend the definition. So, Critias jumps into the discussion and takes over the argument. On the authority of Hesiod, he draws a distinction between *doing* a thing and *making* something and he modifies accordingly the claim advanced earlier by Charmides: now temperance is defined as the doing

---

[4] There is no English word that can fully capture the meaning of σωφροσύνη (translit. *sôphrosynê*) and all its connotations and nuances. Following most translators (e.g. Lamb, Sprague, Jowett), I render 'σωφροσύνη' by 'temperance' and 'σώφρων' by 'the temperate person' or 'the temperate man'. Other translations include 'modesty', which, however, lies closer to the meaning of αἰδώς (a sense of shame), and 'discipline' (Moore and Raymond 2019), which, nonetheless, carries strong behavioural connotations and, moreover, does not adequately capture the epistemic aspects of the Greek notion of σωφροσύνη.

[5] See, notably, the classic study by North 1966.

of good things or the performance of useful and beneficial actions (cf. 163e1–3). This variant too gets refuted when Socrates points out that, assuming that this definition is true, it would seem to follow that the experts in various fields may be temperate and yet ignorant of their temperance (163e3–164d3).

Rather than accept this implication, Critias appeals to Apollo and the Delphic oracle to propose another, altogether new definition: that temperance is knowing oneself (165b4). It is the *epistêmê* of oneself (165c4–7). The meaning of '*epistêmê*' in this and other Platonic contexts is controversial. Up to a certain point in the dialogue, the interlocutors of the *Charmides* use the term interchangeably with '*technê*'[6] to refer to all sorts of arts and crafts, and also sciences or disciplines. Insofar as each of these latter presupposes the mastery of interrelations and rules within its own domain, the most accurate translation of '*epistêmê*' and '*technê*' is 'scientific or expert understanding'. As a shorthand, I follow the scholarly convention of rendering '*epistêmê*' by 'science' or (expert) 'knowledge', and '*technê*' by 'art', 'craft', or 'expertise'. But it should be borne in mind that these expressions are intended to entail the ideas of causal explanation and complete understanding.[7] (This point will become clearer in the later chapters of the book.)

To continue with the summary of the *Charmides*: Critias appears to expect that his definition of temperance in terms of knowing oneself would be acceptable to Socrates (165b3–4). And indeed it evokes in the reader's mind Socrates' own quest for self-knowledge in the *Apology*, the terms in which he develops his conception of this latter, the connection that he draws between self-examination and self-knowledge, and his claim that the unexamined life is not worth living (*Ap.* 38a). Nonetheless, Socrates declares that he cannot accept Critias' definition without submitting it to examination (165b5–c4). On my reading of the text, he thus makes clear that the argument to follow principally regards not his own beliefs about self-knowledge, but Critias' conception of temperance as self-knowledge, whatever that turns out to be.

To begin this enquiry, Socrates uses analogies from specific sciences or arts (*epistêmai* or *technai*) such as medicine and house-building to press the idea that temperance as an *epistêmê* must have an object distinct from itself, and he asks what that object might be (165c4–166b6). Critias argues that, on the contrary, the *epistêmê* equivalent to temperance differs from all

---

[6] I shall say more about this both at the end of the Introduction and in later chapters.
[7] See the argument by Nehamas 1984, which, nonetheless, focuses on Plato's later dialogues.

other *epistêmai* or *technai* precisely because it does not have an object distinct from itself (166b7–c3). From this point onwards, the interlocutors favour the use of '*epistêmê*' over that of '*technê*', presumably because they are focusing primarily on the cognitive aspects of the virtue under discussion.[8] Eventually, with the help of Socrates, Critias articulates his final definition of temperance as follows: temperance is the only *epistêmê* which is of itself and the other *epistêmai* and the privation of *epistêmê*,[9] but of no other object (166e4–167a8). As Socrates phrases it, temperance is an '*epistêmê epistêmês*' (usually rendered as 'knowledge of knowledge' or 'science of science'),[10] but not an *epistêmê* of some distinct object or subject-matter (as well).[11] As we ourselves might put it, Critias contends that temperance is the only knowledge or science which is both strictly reflexive and higher-order: it governs everything that qualifies as an *epistêmê* just insofar as it is an *epistêmê*[12] in addition to being of itself.

Now Socrates wants to know, first, whether such an *epistêmê* could be conceivable or credible and, second, even assuming that it were possible, whether it would be appropriately beneficial (167a9–b4). The elenchus that follows addresses these two questions in turn. Initially, Socrates develops an analogical argument (I call it the Argument from Relatives: 167c8–169c2) which examines different groups of relatives that Socrates takes to be analogous to *epistêmê*: perceptual relatives such as sight and hearing, other psychological relatives such as desire and belief, quantitative relatives such as half and double or larger and smaller, and, finally, cases such as motion and heat. Critias comes to accept that, in some of these cases, strictly reflexive constructions appear very odd and that, in other cases, such constructions seem entirely incoherent. Hence, he reluctantly accepts the tentative conclusion drawn by Socrates that a strictly reflexive *epistêmê* likewise seems incredible if not altogether impossible.

In the next phase of the elenchus, Socrates proposes that they concede for the sake of the argument the possibility of reflexive knowledge in order to address the issue of benefit: assuming that temperance can be an *epistêmê*

---

[8] Compare Plt. 292b: 'we have said that the kingly art is one of the *epistêmai*, I think'. First, the expertise of the statesman is called a *technê* but then it is called an *epistêmê* to emphasise the cognitive aspects of statesmanship, in particular the capacity to form accurate judgements and issue commands accordingly. On Plato's use of synecdoche, see Hulme Kozey 2018 and the remarks in Chapter 8, 172 and note 7.

[9] This exactly corresponds to the text and gets articulated in terms of knowing what one knows and what one does not know (167a5–7).

[10] See notes 5 and 6 in this chapter.   [11] This point is controversial and shall be discussed later.

[12] Hence reflexivity is preserved all the way through. On this point, see Chapters 9 and 10, *passim*, and also Chapter 11, 271 and *passim*.

of *epistêmê* itself but of no other object, what good might it bring? On the basis of this assumption, Socrates develops the last, very impressive argument of the *Charmides* (I dub it the Argument from Benefit: 169c3–175a8). On the reading that I shall defend, this is a cumulative argument which advances in successive stages. First, conceding for the sake of the investigation that an '*epistêmê epistêmês*' may be possible, Socrates questions whether it entails knowledge-what as well as knowledge-that: can its possessor tell *what things* one knows or doesn't know, in addition to being able to judge *that* one person possesses some knowledge but another person doesn't? As the elenchus suggests, since, according to Critias, temperance is an *epistêmê* of itself but of no distinct object or subject-matter, and assuming (as Socrates does) that the content of an *epistêmê* is determined by its proprietary object, i.e. what the *epistêmê* is of, it seems to follow that temperance cannot be substantive knowledge of content (knowledge-what) but only discriminatory knowledge (knowledge-that). Namely, it is a knowledge that enables the temperate person to distinguish knowers from non-knowers, without being able to tell, however, what these knowers are knowers *of*. Second, Socrates points out, counterfactually, the great benefits that temperance would yield if it were substantive knowledge. Then, he briefly suggests that, since temperance is not in fact substantive knowledge and cannot offer great benefits, perhaps it may offer certain lesser benefits. Both interlocutors, however, dismiss this possibility, for it seems absurd.

Third, to help the argument, Socrates proposes another major concession. Let us assume, he says, that temperance is, in fact, substantive understanding entailing knowledge-what: it is knowledge of *what things* one knows and doesn't, as well as knowledge *that* one has some knowledge but another person doesn't. To consider this hypothesis, Socrates proposes a thought-experiment about an imaginary society ruled by temperate rulers endowed with *epistêmê epistêmês*. And although he grants that such a society would function efficiently under the rule of the 'science of science', nonetheless he questions that the city would do well and the citizens be happy. Fourth, continuing with the argument, Socrates extracts from Critias the admission that, in truth, happiness is not the proprietary object of temperance or the 'science of science', but the proprietary object of another *epistêmê*, namely the *epistêmê* of good and evil. Finally, he completes the elenchus by refuting Critias' last suggestion, namely that since the 'science of science' is supposed to be higher-order on account of its reflexivity and hence govern all the other sciences, it governs the science of good and evil as well and can appropriate the peculiar object of this latter. However, Socrates retorts, since the 'science of science' is supposed to have no object other than *epistêmê* simpliciter, it cannot appropriate the proprietary object of any particular *epistêmê*, including, of course, the science of good and evil. Nor can it appropriate the latter's peculiar function and the benefits it brings. The absurd outcome of the investigation is that temperance as Critias defined it would be completely useless.

In his brilliant assessment of the argument (175a9–d5), Socrates registers its major flaws and takes responsibility for having conducted the search in the wrong way. The epilogue of the work points back to the themes of the prologue, but also adds a dark shade of its own. Socrates again addresses young Charmides (175d5–176a5). He restates his own belief that temperance is one of the greatest goods for a human being and suggests that the youth must do everything to cultivate it in his soul. He expresses regret for failing to deliver the 'beautiful words' necessary for applying Zalmoxis' remedy. And he urges Charmides to keep examining and re-examining himself (176a1). The youth appears eager to place himself under Socrates' care. Critias instructs him to do so. And both of them together warn Socrates that he must not oppose their plan, for they are prepared to use force to execute it (175a6–d5).

2 The Historical Subtext

This is what Aristotle might call the plot of the play. It is a very Athenian drama. The action takes place in the early days of the Peloponnesian war, in a wrestling-school in Athens overlooked by one of the city's temples. In the opening scene, Plato's marvellous representation of the ambiance in the gymnasium and of Socrates' entrance evokes the idealised description of Athens and the Athenian way of life in the Funeral Oration that, according to Thucydides, was delivered by Pericles in 431 BCE (approximately two years before the dramatic date of the *Charmides*), in honour of the citizens who fell in battle in the first summer of the Peloponnesian war: courage in war and enjoyment in the hours of peace, strength as well as grace, simplicity of manner and the love of beauty, the importance of leisure and the love of philosophy, and a city unafraid of the enemy, whose greatest adornments derive from the virtue of its citizens and whose values are 'a school for all Greece' (Thucydides, *Hist.* II 37.1–41.4).

The opening scene of the *Charmides* seems an emblematic illustration of these attitudes. Socrates has just returned from a destructive battle but shows no fear or sorrow. His concern is beauty and philosophy and the presence of both in the city. He appears eager to contemplate the former and engage in the latter as soon as he is given the opportunity to do so. As for the other men surrounding the palaestra, their easy manner and pleasantries might make it difficult to believe that they are living in wartime. The same holds for the youths training in the palaestra, for Charmides' admirers, and for Charmides himself. Thus, in these early days of the Great War, Plato depicts Athens full of confidence and hope. The representation has verisimilitude, for Athens could still rely on its army and navy and the fighting spirit of its men. Also, it could still look forward to a new generation of leaders steeped in the values of the city, living the Athenian way of life, and ready to defend Athens and everything it stood for.

Both as narrator and as character, Socrates underscores that prospect.[13] Notably, the description of Charmides' entrance conveys the impression that the young man is vested with a sort of divinity: superbly handsome, impassive like a god, followed by a train of admirers, astonishing and bewildering to everyone who sees him. If only his physical perfection corresponds to perfection in his soul, there is much that he could achieve. Evidently, the concern about Charmides' *kalokagathia*, excellence of body and soul, is not merely a private matter. For given his social lineage and standing, he is expected to someday play a dominant role in Athenian politics. Within the frame of the dialogue, then, Charmides represents a great hope for Athens. This remark applies to Critias as well. He comes from the same stock as Charmides, is worldly, educated, and formidably intelligent, and, therefore, has the credentials to get involved in high-level politics. The narration stresses that Critias is Charmides' guardian and suggests that he exercises considerable influence on his younger cousin. He appears to serve as a model for Charmides and have authority over the youth's education. From within the framework of the dialogue, then, it might seem that Charmides will turn out right, not least because both he and his guardian acknowledge the value of dialectical discussion and Socrates' pedagogical gifts. One might think that the future is open and hopeful for the two cousins, for Socrates, and for Athens as well.

Plato and his audience, however, have the privilege of hindsight and can tell a different tale: of unfulfilled promise and frustrated hope, of foolishness and loss, of ugliness and violence and destruction. Approximately twenty-five years after the fictional encounter narrated in the *Charmides*, Athens lost the war to the Spartan coalition (404 BCE). The Long Walls

---

[13] There is complex irony here. Plato's audiences know that Critias and Charmides do not uphold the democratic values of Athens but are prominent defendants of oligarchy, and eventually will side with Sparta and join the Thirty.

were destroyed, the population was decimated, and the city itself ran the risk of being razed to the ground. The Athenian way of life was lost forever, together with the tolerance and joyful privacy that the Athenians used to enjoy. Democracy was abolished, a military junta commonly called the Thirty and headed by Critias assumed power in Athens, and a similar tyranny was installed in Piraeus under Charmides (404 BCE). Both juntas proceeded to 'purge' the city by summarily executing hundreds of Athenians, and both were overthrown and their leaders killed a few months later (403 BCE). The restored democracy shared only superficial similarities with the polity exalted by Thucydides' Pericles in the Funeral Oration. The confidence, tolerance, and goodwill that the latter attributed to Athenian democracy were replaced by insecurity, intolerance, and the blind determination to eliminate every possible threat to the recently re-established democratic regime. Socrates was perceived as such a threat, and his earlier acquaintance with Critias became one of the liabilities on account of which he was brought to trial and condemned to death (399 BCE).

In outline, these are the historical facts that constitute the background to the *Charmides*. Since Critias and Charmides were Plato's close relatives,[14] their crimes, disgrace, and ignominious death must have affected him deeply, all the more because they also contributed to Socrates' condemnation and execution. Nonetheless, the dramatic date of the dialogue precludes any direct reference by the narrator to those events. It is natural to wonder why Plato chose to set the dialogue so far back in time, and it is also natural to ask why he chose Charmides and Critias as its protagonists. These issues are interrelated and controversial. Also, they bear on another cluster of questions even more difficult to answer; notably, what is the true subject of the dialogue and what is the ultimate purpose for which it was written? An entry point to the discussion of these matters is the dramatic portraits of Socrates' two interlocutors.

3 The Protagonists of the *Charmides*

While the *Charmides* is mostly considered an apologetic work, there is no consensus regarding the nature or the beneficiary of the defence that it is supposed to offer. According to some interpreters, Plato wishes to redress the reputation of his relatives by showing them in a favourable light. On

---

[14] Plato's family tree is complicated. It seems that Plato was Charmides' first cousin through Pyrilampes, the husband of Plato's mother Perictione, and also Charmides' nephew through Perictione herself. Critias was Plato's cousin once removed.

the contrary, according to others, Plato wants to defend Socrates from the taint of association with the Thirty by showing how he disassociates himself from Charmides and Critias and by contrasting the virtues of Socrates with the obvious flaws of the two cousins. Yet other interpreters maintain that Plato's portrait of Charmides is relatively positive but that of Critias negative, and they draw different inferences from that contrast. There are other interpretations as well, covering a broad range of possibilities. All of them, however, share in common the assumption that the date and protagonists of the *Charmides* are determined by quasi-biographical motives: Plato aims to either contribute to Socrates' hagiography or restore his own family pride or, conceivably, both.

In my view, however, Plato's portraits of Charmides and Critias are far more nuanced than they have been taken to be. They are depicted neither as villains nor as flawless characters, but rather are surrounded by ambiguity throughout the dialogue. Dramatically, the appearance of ambiguity is cultivated by the fact that the dialogue can be read from different perspectives. The reader follows the development of Charmides and Critias within the dialogue, and also can look upon them telescopically, from a vantage point resembling Plato's own. The narrator's frame offers a third viewpoint for the reader's use. In relaying the episode, Socrates steps back from the action and occasionally comments on it.[15] In the following chapters, I shall try to keep alive these different perspectives as I develop my analysis and interpretation of the dialogue. Here, I should like to briefly defend a claim that I hope to substantiate in the main body of this monograph, namely that the portraits of Charmides and Critias are ambiguous: e.g. no clear picture emerges regarding their emotional and ethical texture, their dedication to philosophy, or the extent to which they are really willing to submit to Socrates' scrutiny and conduct a philosophical investigation jointly with him.

Beginning with Charmides, on the one hand, he is depicted as a youth of great beauty and distinguished ancestry, inclined towards poetry, gifted at dialectic, and endowed with a sense of decorum and with commendable natural modesty. His guardian extolls his *sôphrosynê* and, indeed, as we shall see, the exchange between Socrates and Charmides establishes that the latter possesses certain aspects of temperance in an ordinary sense. He shows proper deference to his guardian, addresses Socrates respectfully and

---

[15] This could raise the issue of Socrates' reliability as a narrator. Even though Socrates gives us no reason to question his sincerity, we may consider the possibility that Socrates has his own interests and motives for presenting the episode in a certain way.

in a measured manner, shows himself willing to submit to the discourses supposed to instil virtue in the soul, and answers Socrates' questions with modesty and decorum. On the other hand, Charmides also indicates a preference for shortcuts and easy answers, e.g. when he borrows someone else's definition of temperance as 'doing one's own' rather than searching for it within himself. He makes sly remarks about the author of that definition, who, as it turns out, is his own guardian, and appears to enjoy the prospect of upsetting Critias. His successive efforts to define *sôphrosynê* reflect traditional ideals and show no trace of originality or any flicker of imagination. Ominously, towards the end of the dialogue, he reiterates his duty to obey Critias and do his bidding.

Similarly, Critias' character is carefully wrapped in ambiguity from the beginning to the end of the narrative. It is simply not the case that Critias is represented as a purely good or a uniformly bad man. Plato's portrait of him is drawn in chiaroscuro and the effect is sensational. Critias emerges as a personage of great complexity, full of light and shadows, endowed with strong intellect and powerful emotions, seeking truth but also vindication and victory, interested in the nature of virtue chiefly in connection to political rule. Neither as narrator nor as character is Socrates in a position to know how Critias will turn out with the passage of time. But Plato takes pains to direct our attention to the aspects of Critias that will eventually dominate his personality, and he guides us to draw connections between the drama of the *Charmides* and historical reality: between the dramatic date of the narrative and the historical date of the regime of the Thirty, between Critias as he appears in the dialogue and Critias the tyrant, between the former's argumentative ability and the latter's political inept-ness, between the former's conception of a higher-order 'science of science' entitling only the temperate rulers to govern the state and the ideology of cognitive elitism that the Thirty appealed to in order to justify their deeds.

As I hope to show, Plato regularly highlights the tensions marking Critias' character and pointing to different ways in which his historical counterpart might have developed. On the one hand, for instance, the *Charmides* strongly suggests that Critias is one of the Socratics, i.e. people who regularly associate with Socrates, have respect or affection for him, and are keen on his way of thinking.[16] He is almost the first person to greet Socrates upon his entrance to the gymnasium, and he is the one to answer Socrates' query about the state of philosophy and the promising youths of

---

[16] On the criteria of who counts as a Socratic, see Tsouna 2015, which contains references to the secondary literature on that subject.

the day. According to Charmides, Critias was frequently in the company of Socrates, when Charmides himself was but a child (156a). The two older men relate to each other with ease, conspire in order to bring young Charmides in the vicinity of Socrates, and Critias repeatedly expresses his confidence in Socrates' pedagogical gifts. Indeed, in the final scene of the dialogue, he says that he will take as proof of Charmides' temperance the youth's willingness to submit himself to Socrates and remain close to him.

From a philosophical point of view, Critias is the only interlocutor in Plato's so-called Socratic dialogues who, jointly with Socrates, channels the course of the argument. He questions certain premises suggested by Socrates. He rejects Socrates' contention that, if temperance is a form of *epistêmê*, it must have an object or domain distinct from itself, just as all other arts and sciences do. He qualifies his 'yes' or 'no' answers when it seems appropriate, uses rhetorical and literary techniques effectively, and reasons with clarity, elegance, and force. Generally, he appears to appreciate the value of *dialegesthai*, dialectical debate,[17] has excellent dialectical training, and, despite occasional lapses, is mostly able to follow Socrates through the twists and turns of a fiendishly complicated argument. However, Critias' dialectical conduct also exhibits elements alien to Socrates' ethos and goals. Plato underscores Critias' aristocratic pride, his violent outburst at Charmides when the youth makes a joke at his expense, his allegation that Socrates is after victory rather than truth, his concern not to lose face but win the debate, and his effort to evade the issue when Socrates casts serious doubt on the conceptual coherence of Critias' final definition of temperance. In addition to these traces of arrogance, ambition, irascibility, and intellectual dishonesty, the Socratic elenchus brings to the surface Critias' obsession with the exercise of power and his concern to determine the sort of knowledge entitling one to become a ruler. Moreover, the last scene of the dialogue exhibits, albeit humorously, Critias' readiness to use force, if Socrates refuses to take Charmides into his care. At this point, the connection between Critias the character and Critias the tyrant becomes too obvious to require further comment.

In sum, both the dramatic date of the *Charmides* and the ambiguous portraits of the two cousins serve an important dramatic purpose. They

---

[17] In its typical form, training in διαλέγεσθαι involves one-to-one dialectical debate by means of question and answer whose form must be yes or no. The answerer aims to defend a claim p, e.g. 'justice is part of virtue', while the questioner sets out to ask successive questions that will elicit from the answerer premises leading to a conclusion inconsistent with the original claim p. The students were frequently asked to switch roles, and the same student could be asked to defend first a certain claim p and then its contradictory. Critias suggests that his ward has already received some such training, for he says that Charmides is ready to engage in *dialegesthai* (154e6–7).

contribute to embedding the dialectical encounter reported by the narrator in a rich and layered context, which consists of dramatic and philosophical elements as well as historical facts and which offers multiple viewpoints on the dialogue's contents.

Socrates too is a complex character. As mentioned, he has a double role, as narrator of the dialogue and as participant in the reported conversation. In his capacity as narrator, he relays his encounter with the two cousins in a manner evoking the narration of the *Republic*: descriptive and dispassionate, elaborate and systematic, focusing on the physical as well as the verbal behaviour of the personages, and suggesting connections between the character of these latter and the beliefs they put forward. Socrates' narration unfolds in an atmosphere of ease and intimacy between him and a 'noble friend', whose identity and reactions remain undisclosed. We are given to understand that he is an adult, familiar with the location and protagonists of the story, and sufficiently close to Socrates to hear from him a confession of a very private nature. As a character of the narrated story, Socrates exhibits features known to us from the *Apology* and other Platonic writings. He is shown returning from the battlefield to his usual habitat, the public space of Athens. He is acquainted with the people in the gymnasium and recognised by them. Chaerephon and Critias appear to know him intimately; Charmides has heard of him and can easily identify him. He seems unmoved by the dangers of the recent battle and averse to telling tales of heroism and slaughter. Although briefly stirred by Charmides' overwhelming beauty, he remains master of himself. Philosophically, his primary concern is what one might expect: he wants to know 'about philosophy, how it is doing at present, and about young men, whether any among them has become distinguished for wisdom or beauty or both'. He is interested in the beauty of Charmides' soul rather than his body, and he stresses the paramount value of the former compared with the latter. His conversation with Charmides has clear pedagogical aims, the topic is recognisably Socratic, and the same holds for the philosophical method applied throughout the dialogue. We shall discuss these features in some detail in subsequent chapters.

On the other hand, there are ways in which the portrait of Socrates in the *Charmides* is peculiar or unique. First of all, this is probably the only dialogue in which Plato represents Socrates as an early and fairly close acquaintance of the tyrants-to-be.[18] Charmides says that he remembers Socrates 'being with Critias' since the time of his own childhood, but leaves

---

[18] It is controversial whether the character Critias in the *Timaeus* corresponds to the leader of the Thirty or an ancestor of this latter.

unclear the nature of the bond between the two older men. Plato's audience was likely to recall that Critias too had been reputed for his beauty and that Socrates the narrator describes himself as 'a broken yardstick' when it comes to handsome youths: he finds all of them beautiful and is bound to be interested in them.[19] The familiarity between these two characters becomes evident already in the prologue of the dialogue and extends, as it were by proxy, to the relation gradually established between Socrates and Charmides as well. Nonetheless, as just suggested, the narrator does not clarify how deep or steady is the cousins' commitment to Socrates and his values and method. And he is even less revealing about Socrates' attitude towards the two cousins. For instance, in the prologue, Socrates agrees to play the role assigned to him by Critias and pretend to be a doctor that could cure Charmides' headache. But we cannot tell whether he believes that the 'good arguments' prescribed by the doctors of Zalmoxis are likely to work on the youth. Nor can we tell what he really thinks of Critias, even though he preserves a friendly tone towards him and appears mindful of Critias' feelings and pride. Does Plato wish to suggest that, as early as 431 BCE, Socrates had tight connections with the two cousins which, if so, presumably were severed at a later date? Or does Plato intend to show that, despite appearances, Socrates had always kept his distance from Critias and Charmides? Some aspects of the character Socrates seem to point towards the former of these options, while other aspects appear to favour the latter.

More importantly, it is arguable that the philosophical content of the dialogue also contains a certain degree of ambiguity or indeterminacy. Like other so-called Socratic dialogues of Plato, the main part of the *Charmides* consists of several attempts by Socrates' interlocutors to define a virtue, in this case temperance. And similarly to the arguments of other Socratic dialogues, the arguments of the *Charmides* are ostensibly adversarial. They purport to examine the consistency or truth of successive definitions of temperance proposed in turn by each of Socrates' interlocutors, but do not directly concern the views of Socrates himself. At the same time, the *Charmides* is not the only dialogue in which the views advanced by Socrates' interlocutors and refuted by the elenchus have an unmistakably Socratic tinge. Something similar occurs also in, for example, the *Laches*, in which the elenchus refutes Nicias' contention that courage is a kind of knowledge, or in the *Euthyphro*, in which the elenchus refutes the view that

---

[19] Note the parallel with the introduction of the philosopher in comparison with the lovers of sights and sounds in *Rep.* V 474b–476e.

piety is a part of justice. To my mind, however, the *Charmides* stands out in virtue of the fact that it does not challenge just one or two aspects of Socratic philosophy, but rather appears to attack Socratic intellectualism as a whole. As we shall see in more detail later, the central argument of the work appears to challenge, implicitly or explicitly, a set of ideas commonly believed to lie at the heart of the philosophy of Socrates – notably, the ideas that virtue is a sort of expert knowledge, that the endeavour to discover moral truths presupposes a kind of self-knowledge, and that the knowledge equivalent to virtue is able to secure human flourishing. The question arises, then, whether the *Charmides* aims to reject the core of Socrates' philosophy or whether it can be interpreted in some other way, e.g. whether it is intended to suggest that Socratic intellectualism needs to be supported by Platonic epistemology and metaphysics.

Another respect in which the *Charmides* stands out with regard to other dialogues commonly classified in the same group is that it entertains the hypothesis of architectonic knowledge entitling its possessor to rule the state. Again, more will be said later about this subject. For the moment, it is enough to remark that the theme of architectonic knowledge is explored in the so-called middle and late dialogues of Plato, but nowhere else than here in the Socratic dialogues. The only other comparable dialogue in which that theme briefly appears is the *Euthydemus*, whose classification is controversial and its links to the *Republic* under debate. Like the *Charmides*, the *Euthydemus* refutes the idea of a 'kingly art', but the two works achieve that result on different grounds, and also the former goes very much further than the latter. Given that the idea of an architectonic expertise mastered solely by the statesman becomes prominent in Platonic thought, the central argument of the *Charmides* seems especially difficult to interpret, because it seems to cast doubt on the possibility or the benefit of such an expertise. Different interpretative options are possible and each appears to accommodate certain features of the text better than others.

I hope that these examples convey an adequate sense of the sorts of issues at stake in the *Charmides*. Generally speaking, the controversies concerning the nature and status of the philosophical views examined in the *Charmides* often depend on the stance that one takes regarding the dramatic features of the work and, especially, the characters of the protagonists.

When the representation of Charmides or Critias is considered negative, the tendency is to contrast their views about temperance with Socrates' own philosophical beliefs. On the other hand, when the two cousins and in particular Critias are viewed in a positive light, it is frequently suggested that Plato wishes to criticise the philosophy of Socrates and signal a new departure.[20] But in the former case, one wonders where exactly in the *Charmides* Socrates states his own view about temperance[21] or submits it for examination. Or, in the latter case, one needs to explain why Plato would choose Critias, of all people, as Socrates' own spokesman. Why would he choose this infamous character as a vehicle in order to show that he is now leaving behind the philosophy of Socrates and is ready to move on?

Further complications derive from the structure of the *Charmides*, for it appears to many to be composed, after the prologue (153a–159a), of two quite disconnected parts. As indicated, in the first part (153a–164d or 166e), Socrates engages in a dialectical conversation with Charmides with an evident pedagogical goal in mind: to lead him to express and examine his own beliefs about *sôphrosynê*, temperance, and to find out whether or not that virtue is present in him. After the youth is refuted for the third time, Critias takes his place in the debate and attempts to defend anew the last definition proposed by Charmides, according to which temperance is 'doing one's own'. Critias elaborates this formula into 'the doing or making of good things' (164e), thus introducing value into the argument. The central issue of self-knowledge is raised, precisely, when Socrates points out that, if temperance is what Critias says it is, then the first-order experts may have temperance without knowing that they have it. On most accounts, the second part of the dialogue (164d–176d) begins right here, when Critias retorts that, in his view, it is impossible to be temperate without being aware of that fact. For this assertion leads him to think of the Delphic inscription 'Know Thyself' and advance another definition according to which temperance is 'knowing *oneself*'(164d). Subsequently, with the aid of Socrates' questioning, he articulates the latter formula into 'the only science of both the other sciences and itself' (166c2–3), concedes that it is also 'of the privation or absence of science' (166e7–9),[22] and does not object when Socrates refers to it as a 'science of science' (166e7–8) – an accurate and convenient shorthand that I shall borrow as well.

As mentioned, most of the second half of the dialogue is devoted to the development and refutation of Critias' final definition of *sôphrosynê*. But even accepting that the dialogue consists of two fairly distinct parts, how is the first half of the dialogue related to the second? How are the definitions within each part related to each other? How does the prologue bear on the argument in each part or in both? In the end, does the *Charmides* have

[20] There are many other interpretative strands as well: see section 4.
[21] We should also bear in mind the possibility that the target of the elenchus could be some view held by Socrates but not *about temperance*.
[22] See note 8 in this chapter.

philosophical unity and what might it consist in? These questions seem especially disconcerting, because Socrates articulates Critias' definition of temperance as self-knowledge in terms strongly evocative of the *Apology*. But there is no consensus whatsoever as to how Critias' notion of self-knowledge is related to Socrates' own. And, therefore, there is no agreement about the target of the central argument or the purpose of the work as a whole.

4 What Is the *Charmides* About? Rival Lines of Interpretation

To provide a scholarly context for my own interpretation, and also to convey a sense of the depth and significance of the philosophical issues at stake, it seems useful to offer a selective and schematic survey of certain prominent lines of interpretation of the *Charmides*.[23] Several of them can be traced back to nineteenth- and early twentieth-century scholarship and also occur in more recent publications. While in some cases I sketch a line of interpretation exactly as the author develops it, in other cases, for philosophical or practical reasons, I single out certain aspects of an interpretation but leave out others.

As indicated, one fairly common approach is historical and biographical. Depending on whether its proponents take Plato's representations of Charmides and Critias to be positive or negative, they contend that the ultimate purpose of the dialogue is to defend the two cousins or, alternatively, to dissociate Socrates from them by exposing their villainous traits.[24] Certain variants of this approach attempt to map pieces of historical information about Critias and Charmides onto their dialectical behaviour as represented in our dialogue. For instance, it has been suggested that

[23] Tsouna 2017 contains a more extensive presentation and discussion of the material of this section.
[24] Most interpreters who endorse the negative portrait of Critias depicted by Xenophon and other ancient authors (e.g. *Mem.* 1.2.12–16, 29–30) extend that view to Charmides as well, and attribute to Plato a strategy comparable to that of Xenophon: in the *Charmides*, he takes care to stress that Socrates and Critias have different values and therefore the former cannot be held responsible for the evil deeds of the latter when he assumed power. See Hyland 1981; Kahn 1996; Lampert 2010; Landy 1998; Levine 1976, 1984; Schmid 1998. On the other hand, Tuozzo 2011, 51–90, challenges that approach. On the grounds of a careful survey of the ancient evidence, he argues that Critias was a philo-Laconian intellectual, conservative and elitist, who believed that the conservative aristocratic values, including, prominently, *sôphrosynê*, are crucial to beneficial conduct but did not think that the many were capable of cultivating such values. Tuozzo also draws a relatively sympathetic portrait of Charmides. Although I find many of Tuozzo's suggestions attractive, I see no evidence in Plato's text bearing out the claim that, for Plato, Critias 'represent[s] a positive strand of Greek political and cultural thought' (57; see also Notomi 2000). Nor do I agree that 'there is no reason to think that [Plato] traces the disastrous outcome [of the political engagements of his cousins] to moral failings in either of them' (89). In fact, I argue, Plato's ambiguous portraits of the two cousins highlight both their potential to do good if they stick to the principles of philosophical education and their proclivity to do evil if they do not.

Charmides' definitions of temperance, first in terms of quiet and decorous behaviour, and then as a proper sense of shame, reflect his automatic endorsement of conservative values. Moreover, it has often been claimed that Charmides exhibits the tendency to follow the opinions of his guardian without thinking critically about them: he borrows from Critias the definition of temperance as 'doing one's own', without really understanding what this formula means. More importantly, biographical or historical approaches attempt to connect Critias' beliefs as they are expressed in the *Charmides* with the cognitive elitism allegedly endorsed by the historical Critias and responsible for the murderous 'purges' that the latter performed as leader of the Thirty. In fact, certain scholars maintain that Critias' impressive performance in the *Charmides* discloses that Plato felt sympathy for his cousin's ideology, though not for his deeds.

According to Noburu Notomi's interpretation of the *Charmides*, on the one hand Plato acknowledges both Critias' good intentions and his ignorance of the nature of political rule and, on the other, Plato also intimates that the Socratic elenchus can undermine belief in the dominant values of society and thus open the way to political absolutism.[25] Indeed, as Notomi claims, Plato's political philosophy in the *Republic* lies closer to Critias' conception of political rule as expressed in the *Charmides* than to Socratic philosophy and method: the virtuous few who possess higher-order knowledge ought to be the ones to rule. However, Notomi himself notes that, according to the majority of interpreters, the *Charmides* reveals Plato's revulsion towards the beliefs and values of his cousins. As is often contended, Socrates' well-timed references to a state ruled in accordance with a 'science of science' point unmistakably to the central message of the dialogue: the intellectualist conception under examination should be rejected, not only because it is incoherent, but principally because it encapsulates the epistemic arrogance thanks to which Critias and his associates felt entitled to 'purge' Athens in 404 BCE.[26]

Some of these ideas also occur in interpretations attempting to integrate the *Charmides* into broader frameworks which are frequently, but not always, of Straussian inspiration. In his book-length study *The Virtue of Philosophy*,[27] Drew Hyland rejects various analytic treatments of the dialogue[28] for the reason that they fail to take into account its dramatic aspects,[29] and he develops an approach that has been characterised as

---

[25] Notomi 2000.   [26] Dušanić 2000.   [27] Hyland 1981.
[28] E.g. Tuckey 1951; Ebert 1974; Witte 1970. See also Hyland 1981, xii n. 1.
[29] Hyland 1981, ix and *passim*.

existentialist[30] and is accompanied by a hermeneutics aligned with the methods of the Straussian tradition.[31] On this approach, the *Charmides* points to an alternative path lying in between what he calls 'the stance of mastery', which he associates with scientific and technological knowledge, and 'the stance of submission', present in phenomenological or existentialist modes of thinking and in social movements professing detachment and an easy submission to the way things stand.[32] Thus, according to Hyland, the Platonic Socrates exhibits an attitude most fully represented by the dialogue form itself, i.e. an 'interrogative' or aporetic stance identical with Socratic wisdom. The *Charmides*, he thinks, is especially relevant to the understanding of that stance: it illustrates the importance of remaining open and responsive; of adopting an attitude of play; of constantly striving against the tendency to assume the stances of mastery or submission; of being aware of our capacities and possibilities, in particular the potentiality of overcoming human incompleteness through *eros*, love; and of pursuing *sôphrosynê* by redefining the notions of self-knowledge, self-mastery, and self-control. Of course, this is the barest summary of Hyland's agenda. But assuming that it is roughly accurate, it indicates, I think, that the main subject of the *Charmides* is the advancement of the 'interrogative stance' over rival stances and, especially, over the stance of mastery based on technological knowledge.

Although Thomas Schmid's more recent monograph, *Plato's Charmides and the Socratic Ideal of Rationality*,[33] shows that he is aware of analytic approaches to the dialogue, nonetheless his work too mostly belongs to the same tradition as Hyland's.[34] Schmid frequently interprets the interrelation between drama and argument by reading between the lines of the text and by assuming that the dramatic framework serves to disclose in certain ways the philosophical content of the dialogue.[35] His method has far-reaching implications. For instance,

> we cannot take the refutation of a definition at its face-value; what may be refuted is only that definition under a certain interpretation, but not under another interpretation, which may be indicated by the drama but not

---

[30] So Schmid 1998, 189 n. 3.   [31] See Hyland 1981, xii n. 2.   [32] Hyland 1981, 1–17.
[33] Schmid 1998.
[34] See Schmid's citation of the traditions and scholars from whom he has benefited most: Schmid 1998, xiii.
[35] Analytic approaches too explore ways in which the dramatic framework of the Platonic dialogues serves philosophical purposes, but they do so on different assumptions and in different ways than studies following the methods of, for example, Hyland and Schmid.

addressed in the argument. The effect of this approach is to create two different levels of meaning: there is a surface level of meaning, in which definitions are put forward and refuted; and there is a depth level, at which, through various means but especially through the use of dramatic elements, the same definitions, interpreted differently, may be recovered.

Schmid contends that the contrast between these two levels is essential to the *Charmides* and, in his study of the dialogue, he undertakes to show just how it works.[36]

In brief, Schmid contends that the central purpose of the *Charmides*, as indicated by the prologue, is to exhibit Socrates' philosophical outlook and to contrast this latter with the moral ideals and social values predominant in fifth-century Athenian culture. In particular, the dialogue aims to show how dialectical engagement on the subject of *sôphrosynê* can serve to redefine the traditional conception of self-knowledge in terms of the Socratic ideal of rationality, i.e. 'as something achieved *in* rational inquiry through a particular kind of self- and other-relation tied to such inquiry'.[37] According to Schmid, the exploration of this ideal presupposes the introduction of a framework conceptualising the self, an elaborate psychological theory, the rejection of one epistemic model of self-knowledge in favour of another Socratic one, and, in the end, the adumbration of 'Plato's vision of the life of critical reason and its uneasy relation to political life in the ancient city'.[38] Importantly, Schmid's interpretation has a political aspect as well: the *Charmides* is not only Plato's most sustained reflection on the implications of the Socratic knowledge of our own ignorance, but also an attestation that, by rejecting Critias' dysfunctional model of epistemological elitism, Socrates supported democratic relations in the Athenian form of government. While Schmid's book pursues a rich set of topics, for present purposes I wish to stress his suggestion that the dialogue is really about Socratic self-knowledge and aims to advance Socrates' conception of knowing oneself in the context of a metaphysics and psychology of the self.

Laurence Lampert[39] develops his interpretation along similar lines but goes further:

> The very narration of the *Charmides* serves its unstated theme: Socrates attempts to transmit his philosophy successfully by narrating his failure to transmit it to Critias. Socrates honours his auditor [sc. the unnamed 'noble friend' to whom Socrates recites the conversation with Charmides and his

---

[36] Schmid 1998, ix, endorses the principle expressed by Desjardins 1988 and related to the 'pedimental model' or 'two-level' model of literary composition attributed to Plato by Thesleff 1993.
[37] Schmid 1998, x.   [38] Schmid 1998, x.   [39] Lampert 2010, 147–240.

guardian] by presuming that he may be equal to the challenge of piecing together his philosophy from phrases he once transmitted to Critias but that Critias misinterpreted.[40]

And also: '*Charmides* is about the returned Socrates' discovery of the fate of his philosophy in his absence; *Charmides* is about Socrates' philosophy and its transmission to young associates . . .. It is a dialogue in which (Socrates) leaves the essential matters to the inferences of his auditor'.[41] So, Lampert explicitly states a contention that I believe to be present also in the approaches of Hyland, Schmid, and others, namely that the real objective of the dialogue lies below the surface, waiting to be teased out by those in the know. Furthermore, Lampert assumes that Critias' intellectualist view about *sôphrosynê* merely amounts to a misunderstanding of the philosophy of Socrates; it cannot have, as it were, a life of its own. As for Socrates' 'noble friend', the unidentified listener of Socrates' narration of the dialogue, he is expected to 'decipher' Socrates' genuine reflections and guide us to reconstruct the Socratic conception of virtue and self-knowledge by drawing the relevant inferences from his cross-examination of Critias. In sum, the *Charmides* is all about Socrates. It is not about Charmides' or Critias' beliefs concerning the virtue under discussion.

Concerning approaches of clear analytic orientation, in addition to Tuckey's earlier monograph according to which the second half of the dialogue is about knowing that one knows,[42] I should mention, first, Charles Kahn's proleptic interpretation of the dialogue.[43] He proposes that the *Charmides* be read alongside the *Laches*, the *Lysis*, and the *Euthydemus* and, on these grounds, he argues that the refutation of the definition of temperance as 'knowledge of knowledge' or 'science of science' relies on the principle that there is a one-to-one mapping between every specific *technê* and its specific subject-matter (cf. *Charm.* 170a–171a). If so, the refutation of Critias' definition of temperance as *epistêmê* of itself and every other *epistêmê* constitutes, in effect, a serious critique of Socratic self-knowledge or Socratic ignorance. For the elenchus points out that to be able to cross-examine other people about value successfully, as Socrates in the *Apology* claims to have done, one must possess the relevant sort of knowledge; hence, one cannot be ignorant about 'the most important things' or disclaim having understanding of these latter in the way in which Socrates did disclaim it.[44] Hence, according to Charles Kahn, the main purpose of the *Charmides* is to suggest that the successful application

---

[40] Lampert 2010, 157.   [41] Lampert 2010, 156.   [42] Tuckey 1951.
[43] Kahn 1988 and 1996, ch. 7.   [44] See also McKim 1985, cited by Kahn 1988, 549.

of the Socratic method would require Platonic metaphysics and epistemology. On this view, the dialogue offers a positive definition of *sôphrosynê* in
terms of knowledge of the good, implicitly relates that conception of the
virtue to the practice of dialectic and the acquisition of the 'royal art', and
points to the theory of Forms and the Form of the Good.[45]

On the contrary, Harold Tarrant,[46] for example, believes that Socrates'
own possession of *sôphrosynê* is no bar to his own lack of knowledge about it.
Unlike Vlastos[47] and others, who take Socratic interrogation to apply
principally to the beliefs and lives of Socrates' interlocutors, Tarrant maintains that Socrates conducts the main argument of the *Charmides* for the
purpose of self-examination, while the conversation between Socrates and
Critias points to various Socratic *parakousmata*, mistaken or imperfect ways
of understanding major aspects of Socratic ethics. Richard Stalley[48] takes
issue with another widespread assumption: that the intellectualist thesis
dominating the second half of the *Charmides* has little or no connection
with the interlocutors' earlier efforts of determining *sôphrosynê*;[49] these latter
encapsulate the notion of self-restraint and suggest that the virtue should be
defined in terms of order and harmony in the soul. If I understand Richard
Stalley correctly, he suggests that, in fact, the main purpose of the dialogue is
to show the inadequacy of the conception of self-knowledge espoused by
both Socrates and Critias and to point to ways in which self-knowledge or
sôphrosynê may be related to the only truly valuable knowledge; that is,
knowledge of the good.[50] On this approach, then, the notion of 'knowledge
of knowledge' or 'science of science' is taken to be a legitimate development
of Socratic self-knowledge, and the refutation of the former is considered
ipso facto a telling criticism against the latter as well.

Finally, towards the opposite end of the spectrum, Gabriela Roxana
Carone[51] denies that the elenchus actually refutes the notion of 'knowledge
of knowledge', and contends that the latter is closely related to Socratic self-
knowledge in the *Apology* and constitutes a perfectly good candidate for
determining *sôphrosynê* as a core element of human wisdom. One common
point between her approach and that of Tuckey[52] (in a monograph written
over half a century before Carone's article) is that both believe that the
Charmides problematises the notion of self-awareness: what an extraordinary
thing it is to be aware that we know,[53] or, what is the faculty or activity by
virtue of which we apprehend an act of knowledge.[54] In sum, with the main

---

[45] See Kahn's defence of these claims in Kahn 1988 and 1996, ch. 7.   [46] Tarrant 2000.
[47] Vlastos 1983, 25–58, revised by Vlastos 1994, 1–37 (both cited by Tarrant 2000, 251 n. 2).
[48] Stalley 2000.   [49] See, for instance, Irwin 1995, 37 ff.   [50] See, especially, Stalley 2000, 274.
[51] Carone 1998.   [52] Tuckey 1951.   [53] So Carone 1998.   [54] So Tuckey 1951, *passim*.

exception of Thomas Tuozzo,[55] analytic authors tend to relate in different ways self-knowledge in the sense that Socrates uses it in the *Apology*, i.e. knowledge of what one knows and does not know about oneself and others, to self-knowledge in the sense in which Critias develops it in the *Charmides*, i.e. *epistêmê* of itself and everything else qualifying as an *epistêmê*. And although the authors belonging to the analytic tradition both differ methodologically from non-analytic interpreters and focus on different aspects of the dialogue than these latter, nonetheless most representatives of both groups believe that the *Charmides* is mainly devoted to a sustained critique of Socrates' own conception of *sôphrosynê* or self-knowledge, not an alternative conception advanced by Critias.

Before I continue, I wish to register a reaction that I have had to the accounts just mentioned and several others besides: I have felt disconcerted by the fact that, as it seemed to me, most of these accounts could reasonably claim to find support in certain elements of Plato's text, though not in others. I have come to believe that this is probably true of my own interpretation of the *Charmides* as well. Even though I am committed to it and shall try to defend it as convincingly as I can, I do not propose it with the intention of eliminating every other candidate from the map. On the contrary, I believe that the dialectical strategy of the *Charmides* crucially consists in cultivating alternative viewpoints and in inviting the reader to consider competing interpretative options. I should state from the start that my reading of the dialogue is inscribed in the analytic tradition and my discussion focuses chiefly on the argument. At the same time, I assume that literary form and philosophical content are inseparable in the *Charmides* as in all other dialogues of Plato, and that the dramatic elements of the *Charmides* have philosophical significance. As indicated, commentators account for these latter in vastly different ways and, in the present study, I shall try to defend my own view of how the dramatic and philosophical features of the dialogue merge into a conceptually coherent whole.

5 Two Competing Conceptions of Self-Knowledge

At the core of my interpretation lies the contention that two different conceptions of *sôphrosynê* or self-knowledge are present in the dialogue,

---

[55] In the following chapters, I engage with many aspects of Tuozzo's interpretation. To my knowledge, Tuozzo 2011 is the only analytic author who argues in a sustained manner for a distinction between self-knowledge as conceived by Socrates and self-knowledge as conceived by Critias. My debts to Tuozzo are many and, for the benefit of the readers, I shall frequently compare or contrast my approach with his.

one belonging to Critias, the other associated with Plato's Socrates. The former is the direct and primary target of the adversative argument against Critias developed in the second half of the dialogue, while the latter is regularly and importantly evoked for purposes of comparison and contrast and may be indirectly affected by the elenchus as well. The juxtaposition of these two conceptions throughout the dialogue and their interplay with regard to each other are, in my view, the scarlet thread connecting the different phases of the encounter represented in the *Charmides* and cementing the philosophical unity of the work. Also, they bear on the dramatic unity of the dialogue, insofar as each of these two conceptions of *sôphosynê* as self-knowledge is related to a corresponding character and is variously illustrated by reference to that character. Socrates is represented as exhibiting self-knowledge in a recognisably Socratic sense, whereas what we know of Charmides and Critias enables us to explore possible connections between their views about *sôphrosynê* in the dialogue and the deeds of their historical counterparts.

It will simplify matters if I outline from the start what I take to be the two different conceptions of self-knowledge at play. As many have noted to different effects, the text of the *Charmides* appears calculated to regularly remind us of the *Apology* and, in particular, Socrates' description of the verdict of the Delphic oracle that no man is wiser than he is (21a) and of the philosophical mission that Socrates pursued from that point onwards as a service to the god. For instance, at a pivotal point of the *Charmides* where the definition of temperance as self-knowledge is first introduced, Critias refers to the Delphic inscription 'Know Thyself' and contrasts the traditional interpretation of the inscription (which could bear on the Socratic concept of becoming aware of one's human limitations) with his own interpretation of the dictum (154d3–165b4). As Plato's readers will recall, in the *Apology*, Socrates explains to the jury how he acquired an enhanced sort of self-knowledge[56] by trying to understand the meaning of Apollo's verdict, i.e. that no man was wiser than Socrates (*Ap.* 21a). Namely, after he had cross-examined several people who had a reputation for wisdom, he realised that they thought they knew worthwhile things when they did not, whereas he himself did not believe that he knew when he didn't (21d). Although Socrates avoids identifying the worthwhile things in a straightforward manner, nonetheless he makes clear that they differ from the benefits of first-order *technai* (22d–e), and he strongly suggests

---

[56] Socrates does not explicitly say that he acquired self-knowledge, but this is clearly implied by the context.

that they have to do with truth, virtue, and the health of the soul (30a–31c). Socrates' wisdom consists, precisely, in that he does not believe himself to be wise in these 'most important matters', whereas other people lay a groundless claim to such wisdom or expertise. Socrates ventures to call his own sort of wisdom 'human wisdom' (20d–e), but speculates on the basis of his investigations that expertise in 'the most important matters' is 'divine wisdom' possessed, perhaps, only by the gods (20e).

In brief, Socrates' speech in the *Apology* has both a normative and a paraenetic purpose. For Socrates highlights the asymmetry between divine and human wisdom, indicates that the latter consists in self-knowledge of a certain kind, and suggests that we ought to seek the latter in order to correctly assess the limits of human wisdom vis- à-vis the perfect moral wisdom of the gods (23d–e). Socrates is presented as the paradigm of the way of life by which that goal might be achieved: only a philosopher who devotes himself to the dialectical scrutiny of his own beliefs as well as those of others can hope to reach self-knowledge in the sense designated above (28e). It is significant that Socrates describes his search in terms of a divine mission and of labours that he undertook in order to serve the god. For, on a straightforward reading of the text, this suggests that he believes in the existence of divinity, assumes that the gods are far superior to men in moral wisdom (29a), and claims to know that it is necessary for the happiness of humans that they obey the gods' commands. And although Socrates' divinities are probably not identical with those of the city,[57] he is represented as neither an atheist nor an agnostic, but rather as a profoundly religious man.

Critias' conception of self-knowledge, I contend, is of a very different kind. In the first place, it seems to have little to do with one's awareness of the limitations of human wisdom. Instead, Critias' speech about the meaning of the Delphic inscription 'Know Thyself' (164d–165b) intimates that intelligent people, such as the dedicator of the inscription and Critias himself, can understand the true meaning of the inscription and transcend ordinary human limitations in that regard; they alone have access to the mind of the god, while common people do not. In the second place, regardless of how one interprets Critias' definition of temperance, first as knowing oneself, and then, equivalently, as '*epistêmê* (science) of every other *epistêmê* and of itself', it is clear that Critias' model of such an *epistêmê*

---

[57] See, notably, Burnyeat 1997. However, Socrates' appeal to Apollo is, at least rhetorically, an admission that he respects traditional religion. This is an important feature of Socrates' self-representation in the *Apology*.

is both abstract and directive and does not pertain in any evident manner to morality and the care of one's soul. We shall return to this topic later but, for the moment, I wish to stress the following: the text strongly suggests that, according to Critias, temperance or 'the science of science' would be greatly beneficial *precisely because* it is only of itself and of science or every science insofar as it is a *science*. To put it differently, Critias appears to assume that temperance, as he defines it, is enormously profitable just because of its peculiar nature: it is strictly reflexive and, by virtue of its reflexivity, it is higher-order as well.[58] Evidently, these features do not occur in Socrates' conception of self-knowledge in the *Apology* or anywhere else. The difference between the Socratic and the Critianic[59] models of temperance as self-knowledge are marked at the level of language as well. For instance, when Socrates elaborates Critias' definition of temperance as 'science of science' (167a), he employs a cognitive vocabulary strongly reminiscent of the *Apology* and, in particular, favours the use of '*gignôskein*', '*eidenai*', and their cognates ('to know') vis-à-vis '*epistasthai*' and its cognates. Critias and Socrates regularly use these latter to refer to expert knowledge in the arts, and Critias reserves '*epistasthai*', 'to know expertly or scientifically', and '*epistêmê*', science or expertise, for the formulation and defence of the 'science of science' that he takes to be equivalent to temperance. On the other hand, Socrates generally avoids referring to his own 'human wisdom' or the understanding of his own cognitive limitations, as a form of *epistasthai*, let alone an *epistêmê* of some specific kind.[60]

The central argument of the *Charmides* highlights another assumption of Critias' conception of self-knowledge as well: it is supposed to be especially relevant to politics, since one's possession of the 'science of

---

[58] Why does Critias think that? As we shall see, he argues that, unlike all the other sciences or arts, temperance is a science that does not have a specific object distinct from itself, but is only of science (i.e. itself and every other science as well as the privation of science). It is precisely on account of that fact that, according to Critias, the 'science of science' can discern experts from non-experts in every science, correctly delegate tasks, and oversee their successful execution.

[59] I borrow the term from Tuozzo 2011.

[60] Compare the remarks by Burnyeat 1970, 106, on the use of cognitive terms in *Tht.* 201d, which, I believe, point in the same direction as my own remarks here. Burnyeat suggests that, in contexts referring generally to different forms of expertise, ἐπιστήμη is interchangeable with τέχνη and the same holds for their respective cognates. In contexts focusing on the cognitive aspects of expertise, including the discussion of Critias' conception of temperance as 'ἐπιστήμη ἐπιστήμης', 'ἐπίστασθαι' and its cognates are preferred over alternatives. In contexts marking out, specifically, Socratic self-knowledge, 'γιγνώσκειν ', 'εἰδέναι', and related terms are preferred over 'ἐπίστασθαι'. According to Burnyeat, this latter term indicates, generally, various areas or branches of expert knowledge, whereas the former terms are often intended to mark out a particular kind of knowledge, namely Socratic knowledge of what oneself and others know or do not know.

science' entitles one to govern the state. Socrates brings to the fore this aspect of Critianic temperance or self-knowledge by means of a thought-experiment specifically construed for that purpose: an imaginary society governed by temperate rulers who, in virtue of possessing 'science of science', can distinguish true experts from mere charlatans and correctly delegate and supervise the execution of the corresponding tasks. There will be much to say about this thought-experiment, but the point to retain at present is that, unlike Socratic self-knowledge, Critianic self-knowledge as 'science of science' is intended to apply, first and foremost, to the public sphere and points to a technocratic ideal[61] of political governance.[62] Whether or not this model is defensible remains to be seen.

Something should be added about Charmides' attempts to define temperance, even though they do not play as central a role in the argument as the two rival conceptions of self-knowledge just sketched out. Following what Socrates describes as 'the best method' of investigation, the youth 'looks into himself' in order to discern whether he has *sôphrosynê* and, accordingly, form a belief about 'what temperance is or what kind of thing it is'. The first two definitions that he comes up with reflect corresponding features of his character: first, acting in a quiet and decorous manner and, then, acting with modesty or a sense of shame. Indeed, in the prologue and his conversation with Socrates, the young man conducts himself with ease and dignity, expresses himself decorously and well, and appears mindful of what Socrates and others may think of him. His third and last effort to define temperance is based not on introspection but the authority of 'some wise man', who turns out to be Critias himself. Not surprisingly, Charmides does not succeed in defending a definition whose meaning he does not really understand, namely that temperance is 'doing one's own'. But that definition is not without merit, and its strengths and weaknesses become apparent when Critias replaces his ward in the conversation and defends it afresh.

One of the objectives of this study is to explore the dramatic and conceptual interconnections between these definitions, and also show how the conversation moves on to the central topic of self-knowledge and the refutation of 'the science of science' in the second half of the

---

[61] See Levine 1976 and 1984.
[62] Even assuming that Critias develops self-knowledge in terms of strictly reflexive knowledge in order to express a particular conception of value (so Tuozzo 2011, 198–200), few would disagree that his primary endeavour is not the Socratic endeavour to care for one's soul, but rather the concern to determine a higher-order cognitive power authorising the temperate rulers to govern the state in an effective and unchallengeable manner.

dialogue. Even though I take the argument to be adversative in both the exchange between Socrates and Charmides, whose primary aim is peda-gogical, and the debate between Socrates and Critias, whose aim is to test the contentions advanced by Critias, nonetheless I consider how earlier stages of the argument may bear on later ones and earlier definitions may remain alive after they have been refuted. For instance, I suggest that every conception of temperance debated or alluded to in the dialogue can be traced back to the prologue, including the two competing conceptions of self-knowledge that my interpretation attributes respectively to Critias and Socrates, but also the ordinary conception of *sôphrosynê* as self-control, which plays no role in the argument but is present in the dialogue's drama. Moreover, like other scholars, I maintain that Charmides' views about temperance are illustrated by the youth's behaviour in the opening scene but probably undermined by his conduct in the final scene of the narra-tion. Furthermore, I try to show how the view initially defended by Critias, i.e. that temperance is 'doing one's own', serves as a bridge to the second half of the dialogue, and also constitutes the principle according to which the imaginary society of Socrates' 'dream' is supposed to function. And so on.

In sum, I aim to discuss each phase of the dialogue both in connection to other phases and in its own right. I chose for this monograph the form of a running commentary, because it suited me best in order to pursue several different and often complementary tasks: provide a new and detailed analysis of the arguments, discuss the dramatic details of the narration, highlight dramatic and conceptual links lending unity to the work, and gradually develop an overall reading of the *Charmides* which inevitably has common points with other interpretations but also, I hope, a distinctive character of its own.

6   What Is Unique about the *Charmides*? Issues of Philosophy and Method

Perhaps I have said enough to indicate that, although the *Charmides* has dramatic resemblances to other Socratic dialogues of Plato, it also has dramatic elements that set our dialogue apart from others. These include the dialogue's frame, the elaborate and somewhat exotic prologue, and, most importantly, Plato's peculiar choice of protagonists. Now I wish to comment further on certain philosophical features on account of which the *Charmides* stands out with regard to other dialogues classified as 'Socratic', 'early', or 'transitional'. Some of these features are very controversial, while others have received little or no notice in the secondary literature. I shall not engage in any depth with rival interpretations, but only identify methodological and systematic aspects of the *Charmides* which are especially striking or atypical or unique.

At the outset, it should be stressed that several elements of the *Charmides* are typical of the so-called early or transitional or pre-middle[63] dialogues (whether these terms indicate Plato's chronological development or the sequence in which his dialogues are intended to be read). Like other works belonging to these categories, the *Charmides* is a dialogue of definition: Socrates asks the 'what is X?' question, where X stands for the virtue of *sôphrosynê*, and the interlocutors jointly try to answer that question by advancing and examining in turn different definitions purporting to capture 'what *sôphrosynê* is and what kind of thing it is'. The *Euthyphro*, the *Laches*, and the *Meno*, for instance, address the 'what is X?' question in a similar manner with regard to piety, courage, and virtue, respectively. Likewise, the 'what is X?' question motivates the enquiry about the nature of justice in the opening book of the *Republic*, is posed with regard to friendship in the *Lysis*, and is also asked in the *Gorgias* concerning the nature of rhetoric.[64] Moreover, arguably unlike Euthyphro, Laches, and Meno, but like Nicias as well as Gorgias and Thrasymachus, Socrates' interlocutors in the *Charmides* immediately understand what Socrates is looking for when he asks 'what is X?', in this case 'what is temperance?': he is looking for a general formula that can capture the nature of temperance or account for all and only the instances of that virtue. Despite his youth, Charmides is sufficiently familiar with *dialegesthai*, dialectical debate, to offer in turn three answers of the right sort. The same holds, of course, for Critias, who is represented as an exceptionally experienced debater. Furthermore, Charmides' three attempts to answer the 'what is X?' question have intuitive plausibility, just as the definitions of courage advanced by Laches do. This is also true of Critias' claims that temperance is 'doing

---

[63] Kahn 1988 classifies the *Charmides* as a 'pre-middle' dialogue, together with the *Laches*, the *Euthyphro*, the *Lysis*, the *Protagoras*, the *Euthydemus*, and the *Meno*. In his view, these dialogues should be read proleptically, looking forward and not backward for their meaning. They should be read in order to find out not what Socrates said long ago, but how Plato will pursue his paths of enquiry from one dialogue to the next and onto the doctrines of the middle dialogues. According to my reading, however, the intertextuality of the *Charmides* is not exhausted by looking forward to other dialogues of the above group and to the works of Plato's so-called middle period, but also by looking backward, notably to the *Apology*, as well as beyond the *Republic* to the *Theaetetus* and the *Statesman*. On this point see below, section 7.

[64] The *Theaetetus* too addresses the 'what is X?' question: what is *epistêmê*, scientific understanding or, as a shorthand, knowledge?

one's own' in the sense of 'doing good deeds', and then that temperance is
knowing oneself. Many Athenians with oligarchic tendencies would find
plausible the idea that the distinctive mark of *sôphrosynê* is to avoid being
a busybody and instead concentrate on one's own business. And many
would assume that *sôphrosynê* entails self-knowledge of some sort.

Regarding the formal features of the debate, the *Charmides* partly
consists of a series of refutations that, in the round between Socrates and
Charmides, have a clear pedagogical goal (compare, for example, the *Lysis*
and the *Euthydemus*), while in the round between Socrates and Critias the
dialectical arguments aim to examine the consistency of the substantive
view defended by Critias and to discover the truth of the matter. In this
respect, the debate between Socrates and Critias is comparable to, for
example, the elenchus of Nicias' definition of courage in the *Laches*, the
debate between Socrates and Protagoras concerning the unity of the virtues
in the *Protagoras*, and the refutation of Callicles' hedonism in the *Gorgias*.
In general, according to my reading of the dialogue, while the arguments
composing the main body of the *Charmides* may differ in their aim, all of
them are adversative in their form. Namely, the successive definitions
proposed for investigation represent the views of Socrates' interlocutors,
not Socrates himself.[65] Each definition is examined only on the basis of
premises that the defender of the definition concedes and endorses. And
each gets refuted because it is shown that the defender's belief set is
inconsistent or entails absurdities or both. Thus, the *Charmides* raises the
same question that typical Socratic dialogues such as the *Euthyphro* and
the *Laches*, dialogues like the *Protagoras* and the *Gorgias*, and, in some
ways, the *Meno* and the *Euthydemus* also raise: whose arguments are the
arguments conducted in each of these dialogues?[66] Do they belong to
Socrates or his interlocutors or both, and in what way?

As with the aforementioned dialogues, so the *Charmides* prompts us to
wonder just how the investigation taking place constitutes a truly joint
enterprise. For although Socrates says that the search is jointly conducted
between him and his interlocutor, nonetheless the form of the arguments
does not commit Socrates himself to either their premises or their conclusion. Nor, of course, does Socrates need to be committed to any of the
definitions proposed by his interlocutors. For even when these latter can
plausibly be assumed to lie close to his own heart, as is the case with the

---

[65] Socrates does himself suggest the definition of rhetoric in the *Gorgias* and the view that piety is part
of justice in the *Euthyphro*. But these definitions become subjects of cross-examination only after
they are endorsed, respectively, by Gorgias and Euthyphro.
[66] See Frede 1992.

definition of courage as a sort of knowledge in the *Laches* (194d) and the definition of temperance as self-knowledge in the *Charmides* (165b), this does not appear to prevent Socrates from aiming to refute them and succeeding in so doing. I shall argue that, nonetheless, the *Charmides* does mark a new departure with regard to the other dialogues mentioned earlier. For the moment, we should accept that, formally speaking, the *Charmides* resembles other dialogues standardly classified in the same groups in the following ways: the definitions proposed belong in an obvious way to the interlocutors, not to Socrates; and they are refuted as defended by the interlocutors, not by Socrates himself. It is worth noting that the *Charmides* as well as the *Laches* is named after the first and, from the point of view of dialectical maturity, weaker participant.[67] But in both dialogues it is the second participant that carries the greater weight of the conversation, defends a view commonly attributed also to Socrates, and eventually gets refuted.

So much for method and form. In terms of substance too, the *Charmides* exhibits features typical of other dialogues belonging to broadly the same group. For instance, comparably to the *Crito* as well as the *Gorgias*, the prologue of the *Charmides* suggests a conception of virtue, in this case *sôphrosynê*, according to which the latter is a state of health and the source of everything good for a human being. As in the *Laches*, so in the *Charmides* the initial phase of the conversation consists in examining definitions that have been taken to downplay the dispositional aspects of virtue in favour of its behavioural manifestations. Laches defines courage, first, as remaining in one's post and not running away in retreat (190e) and, then, as a sort of psychic endurance (192b–c). In comparable manner, Charmides defines temperance, initially, in terms of conducting oneself quietly and decorously (159b) and, then, in terms of the inclination to act modestly and with a sense of shame (160e). Arguably, in neither case is behaviour severed from one's disposition, but in both dialogues the former is nonetheless more emphasised than the latter.[68]

Importantly, the *Charmides* as well as, for example, the *Laches*, the *Euthyphro*, and the *Meno* entertain the view that virtue is a kind of expert knowledge and consider implications of that view. More generally, these and other dialogues of Plato explore aspects of the stance frequently

---

[67] Arguably this is true of the *Gorgias* as well. For although Gorgias is by far the more venerable speaker, he is also the first and, it seems, the least dialectically strong participant.

[68] Compare a mainstream view according to which, in both the *Laches* and the *Charmides*, the first definition is merely behavioural, whereas the second constitutes an improvement in that it points to a disposition rather than mere behaviour.

labelled 'Socratic intellectualism'. Nicias, the second interlocutor of Socrates in the *Laches*, proposes that courage is a sort of expert knowledge or understanding and expects Socrates to assent to that claim (194d). Euthyphro develops the idea that piety is the part of justice having to do with service to the gods by suggesting that the latter amounts to expert knowledge of proper religious ritual. In the *Meno*, the teachability of virtue appears to depend on whether virtue is knowledge as opposed to mere belief.[69] Likewise, in the *Charmides*, Critias investigates the idea that temperance is a sort of *epistêmê*, science, namely an *epistêmê* of oneself, and he examines jointly with Socrates how the latter might bear on happiness. Finally, like other 'early' or 'transitional' dialogues, the *Charmides* is partly motivated by an *aporia*, a two-horned puzzle motivating the investigation, and also ends in *aporia*, i.e. perplexity.[70] The *Laches* yields no final answer to the question 'what is courage?', nor does the *Euthyphro* settle the question 'what is piety?', nor does the *Meno* tell us, in the end, what virtue really is or whether it is teachable. Similarly, for all its subtlety and sophistication, the *Charmides* does not definitively answer the query whether its young protagonist has *sôphorsynê* or the general question of what *sôphrosynê* is or what kind of thing it is. The central argument shows only that temperance is probably not the sort of *epistêmê* envisaged by Critias and jointly considered by both interlocutors. For the rest, we remain perplexed about the nature of temperance, even though our study of the dialogue can substantially improve our understanding of that virtue and of the important issues at stake.

In many ways, however, the *Charmides* is atypical of the dialogues commonly believed to precede the *Republic*. Formally as well as substantially, it exhibits elements that are not encountered in these latter but occur uniquely in the *Charmides* or point towards dialogues traditionally taken to belong to the middle and later periods of Plato's production.

From the point of view of structure, while the prologue of the *Charmides* is comparable to that of the *Laches* in terms of length, the former far exceeds the latter in thematic complexity and philosophical significance. For instance, Critias' ruse to assign to Socrates the role of doctor, Socrates' acquiescence in that plan, the effects of Charmides' spectacular entrance to the gymnasium, the atmosphere of stifling sexuality surrounding the youth, the overwhelming influence of his beauty on everyone present including Socrates, and the latter's encomium of Charmides' ancestry

---

[69] Interpreters disagree about this point, but here I shall not enter the controversy.
[70] On the different senses of *aporia*, see Politis 2006, 2008; Wolfsdorf 2004.

and lineage (which is also Critias' lineage as well as Plato's) are elements unique to our dialogue. The same holds for Socrates' evocation of the divinity of Zalmoxis, the radical holism attributed to the Zalmoxian doctors, the drugs and charms allegedly used by them, and Socrates' apparent readiness to apply their techniques in order to treat the young man. Furthermore, no other Platonic dialogue is comparable to the *Charmides* regarding either the choice of characters or the ambiguity of their portraits. And also, with the possible exception of the *Phaedrus*, no other Platonic dialogue has raised so much controversy regarding its thematic unity. The selective survey of rival interpretations offered earlier indicates the range of different hypotheses as to how the parts of the *Charmides* fit together or how they contribute, jointly or severally, to the main subject and purpose of the work.

From the point of view of methodology, the *Charmides* stands alone because it contains clarifications but also explicit criticisms of the Socratic way of conducting an investigation. For example: when Socrates tries to encourage Charmides to answer the question of whether he has temperance or is temperate, he outlines 'the best method of enquiry' (158e). He suggests that Charmides should look into himself to discern whether he has temperance: if the virtue is present in him, he is bound to have a sense (*aisthêsis*) of it and to be able to form a belief (*doxa*) about its nature; and since he speaks Greek, he should be in a position to express that belief and submit it to examination. To my knowledge, this is the only passage in the Socratic dialogues of Plato which refers to these psychological assumptions of the Socratic method in a protreptic and pedagogical context.

More importantly, the *Charmides* contains the only sustained challenge to Socrates' use of the so-called *technê* analogy, whose core consists in the assumptions that virtue resembles the first-order *technai*, namely expertise in particular fields, and that virtuous people relevantly resemble experts in such first-order fields. According to a fairly traditional scenario, in Plato's Socratic dialogues, Socrates relies on the *technê* model to explore the idea that virtue is a sort of expert understanding and consider its implications. And he operates with a rationalistic conception of *technê* intended to match his rationalistic conception of virtue. Notably, he suggests that, like every genuine expertise, virtue should be supposed to consist in the expert mastery of a body of knowledge that uses a particular set of methods and tools, has a distinctive function or does a distinctive work (*ergon*), and pursues its own proprietary goal in a systematic manner. Importantly, like every other *technê*, virtue is just the sort of knowledge susceptible to giving a certain kind of *logos*, i.e. a causal explanation of its own practices. And because of the latter feature, one may expect that virtue, like every other *technê,* should be transmissible from one person to another and can be taught.

In addition, Plato's Socrates intimates that, as every first-order *technê* is set over a distinct domain and governs what falls within that domain, so virtue too must be set over a distinct (if greatly extended) sphere and govern everything belonging to that sphere. Socrates repeatedly underscores the prudentially beneficial character of the *technai* and the difference that they make to the preservation and comfort of human life. Likewise but infinitely more so, he suggests, virtue is supremely beneficial in relation to its own function and goal; in fact, its work (*ergon*) is to achieve and maintain happiness. These and other related ideas are repeatedly encountered in Plato's Socratic dialogues and, arguably, indicate that Socrates views virtue as a form of expertise, which constitutes the crowning achievement of human rationality and the essential component of the good life.[71]

The *Charmides,* however, contains a rare instance of explicit criticism directed at a particular aspect of the analogy between the virtue of *sôphrosynê* and the first-order *technai.* To be brief, when Socrates presses Critias to clarify his definition of temperance as a science of oneself (*epistêmê heautou*) by drawing attention to the logical and semantic behaviour of '*technê*' or '*epistêmê*'[72] and by pointing out that every art or science must be *of something,* i.e. it must have an object or subject-matter distinct from itself, Critias responds that, in fact, the 'science of science' equivalent to temperance differs from all the other sciences in this: it alone is of itself and the other sciences,[73] but has no object or domain distinct from itself (165c–d, 166a–b). Thus Critias attacks the *technê* analogy at its core. For he both raises the methodological worry that Socrates' use of the *technê* analogy is at odds with the problem under discussion (165e) and rejects a central aspect of that analogy. What is more, Socrates eventually concedes the contention that temperance alone is a 'science of science' but of nothing else, and accepts to examine together with Critias whether this could be accepted as the definition of temperance. According to dominant interpretations, generally, of Socratic philosophy or, specifically, of the *Charmides,* Socrates rejects here the *technê* model of virtue and never uses it again. This issue is absolutely crucial both for the interpretation of the

---

[71] The nature and scope of the *technê* model are under debate. See Chapter 8, 172 and note 5.

[72] In this context, Socrates uses these terms interchangeably: see note 8 in this chapter and Chapter 8, note 2.

[73] This amounts to the claim that temperance alone is a 'science of science' *simpliciter*: see Chapter 9, 188 and note 1.

argument in the second half of the *Charmides* and in its own right. An important task of the present monograph will be to explore the implications of Critias' stance vis-à-vis Socrates in respect of the *technê* analogy, and revisit the issue of whether the argument in the *Charmides* could be intended to show that the *technê* model is flawed and should be abandoned altogether.

In general, so far as methodology is concerned, Socrates as a character appears more self-conscious in the *Charmides* than in any other Socratic dialogue of Plato. On the one hand, he defends the impartial nature and truth-seeking goal of Socratic investigation against an opponent who accuses him of aiming at victory rather than truth (166c–d), and he highlights the therapeutic and pedagogic power of philosophical discourses to engender virtue in one's soul (157a–b). On the other hand, he regularly draws attention to the dialectical character of crucial premises, casts doubt on the legitimacy of certain moves, and assesses critically the *status questionis* at pivotal turns of the argument in ways that find no close parallel in other so-called early or transitional dialogues. The fact that he steps back from and criticises his own method is especially evident towards the end of the *Charmides*, in his final summary of the argument occupying the second half of the dialogue (175a–176a). To account for the failure of the search, he points to the arbitrary character of the pivotal concessions that he and Critias made (175b), the irrationality of an assumption that both of them took for granted (175c), and the blatant absurdity of the conclusion of the elenchus (175a–b). As he suggests, their failure to determine the nature of temperance is due not only to the sloppy manner in which he and Critias conducted the investigation (175a–b, e), but also to the method of investigation itself (175c–d). Also unique to the *Charmides* is the fact that Socrates blames himself more than Critias for the disappointing outcome of the enquiry (175a). This is the only instance in Plato's Socratic dialogues in which Socrates underscores the responsibility of the questioner as much as of the answerer regarding the quality of a dialectical search.

We should pause to ask where these methodological criticisms leave Plato, and where they leave us. There is no doubt, I think, that the *Charmides* points to some serious limitations and shortcomings of the Socratic method. Pedagogically, we suspect that Charmides learned little from the conversation and we know that, despite his eagerness to place himself under Socrates' care and submit to the charm of Socratic discourses, finally he did not resist the snares of power in real life. It is tempting to entertain a similar thought with regard to Critias, who, as mentioned early in the dialogue (156a), befriended Socrates at a time when

Charmides was a mere child. In this case too, we may surmise, the Socratic method of doing philosophy did not prevent Critias from becoming a lover of power and eventually a tyrant. It is hard to tell what lesson we are to draw, but perhaps it is something like the following: the scrutiny of one's beliefs by means of Socratic *logoi* is an important step in the right direction, but more is needed in order to perfect a young person's character and secure happiness for the individual, let alone the state. In addition to the ethical and pedagogical shortcomings of the Socratic method, the *Charmides* highlights also its logical and epistemological weaknesses and directs us to consider other methods of enquiry. For example, at the close of the Argument from Relatives, Socrates says that he himself is unable to settle the question of whether there can be relatives exclusively orientated towards themselves or whether the *epistêmê* equivalent to temperance is among them; rather, some 'great man' is needed to draw the necessary divisions (*diairêsetai*: 169a) and thus solve the issue under debate in a decisive and satisfactory manner (169a–b). Socrates, then, appears to realise that his own method cannot deal with such substantive issues in a satisfactory manner. And he indicates how to move forward.

From the philosophical point of view, the *Charmides* is atypical or unique in many ways. In addition to the fact that it provides materials in order to entertain side-by-side competing conceptions of intellectualism, the dialogue is an exciting exploration of different facets of *sôphrosynê* that are rarely (if ever) considered together in a single philosophical enquiry. We acquire new and valuable insights into behavioural, dispositional, affective, cognitive, logical, semantic, and political aspects of the virtue – some of them closely attached to the conceptual and cultural context of the *Charmides*, many others of direct philosophical concern to ourselves as well. On balance, as I hope to show, the ideas entertained in the dialogue are worthy of serious consideration, and the arguments of the first part deserve more credit than they have been given. As for the two-pronged refutation of Critias' definition of temperance as a unique, strictly reflexive science, I claim that it is a highly original and successful dialectical argument that involves, among other things, seminal work on relatives, logical and semantic problems bearing on reflexivity, sustained criticism of the ideal of technocratic governance, and the eminently sound suggestion that, insofar as the latter involves no conception of the moral good, it cannot by itself secure the happiness of individuals and the well-being of the society in which they live. I should like to say something more about some of these claims.

Starting with the opening scene of the *Charmides*, even though the idea of virtue as a kind of psychic health occurs in several Platonic works, the prologue of our dialogue makes the further move of combining that idea with psycho-physical holism. According to the view that Socrates attributes to the doctors of Zalmoxis, *sôphrosynê* is the source of health for the whole person conceived as a psycho-physical unity. This sort of holism[74] prompts questions concerning the relations between the soul and the body as well as between the self and the body, and also raises questions concerning the dependence or independence of physical disease with regard to one's psychic condition. Even though these issues are not pursued in the *Charmides*, Socrates takes care to make us aware of them and repeatedly gives us the opportunity to consider them both in the context of the dialogue and in their own right.

The conversation between Socrates and Charmides has its own philosophical virtues as well. Despite the youth's inexperience in dialectic, his definitions of temperance are not implausible and the arguments by which they get refuted are not nearly as weak as they are frequently taken to be. For example, the elenchus of Charmides' first definition of temperance as a form of 'quietness' does not suffer, I suggest, from vicious ambiguities concerning the notion of *hêsychiotês*, but exploits ingeniously the semantic nuances of that concept to defend a plausible conclusion. Or, the brief elenchus of the definition of temperance as *aidôs* (modesty or a sense of shame) is not affected by a paralogism, nor does it rely on appealing to authority. In fact, I maintain, there is no fallacy here, and the single counterexample adduced by Socrates constitutes adequate grounds for the refutation. The attempt by Charmides and then by Critias to define temperance in terms of 'doing one's own' raises interesting queries as well. As is well known, this formula is used to define justice in the *Republic*, but what meaning may it have in the present context? What could be the systematic relations between virtue and a kind of *praxis*, having temperance and doing the sorts of things that properly belong to oneself? Or, to put it differently, how does the latter kind of *praxis* qualify as *virtuous* or, specifically, *temperate*? Again, such questions serve as entry points to the interpretation of the relevant passage in the *Charmides*, but also have philosophical interest in their own right.

As mentioned earlier, the elenctic refutation of the latter definition brings to the fore an important and, to my mind, defensible assumption: virtue cannot be merely a matter of performing good actions; the virtuous

[74] Compare *Rep.* 403d.

agents must also *know* somehow the value of their actions, i.e. they must know them to be *good*. In other words, according to the interlocutors of the *Charmides*, one's possession of temperance must crucially involve a sort of self-knowledge. This assumption is both pivotal for the development of the argument in the *Charmides* and central to contemporary discussions in moral philosophy. To be sure, Critias acknowledges its legitimacy and, therefore, advances the view that, in truth, temperance is equivalent to 'knowing oneself'. On my reading, the chief and ostensible aim of the second half of the *Charmides* is to articulate and examine that view as Critias understands it: temperance as a 'science of itself and the other sciences' or, for the sake of brevity, a 'science of science' simpliciter.[75]

This is not Socrates' view. Nor, I believe, is it tenable. Against interpretations that find attractive the hypothesis of a 'science of science' both strictly reflexive and higher-order and, consequently, disvalue the two-pronged elenchus[76] by which it is refuted, I contend that the arguments constituting this latter are philosophically valuable and dialectically successful. In brief, they are not intended to attack every sort of reflexive knowledge, but only the strict reflexivity involved in Critias' conception of a 'science of science' – incidentally, this is the first and only time that the property of strict reflexivity is discussed in the Platonic corpus. There are several reasons that can explain Plato's interest in that property. As many have suggested, reflexive expressions such as 'science of science' occurred in logical puzzles and were probably used for sophistical or eristic purposes. Plato's interest may have been triggered by such uses, but also, far more importantly, by his own endeavours to understand relatives and relations, his work on self-predication, and his ideas concerning the reflexive character of rationality, human or divine.[77]

Be that as it may, in the *Charmides*, the Argument from Relatives (167c8–169c2) rightly suggests that the conception of strict reflexivity is deeply problematic. As mentioned, Socrates and Critias entertain several different groups of relatives that Socrates takes to be analogous to *epistêmê*, and they conclude that, in some of these cases, strict reflexivity appears strange, while, in other cases, it seems impossible. As for the Argument from Benefit (169d2–175a8), it plausibly suggests that, even conceding that

---

[75] Although the expression 'science of science' (*epistêmê epistêmês*: 166e) is introduced by Socrates and not Critias, this is not something to puzzle over: see Chapter 9, 188 and note 1, and compare Tuozzo 2011, 203–4.

[76] As indicated, this consists of two interrelated arguments that I call, respectively, the Argument from Relatives and the Argument from Benefit.

[77] Consider, for instance, *Alc.* I 132c–133c.

there is such a thing as a strictly reflexive science, it wouldn't bring any real benefit because it could have no substantive content and no function of its own. According to my interpretation of these arguments, the upshot is not, as many have feared, that if we take them seriously, we must conclude that Socrates or Plato reject the possibility of self-knowledge, or of reflective understanding, or of an architectonic science aiming at the good governance of the state. In fact, the second part of the *Charmides* does not attack these ideas in any general way. Socrates questions just one sort of reflexivity, what I call strict reflexivity, and he brings into the open a cluster of logical, semantic, and philosophical problems related to that phenomenon. I shall aim to show that the Argument from Relatives and the Argument from Benefit, severally as well as jointly, support the conclusion that strict reflexivity appears to be an odd or incoherent notion. If this is right, these two arguments provide grounds for rejecting Critias' claim that temperance is a strictly reflexive *epistêmê* orientated towards *epistêmê* alone but nothing else.

In ending this section, I wish to stress again that the two arguments that establish (albeit tentatively) the aforementioned conclusion are of major philosophical importance and have no close parallel anywhere in Plato. Clearly, the Argument from Relatives is for Plato a new and major departure[78] comparable, for example, to the theory of causation dominating the *Phaedo*. It contains seminal work on relatives and relations and points forward to puzzles concerning self-predication and, generally, Plato's theory of Forms. Also unique, and terribly important, is the Argument from Benefit, because it appears to challenge two views lying at the heart of Socratic philosophy, namely that virtue is a sort of *epistêmê*[79] and that virtue as a higher-order *epistêmê* is sufficient for happiness. In addition to its singular target, the Argument from Benefit is remarkable also on account of its structural complexity and several interim inferences and claims. These include the contention that, because of strict reflexivity, the 'science of science' could have no substantive content; that even if it did have substantive content, it is still dubious that it could bring any real benefit to the individual or the state; and that happiness could never be the object of such a science, first of all for formal reasons having to do with the view of relatives and relations at play. In sum, there is much at stake,

---

[78] The Argument from Relatives can be compared to the discussion of likes and unlikes in the *Lysis*, but the former passage goes so much further than the latter that no substantial parallel can be drawn between the two works.

[79] This idea is challenged also in the *Euthydemus*, but the *Charmides* is the only dialogue that deploys a systematic argument to that effect.

philosophically, in these arguments, and they deserve to be revisited with an open mind.

7   Intertextuality

The *Charmides* is by no means the only dialogue by Plato which directs its readers to reach beyond its own frame to other works of the corpus. In fact, most Platonic dialogues lend themselves to such intertextual associations and can simultaneously address different audiences.[80] However, I think that the *Charmides* stands out in this regard as well, for the intertextual connections it prompts us to seek appear to constitute an integral part of Plato's dialectical strategy in this dialogue, and can enrich substantially our understanding of both the drama and the argument. Also, regardless of whether the dialogue is viewed from a developmentalist or a unitarian perspective, the intertextual associations it evokes point not only forward to the *Republic* and other 'middle' dialogues, but in other directions as well, i.e. Platonic dialogues traditionally classified as 'early', 'transitional', or 'late': the *Apology* and the *Crito*; the *Laches* and the *Euthyphro*; the *Gorgias*, the *Protagoras*, and the *Meno*; the *Lysis* and the *Euthydemus*; the *Symposium* and the *Phaedrus* as well as the *Republic*; beyond them, importantly, the *Parmenides*, the *Theaetetus*, the *Sophist*, and the *Statesman*; also, occasionally, the *Timaeus* and the *Laws*.

I shall refer to these dialogues fairly frequently in order to illustrate, elaborate, corroborate, or question features of the *Charmides*: dramatic elements too, but mainly ideas and claims that remain undeveloped or require further support. However, it is important to clarify at the outset what I intend to be the status and function of such intertextual connections in my analysis. First, these latter are bound to have a strong subjective element, since they reflect associations that have occurred to me and serve the interests of my own interpretation. I hope that they may prove interesting and stimulating, but they are not intended to be exclusive or exhaustive. Second, while the intertextuality built into the *Charmides* can substantially contribute to its dramatic attractiveness and dialectical success, nonetheless, in my view, the dialogue is philosophically self-standing and its arguments should be assessed primarily in their own right. Third, I should like to make plain that I find no indication whatsoever that the *Charmides* has some hidden meaning accessible only to the privileged few. The text is there for all to read, and the fact that it bears on many other

---

[80]   See Rowe 2007.

Platonic texts and invites many different readings has nothing to do with some secret agenda on Plato's part. Fourth, while the focus of the present study will remain fixed on the *Charmides*, the readers will be given opportunities to revisit traditional views and acquire new perspectives on other dialogues as well. Immediately below, I give examples of the ways in which the *Charmides* may be pointing to other works by Plato, and I try to convey a sense of the unusual complexity of such connections and their vast scope.

The *Apology* constitutes the main point of reference for the conception of Socratic self-knowledge alluded to in the prologue of the *Charmides* and implicitly contrasted with Critias' conception of self-knowledge in the central argument of the dialogue. For instance, if we read the *Apology* together with the *Charmides*, we are likely to achieve a better understanding of Socrates' claim in the prologue of the *Charmides*, i.e. that, according to the doctors of Zalmoxis, virtue and in particular temperance is the source of every good for a human being and can be acquired by means of *logoi kaloi*, fine words or arguments (157a) – a charm that Socrates is able to administer. Or, the *Apology* lends perspective on Socrates' articulation of Critias' notion of *sôphrosynê* as 'science of science' in terms of the temperate person's ability to judge what they and others know or do not know and thus distinguish between experts and charlatans. The fact that Socrates elaborates Critias' definition of *sôphrosynê* as reflexive science in terms strikingly similar to his own description of Socratic self-knowledge in the *Apology* should give us pause. We should entertain the possibility that the elenchus ostensibly directed against Critias' 'science of science' may point to problems in Socratic philosophy and method as well. The *Crito* and the *Gorgias* provide other points of comparison and a broader context for several features of the *Charmides*: Socrates' interest in Charmides' soul rather than his body, the claim that virtue is the source of every good, the contrast between Socratic *dialegesthai* and Critias' rhetorical speech about the meaning of the Delphic inscription 'Know Thyself', the fact that the nightmarish society of the 'dream' is governed solely by the 'science of science' but not by law, and so on.

As indicated, the *Charmides* has evident commonalities with dialogues such as the *Laches* and the *Euthyphro*, which also belong to the group of Plato's 'Socratic' dialogues and are commonly supposed to have been written during the same period as the *Charmides* or, alternatively, to be so crafted as to be read in close sequel to the latter. In addition to the fact that a comparative examination of the treatment of the 'what is X?' question in these works is likely to enhance our understanding of the

Socratic method and its applications, the first two definitions of *sôphrosynê* in the *Charmides* are structured in ways pointing to their counterparts in the *Laches* and the same holds for their development and refutation. Socrates' description of the 'best method' in the former work can be fruitfully compared to Nicias' account of the Socratic method and its effects on people's lives in the latter (*Lach.* 187e–188c). Certain dialectical initiatives that Socrates takes in the *Charmides* are comparable to the initiative that he takes in the *Euthyphro* to propose to his interlocutor for consideration the view that piety is part of justice (11e–12d). Considered together, these initiatives lead to a better appreciation of the questioner's role in the elenchus and prepare us for Socrates' self-critical comments on method towards the end of the *Charmides*.

Similar remarks apply to intertextual comparisons that can be drawn between the *Charmides* and dialogues commonly believed to be more advanced than the *Laches* and the *Euthyphro* either in respect of their relative chronology or in respect of their intended order of study. Such dialogues include the *Meno* and the *Protagoras*. For example, it is worth entertaining the idea suggested by some scholars that Socrates' 'best method' in the *Charmides* looks forward to the theory of recollection in the *Meno* or can be fruitfully considered from the vantage point of the latter dialogue. In both these works there is talk about a belief extracted from within us and expressible in language, and in both it is suggested that the belief could turn into knowledge through repeated and systematic questioning. Or, we may want to compare versions of intellectualism as they are developed, respectively, in the *Charmides* and the *Protagoras* and explore the implications of such a reading for either or both works. The *Charmides* and the *Protagoras* can also be read in parallel with regard to the role of expert knowledge in ruling. On the one hand, the conversation between Socrates and Protagoras raises the worry that democracy may be unable to accommodate and benefit from true political expertise. On the other, the debate between Socrates and Critias represents a failed attempt to defend a certain conception of a higher-order expertise, i.e. a 'science of science' that, according to Critias, would enable its possessor to govern the state well. As we shall see, the relevant argument in the *Charmides* is far more thorough and promising than the corresponding argument in the *Euthydemus*, and it points forward to two different elaborations of its main theme, one undertaken in the *Republic*, the other in the *Statesman*. I shall briefly comment on each of these dialogues in turn.

At the dramatic level, the intertextual affinities between the *Charmides* and the *Republic* are underscored by the fact that both dialogues have

Socrates as narrator and both have Plato's relatives as protagonists. At the philosophical level, the *Charmides* can be considered in certain ways a mirror image of the *Republic*. For the former dialogue focuses on a form of intellectualist elitism that can easily be associated with the elitist ideology of the Thirty, while the latter elaborates and defends an elitist conception of political governance centred on the supreme value of philosophical education. But the theme of a higher-level *epistêmê* is central to both dialogues, as is the idea that such an *epistêmê* empowers its possessor to rule. How exactly the two works may be related, however, is not a clearcut matter. On one approach, there is continuity between Critias' hypothesis of a strictly reflexive *epistêmê* enabling the temperate person to govern well and the theoretical understanding that the Philosopher-King brings to bear on the affairs of the state. In both cases, the ruler's knowledge ranges over the first-order arts and sciences, determines their application and use, delegates tasks to the relevant experts, and, generally, supervises and orchestrates from above all activities in the state. In sum, according to this interpretation, the same line of thought stretches through the *Charmides* and the *Republic* as well as the *Euthydemus* and the *Statesman*.[81]

On a different approach, however,[82] the 'science of science' in the *Charmides* does not preannounce the ideal of the Philosopher-King, but points in an altogether different direction. While the interlocutors of the *Charmides* articulate the 'science of science' as an architectonic sort of expertise whose application by the ruler is direct and empirical, the *epistêmê* of the Philosopher-King consists in the theoretical understanding deriving from the contemplation of perennial realities, the Forms. Critias' temperate rulers would govern by virtue of their capacity to distinguish science from non-science and experts from non-experts, and to delegate and supervise tasks accordingly. The Philosopher-King is on the contrary supposed to govern by somehow bringing to bear on empirical affairs a kind of knowledge that transcends these latter and includes, all importantly, the contemplation of the Form of the Good. On this latter approach, the abstract, unspecified nature of the 'science of science' defended in the *Charmides* must not mislead us: it has little to do with the philosophical knowledge achieved by the Philosopher-King. Rather, as we shall see shortly, it lies closer to the 'kingly art' of the *Euthydemus* and points towards the *epistêmê* of statesmanship in the *Statesman*.

---

[81] See Kahn 1988 and 1996, ch. 7: 183–209.

[82] See Schofield 2006. As Schofield 2006, 145, remarks, the fundamental task of philosophy and the aim of Socratic enquiry is to find out the nature of the good and determine what knowledge of the good would consist in. But neither the *Charmides* nor the *Euthydemus* undertakes this task.

Yet, there are many other respects in which the *Charmides* appears to gesture towards the *Republic* as well as beyond it. For instance, the third definition of temperance as 'doing one's own' overlaps with the definition of justice in *Republic* IV, even though the formula does not mean the same thing in the two works.[83] Besides, it occurs as a virtual quotation in the *Timaeus* (72a–b), where 'doing one's own' is not treated as a view of *sôphrosynê* that has been rejected. Also, the *Charmides* suggests a distinction between makers and users, which turns out to be crucial for the argument in the *Republic* and, specifically, for the contention that only users have real knowledge, whereas makers have true belief and imitators have neither. Moreover, towards the end of the *Charmides*, Socrates extracts from Critias the admission that the only *epistêmê* pertaining to individual and civic happiness is the *epistêmê* of good and evil – an idea that Socrates elaborates in the *Republic* in connection with the ideal of the Philosopher-King. And furthermore, importantly, the *Charmides* is sprinkled with terms and phrases used also in the *Republic* in connection with the metaphysics and epistemology of Forms. Notable examples occur in the Argument from Relatives and will be discussed in due course. Again, my proposal is not that we fill the Argument from Relatives or any other argument of the *Charmides* with premises drawn from other Platonic works. I only suggest that intertextual parallels can provide a broader context for certain seemingly arbitrary elements of the *Charmides* and thus help us assess such elements in a fuller and more favourable light. It is up to the reader to decide whether or not they will want to take such suggestions into account.

Whatever stance one takes regarding the relation between temperance as 'science of science' in the *Charmides* and the *epistêmê* of the Philosopher-King in the *Republic*, it is clear, I think, that the *Charmides* explores an ideal that also surfaces in the *Euthydemus* and is fully developed in the *Statesman*: an architectonic *epistêmê* that extends over every specialised art or science, delegates and oversees the activities of the first-order experts, and secures the good governance and well-being of the state.[84] Even though there are marked differences between Critias' 'science of science' and the 'kingly art'

---

[83] In the *Republic* IV, justice is not identified with 'doing one's own'. It is the condition of a soul or a city when its three constitutive parts are each doing their own.

[84] Schofield 2006, 136–93, explains how Plato's ideal of architectonic knowledge inspired John Stuart Mill's technocratic model of government. He compares and contrasts this latter with Jowett's favourite model, which was inspired by Plato's answer in the *Republic* as to who is fit to rule: the true statesman is not the technocrat but the philosopher, who rules successfully and well by harmonising practice and contemplation.

(*basilikê technê*) entertained in the *Euthydemus*, nonetheless, in these two cases, the argument is motivated in similar ways and the conclusions are interestingly comparable. On the one hand, the *Charmides* investigates what *sôphrosynê* is and eventually raises the question of whether a reflexive *epistêmê* supposedly equivalent to temperance suffices to ensure happiness in the state. On the other hand, the *Euthydemus* supposes that a certain *epistêmê* is needed for happiness and undertakes to specify what *epistêmê* this is. In response, both dialogues entertain the idea of an architectonic form of *epistêmê* that might be able to achieve the desired result. And both eventually refute the possibility of an architectonic sort of *epistêmê*, while the *Charmides* offers a fuller and more substantial argument to that effect. Moreover, a main reason why the hypothesis of an architectonic science fails in the *Euthydemus* is that it involves a certain kind of reflexivity probably leading to regress (cf. 291b–292e). Another, related reason for that failure is that no connection is secured between the architectonic science supposedly leading to happiness and the good, and both these elements are prominent, as indicated, in the *Charmides* as well. In sum, I believe that we gain a fuller philosophical perspective of certain key ideas of these two works if, in addition to studying each of them independently, we also consider them in parallel to each other and, moreover, read either of them or both in connection with the *Republic*. For example: jointly the aforementioned passage of the *Euthydemus* and the critique of reflexive knowledge in the *Charmides* can be read as showing Socrates' own admission that, in equating the good with knowledge or wisdom, he has initiated a potentially vicious regress (cf. *Rep.* VI 505b) which the *Republic* will block by introducing Plato's Form of the Good. Such a reading can be used to support the idea that, in the *Charmides*, Plato is making moves to distance himself philosophically from Socrates as represented in the so-called early dialogues.[85] I now wish to pursue a little further the theme of architectonic science that, in my view,[86] runs through the *Charmides* and the *Statesman*.

The leading question of these two dialogues differs, since the former asks the Socratic question what is *sôphrosynê*, whereas the latter is driven by a concern dominating Plato's substantive philosophy, namely the nature of true political expertise and the entitlement to rule deriving from it. Nonetheless, both the drama and the argument of the *Charmides* prompt reflection on central issues addressed in detail by the *Statesman* and, in a different way, by the *Republic* as well: who ought to govern the ship of

---

[85] I thank David Sedley for his comments on this point.

[86] See also the reference to Schofield 2006 in note 84.

state? What sort of expertise should qualify them for that task? How is it to be applied in practice? How does the ruler's expertise bring about the unity and good governance of the state as well as the happiness of its citizens? The *Charmides* does not systematically discuss these matters, nor does it propose a coherent view of the proper qualifications for statesmanship. However, it is clear that Critias has a deep concern for this latter issue, and many of Socrates' interventions seem calculated to highlight that fact. I suggest that Plato chooses Critias as a principal interlocutor partly because he wishes to signal the unsuitability of the 'science of science' as a political ideal: in all probability, the temperate ruler as Critias conceives of him would be entirely inappropriate to steer the ship of state. The central argument of the dialogue offers grounds that can support that suggestion. Not only is Critias' view of the ruler's *epistêmê* conceptually problematic, but also the latter probably couldn't have any substantive content or any substantive connection to the good. Socrates' thought-experiments, especially the 'dream', illustrate that point and, moreover, bring to the fore the putative ruler's inability to create and preserve a sense of community and cohesion. Thus, the *Charmides* shows among other things the need to redefine the sort of architectonic *epistêmê* pertaining to the ruler, propose a better model of successful political governance, and determine anew the cognitive and moral desiderata for such a model.

The *Statesman* pursues these and other related issues, and one of its most important contributions is that it proposes a fully worked-out conception of an architectonic science of political governance and of the statesman in possession of the latter.[87] Crucially, this conception comprises the idea that ruling involves a certain kind of theoretical understanding enabling the statesman to direct activities in the state; the metaphor of the ruler as a weaver; the distinction between weaving and contributory activities; and the description of the ruler in terms of the 'supreme orchestrator' of everything that takes place in the state.[88] Assuming that the statesman is able to properly exercise his art, the results that he achieves for individual citizens and for society as a whole comprise elements conspicuously absent from the imaginary society of Socrates' 'dream' in the *Charmides*. For, unlike the temperate rulers of this latter, the statesman

---

[87] On the political argument of the *Statesman* and the methodological approach Plato follows in that dialogue, see notably Lane 1998.
[88] See Schofield 2006, 168.

brings their life [sc. the life of the citizens] together in agreement and friendship and makes it common between them, thus completing the most magnificent and best of all fabrics and covering with it all the other inhabitants of cities, slaves as well as free people; and it holds them together with this twining and rules and directs and, so far as it belongs to a city to be happy, it does not fall short of that in any respect. (*Plt.* 311b–c)

Arguably, the *Charmides* fulfils a double function in respect of the ideal advanced in the *Statesman*. On the one hand, the former dialogue sets up the agenda pursued in the latter but, on the other, Plato's choice of protagonists in the *Charmides* serves to alert us to the dangers lurking in the ruler's absolute power. Consider, for instance, an idea prominent in the *Statesman*: that the expertise of the wise overrides every other normative element, including the laws of the state. According to the Eleatic stranger, the art of kingship entitles the wise and just ruler occasionally to act against both law and custom, forcing the citizens to do what is best (296b–c) and even using purges when they are needed. The *Charmides*, however, provides a useful reminder of what can happen when absolute rulers merely believe themselves to be wise and just, and on the basis of that mistaken belief undertake to 'purify' the state.

   Turning away from the *epistêmê* of ruling to *epistêmê* simpliciter, we may consider reading the *Charmides* in relation to the *Theaetetus*. In some ways, the latter is sharply different from the former. For, unlike the *Charmides*, the *Theaetetus* is generally believed to be a later work of Plato, is widely acknowledged to have philosophical pertinence and value, and constitutes an outstanding example of a cooperative dialectical enquiry between Socrates and interlocutors of similar ilk. In other ways, however, the two dialogues appear to be crafted so as to point to each other. Methodologically, both of them conduct their respective investigations by means of the Socratic method and lead to an aporetic result. But also, each of these dialogues arguably indicates a distance between Socrates as character and Plato as author, albeit in a different manner and to different effect.[89] Philosophically, the study of reciprocal connections between the two dialogues may enrich our understanding of either or both. Not only are their respective subjects closely related, so that the investigation of the

---

[89] In the *Charmides*, Socrates points to some serious limitations and shortcomings of his own method of investigation: see above, 35–6. It seems plausible to infer that the character Socrates voices Plato's criticisms of his mentor's method and his readiness to move on. Regarding the *Theaetetus*, see, notably, the interpretation defended by Sedley 2004.

nature of *epistêmê* in the *Theaetetus* provides a broader epistemological context for our understanding of a specific kind of *epistêmê*, i.e. the 'science of science', in the *Charmides*. Also, the *Theaetetus* speaks to Socrates' worry in the *Charmides* concerning the conceptual coherence of the hypothesis that there can be a science orientated solely towards itself.

Towards the end of his criticism of the aviary, Socrates considers and discards various hypotheses in turn (*Tht.* 200b). The last of them raises the possibility that there might be a second-order set of *epistêmai* of first-order *epistêmai* and the lack thereof, which might exist in some other aviary. As the interlocutors intimate, this hypothesis involves a sort of reflexivity, and it is dismissed because it leads to regress. Even though the *Charmides* examines reflexivity from a different perspective and questions it on different grounds, it is important that both dialogues construe their hypotheses of reflexive *epistêmê* by attributing to the latter a higher-order function, both problematise reflexivity in connection to that function, and both eventually reject the hypotheses under consideration. The *Theaetetus*, then, corroborates the intuition motivating the Argument from Relatives in the *Charmides*, namely that the strict reflexivity exhibited by the 'science of science' is at the very least problematic. And both dialogues provide incentives for us to think harder about reflexive relatives and relations and try out alternative options of construing *epistêmê* in ways that involve reflexivity of some innocuous kind. In addition, these two works raise similar clusters of issues related to the question of whether the central argument in each work requires the assumption that there are Forms or can function without appealing to these entities.[90] Is this similarity a mere coincidence? Or is it due to a deliberate choice that Plato makes, i.e. to follow the same strategy in both dialogues? In my analysis, I occasionally draw attention to such questions, and I hope that some readers will take them up.

At the level of drama too, there are striking parallels between the *Theaetetus* and the *Charmides*. War and death cast their long shadow on both dialogues. The former is a sort of funeral oration for the great mathematician Theaetetus, as he is brought back mortally wounded from the battlefield. The latter relays, as mentioned, an encounter supposed to have taken place upon Socrates' return from the battle of

---

[90] Cherniss 1936, 447 n. 11, cites *inter alia Charm.* 176a as evidence for the claim that 'the dialogues of search, by demonstrating the hopelessness of all other expedients, show that the definitions requisite to normative ethics are possible only on the assumption that there exist, apart from phenomena, substantive objects of these definitions which alone are the source of the values attaching to phenomenal existence'.

Potidaea, which took the lives of many Athenians and gave a foretaste of heavier losses to come. In sharp contrast to their historical settings, the narratives constituting the main body of both works convey the liveliness and pleasure of dialectical exchanges and show how these can be used for philosophical and pedagogical ends. In addition to these general similarities, however, there are also dramatic elements that are most fully understood if we read the *Charmides* in the light of the *Theaetetus* and vice versa. One such example concerns the respective protagonists of the two dialogues and the relations they are depicted as having with each other.

In the *Theaetetus*, Socrates famously describes himself as a barren midwife, who is able to assist men pregnant with thoughts to bring forth their offspring, examine whether these latter are real or merely wind-egg, and also act as a sort of matchmaker. Assuming that philosophical education differs from sophistical education, Socrates can distinguish youths disposed towards the former from others inclined towards the latter and pair each of them with an appropriate mentor. The *Theaetetus* exhibits Socratic midwifery at its best. Socrates is represented as applying his skill to a youth who has an active and creative mind, has received excellent mathematical training, has acquired the ability to think theoretically and abstractly, and is likely to be pregnant with thoughts. He is modest and appropriately respectful, but intellectually enterprising and independent. He shows no trace of reluctance, cowardice, or deference to authority. On the contrary, he labours bravely to give birth to his ideas and makes substantial progress in trying to defend them. Theaetetus grows in self-knowledge right before our eyes and, as Socrates observes, he appears ready to explore new theories and likely to show gentleness to other people less gifted than himself. The opening scene of the *Theaetetus* confirms what we know from independent evidence as well, namely that Theaetetus lived up to promise. Within the frame of the dialogue, Theaetetus finds in Socrates the right match and draws from Socrates' midwifery a net gain: he gradually improves in self-understanding and shows himself keenly aware of the advances that the Socratic method enabled him to make (*Tht.* 200b–c).

Consider now the *Charmides* in the light of the above remarks. From the very beginning of the dialogue, one cannot suppress the suspicion that Charmides may not be able to benefit from talking with Socrates but is more likely to gravitate towards a different sort of mentor. While Charmides appears *prima facie* promising on account of his beauty, ancestry, education, and manner, it becomes increasingly more questionable whether he really has a talent for philosophy or the tenacity to pursue the enquiry about temperance beyond a certain point. After two failed attempts to define the virtue by looking into himself and expressing his own belief about temperance, he gives up. Rather than examining himself and his own beliefs, he submits for investigation the claim of someone else, namely his guardian Critias. And when Critias takes over, the youth withdraws from the conversation and reappears only in the last scene. Generally, Charmides' definitions of temperance as well as his attitudes and demeanour indicate a deferential attitude towards tradition, a certain intellectual laziness, and a docile and passive mind. Even though he is portrayed at a slightly younger age than Theaetetus, he appears far more immature than Theaetetus regarding his mental and psychological development. He shows nothing like Theaetetus' intellectual drive or his ability to conceive and bring forth his own thoughts.

In the last scene of the *Charmides*, the young man pleads menacingly with Socrates to take him into his care, and we are left to wonder whether this will happen. The *Theaetetus*, however, gives us reason to suspect that the association between Charmides and Socrates could never work. In the midwifery passage, Socrates says that, while he exercises his art to help men who seem pregnant to bring forth their thoughts and determine whether these latter are fertile truths or mere phantoms (*Tht.* 150b–151a), he declines to attend to people who somehow do not seem to him to be pregnant or have need of him (151b). In such cases, he continues, with the best will in the world he acts as a matchmaker and sends the barren youth over to Prodicus or some other *sophos*, wise man or sophist (151b). In the *Charmides*, Socrates characterises Critias, without naming him, as a *sophos*, wise man or sophist, and points to him as the likely source of the definition of temperance as 'doing one's own' (161b4–c1). Even though Critias was not a professional teacher like Hippias or Prodicus, he was familiar with the sophists' teachings and was probably perceived as a sophist by many. As for Charmides, when we compare him with Theaetetus, we get the impression that his mind is rather barren and, unlike Theaetetus' mind, it needs to be sown by something else's seed.[91] The last scene of the *Charmides* suggests that, in fact, a matchmaking has already taken place and Socrates' services will not be needed. Charmides is portrayed as being already under the influence of Critias, and as for Plato's

---

[91] As Burnyeat 1977 notes, from the point of view of Socratic midwifery Charmides and Socrates are a bad match. See Chapter 12, 298–9 and notes 50 and 51.

audiences, they are in a position to know that the seeds that Critias will plant in his ward's soul shall bring a bitter harvest.

8 Why Did Plato Write the *Charmides*?

In the end, why did Plato write the *Charmides*? To my mind, there is no single or definitive answer to that question, nor is it fruitful to look for one. Although Plato's choice of interlocutors and of the views defended by them (and especially by Critias) may be intended to anchor the dialogue in historical reality, we simply do not have available the sort of information that would enable us to distinguish firmly between the real and the fictional elements of Plato's craftsmanship. Even greater opacity surrounds Plato's own attitudes and feelings towards his own relatives. Their ambiguous portraits in the *Charmides* may reflect his ambivalent feelings towards them, or serve dramatic and philosophical purposes, or both. Furthermore, although the *Charmides* drives a sort of wedge between the character Socrates and his interlocutors and indicates that the former cannot be held responsible for the thoughts and deeds of the latter, there is no firm evidence that Plato composed the dialogue primarily for apologetic purposes.

In short, we cannot really tell whether or to what extent the *Charmides* is a biographical text. As I have said, my own study of the dialogue does not exclude the possibility of such readings, but also does not pursue or confirm it. To put my cards on the table, I assume that the main reasons why Plato wrote the *Charmides* are philosophical.[92] And while the drama and the argument are intermeshed so as to form a coherent whole, the plot and characters of the work are chosen chiefly for the sake of its philosophical content and not the other way around.[93] Of course, these assumptions need not be accepted by every interpreter of the dialogue; in fact, many would reject them. However, they do shape in part the perspective and goals of my own approach, and do underpin the interpretation of the dialogue that I offer.

I hope to show that the philosophical value of the *Charmides* is considerable and lies in the systematic exploration of its stated topic: the nature of *sôphrosynê*,[94] as well as the pros and cons of different accounts of *sôphrosynê*; first in terms of ways of behaving, then in terms of good actions falling

---

[92] As indicated, there is no scholarly consensus on that point.
[93] Compare Myles Burnyeat's remarks with regard to the character of Thrasymachus in Burnyeat 2003.
[94] See also Tsouna 2017.

within the domain of one's expertise, and finally in terms of self-knowledge understood in a certain manner, namely as a strictly reflexive, higher-order scientific knowledge. I take it that a crucial element of the dialogue is the regular if implicit contrast that Socrates suggests between Critias', as it were, technocratic conception of self-knowledge as a 'science of science' and a different conception attributed, within the *Charmides* as well as in other texts, to Socrates himself. The philosophical importance of that contrast is this: it forces us to reflect critically about the ideal, defended by Critias, of a higher-order scientific knowledge both reflexive and directive that represents a model of successful political governance. Comparison and contrast of this latter with the model of Socratic self-knowledge – a sort of knowledge that is neither reflexive nor directive but necessary for personal improvement – is a strategy designed to help the readers of the dialogue discern the weaknesses of the Critianic model, but also the shortcomings of Socrates' philosophy and method. Thus, the readers are guided to look towards alternative models of an *epistêmê* related specifically to political governance. Two of them are developed, respectively, in the *Republic* and the *Statesman*, but nothing prevents the readers of the *Charmides* to pursue some of its themes outside Plato's works as well.

Independently of its relevance to political governance, the conception of temperance as a 'science of science' is philosophically remarkable in its own right. To my mind, an important part of Plato's motivation for composing the *Charmides* is, precisely, the elaboration, criticism, and refutation of that view and, in particular, of the idea that there can be a strictly reflexive *epistêmê*, i.e. a science uniquely and exclusively related to itself and not to any object distinct from itself. Whether this position circulated in intellectual circles or was invented by Plato, I believe that Plato takes it seriously[95] and is genuinely intrigued by the logical, psychological, ethical, and political issues that can be raised in that connection. He takes care to show to his audiences why the view under discussion might be attractive and to whom. And he undertakes to explore it in earnest. This is an important task. Historically, some version of the view under consideration can be associated with the ideology of the Thirty, but also is present in the model of governance proposed by John Stuart Mill,[96] as well as in contemporary models that assign to expert technocrats a prominent role in politics. Logically and epistemologically, the investigation launched by Plato's Socrates regarding the conceivability of a strictly reflexive *epistêmê* or the

[95] On the question of why Plato would be interested in such a concept, see also above, 25–7, 38.
[96] See Schofield 2006, ch. 4: 136–93.

benefits that might derive from it constitutes a platform for Plato in order to do significant work on relatives and relations,[97] expose certain syntactic and semantic aspects of reflexivity, and explore specifically the notion of reflexive *epistêmê* and its purported function and content. Ethically, the investigation of the 'science of science' in the *Charmides* highlights the eudaemonistic expectations underlying the idea of political expertise and, I believe, intimates that we should search for other forms of higher-order understanding involving some sort of reflectiveness and also bearing on ethics and the well-being of society.

There is yet another cluster of reasons why, it seems to me, Plato chose to write the *Charmides*. They are related, I think, to indirect criticisms concerning certain aspects of Socratic philosophy as it is represented in Plato's so-called Socratic dialogues. On my reading, the Socratic notion of self-knowledge is only obliquely present throughout the dialogue. But even though it is not the direct target of the elenchus, the argument in the second half of the *Charmides* guides us to examine whether Socrates' claim of being able to detect knowledge and ignorance in both oneself and others, as well as the method by which he is supposed to achieve that result, may not be vulnerable to some of the objections raised against the 'science of science'. On the one hand, Socratic self-knowledge, i.e. the capacity of judging what oneself and others know or do not know by means of the elenchus, does not involve strict reflexivity and hence is not vulnerable to objections raised by the Argument from Relatives. On the other hand, towards the end of the dialogue, Socrates himself raises the worry that it may be 'impossible for a man to know, in some sort of way, things that he does not know at all' (175c). Whether this is as serious a problem for Socratic self-knowledge remains to be examined by those who are inclined to do so.[98] In any case, the fact that, in his final summary of the refutation of the 'science of science', Socrates criticises his own method strongly suggests that Plato composed the *Charmides* in a critical mode and probably with this aim in mind: to disengage himself in an oblique and qualified manner from the Socratic views and method, and direct his audience towards the substantive philosophical doctrines and methods elaborated in the so-called middle and late Platonic works.[99]

A serious criticism against Socrates bears specifically on the political dimensions of the argument in the *Charmides*. Not only does the investigation reveal the fatal flaws of Critias' conception of temperance as

---

[97] See Duncombe 2020, *passim*.   [98] On this point, see Tsouna 2017.
[99] See also above, 35–6, and Chapter 12, 273–86.

a 'science of science' conveying supreme cognitive authority to the temperate ruler. It also brings into the open Socrates' fundamental inability to provide an alternative model to the nightmarish society of the 'dream'. Indeed, Socrates' dialectical moves, which include the promising suggestion that happiness is the exclusive object of the *epistêmê* of good and evil, concern the happiness of the individual but not of the political community in its entirety. Recall that, in the *Apology*, Socrates confirms that his endeavours to gain self-knowledge and improve the souls of his fellow-citizens were conducted on a strictly private basis; more active involvement in politics would have been incompatible with his philosophical mission and would have put his life at risk. Consistently with these claims, the *Charmides* suggests that Socrates' philosophy and method can make us better people, but cannot improve society as a whole. To pursue this latter goal, we need to leave behind the ethical paradigm offered by Socrates and consider the paradigms of the statesman or of the Philosopher-King.

This is all I have to say in the way of an introduction to the main part of this book. I hope to have given some sense of the agenda that I shall follow, and also I hope to have made sufficiently clear my intention to engage with the *Charmides* and the secondary literature in a dialectical spirit rather than a dogmatic mode.

9 Postscript: Practical Matters

The book is divided into twelve chapters. The current chapter has presented a fairly detailed introduction that aims to convey a sense of the main dramatic and philosophical issues of the *Charmides*, outline its historical subtext, and provide a scholarly context for the interpretation that I shall defend. Chapters 2 to 12 roughly follow the drama and argument as they are developed in the *Charmides*. Chapter 12 serves also as a conclusion to the book, since it discusses how Socrates draws together the results of the argument that we have gone through, especially in the second part of the dialogue, and also comments on the dramatic closure of the work. Even though this structure largely reflects what I take to be natural pauses or, if you wish, natural joints of Plato's text, there is nothing rigidly normative about it. The boundaries of the successive phases of argument can be blurry, and it is worth exploring different ways of carving it up. The chapters' length is unequal. It depends partly on the length of the passage under discussion in each chapter and the wealth of dramatic detail, but also, first and foremost, on the importance of the philosophical issues that are raised and debated by the dialogue's interlocutors. In the earlier chapters I have translated excerpts of the Greek text, but the Argument from Relatives is translated in its entirety and the Argument from Benefit is translated for the greatest part. These arguments are especially complicated and difficult to follow, and I believe that it will be helpful to the reader to have the text under their eyes in order to assess more easily the analysis that I propose. Stephanus page references usually include line numbers, but in the current chapter, for instance, they do not because such degree of precision is not necessary. A new translation of the *Charmides* is also included in an Appendix at the end of the book.

I wish this book to be accessible to philosophers as well as classicists, and experts that do not read Greek as well as those who do. To that end, Greek words and phrases are standardly transliterated in the main text and always translated or glossed over in their first occurrence, as well as at regular intervals throughout the discussion. I use Greek characters in the footnotes when I deem it important to cite parts of the text or when I address specifically linguistic or technical issues. Frequently occurring terms, in particular '*sôphrosynê*', '*epistêmê*', '*technê*', and '*kalon*', are always transliterated in the main text and frequently transliterated in the footnotes as well. In these cases too, I translate the terms on their first occurrence in every chapter and then use, indiscriminately, either the transliterated term or the corresponding translation or both. To mark the striking peculiarity of the definitions of temperance as 'doing one's own' and, later in the dialogue, as 'science of itself and the other sciences' or 'science of science' simpliciter, I use quotes. The use of emphases in the translation in some cases renders what I believe to be emphasised, for example, by word-order in Plato's text, while in other cases it aims to highlight points taken up in interpretation. As indicated, I take it that the terms '*technê*' (art or craft or expertise) and '*epistêmê*' (science, expertise, scientific knowledge, scientific or expert understanding) are used interchangeably in some contexts but synecdoch-ically in others: '*epistêmê*' captures the specifically cognitive aspect of expert knowledge in a way that '*technê*' does not, and this explains why '*epistêmê*' and not '*technê*' is the term used to convey Critias' definition of temperance as a governing science orientated solely towards itself. I try to render these nuances in both the translation and the evaluation of the dialogue's arguments.

The Bibliography contains the books and articles that inform my own interpretation. To the extent that it proved possible, I acknowledge my engagement with the secondary literature in the footnotes. However, it seems appropriate to single out the book by Thomas Tuozzo, *Plato's Charmides: Positive Elenchus in a 'Socratic' Dialogue* (Cambridge, 2011), which has been for me a valuable source of historical information and philosophical reflection; Matthew Duncombe's PhD dissertation and his monograph *Ancient Relativity* (Oxford, 2020); published work by Victor Caston, Thomas Johansen, and M. M. McCabe on the Argument from Relatives (or, as some call it, the Relations Argument); van der Ben's commentary on the *Charmides* (Amsterdam, 1985); and also the monographs by T. G. Tuckey (Cambridge, 1952), B. Witte (Berlin, 1970), and W. T. Schmid (Albany, NY, 1998). David Sedley's interpretation of the *Theaetetus* informs the parallels that I draw between that dialogue and the *Charmides*, and Malcolm Schofield's account of Plato's models for political science is fundamental for my own discussion of the political aspects of Critias' conception of a 'science of itself and the other sciences'. Myles Burnyeat's remarks on the complex roles of Platonic characters lie at the basis of my approach to the characters of Charmides and Critias, and his analysis of the 'dream' in the *Theaetetus* inspires my attempt to make sense of the harrowing 'dream' of the *Charmides*. I anticipate with interest and pleasure Raphael Woolf's book *Plato's Charmides*, which will be part of the series *Cambridge Studies in the Dialogues of Plato* edited by M. M. McCabe and published by Cambridge University Press. So far as we are able to judge, our studies will not overlap but rather complement each other. My translation is greatly indebted to the translations by W. R. M. Lamb and R. K. Sprague, and occasionally to other translations of the dialogue as well, for instance the recent translation by C. Moore and C. C. Raymond (2019). It is divided in sections approximately corresponding to the chapters of the book and their subdivisions. Generally, I tried to make the volume as reader-friendly as I could, and I hope that the reader will not be too frustrated in places where I have not succeeded in that aim. Without any further delay, we should now turn to our text.

CHAPTER 2

The Prologue (153a1–159a10)

1 Setting the Stage (153a1–154b6)

We had arrived the previous evening from the camp at Potidaea and, having arrived after a long absence, I gladly headed for my regular haunts. And so it was that I went into the gymnasium of Taureas opposite the temple of Basile and came upon a great many people there, some of whom were actually unknown to me but most of whom I knew. And as soon as they saw me unexpectedly entering the wrestling-school, they greeted me from a distance from wherever each of them was. Chaerephon, however, acting like the madman that he is, jumped up from the middle of the crowd, ran towards me, and, taking hold of my hand, asked, 'Socrates, how did you survive the battle?'. True, shortly before we came away, there had been a battle at Potidaea that the people here had only just got news of. (*Charm.* 153a1–b6)

The opening lines of the *Charmides* circumscribe the dialogue's frame, distinguish the level of the narration from that of the action, and specify the spatio-temporal parameters of the encounter that will be related. Speaking in the first person and the past tense and addressing his anonymous friend, Socrates as narrator immerses us directly in the episode's context and action. The dramatic date of the latter is one of the earliest in Plato. Socrates (as character in the narration) has just returned home, together with other survivors,[1] from the camp of Potidaea in Thrace, shortly after a very severe battle that took place either in 432 BC or, more likely, 429 BC.[2] The place is Athens and, more specifically, one of the city's

---

[1] The very first word of the dialogue, translated as 'we had arrived' (ἥκομεν: 153a), is not in the singular but the plural and probably indicates that several survivors of the battle of Potidaea, including of course Socrates, left the camp together and headed for their city. Socrates' use of the first-person plural is significant: contrary to Critias who has led a sheltered and privileged life in Athens during the months of the siege, Socrates views himself as one of many Athenian soldiers who participated in the Thracian Campaign of 432–429 BCE and faced its perils.

[2] Many commentators assume that there was only one battle at or near Potidaea, that it is the one mentioned both in *Charm.* 153b5–7 and *Symp.* 220d5–e7, and that it took place in the autumn of 432

wrestling-schools, the palaestra of Taureas. We are told that this was one of Socrates' regular haunts and that he was pleased to enter it again[3] after a relatively long absence. We are thus led to think of the habitual interests and activities of Plato's Socrates and consider the associations suggested by the narrator's meticulous depiction of the dialogue's setting.[4]

Potidaea was one of the causes of the great conflict which ended with the defeat of Athens, the demolition of its walls, and the imposition of the rule of the Thirty. Socrates confirms that the battle that he fought there was especially violent and that many Athenians had lost their lives (153b9–c1). Potidaea, therefore, is a location associated with defeat and loss. Within the city of Athens, the shrine of Basile standing across from the gymnasium of Taureas carries similar associations, since it was probably dedicated to Persephone, queen of the underworld.[5] By leaving behind the military camp in northern Greece and heading towards the south and his native city, and then turning his back on the temple of Basile in order to enter the gymnasium, Socrates is shown to move away from the realm of the dead in order to eagerly join the world of the living.

The sequel of the narrative indicates that this is a deliberate choice on Socrates' part. Even though he accepts Chaerephon's exhortation to sit down and give a full account of the recent battle (153c5–6), he seems unwilling to talk much about it. When Chaerephon asks him how he managed to survive, he merely replies: 'exactly as you see me' (153b7–8). He is equally laconic in confirming the exceptionally fierce character of the conflict and its grim outcome (153c9–d1). As narrator, he mentions that he answered the questions that the people in the gymnasium asked him

---

BCE under the command of Callias (Thucydides, I.62–3). Consequently, they fix the dramatic date of the dialogue at 432 BCE: for example, see Dušanić 2000. However, a convincing case has been made by Planeaux 1999 that, in fact, in the *Symposium* Alcibiades implies that there was more than one battle, and that the battle to which the *Charmides* refers is not the battle of 432 BCE in which Alcibiades received an award, but the bloody battle in the spring of 429 BCE at Spartolus near Potidaea under the command of Xenophon, which was followed by the disbanding of the Athenian forces and the return of Athenian survivors to Athens (Thucydides, II.79). Planeaux's argument aims to show that Plato is interested in historical detail, and his concern for biographical realism is greater than is generally acknowledged.

[3] ἐπὶ τὰς συνήθεις διατριβάς: 153a3.

[4] Depending on the context, I use 'dialogue' either to refer to the *Charmides* as a whole consisting of both the frame of the narration and the episode that the narrator relates or, alternatively, to refer only to the related conversation between the three main characters.

[5] We know very little about this shrine. It is mentioned in a Greek inscription (*IG* 2d.ed., 94), but the identity of the Basile cannot be inferred with any certainty. Most probably, Basile is the bride of Hades, Persephone (Schamp 2000, 111–12). Other views include: that Basile was a personification of Athenian royalty (Sprague 1993, 57 n. 3), that it personified an aristocratic Athens (Shapiro 1986; Witte 1970, 40–2), and that the temple of Basile was related to the care of the soul, as opposed to the palaestra, which was related to the care of the body (Rotondaro 2000, 217).

(153c9–d1), but does not dwell further on this matter. In the capacities of both narrator and character, Socrates appears disinclined to linger on the subjects of war, violence, and death. And while he is portrayed as quite unmoved by the mortal risk that he has run, he shows no penchant for heroics.

A first connection can be traced between the literary form and the philosophical subject of the dialogue. Unlike the 'manic' Chaerephon[6] who does not control his emotions and gestures, Socrates appears to be master of himself. If he has experienced fear at the sight of death or relief at its escape, sorrow about those that have been lost in battle or elation for being back in his city and amongst his friends, he does not betray such emotions but can control them so that they do not affect his behaviour. In other words, he is depicted as having *sôphrosynê*, temperance, in this ordinary sense of the term. Another feature of the opening lines of the dialogue bears on both the drama and the argument, namely an initial hint that Socrates and Critias are known to be friendly with each other. For, when Chaerephon asks Socrates to tell them more about the battle of Potidaea, he leads him to a seat next to Critias (153c6–7), presumably taking for granted that this vicinity would not displease Socrates.[7] Moreover, while he was taking his seat, he warmly greeted[8] Critias and everyone else sitting nearby (153c8–d1). The ambiance is one of easy familiarity – an impression that will be reinforced later in the dialogue's prologue. Socrates does comply with his countrymen's requests to provide information about the recent battle, but it is clear that his own interests lie elsewhere. The following passage reveals what they are.

> When we had enough of these things, I turned to questioning them about affairs at home, namely, about philosophy, how it was doing at present, and about the young men, whether any among them had become distinguished for wisdom or beauty or both.[9] And Critias, looking away towards the door and seeing some young men who were coming in railing at each other

---

[6] μανικός: 153b2.

[7] Plato's audiences know that Chaerephon and Critias eventually found themselves in opposite camps. Chaerephon was a democrat who fought with Thrasybulus to overturn the dictatorial regime headed by Critias and restore democracy. Surely it is not accidental that, in the prologue of the *Charmides*, Chaerephon and Critias are depicted as being on friendly terms. Their presence points unmistakably to the political subtext of the dialogue and refers its readers back to a time when political tensions festered beneath the surface of the Athenian democracy's precarious stability.

[8] ἠσπαζόμην: 153c8. LSJ refers to this passage, rendering the verb by 'salute from a distance' when it is preceded by πόρρωθεν. However, the latter adverb does not occur in our passage and, in the absence of that qualification, I take it that, here, the verb ἀσπάζομαι does not mean merely 'to greet' or 'to salute', but to do so with joy and frequently also with a hug or a kiss.

[9] ἢ σοφίᾳ ἢ κάλλει ἢ ἀμφοτέροις: 153d4–5.

followed by another crowd of people behind them, said 'As for the beautiful youths, Socrates, I expect that you will get to know at once; for these who are coming in happen to be the entourage and lovers of the youth who, at least for the moment, is believed to be the most beautiful; and I imagine that he himself is already on his way and somewhere close by'. (153d2–154a6)

Socrates identifies two objects of primary concern to him, namely the current state of philosophy and the excellence of youths in respect of *sophia*, wisdom, or *kallos*, beauty, or both. While he does not state how these themes are related to each other, the fact that he mentions them in close succession intimates that they are interconnected: Socrates wants to know whether there are any young men of exceptional promise who have an inclination to philosophy. Assuming that this is so, on the one hand, Socrates ostensibly observes conventional standards according to which youths are praised in encomiastic poetry and other kinds of literature,[10] but, on the other, he gestures towards the peculiarly Socratic idea that a youth's excellence in wisdom crucially bears on his aptitude and attitude towards philosophy. Already at this point, experienced readers of Plato are in a position to surmise that, in the eyes of Socrates, a young man's beauty has to do with his soul as well as his body, his philosophical nature as well as his physical form (cf. *Men.* 76b, *Tht.* 185e).

The man who answers Socrates' query is Critias, in his first direct intervention in the dialogue. It is worth noting that, initially, he does not say anything about wisdom. Concentrating on beauty alone, he assures Socrates that he will soon see the most beautiful youth of the day. Moreover, he informs Socrates that those accompanying the young man are his lovers (*erastai*: 154a5), highlighting the intuitive connection between *kallos*, beauty, and *erôs*, love. Thus Critias introduces an element of eroticism, even before mentioning the young man's name. It is only when Socrates prompts him (154a7) that he identifies the youth as follows: 'Charmides, son of our uncle Glaucon,[11] and my cousin' (154b1–2).[12] Reaching out of the dialogue to historical reality, Plato thus makes explicit the family ties between Critias and Charmides, and also between the two cousins and himself. And he also alludes to Socrates' familiarity with the

---

[10] See, for instance, Pindar, *Olymp.* X, 97–105, Isocrates, *Evag.* 22–4, and the discussion in Tulli 2000, 262–3.

[11] This Glaucon is probably the grandfather of the Glaucon of the *Republic*.

[12] Planeaux 1999 fixes the dramatic date of the *Charmides* at 429 BCE on the grounds that Socrates must have been absent from Athens long enough for Charmides to pass from boyhood to adolescence.

members of his own family. For, according to our dialogue's narrator, Critias remarks that Socrates must have met Charmides in the past, but would not recognise him now, since he went on campaign away from Athens when Charmides was still a child (154a8–b1). Indeed, Socrates emphatically confirms that he knew Charmides and adds, ambiguously, that he was not ordinary (*ou phaulos*: 154b3) even in childhood (154b3–5).

Much has been achieved in these opening lines of the *Charmides*. The frame of the dialogue has been sketched and space has been created between the frame and what lies within it. The readers are now able to adopt different perspectives with regard to the dialogue's contents and to assess the action from different moments in time.[13] Socrates' double role, as narrator and as participant in the narrated episode, has become clear-cut,[14] what Plato has at stake has been indicated, and his authorial presence in the background has been felt. All the principal characters have been introduced, some information has been given regarding their relations to each other, and some features of their portraits have been sketched.

Both as narrator and as protagonist, Socrates is portrayed in a familiar way that brings to mind, notably, the *Apology*, the *Laches*, and Alcibiades' speech in the *Symposium*: friendly but not over-familiar, dispassionate and even-tempered, brave in the face of physical danger but making no display of his courage, entering an Athenian public space in search of company and conversation, passionate about philosophy and looking for youths of talent and beauty. For the moment, we can infer almost nothing about the

---

[13] While the dramatic date of the narrated episode is 432 BCE or, more likely, 429 BCE, the date at which Socrates' narration to his anonymous listener is supposed to take place remains vague. As for the date of the composition of the *Charmides* by Plato, opinions vary but the dialogue is generally located sometime in the 380s. According to Dušanić 2000, Plato wrote the *Charmides* in 382 BCE, probably after Lysias' speech *On the Scrutiny of Evandrus* (cf. XXVI.3, 5) and after Isocrates' *Helen* (cf. X.1, 5). On the other hand, Witte 1970, 44–5, points to close parallels between the *Charmides* and Lysias' speech and contends that the speech post-dates the dialogue by a few months and that its author deliberately imitates features of Plato's text. Witte and especially Dušanić argue in favour of the relevance of Critias' political heritage at the time of the composition of the *Charmides*. In fact, Dušanić contends that Plato's positive representation of Critias in the latter dialogue constitutes an implicit criticism of the support that Athenian democrats wanted to lend to Thebes in 382 BCE. According to Dušanić, by portraying Critias in a favourable light as a proponent of the aristocratic virtue of *sôphrosynê*, and by pointing to the similarities between the immediate aftermath of the battle of Potidaea and the political conditions of 382 BCE, Plato warns his fellow-citizens against demagogy, imperialism, and hostility towards Sparta (Dušanić 2000, 60–3).

[14] Rotondaro 2000, 214, maintains that, as narrator, Socrates uses a mixed form of speech consisting of both narration (διήγησις) and imitation (μίμησις), whereas, as participant in the narrated episode, he uses only imitation (μίμησις).

nameless character who is listening to Socrates' narration.[15] In the course of the prologue, we shall gradually form the impression that he knows (or knows of) the places and the personages that Socrates mentions, is somehow associated with Socrates,[16] and is probably sufficiently intimate with him to receive from Socrates a confession of a personal nature.[17]

In addition to these characters, we get briefly acquainted with the 'manic' Chaerephon, clearly very attached to Socrates but over-emotional and uncontrolled. He will play a small part in the prologue and then drop out of sight. Critias, however, is there to stay. As mentioned, he is portrayed as a relatively close acquaintance of Socrates or even a family friend. His behaviour appears unexceptional and his exchange with Socrates exhibits something of a rhetorical pace and structure. First he tells Socrates that there will soon be an answer to his query about beautiful youths, next he shows to him the admirers of 'the most beautiful youth of the day' but does not name him, then he reveals Charmides' name and that of his father and, in the end, he states his own family connection to the young man. We should remember that Critias initially identifies Charmides as the most beautiful boy of his age group, but does not say that he is also the wisest of his peers. As for Charmides himself, even though he has not yet made his entrance, we already know several things about him. He is the son of Glaucon, cousin of both Critias and Plato, known by Socrates since he was a child, now grown into adolescence, and an exquisitely handsome creature courted by many and admired by all.

2   A Most Poetic Youth (154b6–155a7)

You will know immediately, he [sc. Critias] said, both how much and in what way he [sc. Charmides] has grown. And as he was speaking these words, Charmides came in.

---

[15] Van der Ben 1985, 4, suggests that the anonymous listener appears to be quite young.

[16] The vocative 'my friend' (ὦ ἑταῖρε: 154b) may point to a quite close relationship between Socrates and the listener (cf. *Phd.* 89e; also Xenophon, *Mem.* 2.8.1). Socrates' later address, 'my noble friend' (ὦ γεννάδα: 155d3), may indicate even a love relation of a certain kind. As McAvoy (1996, 77–8 n. 33) remarks, this is the unique occurrence of the vocative in Plato; the only other use of the word γεννάδας found in the Platonic dialogues occurs in *Phd.* 243c3 where Socrates, repenting of his first speech which compares lovers to wolves, implores someone 'of a noble and gentle nature' in love with a person of the same kind not to be offended and not to think Socrates entirely ignorant of genuine *erôs*, love.

[17] Arguably, only a noble lover would be an appropriate audience for the confession made by Socrates at 155d3–e2. Moreover, only someone well versed in Socratic dialectic would be able to follow Socrates' narrative beyond the prologue and through the argument. For these reasons, it has occasionally been suggested that the anonymous listener represents Plato in his youth.

Now truly, my friend, I cannot measure anything. So far as beautiful youths are concerned I am merely a blank ruler. For, somehow, almost all youths who have just come of age appear to me beautiful. Indeed this is so, and especially on that occasion the youth appeared to me marvellous in stature and beauty. As for all the others, they were so astonished and confused when he entered that they seemed to me to be in love with him. Moreover, many more lovers were following in his train as well. Of course this was not so surprising on the part of men like ourselves. However, I was also observing the boys and noticed that not a single one of them, even the youngest, was looking elsewhere but all gazed at him as if he were a statue. (154b8–c8)

In an apostrophe to his anonymous auditor, Socrates reveals something about himself, namely that he is a 'white measuring-line' or a blank ruler[18] that cannot measure the beauty of one young man in comparison to that of another: all of them appear the same to him in that regard.[19] Why wouldn't Socrates be able to do what everyone else can do; that is, judge the beauty of one person in comparison to that of another? His metrical ineptitude could not derive from excessive proneness to sensuality, for this hypothesis is largely incompatible with Socrates' persona and with the self-restraint that he shows at a later stage of the opening scene. Nor, on the other hand, can his ineptness result from indifference, since he has already expressed interest in the beautiful youths of the day and has just told his anonymous friend that Charmides appeared to him marvellous in beauty and stature. Perhaps, then, Socrates has in mind something else – an idea developed by Diotima in her account of a lover's ascent to the scale of perfection in the *Symposium* and in the *Republic* (474 c ff.).

According to Diotima, as the candidate for initiation in the mysteries of love is going up the ladder, in his initial steps, first, he falls in love with the beauty of one individual body; next, he comes to realise that the beauty of one body is the same as the beauty of another and thus becomes a lover of every beautiful body; and then he grasps that the beauty of the soul is

---

[18] ἀτεχνῶς γὰρ λευκὴ στάθμη εἰμὶ πρὸς τοὺς καλούς: 154b8–9. Reece 1998, 66, renders the expression by 'blank ruler', Sprague 1993 by 'broken yardstick'. Reece remarks that the image of a white measuring-line is especially appropriate on this occasion, since Socrates is looking at a young man who is like an ἄγαλμα, a statue of white marble or stone. I am not sure about this suggestion, for, so far as I know, ancient statues were usually painted.

[19] Those familiar with Lorenzo Da Ponte's libretto of Mozart's *Don Giovanni* might be tempted to compare Socrates' metrical ineptness with regard to beauty with Don Giovanni's lack of discrimination with regard to womanhood: 'non si picca se sia ricca, / se sia brutta, se sia bella;/ purché porti la gonnella, voi sapete quel que fa!' (*Don Giovanni*, Act 1). Compare Nehamas 2007, 112–14, with notes, who explains the 'extraordinary convergence between Plato and Mozart' by tracing the connections between the philosophical lover in the *Symposium* and Leporello's area through Lucretius and Molière.

incomparably superior to the beauty of the body and hence overwhelmingly attractive even in the sight of a plain or ugly physique (*Symp.* 210a–b). Considered in these terms, Socrates' confession that, when it comes to beautiful youths, he is a 'blank ruler' indicates that he has reached at least the second step of the heavenly ladder: he understands that the beauty of each and every body is the same and, accordingly, does not judge the beauty of one boy in comparison to that of another but is a lover of beauty in all beautiful boys alike (cf. 210a8–b6).[20] The parallel between the two dialogues need not go further and, therefore, need not introduce transcendent Forms. In the *Charmides*, Socrates has come to realise that all beautiful youths are alike in respect of beauty, and also that the beauty of the soul is incomparably superior to that of the body. But so far there is no indication that he has moved beyond that point.

Enter Charmides. The narrator vests him with the elaborate imagery of divinity. He is both preceded (154a4) and followed (154a5) by adherents, and he has a terribly powerful impact on everyone except Socrates. His admirers are astounded and overpowered, confused and bewildered,[21] much as people are when they fall under the spell of erotic passion or, in myths, when they encounter some god. Socrates himself marvels[22] at both the young man's physical beauty and people's uniform reaction to him.[23] For, regardless of their age, all of them gaze at Charmides[24] with a sort of fixation and seem incapable of turning their eyes away. Socrates says that he found especially astonishing the fact that not only mature men but also the youngest boys looked at Charmides in that manner (174c5–8). Presumably, the reason was this: while he could explain the behaviour of the former by surmising that they experienced intense physical desire, he could not find a ready explanation for the behaviour of the latter. He seems to think that, even if very young boys (*paides*: 154c6) feel sexual desire of some sort, this does not amount to fully fledged sexual passion, nor does it have such compelling force.

Socrates compares the way in which the people in the gymnasium gaze at Charmides with the way in which one stares at a statue.[25] The metaphor carries significant connotations that bear on the sequel of the prologue and

---

[20] Diotima's ladder can also be considered relevant to Socrates' expressed interest in Charmides' soul rather than his body (*Charm.* 154e). For this suggests that, in the terms of the divine ladder of the *Symposium*, he has effected the ascent to the third step as well, where the lover of beauty in every youth alike fixes himself on a youth's soul rather than his body and endeavours to conduct the sort of *logoi*, discourses, that will benefit the young men and improve their character (*Symp.* 210b6–c3).
[21] ἐκπεπληγμένοι τε καὶ τεθορυβημένοι: 154c3.   [22] Cf. θαυμαστός: 154c1.
[23] θαυμαστὸν ἦν: 154c5–6.   [24] ἐθεῶντο: 154c8.   [25] ὥσπερ ἄγαλμα ἐθεῶντο αὐτόν: 154d1.

foreshadow some of its themes. Statues frequently represent divine or quasi-divine beings, and the members of Charmides' retinue stare at him as if he were a god or a sculpture representing a god. Arguably, in the eyes of the spectators classical statues primarily represent ideals rather than elements of individuality. Likewise, as they gaze at Charmides, his admirers primarily perceive the beauty and harmony of his form rather than features of his personality or character. Indeed, Charmides is depicted through the prologue as a lad of such perfection that his beauty resembles that of an art object:[26] a sculpted human form.[27] Also, a statue is passively available to the eye of the beholder but cannot interact with him. In comparable manner, the narrator gives us to understand that, at first, Charmides was entirely passive.[28] Everybody stared at him but he did not stare at anyone in return. His admirers seem passionate about him but he appears completely detached. Everyone is in love with him but there is no indication that he is even aware of it. People are talking about him but he hasn't yet uttered a word. These features are even more prominent in the sequel of the narration, when Chaerephon's praise of the youth's beauty almost violates wrestling-school protocol and prompts a remarkable exchange between the other two older protagonists.

> Then Chaerephon called me and asked, Socrates, how does the youth seem to you? Does he not have a beautiful face? – Very much so, I replied. – And yet, he said, if he were willing to take his clothes off, it would seem to you that he has no face, so great is the beauty of his bodily form. All the other men too agreed with Chaerephon's claim. – By Hercules, I said, you make the man seem irresistible, if indeed he has in him one more advantage – a small one. – What? asked Critias. – If he happens to be beautiful with regard to his soul, I replied. But somehow he ought to be of such sort, Critias, since he belongs to your family. – Well, he (sc. Critias) said, he is very beautiful and good in this respect too. – Why then, I said, did we not strip that very part of him and view it first, before his bodily form? For, in any case, at his age, he surely will be willing to engage in dialogue. – Very much so, said Critias, since in fact he is a philosopher and also, as it seems to both himself and others, he is quite a poet.[29] – That fine gift, I said, my dear Critias, exists in your family from a long time back and derives from your kinship with Solon. (154c8–155a3)

Chaerephon's intervention is especially revealing about the manner in which he and his peers perceive Charmides and suggests a contrast between, on the one hand, Chaerephon and other mature men in the room and, on the other, Socrates and possibly Critias as well. In accordance with his 'manic'

[26] Charalabopoulos 2008, 513, and 2014.   [27] Reece 1998, 66.   [28] McAvoy 1996, 84.
[29] πάνυ ποιητικός: 155a1. On the meaning of ποιητικός see below, 68–9.

temperament, Chaerephon presses Socrates to acknowledge emphatically[30] that Charmides is indeed *euprosôpos* (154d2), he has a beautiful face, and then goes on to remark that, should the youth agree to stand naked in front of them, his face would be totally eclipsed: Charmides would seem *aprosôpos*, faceless (154d4–5). Chaerephon's meaning is not entirely clear. Given his impulsive character and his evident susceptibility to passion, I think that his point is not that one cannot contemplate two kinds of beauty at the same time,[31] or that Socrates should look towards the universal, Form-like aspects of Charmides as opposed to his individual, face-like aspects.[32] Rather, Chaerephon says that, however beautiful the young man's face may seem, its beauty would be completely obliterated by the beauty of his naked body. And the likely reason why Chaerephon makes this claim is that he passionately desires the youth's body. The same probably holds for other mature men in the room who agree with Chaerephon (154d6).

Charmides, then, is both fragmented and reified by these older men. Unlike Socrates who has been away for several months, these men must have had many opportunities to see the youth exercising naked in the palaestra. And, unlike Socrates, they had probably experienced the overwhelming effect of that sight many times. Presently driven by desire, they disconnect the youth's face from his body and become oblivious to the former but focus their gaze exclusively on the latter. They see only a part of the young man, but cannot view him as a whole. And insofar as a person's face is linked to his/her individuality, Chaerephon's remark intimates that he and his companions are blind to Charmides' personality but view him only as an object of desire. Should the young man consent to remove his clothes, he would strip himself of his identity as well as his garments.[33] Note that, even though Chaerephon makes the stripping conditional upon the young man's consent,[34] Charmides' fragmentation in the eyes of the beholder and his transformation into a faceless figure would be something that he would merely suffer, much as a lifeless

---

[30] ὑπερφυῶς: 154d3.   [31] So Bruell 1977, 144.

[32] Benardete 1986, 13, maintains that Chaerephon points out to Socrates the Form-like aspects of Charmides. In his view, Socrates is not interested in σωφροσύνη as knowledge of the self – that is, of a unique bundle of individual features – but in σωφροσύνη as class-knowledge.

[33] Compare the end of Socrates' first speech in the *Phaedrus* (237a–241d), where the speaker points out that, in many cases, the fondness of the lover for the beloved is not motivated by goodwill towards the beloved but by erotic appetite: 'just as the wolf loves the lamb, so the lover is fond of the beloved' (241d). The wolf looks on the lamb as food, not as Wooly. Likewise, the lover sees the beloved as an object intended for the satisfaction of his own needs, not as an individual that has value in his own right (cf. 240c–d).

[34] εἰ ἐθέλοι: 154d. Although Chaerephon's appreciation of Charmides' body is indicative of his passionate nature and his susceptibility to sexual desire, it does not amount to an 'eroto-violent suggestion' to strip Charmides naked (*pace* McAvoy 1996, 83).

object would. From this perspective too, the young man's passivity is comparable to that of a statue. Things are done to him, but he does not react in return.

So far as one can tell, Critias is in the same position as Chaerephon and the other men mentioned by the narrator. He too has probably often seen his ward naked in the palaestra, and we cannot know whether he agrees with Chaerephon for he says nothing to that effect. The only man in the room who has not been privy to the youth's physical charms is Socrates, since he left Athens to go to war when Charmides was still a child. Therefore, he is still unaffected by passion and able to perceive the young man, so to speak, from a distance as a whole person. Not only does he perceive the latter's exquisite face as well as his body, but also he wants to move beyond Charmides' physical appearance and gaze at his soul. In typical manner, he changes the course of the conversation at a single stroke: the youth would be really irresistible if, in addition to the beauty of his body, he also had 'one more small advantage'; that is, a beautiful soul (154d7–8). Thus, Socrates expresses the hope that the youth's outward perfection may correspond to something equivalent within, and indicates that, for his own part, he is far more interested in beauty of the soul than of the body.

Next, specifically addressing Critias, he tells him that, since Charmides belongs to the same house as Critias, he *ought* (*prepei*: 154e1) to have a fine soul. One cannot mistake his meaning: given Charmides' aristocratic origins and hereditary gifts, he is expected to live up to the loftiest expectations. Socrates will say more on this subject later, but for the moment we should note the earnest tone of his remark, which, I believe, is not ironical in the least. On the contrary, he underscores that young Charmides was perceived as representing a unique chance for his city, his family, and perhaps also philosophy itself; and everything depended on one 'small' condition, namely whether he had (or could acquire) a well-formed soul. Within the frame of the dialogue, there seems to be every reason for optimism. Indeed, Critias hastens to respond that, in respect of his soul too, his young ward is 'both beautiful and good' (155e4),[35] thus claiming, in effect, that the youth embodies the ideal of *kalokagathia*: physical beauty and moral perfection both occurring in the same person.

At first glance, Socrates' proposal that they strip the youth's soul before they look at his body (154e5–6) might appear continuous with Chaerephon's earlier remarks. In truth, it shifts attention away from Charmides' physical charms, diffuses the ambiance of eroticism lingering in the gymnasium, and suggests a startlingly novel way of thinking and

---

[35] πάνυ καλὸς καὶ ἀγαθός: 155e4. The word πάνυ very much governs both adjectives.

talking about the soul. As the body can be stripped of its clothing, so the soul can be peeled of its trappings, and as the former can become the object of contemplation, so can the latter. There is nothing mysterious and inaccessible, generally, about the soul or, specifically, about Charmides' soul. It can be exposed and scrutinised, and both Socrates and Critias seem to think that this would be of great benefit to the young man.[36] We should register that Socrates and Critias are portrayed as having ostensibly similar attitudes in that regard. Unlike Chaerephon, whose interest in Charmides is tainted by sensuality, the other two older characters agree that the condition of Charmides' soul is much more important than that of his body and must be the first to be looked at. Moreover, they agree about the means by which that goal should be pursued: *dialegesthai* (154e7) – one-to-one dialectical cross-examination by question-and-answer.

Socrates assumes that Charmides is ready and willing[37] to engage in this sort of dialogue (154e5–7) and Critias emphatically assures him that this is so. But the reason he gives is very puzzling: not that the youth has reached an age at which he should be able to take part in a dialectical discussion (as Socrates suggests), but that he is *philosophos* (154e8–9), a lover of wisdom, and *panu poiêtikos* (155a1) – an expression that can mean a 'very good poet', but also 'greatly susceptible to poetry', 'very poetical', or 'much celebrated by poets'.[38] In what way might Charmides qualify as *philosophos* and how might this be related to his gift for poetry? Of course, Critias cannot mean that Charmides is a philosopher in any technical sense of the term, for no such sense of 'philosopher' or 'philosophy' is available in the dialogue. All that Critias can mean is that his ward loves to learn and, therefore, will be eager to engage together with Socrates in *dialegesthai*, i.e. participate in the dialectical investigation of some issue or other. It is more difficult to ascertain just how Charmides is 'very poetic'. If Critias is claiming that his ward is a really good poet,[39] and if he assumes that there is some connection between the young man's love of wisdom and his ability to

---

[36] See the excellent discussion of this passage in Charalabopoulos 2008, 518 and also the paper by Papamanoli (unpublished).

[37] ἐθέλει: 154e7.

[38] The entire phrase is this: ἐπεί τοι καὶ ἔστι φιλόσοφός τε καί, ὡς δοκεῖ ἄλλοις τε καὶ ἑαυτῷ, πάνυ ποιητικός (154e8–155a1). The word πάνυ governs only ποιητικός and does not apply to φιλόσοφος: cf. Tulli 2000, 260.

[39] Most translators render πάνυ ποιητικός (155a1) in that way: e.g. Lamb 1927; Sprague 1993. On the one hand, it seems unlikely that Critias would judge Charmides to be a good poet: the phrase ὡς δοκεῖ ἄλλοις τε καὶ ἑαυτῷ (155a1) seems politely worded to save Critias himself from agreeing in that judgement. On the other hand, Critias appears inclined to flatter Charmides and attribute to him exceptional gifts, and the capacity to write good poetry seems to be one of them.

write in verse, it is not at all clear what this connection might be.[40] The same observation holds if we take '*pany poiêtikos*' to mean 'susceptible to the charm of poetry', 'inclined towards the composition of poems', or 'celebrated by poets'. None of these options is especially helpful in order to explain how being *poiêtikos* might bear on being a lover of wisdom or, specifically, on pursuing wisdom by means of *dialegesthai*. Perhaps the thought to retain is this: if Critias believes that poetry, philosophy, and dialectical practice ideally go together, his conception of the ultimate goals of *dialegesthai* is likely to differ from Socrates' own.

Anyway, Socrates proposes to Critias to summon the young man to where they are sitting and introduce him. As he points out, even if Charmides were younger than he is, Critias' presence in the room would totally guarantee the propriety of the encounter, since Critias is Charmides' guardian as well as his cousin (155a3–7). We cannot help comparing Socrates' meticulous concern for decorum with Chaerephon's indiscretion and vulgarity. Nor can we be sure, however, about the totality of Socrates' motives. He may be truly indifferent to Charmides' physical attractions and hence easily follow the etiquette of relations between older and much younger men. Or, conceivably, he may be assuming the position of a potential lover of the right sort: an older and dignified man, who implements a strict code of conduct[41] to the point of making it impossible to guess whether or not he intends to court the youth.[42] In either case, Socrates appears to be in complete control of his feelings and actions and anticipates his talk with Charmides with perfect confidence.

3   The Fawn and the Lion (155a8–e3)

To bring Charmides near Socrates, Critias uses a ruse that, he is sure (155b8), will work: he commands a servant to tell the youth that Critias wishes to introduce him to a doctor able to treat Charmides' morning

---

[40] Several commentators point out that, according to Plato, poetry is incompatible with the practice of philosophy: if Charmides is a good poet or, alternatively, someone very susceptible to poetry (Tulli 2000, 260), it would seem to follow that he can't be a philosopher as well. However, Socrates does not say anything against poetry in the *Charmides*. Also, it would be unlikely for Critias as a character to believe that poetry and philosophy are incompatible, since his historical counterpart was a poet who held philosophical views as well, and the same was true of his ancestor, Solon.

[41] Reece 1998, 67, makes the perceptive remark that 'by having Socrates bring up the issue of wrestling-school protocol, Plato makes the reader aware that this meeting does at least have the appearance of a seductive approach'.

[42] Compare the supposed non-lover in the *Phaedrus*: a crafty older man, who was as much in love with an exquisite youth as many others, but managed to convince the youth that he was not in love at all (*Phd.* 237b).

headaches – an ailment that Charmides has been complaining about (155b1–3). Surprisingly, Socrates says that nothing prevents him from impersonating a physician (*prospoiêsasthai*: 155b5) and agrees to do so. Many elements of that part of the narrative are perplexing. Why does Critias prefer to use a ploy rather than invite his ward to come and sit with them? What prompts him to think of that particular ruse, namely the pretence that Socrates is a doctor? What are we to make of Charmides' malady, i.e. the morning headaches that Socrates is supposed to treat? And since Socrates is not a physician, why does he consent to be introduced as such? In fact, Critias' ruse fits well with both what precedes and what follows, and adds to the ambiguity of the characters and the complexity of their interactions.

Recall that Socrates has just expressed the wish to strip Charmides' soul, while Critias has claimed that his ward excels in his soul as well as his body and, moreover, is ready to submit to psychic stripping by means of dialectical cross-examination. The metaphor of taking someone's clothes off in order to ascertain what lies underneath brings associations of medical diagnosis, treatment, and healing. Given Socrates' known ability in *dialegesthai*, it is quite natural for Critias to come up with the idea of presenting Socrates as a healer who can strip Charmides' ailing parts in order to diagnose the malady and cure it.[43] This stratagem makes sense from Charmides' own perspective as well. A direct invitation issued by his guardian to come and meet Socrates – an older man and hence a potential lover – could be understood as an erotically charged message,[44] whereas the ruse invented by Critias seems innocent enough.

From the philosophical point of view, Critias' story is suggestive of the medical metaphor of the philosopher as a doctor of the soul, and of the idea that Socrates is indeed a therapist of that kind. We cannot tell whether Critias does think of Socrates as a physician of the soul, or merely presents him as a doctor in order to bring Charmides over. Likewise, we cannot yet be certain whether or to what extent Socrates endorses the medical metaphor and views himself as a healer of the soul. Further ambiguities surround Charmides' malady as well as Socrates' aptitude to treat it. On the one hand, the youth's morning headaches can be taken, specifically, as a sign of fast or even promiscuous living[45] and a bad omen for the youth's future. On the other, they can be read, more generally, as a symptom

---

[43] See McAvoy 1996, 83–4.
[44] See Reece 1998, 67. Bruell 1977, 145, suggests that perhaps Critias uses a ruse in order to put an obstacle in the way of Socrates' wish to converse with Charmides, but this proposal finds no support in Plato's text.
[45] So Hyland 1981, 32–6, 40–2.

indicating that the young man is not altogether healthy: somewhere in him there is a sickness, a disorder, a deeper cause for his malaise[46] that Socrates may or may not be able to detect and heal. In the end, as Critias had predicted (155b8), the ruse proves successful and Charmides approaches the bench where the older men are sitting.

> This is exactly what happened. Indeed he did come, and he gave rise to much laughter. For each of us who were seated tried to make room for him by pushing hard at his neighbour so as to have him sitting next to oneself, with the result that the man sitting at one end of the bench was forced to get up, whereas the man sitting at the other end was tumbled off sideways. In the end, Charmides came and sat down between me and Critias. (155b9–c5)

This scene might have belonged to a comic play. The commotion provoked by the arrival of a handsome young man or one's attempt to make room for him somewhere close to oneself are familiar *topoi*, also occurring in Plato's *Symposium*. Compare the piece of vaudeville narrated in the above passage with the scene of Alcibiades' arrival at Agathon's house (*Symp.* 212c–e). In this latter too there is noise, music, and brawling, and Socrates makes room for Alcibiades to sit between Agathon and himself (213a). As in the *Charmides*, so in the *Symposium* there is burlesque behaviour, intense physicality,[47] congeniality, and laughter.[48] And as in the former case, so in the latter an atmosphere of eroticism and sexuality surrounds the protagonists, even though it manifests itself in different ways in the two dialogues.

As mentioned, it is reasonable to surmise that many of the older men on the bench have seen Charmides naked in the palaestra and many, if not all, have had the experience relayed by Chaerephon: they have gazed at the perfect beauty of his body in total oblivion of his face, i.e. his personality and individuality. Hence there can be little doubt about the reason why each of these men is battling[49] to push away his neighbour and have the youth sit right next to himself. Eventually, Charmides takes his place between Critias and Socrates, and this detail can but need not be vested with symbolic significance. Within the dialogue frame, Charmides makes

---

[46] So Benardete 1986, 18 and Solère-Quéval 1993, 11.   [47] Charalabopoulos 2008, 521.

[48] The narrator's description of the laughter occurring among the older men sitting on the bench fulfils a meta-textual function: it invites the anonymous listener as well as the audience to step into the dramatic frame of the incident and join in the fun. Bernardete 1986, 15, contends that there was really no laughter in the palaestra, but the laughter belongs exclusively to the narrative level: it is not the characters but the auditors who are supposed to find the scene funny.

[49] Charalabopoulos 2008, 523, points out that the terminology of the episode has military connotations.

the natural choice of sitting between his guardian, who has summoned him, and the man whom Critias presents as a doctor. In the light of historical events, however, the youth's choice acquires special meaning. He places himself between two very different men and could turn towards one of them and away from the other. In the sequel of the dialogue he will engage mainly with Socrates, but in real life he will attach himself to Critias and fall together with him. Now, the narrator's tone changes. Addressing his anonymous listener in a direct and intimate fashion,[50] he proceeds to give an account of his own state.

> By that time, my friend, I already began to feel perplexed,[51] and the confidence that I had possessed earlier, because I had anticipated that it would be very easy to talk with him, was quite gone. And when Critias said that I was the person who knew the remedy, and he looked me straight in the eyes[52] in an indescribable manner, and seemed ready to ask a question, and all the people in the gymnasium surged around us in a circle, then, my noble friend,[53] I both saw what was inside his cloak[54] and caught fire[55] and was quite beside myself.[56] And I thought that nobody was as wise in matters of love as Cydias, who, referring to a handsome boy and giving advice to someone else, said, 'The fawn should beware lest, by coming before the lion, he should be seized as a portion of meat'. For I felt that I myself had been seized by such a creature. (155c5–e2)

The first thing to notice in this passage is Socrates' unusual reference to an *aporia* or perplexity that does not directly bear on the puzzlement motivating a dialectical debate[57] or resulting from the inconclusive end of such.[58] Rather, Socrates uses a form of the verb *aporein*, feeling perplexed, to indicate an emotional reaction that does not pass through the intellect:[59] a sort of paralysis caused by Charmides' physical proximity, which renders Socrates at a loss for words. While up to this point he has been unmoved by Charmides' great beauty, now he experiences its full effect. According to the narration, three events occur almost simultaneously: Critias introduces the other two characters to each other by identifying Socrates as the doctor who can treat Charmides; Charmides

---

[50] ὦ φίλε: 155c5.   [51] ἠπόρουν: 155c5.
[52] For this meaning of ἐμβλέπω, see *Alc.* 132e. A related meaning, 'to look deep into something', in this case into oneself, occurs at 160d6.
[53] ὦ γεννάδα: 155d3.   [54] τὰ ἐντὸς τοῦ ἱματίου: 155d3.   [55] ἐφλεγόμην: 155d4.
[56] Sprague's (1993) successful translation of οὐκέτ' ἐν ἐμαυτοῦ ἦν (155d4).
[57] Politis 2006 and 2008 convincingly argues that Socrates uses ἀπορία and its cognates not only in order to refer to the state of mind resulting from a dialectical argument's failure to reach satisfactory conclusions, but also in order to indicate the motivation or starting-point of a dialectical debate.
[58] See, e.g., Wolfsdorf 2004.   [59] Cf. McAvoy 1996, 87 n. 54.

turns his eyes on Socrates and is about to ask him something; and the other bystanders move closer, forming a circle around the protagonists. Each of these events requires brief comment.

First of all, by introducing Socrates as a physician, Critias keeps up the ruse by which he brought his cousin over to the bench. Note that Socrates does not react, nor does he tell Charmides that he is not a doctor, but plays along. Next, the moment that Charmides turns his eyes on Socrates and seems ready to ask a question is the first instance in which the young man is portrayed as coming alive: for the first time, he is active and not merely passive, he is looking at someone and is not merely being looked at, and he is about to talk. There is uncertainty about the significance of his gaze. Does Charmides simply turn his eyes on Socrates in order to address him, or does he look at him provocatively, straight in the eyes?[60] Does Socrates' characterisation of the youth's gaze as '*amêchanon*', indescribable or irresistible (155d1), refer to the overwhelming power of the youth's gaze or to Socrates' own feelings of helplessness?[61] One interpreter suggests that the young man's gaze is aggressive, narcissistic, seductive, and hypnotic, that it aims to conquer, and that it shows that Charmides knows well how to wear the mantle of innocence to get exactly what he wants.[62] Others, however, take Charmides' look to express incredulity: since Charmides knows who Socrates is, he must also know that he is not a doctor and therefore feels confused. While the narrator leaves room for such speculation, he only relays explicitly how the young man's gaze affected him at the time: he found it indescribable and absolutely overpowering.[63] At that crucial moment, the bystanders closed in on those sitting on the bench and, presumably, caused some shifting and shuffling. This explains how Socrates accidentally saw what was inside Charmides' cloak, was set afire, and was no longer able to contain himself (155d3–4).

Dramatically, the condition that Socrates found himself in constitutes the high point of a psychological escalation. When Charmides first entered the room, Socrates observed his beautiful face and stature in a detached manner and from a distance. He expressed a greater interest in the youth's soul than his physical beauty and appeared quite unmoved by the latter. Then, when Charmides sat beside him on the bench, he started feeling confused (155c5). Next, when the young man fixed his gaze on him, his perplexity increased to the point of making him feel unable to speak

---

[60] This depends on how one takes the dative ὀφθαλμοῖς in 155c8: Schwyzer 2002, 211, 237.
[61] See Charalabopoulos 2008, 524 n. 117.   [62] Charalabopoulos 2008, 524, defends these claims.
[63] The term 'ἀμήχανον' has all these connotations and some others besides, notably the connotation of something allowing for no help or remedy.

(155c6–7). In the end, when he glanced into the youth's garment, he was set ablaze and was no more 'within' himself (155d4). A primary factor through which Socrates' condition gradually changes is perception and, specifically, sight. Socrates will return to the topic of perception later on, at a pivotal point of his argument with Critias.

There can be little doubt, I believe, that the passage under discussion has a sexual meaning.[64] First, many syntactical, grammatical, and lexical elements of the narration point firmly in that direction. The neuter plural article rendered by 'what' was inside Charmides' cloak[65] points away from the feminine singular noun 'the soul',[66] which in any case occurs considerably earlier in the context. Typically, the expression 'I caught fire'[67] refers specifically to erotic excitement.[68] As for the phrase 'I was no longer within myself' and other similar phrases, they standardly render one's loss of self-control because of a strong emotion or passion. Besides, this reading of the incident makes excellent philosophical sense: it lends more depth to the persona of Socrates as moral paradigm, and flags an ordinary aspect of *sôphrosynê* that receives little attention in the sequel of the dialogue, i.e. self-control, but also illustrates one of the dialogue's central themes, namely the relation between *sôphrosynê* and self-knowledge. In brief, while earlier in the prologue Socrates appeared impervious to excessive emotions, he is now shown as vulnerable to passion as all men must be. Like his peers in the gymnasium, he too proves to be vulnerable to the power of sexual desire and feels its full impact. Unlike Chaerephon, and perhaps unlike Critias too, he experiences this susceptibility as a major danger to himself. And precisely because he realises his own weakness, he is able to make a concerted and successful effort to counteract the pull of sexual passion and retrieve his self-control. He appeals to an otherwise unattested

---

[64] This is the traditional interpretation of the passage, and most interpreters follow it. However, it has been radically challenged by McCabe 2007a. According to McCabe, the content of Socrates' seeing remains deliberately ambiguous: he does not state whether what he saw inside Charmides' cloak was the most exciting parts of the youth's anatomy or, alternatively, the youth's soul. If I understand McCabe correctly, she favours the latter option because she takes it to illustrate a philosophical approach to perception suggested by the 'Relations Argument' (or, as I call it, the Argument from Relations). Namely, perception is 'civilised' in the sense that its objects need not always be physical. Hence the 'Relations Argument' does not go through either for perception or, analogically, for knowledge: contrary to what the argument purports to show, in fact reflexivity and higher-order functions are possible for *aisthêsis*, perception, and *epistêmê* (scientific) knowledge. While I disagree with McCabe on both counts for reasons stated both here and in the Argument from Relations, her interpretation must be reckoned with because it has far-reaching implications both for our understanding of the drama and argument of the *Charmides* and for Plato's approach to perception.

[65] τά at the beginning of the phrase τὰ ἐντὸς τοῦ ἱματίου: 155d3.

[66] ἡ ψυχή: 154e1. Compare McCabe 2007a.   [67] ἐφλεγόμην: 155d4.

[68] See Eisenstadt 1981, 127.

fragment of the poet Cydias,[69] whose vivid imagery also expresses Socrates' own fear: of being captured and swallowed alive by sexual passion, as a fawn is seized and devoured by a lion (155d6–e1). According to the narration, Cydias used that metaphor as a warning to a man in love with a beautiful boy (155d5–6), and Socrates quite explicitly compared the position of that man with his own. When he was in the throes of passion, he thought of Cydias' verse and felt that he too had been seized by a wild beast (155e1–2).

Let us look more closely at this metaphor in connection to other elements of the prologue. In view of Charmides' earlier representation as a creature resembling a young god, the opening scene can be placed in the context of a rich mythological and religious tradition preserving firm boundaries between divinities and humans, and also determining relations within each realm. Divinities diminish or annihilate the consciousness of those who come near and, likewise, Charmides' physical proximity paralyses Socrates and weakens his spirit. Medusa turns those who stare at her into stone[70] and, in comparable manner, Charmides' gazing at Socrates causes confusion and speechlessness. In Homer, the breast-band of Aphrodite saps the resolve of gods and men,[71] and Charmides appears to have such a catalytic effect on everyone present. Men are often punished for violating the privacy of gods and goddesses or for transgressing in any way the limit between gods and humans. Some lose their perceptual powers, others are consumed by fire, and others suffer annihilation or transformation of their identity.[72]

Something like this happens (albeit temporarily) to Socrates: he sees a part of Charmides that was intended to be hidden and is set afire. In short, Socrates employs the imagery of myth in order to convey the formidable power of the youth's bodily beauty and of the desire that it gives rise to. Besides, Socrates appeals to Cydias' metaphor for erotic capture in a way that was familiar to Plato's audience. A predator seizing its quarry often represents a lover who acquires the object of his desire.[73] Typically, it is the older man who is the predator, whereas a youth is his prey.[74] In this instance, however, Socrates inverts the image, by identifying himself as the fawn and

---

[69] The *Charmides* is our only source of the fragment of Cydias, and that fragment is all we have from the poet.

[70] See the discussion of this mythological archetype in Charalabopoulos 2008, 527–8.

[71] Homer, *Il.* 14. 257–67.

[72] E.g. Teiresias was blinded because he saw Athena naked, Semeli asked Zeus to show himself to her in all his glory and burst into flames, and Marsyas was flayed alive by Apollo, who then transformed him into a stream.

[73] Theognis 1278c–d, cited by Reece 1998, 70.   [74] See Plato, *Phd.* 241d.

Charmides as the lion who might devour him.[75] By casting Charmides in the role of the lover, the pursuer, and himself in the role of the beloved, Socrates foreshadows a reversal that will occur in the dialogue's last scene (176c–d).[76] Finally, the description of this episode enjoys special authority, even though it need not be taken to be infallible. Since the narrator and the principal character are the same person represented at different points in time, and assuming that the narrator is sincere, he is in a unique position with regard to the event under discussion. He can tell us, truthfully if not incorrigibly, what he remembers having felt and thought on that occasion. And we should take him at his word when he says that he felt seized by a powerful beast threatening to devour him. Indeed, the wisdom of Cydias' verse seems to have helped Socrates to compose himself and regain his speech. Thus he managed, though barely so,[77] to answer the question that Charmides has intended to ask him for some time, i.e. whether he really knew the remedy for headaches. Socrates replied that he did (155e2–3).

4   A Leaf and a Charm (155e4–156a8)

According to the narrator, Charmides referred to the medical knowledge that Socrates was supposed to have by using a strong cognitive verb: *epistasthai*,[78] to know simpliciter or, specifically, to know in an expert or scientific manner.[79] The same holds for Socrates, who replied to the youth's question that he did know (*epistaimên*: 155e3) the cure for his malady. Given that he is playing the part of a doctor, he can naturally be taken to assert that he knows the drug in the way that an expert would. Even if this is so, there is no inconsistency, as many have feared, between Socrates' disclaimer of knowledge in other dialogues and the reply that he presently gives to the young man. For while the disclaimer of knowledge concerns expert knowledge of virtue, Socrates' *epistêmê* in treating headaches will amount, as we shall see, to an epistemically less demanding and

---

[75] McAvoy 1996, 90 and Reece 1998, 70–1 convincingly read the metaphor in that way. As Reece points out, several translators and interpreters stretch the text to make Socrates' use of the metaphor conform to its traditional usage: e.g. Jowett 1961, *ad loc.* and Nussbaum 1986, 92.

[76] Compare *Symp.* 222a–b.   [77] μόγις πως: 155e3.   [78] εἰ ἐπισταίμην: 155e2.

[79] Hulme Kozey 2018 convincingly argues that the verb 'ἐπίστασθαι' and its cognate noun 'ἐπιστήμη' have a relation to 'γιγνώσκειν' and 'γνῶσις' comparable to the relation between 'ἐπιστήμη' and 'τέχνη'. Namely, while 'ἐπίστασθαι' and 'γιγνώσκειν' are used interchangeably in certain contexts, they are not strict synonyms and cannot be inter-substituted in all contexts but have a relation of synecdoche. I hope to show that, in the *Charmides* and especially in the second part of the dialogue, 'γιγνώσκειν' will mostly point to Socratic self-knowledge, whereas 'ἐπίστασθαι' and 'ἐπιστήμη' will mainly refer to Critias' conception of temperance as a 'science of itself and the other sciences' and will carry the overtones of scientific knowledge or scientific expertise.

less lofty kind of expertise, consistent with his profession of ignorance as well as with his mission in the service of Apollo.

Borrowing on a generic religious practice common to several Indo-European cultures,[80] Socrates identifies the remedy for headaches with a certain leaf[81] and says that a charm or incantation[82] must be administered in addition to[83] the leaf. He adds that the leaf and the charm ought to be applied '*hama*',[84] without specifying, however, the exact meaning of that term. The word '*hama*' could mean 'together' in a temporal sense, i.e. in the sense that taking both the leaf and the incantation *at the same time* would be sufficient for the cure. But this would be incompatible with something that Socrates says soon afterwards: the incantation must be chanted *before* the application of the medicine (157b2–4), unless one possesses sufficient[85] temperance in one's soul to take the drug straight away (158b5–c1).[86] A natural meaning of the expression '*a hama kai b*' is 'both a and b'. Socrates' point is, I suggest, that if one takes *both* the leaf and the charm, then one will be totally cured (155e7–8).[87]

Charmides seems convinced about the proposed treatment. And he promptly declares he will write down the charm at Socrates' dictation (156a1–2). Socrates asks him whether he intends to do so with or without persuading him to disclose the incantation (156a3),[88] and the youth laughs and replies that of course he would do so with the older man's consent (156a4), addressing Socrates by his name for the first time. Not only does he thus make clear that he knows who Socrates is, he also adds that he has childhood memories of Socrates as Critias' companion,[89] and has frequently talked about Socrates with his own peers (156a4–8). In any case, the young man's assertion that he shall take down the charm in writing raises questions. Since he knows who Socrates is, he also must know that Socrates is not a doctor. Why, then, does he appear eager to have the charm? Evidently, when he was first introduced to Socrates, he immediately understood his guardian's ruse and decided to play along with it: that is, to act as if he believed that Socrates was a physician. It is equally evident

---

[80] See Brisson 2000.   [81] φύλλον τι: 155e.   [82] ἐπῳδή τις: 155e.   [83] ἐπὶ τῷ φαρμάκῳ: 155e6.
[84] ἅμα: 155e6.
[85] σώφρων ἱκανῶς: 158b6. On the idea that people have different degrees of temperance, see below, 97–8.
[86] See the analysis of Coolidge 1993, 25 and *passim*.   [87] Cf. παντάπασιν ὑγιᾶ: 155e.
[88] ἐάν με πείθῃς: 156a3.
[89] The participle συνόντα (156a8) does not indicate the exact nature of the relationship between the two men. Socrates may have been one of Critias' acquaintances or friends, or he may have been Critias' lover. The historical Critias was famed for his beauty, just as Charmides is portrayed as being.

that the two older men realise this. All three protagonists, then, are in the know. And all three undertake to play their respective parts in the play crafted by Critias, each for his own reasons.[90]

The scene hints at certain features of Charmides' character, but discloses nothing definite about him. His eagerness to record the remedy in writing may be an expression of youthful spontaneity or a preference for easy solutions and shortcuts. Socrates' question whether the dictation of the incantation will happen with or without his own consent may be a playful query, or, alternatively, an early diagnosis of a wilful and narcissistic streak in the youth's character. Indeed, Charmides does not ask whether Socrates is willing to dictate the incantation to him, but takes it for granted that the latter will do his bidding.[91] And the reason why he is so certain about this is, probably, that he is aware of the impression that he has made on the older man.[92] If we look forward to the final scene of the dialogue, however, we shall find that the theme of consent and compulsion emerges again: there will be apparently playful talk about forcing Socrates to become Charmides' mentor if he will not be persuaded to do so (175d5–176d5). On both these occasions, Charmides makes a demand on Socrates and anticipates his consent. And on both occasions, we have the opportunity to speculate on what would happen if Socrates refused, or reflect on what might have happened in reality when Socrates refused to comply with the orders of the Thirty (Ap. 32c–d). On the positive side, the fact that Charmides laughs when Socrates asks him whether he intends to write down the incantation with or without Socrates' consent may indicate embarrassment at his own presumption and a sense of shame. As for his reply, that of course he meant to obtain Socrates' consent (156a4), it shows that the youth has taken the point and perhaps has realised that he behaved wrongly.[93] He addresses Socrates by his name (156a4), mentions that he and his peers frequently talk about Socrates (156a6), and, generally, makes an effort to bridge the distance between himself and his interlocutor and establish some sort of familiarity between them.

---

[90] In a way, this is a story within a story. Within the framework set by the narrator and his auditor, a story is told about an encounter based on yet another story: of Socrates as a doctor in possession of a remedy that he is expected to administer to Charmides in order to cure him.

[91] Charmides seems certain about this: note his use of the future indicative ἀπογράψομαι (156a1).

[92] Some interpreters suggest that Charmides meant to show his nakedness to Socrates, but the text does not support this contention. According to McAvoy 1996, 84, Socrates convinces Charmides that it is better to use persuasion than to rely on the force of his presence.

[93] εἰ μὴ ἀδικῶ γε: 156a6. McAvoy 1996, 84–5, believes that this line contains an allusion to a possible injustice.

Overall, this is a promising beginning. Charmides is no longer passive, but plays an active role. And he responds rather well to both Socrates' promise of a cure and what seems like an indirect reprimand. Socrates has partially recovered from his earlier experience and has been able to reply to the youth's query and begin a conversation. As for Critias, after setting up the ploy and distributing the parts to the other two characters, he temporarily recedes into the background.[94] Mutual recognition has occurred, Critias' ruse has come into the open, and everyone is in the know.[95] Now Socrates will give more details about the drug that he proposes to administer.

5   Speaking More Freely: The Holism of the 'Good Doctors' (156a9–c9)

> Well done, I said. For it means I shall speak to you more freely about the incantation and what its nature is, whereas just now I was perplexed as to how to indicate its power to you. For, Charmides, it is of such a nature that it cannot bring health only to the head, but, as perhaps you too have already heard the good doctors mention, when a patient comes to them with a pain in his eyes, they say something like this: that it is not possible for them to attempt to heal the eyes alone, but that it would be necessary that they treat the head along with them, if the condition of the eyes were going to be in good order too. Moreover, they say, it is utter folly to believe that one could ever cure the head on its own apart from the whole body. Following this principle, they apply regimens to the body in its entirety, trying to treat and heal the part together with the whole. Or have you not been aware of the fact that this is how they talk and how things are done? – Very much so, he said. – And do you believe that this principle is a good one and do you accept it? – More than anything, he said. (156a9–c9)

What does Charmides 'do well',[96] so that Socrates is relieved of his puzzlement[97] and capable of speaking more freely[98] about the nature of

---

[94] It is significant that the historical Critias *was* a playwright. McAvoy 1996, 85, compares Critias to a playwright who did not anticipate what Socrates might do with his own part of the play.

[95] This point could be pressed to suggest that all three protagonists have a sort of knowledge of knowledge, i.e. each of them knows what the other two know. If so, this seems a defensible notion of knowledge of knowledge to be contrasted with the notion of a 'knowledge of knowledge' or 'science of science' elaborated and then refuted in the second half of the dialogue.

[96] καλῶς ποιῶν: 156a9.

[97] Unlike other translators, Lamb accurately renders the γάρ at 156a9 and thus highlights the causal connection between what Charmides did well (καλῶς ποιῶν, 156a9) and the fact that, as a result, Socrates is now able to speak more candidly to the youth.

[98] μᾶλλον παρρησιάσομαι: 156a9–b1.

the charm? It is natural, I think, to take the expression 'well done' (156a9) to refer to the immediately preceding context. Charmides has done two things right: he has correctly identified Socrates by name (156a4), and he has accurately remembered that Socrates was Critias' companion at the time when Charmides himself was a child (156a7–8). In that way, he conveys to Socrates that he knows something about him and his ways and, furthermore, that he is ready to trust Socrates as a family friend. Consequently, Socrates now feels at ease to talk to the young man in the manner that he deems best: with greater *parrhesia*, more openly, more outspokenly than he would have done if they were complete strangers to each other. He has reason to hope that the youth will listen to him attentively and won't think him insincere or foolish. Earlier on he experienced *aporia*, perplexity, because it suddenly seemed extremely difficult to him to talk to Charmides (155c5), and his nerve (*thrasytês*) failed him completely (155c6). Now, however, his *aporia* has been lifted and his self-confidence will fully return in due course (156d1). On both occasions, the *aporia* does not indicate the failure to conclude a search in a satisfactory manner, but refers ostensibly to a practical issue: in the former case, how to talk to the youth, and in the latter, how to explain to him the nature of the incantation. In the end, however, both occurrences of *aporia* have to do with Socrates' concern to appropriately engage Charmides in dialogue and hence constitute the starting-points of the dialectical examination to follow.

The passage just cited contains the first part of Socrates' explanation of the remedy for the headache and the manner in which it is supposed to work. He appeals to the practice of certain 'good doctors' who endorse a sort of bodily holism based on the principle that it is impossible to treat the part independently of the whole. Rather, they consider it necessary to cure, for example, the eyes together with the head, the head together with the body, and, generally, the part together with the whole.[99] In accordance with this principle, they prescribe therapies that act holistically, aiming primarily at whatever whole the ailing part is a part of. The bodily holism of these physicians, then, is not just a matter of theory but also a matter of established medical practice. The fact that Socrates refers to them as 'good doctors' suggests that there are doctors that don't follow that approach.

---

[99] Like 'ἅμα' at 156b8, the use of that word at 155e6 need not be chronological in a narrow sense. In the former instance the word conveys the idea that the leaf and the charm should be taken together, but not necessarily at exactly the same time. In the latter occurrence, Socrates need not mean that the part and the whole should be treated at exactly the same time, but only that the one should be treated in close connection to the other. A different view is defended by Coolidge 1993.

Socrates suggests that those who do so have a correct understanding of the physical health of living organisms, in particular human organisms, and are rather successful in treating their patients.

This much is sufficiently clear. Nonetheless, there is disagreement as to whether these physicians are Greek,[100] and whether the bodily holism ascribed to them was a real medical theory or Plato's own invention. The former issue is easier to settle, for even though Socrates does not specify the ethnicity of the physicians in question at first, later in the prologue he says that, according to one of the Thracian doctors of Zalmoxis, the teachings of the Greek [doctors][101] that he (sc. Socrates) 'was just talking about' were good so far as they went, but did not go nearly as far as the teachings of Zalmoxis himself (156d6–7). What Socrates 'was just talking about'[102] could only be the bodily holism of the 'good doctors'. Hence we can safely identify them with the Greek doctors that the Zalmoxian physician refers to.

But are these Greek doctors historical figures? Did any group of Greek doctors actually hold the theory dubbed as bodily holism? A passage from Plato's *Phaedrus* (269e–270d) might seem to suggest an affirmative answer to these questions. There, in an attempt to account for Pericles' exceptional rhetorical skill, Socrates suggests that the Athenian statesman became familiar with Anaxagoras' meteorology (269e–270a), thus acquired the ability to grasp the nature of mind and mindlessness, and applied Anaxagoras' cosmological theory for rhetorical purposes (270a). As the argument goes, this shows that to understand the nature of the soul (*psychês physin*) and become an expert orator, one must understand the nature of the whole (*tên tou holou physin*). Phaedrus adds that, according to Hippocrates, one must understand the nature of the whole in order to understand the nature of the body (270b–c). For his part, Socrates asserts that he accepts that view and promptly undertakes to give a more detailed description of what he presents as Hippocrates' own method. On one account, since the latter posits that we should consider whether the object under investigation is simple or complex, to determine the nature of the object, we should first divide a concept corresponding to reality as a whole into body and soul.[103] Then, assuming that the powers to act and to be acted upon are common to all things including bodies and souls, we should try to establish what causal powers the object of our investigation has and how it generally behaves.[104] Because of the holistic assumptions that appear to govern the aforementioned method, one might infer that the theory of bodily holism

---

[100] See, e.g., Bruell 1977, 147.   [101] ἰατροί secl. Cobet.   [102] ἃ νυνδὴ ἐγὼ ἔλεγον: 156d7.
[103] On this point, see the different approaches of Gill 2003 and Mansfeld 1980.
[104] The exact nature of this method is hugely controversial and has to do with the so-called Hippocratic question, but this topic lies beyond the scope of the present study.

that Socrates attributes to the 'good doctors' is closely similar to the approach assigned to Hippocrates in the *Phaedrus*.

In fact, however, these two views are not closely comparable, nor can they be identified with each other. While in the *Phaedrus* Socrates' mention of Anaxagoras' meteorology strongly suggests that 'the whole' is the whole of nature as the Ionian philosophers conceived it,[105] in the *Charmides* the whole that the 'good doctors' refer to is the whole body of which, for example, the eyes or the head are parts. And while Socrates' account of the method of Hippocrates arguably implies the use of the method of division, his summary reference to the bodily holism of the Greek doctors does not include any such element. Rather, it evokes in a general way the approach adopted by the physicians who belong, broadly speaking, to the Rationalist tradition with regard to the relation between physiological theory and medical practice, i.e. that the theory should determine the choice and application of the treatment. According to Socrates, the 'good doctors' hold a theory, bodily holism, which shapes their healing practices. They believe that no healing can take place unless the part is treated together with the whole (156b6–c1) and dismiss as utter nonsense any attempt to do otherwise (156c1–3). In short, they seem quite dogmatic about the theoretical basis of medical treatment, and appear adamant in their conviction that the former should determine the latter. The fact that Socrates characterises them as 'good doctors' indicates that he considers them competent physicians with proper scientific training, as opposed to healers who learn what to do by trial and error.[106]

Socrates does not specify what exactly, according to his own claim, the Greek physicians take to be the connection between the whole and its parts. It seems that, on the view that Socrates ascribes to them, the parts of the human body and the body as a whole are functionally interconnected, and the unimpeded function of each part is dependent upon the healthy condition of the whole. But this does not explain how, precisely, the treatment of one's body as a whole causes the cure of a diseased part of that body. One possibility is that, according to Socrates, the 'good doctors' commit the fallacy of composition by assuming that the properties of the parts are the same as those of the whole. Another, more attractive hypothesis that Socrates may be pointing to is that the 'good doctors' defend bodily holism by appealing to underlying causes that are operative in the same way on the entire human body as well as every part of it. On the latter scenario, they would proceed much as the so-called Rationalist physicians are known to have proceeded: by giving a theoretical causal account of

---

[105] See Mansfeld 1980, 353–4.   [106] See Frede 1987a, 231–2.

everything occurring in the human body, and in particular of the diseases affecting the entire body or some part of it. Moreover, like many Rationalists,[107] they would be inclined to postulate that reason alone enables the doctor to determine the nature of the malady of a bodily part, find its deeper cause concerning the whole of the body, and, accordingly, prescribe the appropriate treatment.

Once he has sketched out the approach of the Greek physicians, Socrates asks Charmides whether he knows of their theory and practice (156c5–6) and whether he accepts it (156c8), and the youth answers affirmatively on both counts (156c7, 156c9). Given his young age, how plausible is it that he would know the 'good doctors' and their therapeutic principle? And even assuming that he did, how plausible is it that he would have considered their approach and endorsed it? On the one hand, we may think, since Charmides belonged to the upper class of Athenian society, he might have been exposed to informed talk about the physicians of the day and their methods of treatment. On the other, his emphatic assertion that he endorses the principle of bodily holism (156c8) could not have had a solid basis. Charmides was simply not in a position to make such a commitment, let alone make an informed comparative judgement according to which he preferred bodily holism to rival medical approaches (156c8).

In this instance too, then, the character of Charmides is cast in an ambiguous light. He may have overstated his inclination towards the holistic principle merely in order to encourage Socrates to say more about the leaf and the charm. Or he may be entirely clueless about the 'good doctors' and their method. In any case, the youth's unreserved approval of the principle of holism restores Socrates' confidence (156d1–2) and revives him, so to speak, by rekindling in him a different sort of fire (156d2–3): presumably, the ardent desire to elaborate further the idea of holistic health and thus prompt Charmides to engage in dialogue.

6 The Doctors of Zalmoxis: Psychosomatic Holism (156d3–157c6)

> Such, then, Charmides, is the nature of this incantation [or charm]. I learnt it over there, on campaign, from one of the Thracian doctors of Zalmoxis, who are said even to aim at immortality.[108] This Thracian said that the

---

[107] See Frede 1987a, 225–42, and especially 234–5.

[108] Compare ἀθανατίζειν in Herodotus, *Hist.* IV.93–4. Van den Ben 1985, 11–14, argues that, in *Charm.* 156d6, ἀπαθανατίζειν is intransitive, whereas Murphy 2000 and others take it to be transitive. See nn. 111 and 112 in this chapter.

Greeks spoke well when they stated the doctrine that I have just mentioned. However, he said, Zalmoxis our king, who is a god, declares that, just as one should not attempt to treat the eyes without treating the head nor to treat the head without treating the body, so one should not treat the body without treating the soul. In fact, he said this was even the reason why most diseases evaded treatment by the Greek doctors, namely that they neglected the whole that they should have attended to, since when this does not fare well it is impossible for the part to fare well. For all evils and goods for the body and for the entire human being, he said, spring from the soul and flow from it, just as they flow from the head to the eyes. Hence this [sc. the soul] is what one ought to treat first and foremost, if the condition of the head and that of the rest of the body are going to be good as well. And the soul, my good friend, he said, is treated by means of certain charms or incantations, and these incantations are beautiful [or fine] discourses. Temperance derives from such discourses and is engendered in the soul, and once it has been engendered and is present, one can easily supply health to the head and to the rest of the body as well. So, as he was teaching me both the remedy and the incantations, he said, 'Let nobody persuade you to treat his own head with this remedy who has not first submitted his soul to be treated by you with the incantation'. For at present, he said, this is the error besetting men, that certain doctors attempt to manage without each of the two – that is, without both temperance and bodily health. And he very strongly instructed me not to allow anyone to convince me that I should act in a different way, regardless of how wealthy, brave, or handsome that person might be. As for myself, therefore, I shall do as he bids, since I have sworn an oath to him and must obey him. And if you decide, in accordance with the stranger's instructions, to submit your soul to be charmed first by means of the Thracian's incantations, I shall apply the remedy to your head. Otherwise, my dear Charmides, we would be at a loss as to what to do to help you. (156d3–157c6)

The main known source of information for the story of Zalmoxis is Herodotus' *History* (4.94–5).[109] In the first part of his account (4.94), Herodotus says that there is a tribe in Thrace, the Getae, who worship Zalmoxis (or, as Herodotus calls him, Salmoxis) and who *athanatizousin*,[110] 'are immortal' or 'make one immortal'.[111] In particular, they believe that they will never die, but will pass out of life and join

---

[109] Tuozzo 2011, 115–18, offers a detailed discussion of the relevant passages from Herodotus and the relation between their content and the content of Socrates' story. Since I am largely in agreement with his analysis, my own comments will be brief.

[110] ἀθανατίζουσι. As Tuozzo 2011, 116, remarks, we do not know Herodotus' sources for this part of the story.

[111] Compare ἀπαθανατίζειν at 156d6. In neither case is it clear whether the verb is intransitive or transitive. See the discussion immediately below and note 108.

themselves to the god Zalmoxis. In the second part of his account (4.95), Herodotus says that, according to the Greeks of the Hellespont, Zalmoxis was a slave of Pythagoras who, upon gaining his freedom and great wealth, returned to his own country and convinced his fellow tribesmen about immortality in the following manner: after feasting with them and teaching them that neither he nor his fellow-symposiasts nor their descendants would ever die but would transmigrate to a place where they would enjoy all good things and live forever, he hid for three years in an underground chamber, thus making his followers believe that he had died, and then he reappeared to them as if he were returning from the netherworld. While Herodotus remains sceptical about the truth of that story, and especially about the issue of whether Zalmoxis was a man or a Thracian god, he refers us to the Greek institution of symposia in connection to a closed society that supposedly consisted of Zalmoxis and his drinking companions and promised immortality to the symposiasts as well as their descendants. We encounter similar ideas in the teachings of the Orphics and the Pythagoreans, which point to initiation cults and to other practices aiming to secure post-mortem existence and eternal bliss after death.[112]

Socrates' tale evidently relies on Herodotus, but also deviates from Herodotus' account in important ways. On the one hand, following Herodotus, Plato's Socrates preserves some of the language and connotations of mystery rites, and attributes to the aforementioned Thracian doctor the claims that Zalmoxis is a god and that the Zalmoxian physicians aim at immortality.[113] On the other hand, several elements in Herodotus are entirely absent from Socrates' story. Unlike Herodotus, Socrates does not mention the tribe of the Getae, does not explicitly refer to Pythagoras, does not allude to any possible connection between Zalmoxis and Pythagoras,[114] does not explain how Zalmoxis convinced his followers of his own divinity and of human immortality, and does not express any scepticism about the truthfulness of what the Thracian says. He modifies Herodotus' rare term '*athanatizein*' into '*apothanatizein*' – also a rare and ambiguous verb that may mean that the Zalmoxian doctors are themselves immortal or that they are capable of making others immortal.[115] Most importantly, he attributes to Zalmoxis and his followers a theory that Herodotus does not mention, i.e. a kind of holism that comprises the

---

[112] See Tuozzo 2011, 117.   [113] ἀπαθανατίζουσιν at 156d6.
[114] Herodotus' cautious report that the Greeks of the Hellespont connected Zalmoxis to Pythagoras could be historically accurate, since the Hellenic populations of the Hellespont may well have been familiar with both Thracian and Pythagorean lore.
[115] See notes 108 and 112 in this chapter.

soul as well as the body and thus is far more radical and more comprehensive than the bodily holism attributed to the Greek doctors. Those readers of the *Charmides* who are familiar with Herodotus' version of the story of Zalmoxis cannot miss the differences between these two narratives or fail to register that Plato's Socrates decisively distances himself from Herodotus in order to relay the Thracian's tale. Moreover, it is immediately apparent to Plato's audiences that the latter is structured so as to highlight central Socratic themes: the priority of the soul over the body, the causal powers of the soul for good or bad, the cardinal importance of taking care of the soul and of engendering virtue, belief in the soul's immortality, and perhaps some sort of deification. A closer examination of the Thracian's story will give us further insight into these themes and will disclose aspects of Socrates' pedagogical agenda.

Socrates places the encounter that he will relate to Charmides at a remote time and place, when he was on campaign in the north of Greece. Significantly, the first thing he says about the physician that he met there is that the latter was one of the believers in immortality. Thus he brings to the foreground the idea that the soul is infinitely more important than the body – an idea central to the criticism that the Thracian physician levels against the 'good doctors' on the basis of a therapeutic principle stated by Zalmoxis, his own king and a god. At the outset, we should note that, from this point onwards, the narrative moves at several levels simultaneously: the frame set by the narrator, the story told by Socrates as character, the principle stated by Zalmoxis, and the critical application and elaboration of that principle by Zalmoxis' follower. According to the Thracian, then, Zalmoxis, who is a divinity, articulated a kind of holism that goes far beyond the holism of certain Greek doctors on the grounds of an analogy with assumptions endorsed by these latter: as the eyes should not be treated apart from the head and the head should not be treated apart from the rest of the body, so the body should not be treated apart from the soul (156d8–e2).[116] Thus, Zalmoxis proposes a holism that concerns not only the body and its parts but also the soul, which, as it turns out, constitutes the core of Zalmoxian therapy.

The Thracian doctor's criticism of the aforementioned Greek doctors derives precisely from his endorsement of the Zalmoxian principle of psychosomatic holism. According to Socrates' narration, while the

---

[116] I take it that this view is traced back to Zalmoxis himself, while the rest of the story, including the criticism of the Greek doctors, is attributed to his Thracian follower (see 156c6–7). Consequently, I emend Burnet's comma after ψυχῆς at 156e2 to a semi-colon.

Thracian approves of what Socrates 'was just saying' (156d7), i.e. the holism defended by the Greek doctors, he finds fault with them insofar as they concern themselves with the part, i.e. the body, but neglect to attend to the whole.[117] They profess to treat the whole together with the part, but mistakenly identify the whole with the body and the part with parts of the body, leaving out the patient's soul. They view each patient as a mere physical entity, whereas in fact he/she is a complex psycho-physical entity whose condition is causally determined by the powers of the soul. On the other hand, the physicians of Zalmoxis fully acknowledge the causal effects of the soul on the body and the whole human being. They view the soul as the source from which derives every good or evil for the body and the whole person (156e6–157a1). And while the Thracian leaves it uncertain whether the health of the soul is a sufficient condition for bodily health, he explicitly states that the former is a necessary condition for the latter: one's body cannot be healthy if one's soul is not. Therefore, the physicians of Zalmoxis are able to treat successfully many maladies that the Greek doctors cannot (156e3–4). In sum, Socrates relays that the Thracian doctor elaborated the central idea of Zalmoxian therapy mainly in terms of psychic causation. Leaving aside the details, the chief contention is clear: it is the soul and not the body that ought to constitute the principal object of therapy. Furthermore, the physician of Zalmoxis discloses to Socrates that the proper treatment of the soul consists in *epôdai*, incantations or charms, that he describes as 'beautiful [or fine] discourses'[118] without specifying, however, just what these discourses may be. And he also claims that such discourses engender *sôphrosynê* in the soul, strongly suggesting that this virtuous condition is equivalent to psychic health: if one's soul is temperate and thereby healthy, one's head and the rest of one's body will be healthy too (157a5–b1).

So much is quite straightforward, but if we examine the Thracian's story more closely, we find that it suffers from imprecision and residual tensions. First, the part/whole relation is problematic, if the body is taken to be the part and the soul is taken to be the whole. For in what sense could the soul be the whole? And if the soul is not the whole, what is? Second, does the presence of temperance in the soul always suffice in order to heal the body, or can the body suffer from some physical ailment even if the soul is temperate and healthy? Is Zalmoxian holism compatible with our intuitions about this issue? Third, even if we can figure out what kind of

---

[117] τὸ ὅλον ἀγνοοῖεν mss τοῦ ὅλου Burnet; τοῦ ἄλλου ἀμελοῖεν Stobaeus.
[118] τοὺς λόγους εἶναι τοὺς καλούς: 157a4–5.

discourses are the 'beautiful discourses' constituting the charm, it is not clear to what extent the Thracian claims them to be effective. Are these discourses supposed to invariably instil temperance in the soul, or can they also fail to do so? Finally, why does Socrates mention that the doctors of Zalmoxis 'are immortal' or 'can make people immortal'? While the narrative suggests that there is some connection between Zalmoxian holism and the belief in immortality, neither Socrates nor the Thracian doctor state what that connection might be. These are controversial issues and I shall address them in turn.

Insofar as the holism of the Greek doctors is concerned, the part/whole relationship is relatively unproblematic. On the basis of Socrates' examples, we can infer that the part/whole relationship is primarily functional and holds, on the one hand, between different parts of the living body whose functions are directly related to each other and, on the other hand, between a part of the living body and the living body as an organic whole. To treat the eyes (part), the physician must also treat the head (whole), and to treat the head (part), he must also treat the patient's entire body (whole). Zalmoxian holism, however, introduces a new factor that complicates matters, namely the soul.[119] According to many interpreters, the principle articulated by Zalmoxis at 156b8–e2 implies that, as the eyes stand to the head and the head stands to the body, so the body stands to the soul. Therefore they infer that the soul is the whole of which the body is part, and the same holds for the Thracian doctor's contention that the Greek physicians frequently fail to cure their patients because they fail to realise that the part (the body or a bodily part) cannot be well unless the whole, i.e. the soul, is well.[120] The latter idea has seemed puzzling, reasonably so.[121] For it seems counterintuitive, if not plainly wrong, to view the soul as the whole of a human being. Moreover, the suggestion that the relation between the body and the soul is a part/whole relation is extremely problematic, not only because it is not clear in what sense the soul is a whole, but also because the body and the soul are widely believed to belong to different ontological categories. Therefore, it seems wrong to assume that they are related to each other as part to whole in the same way that, for example, the eyes and the head or the head and the body are

---

[119] On the sort of expertise that the doctors of Zalmoxis must be supposed to have, see Murphy 2000, 291–5 and Coolidge 1993, 26–7.

[120] The passages adduced in support of that claim include, notably, 156e2–6 and 157a3.

[121] See, notably, Anagnostopoulos 1972; Hazebroucq 1997; Hogan 1976; Levine 2016; McPherran 2004; Rowe 1998, 88; Steiner 1992; and Tuozzo 2011, 118–21. Tuozzo 2011, 118–21, offers a survey of the competing views. A different sort of survey is given by Korobili and Stefou in press.

related to each other as part to whole. Further worries concern the compatibility of the idea that the soul is the whole while the body or the person is the part with the Thracian doctor's claim that the soul is the source of every good or evil for the body and the whole person. Various attempts to wriggle out of these problems, sometimes by proposing metaphorical readings of the passage, have proved futile.[122] The tensions remain, even when the Zalmoxian principle is rephrased in metaphorical terms.

One line of interpretation that might ease such tensions is this. According to the principle of Zalmoxian holism, the whole/part relationship is not metaphysical, but psychological and causal. Thus, perhaps the soul could be considered a whole just in the sense that the health of everything about one's body and generally one's person (156e7–8) depends on and is caused by the condition of the soul. If so, the Thracian's claim that the soul is a whole would not be very vulnerable to the objection that, in truth, the soul is only a part of ourselves as living beings, not the whole of ourselves. One's acceptance of the contention that the soul is a whole in the psychological/causal sense indicated above depends on one's endorsement of the view that the soul has causal priority over the body and the entire human being. If one accepts that the soul is the ultimate source of the goods and evils that affect every aspect of our being, including our physical health, one might also be inclined to accept that the soul represents the whole of us in just that sense. An alternative line of interpretation might have metaphysical dimensions. In the *Phaedo*, the *Phaedrus*, and *Alcibiades* I, Socrates suggests that the soul is identical with the self. If so, the soul could be considered a whole in the sense that it is essentially who one is, whereas the body or the human being (viewed compositionally as the sum of its constituents) would correspond to a part or aspect of oneself but not to one's whole self.[123] The aforementioned dialogues might be brought to

---

[122] As Korobili and Stefou in press remark, the interpretations of this passage can be divided, roughly, into three groups. Namely, some of them downplay or disregard the part/whole relationship but focus on the causal priority of the soul over the body. Others retain the part/whole relationship, identify the whole with the living human being as a soul/body composite, and take the Zalmoxian approach to entail that if a (body) part is to be well, both that part and the whole of us as a soul/body composite must be treated together. Yet other interpretations try, in different ways, to ascribe equal importance to the part/whole relation and the causal priority of the soul. Tuozzo 2011, 119–22, proposes an operative distinction between πᾶν and ὅλον, according to which the latter term refers to something beyond the mere sum of the parts, whereas the former term refers merely to the sum of the different parts constituting the whole. A similar approach but on the basis of different premises is defended by Korobili and Stefou in press.

[123] According to McPherran 2004, 18–21, we may think of the bodiless soul as an eyeless head: it can think but cannot see the world. However, it governs the body and acts as 'the ordering intelligence and animating principle of the whole person'.

bear on our passage in order to *both* determine a sense in which the soul can be the whole *and* strengthen the connection between Zalmoxian holism and the belief in immortality. Whether the priests of Zalmoxis believe that they themselves are immortal and/or able to make others immortal, immortality entails the perennial survival of the self. Assuming that the self is identical with the soul, the principle of attending to the soul before attending to the body or anything else amounts to an exhortation to take care of one's self and thus gain eternal life.

Despite their merits, both these lines of interpretation face a major problem: they require a sense of 'whole' that is unattested and may even be impossible. So far as I can tell, the only way of circumventing that problem is to reject the claim that, according to Zalmoxian holism, the soul's causal primacy follows from its being a whole.[124] When the Thracian doctor accuses the Greek physicians of failing to cure their patients because they fail to realise that the well-being of the part depends on the well-being of the whole, and because they attend to the body but neglect the soul, he does not mean to equate the soul with the whole. Neglecting the soul is neglecting the whole not because the soul is the whole, but perhaps just because if you neglect a part (the soul), you can't be taking care of the whole (yourself as a human being). On such a reading, the soul is causally prior not because it is the whole, but because of other considerations that the Zalmoxian physician does not develop but that are familiar to Plato's readers, e.g. that the soul is the natural ruler of the body or that the soul is the self. If so, the series of analogical relations at 156e1–2 need not be mereological but could be, so to speak, contextualisations: you can't take care of any part of yourself unless you see it in a broader, holistic context; this crucially involves paying attention to the all-important aspect of you that is the soul.

Turning now to the incantation consisting of 'the beautiful discourses' (*hoi kaloi logoi*: 157a4–5), it seems to me virtually certain that these are philosophical arguments conducted by the dialectical method of question-and-answer and aiming to discover or approximate the truth.[125] Socrates declares that he will follow the instructions of the Thracian doctor and won't administer the medicine for the head unless the patient first submits his soul to Socrates to be charmed by means of the incantation (157b2–4).

---

[124] I am indebted to David Sedley for this suggestion and for written comments.

[125] On the quasi-magical power of Socratic discourses, see *Meno* 80a. Many authors assume that the καλοὶ λόγοι mentioned here are equivalent to Socratic dialectic (Reece 1998, 74). On the other hand, doubts about this identification have been expressed by McPherran 2004, 23–6 and Schmid 1998, 15.

Charmides decides to do so (158e4–5), and what follows soon afterwards is, precisely, the treatment of Charmides' soul by means of the Socratic method of dialectical argumentation.[126] The intended result of this treatment is, specifically, to instil *sôphrosynê* in the patient's soul (157a5–6), for its presence in the soul 'already makes it easy to procure health for the head as well as the rest of the body' (157a6–b1).

Whether the 'beautiful discourses' are necessary or sufficient to engender *sôphrosynê* in the soul is debated. However, I suggest that a glance beyond the dialogue frame of the *Charmides* to the relevant historical facts confirms that 'the beautiful arguments' cannot guarantee the desired result. Even though Charmides probably enjoyed for a while the privilege of conversing with Socrates, he did not become virtuous. As for the vexed question of whether the healing of the soul by means of 'beautiful arguments' can also establish complete physical health, I think that it cannot be decisively settled. According to the Thracian physician, the treatment of the soul cures many diseases that the Greek doctors cannot cure (156e3–6); we may surmise, therefore, that, in these cases, the cure of the soul is necessary in order to cure the relevant physical ailments. However, it does not follow that every bodily ailment can be healed through the treatment of the soul. Nor does it follow that a person with a healthy soul can never be affected by a malady of the body. Socrates phrases the interim conclusion of his tale very carefully indeed. He says that the presence of *sôphrosynê* in the soul 'already makes it easy'[127] to bring about bodily heath. But he neither says nor implies that temperance necessarily brings about physical well-being. Rather, he seems to allow for the supposition that a psychologically healthy person could suffer from some bodily ailment that requires independent medical treatment.

Socrates' binding oath to follow the Thracian's instructions regarding the administration of the drug prevents him from giving the drug to Charmides straightaway. For while he knows the youth to be well born,

[126] According to the study of Laín Entralgo 1970, 108–38, this is one of the many instances in which Plato's Socrates deliberately rationalises for philosophical purposes the *epodai*, conjurations, commonly attributed to magicians and charlatans. Contrary to Boyancé 1937 or Dodds 1951, Laín Entralgo contends that this semantic shift is not a simple metaphor, i.e. an arbitrary verbal linking of two items completely different from each other, but presupposes a substantive similarity between the magic ἐπῳδαί and the charm of οἱ καλοὶ λόγοι: the idea that there is power inherent in the word itself, which, under the appropriate set of circumstances, can bring about the desirable effect. On the basis of the story of Zalmoxis as well as other Platonic passages, Laín Entralgo concludes that Plato is the inventor of scientific (κατὰ τέχνην) verbal psychotherapy. It is worth noting that, on this latter approach, the tale of the Zalmoxian charm implies recognition, on Plato's part, that the soul has both rational and irrational aspects.

[127] ῥᾴδιον ἤδη: 157a7.

wealthy, and beautiful (157b8), he does not know yet whether the latter has *sôphrosynê* and he therefore cannot give to Charmides the leaf curing the headache without first submitting his soul to the Zalmoxian incantations (157b7–c6). So, he invites Charmides to make a choice: submit himself to the charm of Zalmoxis, or receive no treatment at all. In this manner he highlights a crucial element of philosophical therapy: the decision to entrust oneself to the healer must be the patient's own. Critias' own reaction to what Socrates proposes is both revealing and important.

> Socrates, he said, if on account of his head Charmides will also be forced to improve his mind, then the malady of the head would turn out to have been for the young man a gift of Hermes [sc. an unexpected piece of good luck]. But let me tell you that Charmides is believed to surpass his peers not only in bodily looks, but also in the very thing that you claim to have the incantation for – you say it is temperance, do you not? – I do indeed, I said. – Well then, you must know that he is believed to be by far the most temperate youth of the day, while, considering his age, in every other respect too he is second to none. (157c7–d8)

On the one hand, Critias implicitly congratulates himself on the success of his own ruse: because Socrates enacted the role of a doctor able to treat the headache, Charmides is likely to receive a much greater benefit, namely to improve his mind (*dianoia*) by means of the beautiful arguments that he will be treated with (157c7–d1). On the other hand, however, Critias undercuts the idea that his ward stands in need of improvement. For he declares that the youth excels not only in beauty, but also in *sôphrosynê*, i.e. the very quality that the beautiful arguments are supposed to engender in the soul (157d1–8). In any event, unlike Socrates who gives Charmides the choice of accepting or declining the proposed treatment, Critias uses the language of passivity and compulsion. He remarks that, if the young man is compelled[128] to become better in respect of his *dianoia*, mind, this will be a stroke of luck for him (157c7–d1). This phrasing intimates that the young man's mind will be improved mainly by external factors, without the active participation of Charmides himself. It will be a lucky side-effect of the therapy that he will receive for his morning headaches, not a goal that he will independently value and pursue for its own sake. Furthermore, Critias does not specify exactly how he expects his ward's mind to be improved by the incantation. While the charm of Zalmoxis aims at the treatment of *psychê*, soul, Critias speaks about the betterment of his ward's '*dianoia*', mind. If Critias uses this word as a synonym for 'soul', there would be

---

[128] ἀναγκασθήσεται: 157c9.

reason to believe that Critias' appreciation of 'beautiful arguments' coincides with Socrates' own: such *logoi* can instil virtue in the soul and bring about psychic health. If, however, Critias means that the fine arguments of the charm will serve to sharpen Charmides' wits and make him a more skilful debater, then his conception of the relevant *logoi* would be instrumental and pragmatic and, in all likelihood, different from Socrates' own. In the latter case, the youth's improvement would have little to do with moral advancement and self-understanding, whereas in the former case the opposite would hold true. In sum, already at this early stage of the dialogue, we may begin forming the suspicion that, despite their long-standing acquaintance and familiarity, Socrates and Critias may have very different views about the ultimate purpose of the practice of *dialegesthai* and the arguments developed in the course of a dialectical investigation. Relatedly, we may also suspect that these two characters have different conceptions of virtue, of psychic therapy, and of the importance of this latter for one's well-being. These suspicions will be confirmed as the action of the dialogue unfolds.

7   In Praise of Charmides (157d9–158c4)

Of course, I said, it is only right, Charmides, that you should surpass the others in all such things. For I don't suppose that anyone else here could easily point to a case of two such Athenian families united together and likely to produce offspring more beautiful or nobler than those you have sprung from. For your father's family, the house of Critias son of Dropides, has been praised for us according to tradition by Anacreon, Solon, and many other poets for excelling in both beauty and virtue and everything else called happiness. Again, your mother's family is also praised in the same way. For it is said of your uncle Pyrilampes that no one in the entire continent[129] was believed to be superior in beauty or influence whenever he came as an ambassador to the Great King or anyone else in the continent, and this whole side of the family is viewed as not in the least inferior to the other side. Since you have sprung from such ancestors, it seems likely that you will be first in all things. And indeed, dear son of Glaucon, you seem to me not to have fallen behind any of your ancestors in any respect with regard to your looks. But if, in addition, you have sufficiently grown in respect of temperance and those other qualities as your guardian here says, then, I said, dear Charmides, your mother gave birth to a blessed son. (157d9–158b4)

[129] Ast (1819–32) followed by Croiset 1921 and Sprague 1973 remove the phrase τῷ ἐν τῇ ἠπείρῳ at 158a5, while I follow the manuscript reading, as does Lamb 1927.

Socrates' short eulogy of Charmides' house is sincere[130] as well as effective. It points to some well-known facts about Charmides' noble origins, which are also Critias' origins and Plato's own. And it has a twin function. On the one hand, it gives reasons why Critias and many of his contemporaries probably took for granted that Charmides would be good as well as beautiful and perceived him as of great promise for the future of Athens. On the other hand, the eulogy is crafted so as to suggest that Socrates distances himself from these assumptions and is sceptical both regarding the true worth of Charmides' ancestors and their achievements, and regarding the expectations that the latter might raise about the young man himself. For the purposes of illustration, let us look, selectively, at certain features of the encomium.

At the outset, we should note that many of the statements made in the speech represent the beliefs and perceptions commonly associated with the aristocratic segment of Athenian society rather than with Plato's Socrates. They are descriptive rather than prescriptive, and convey what the general run of Athenians may have considered likely, not what Socrates expects will happen. Thus, when Socrates says at the beginning of the speech that it is right (*dikaion*) that Charmides would be superior to the other lads of his age in temperance and all such things, he need not be understood as placing the youth under the ethical obligation of maintaining the reputation of his noble house.[131] Rather, he expresses a social norm that a young aristocrat like Charmides probably endorses. 'It is likely' (*ek tôn eikotôn*: 157e3), says Socrates, that the offspring of two such houses will be second to none (157e1–4). He does not say what *he* thinks; he merely repeats an aristocratic commonplace according to which virtue as well as beauty is treated as a hereditary property passing from one generation to the next within the same house. The reason is probably pedagogical: he hopes to motivate the young man to do as well as he can in the conversation to follow.

Socrates' remarks concerning the two sides of Charmides' family exhibit a similar pattern. He relays some of the praise heaped by tradition[132] on both sets of the youth's ancestors, but does not disclose his own opinion on the matter. Moreover, he focuses his remarks on the beauty (*kallos*) and excellence or virtue (*aretê*) attributed to Charmides' forerunners,[133] but he

---

[130] Bruell 1977, 150, claims that Socrates' words indicate 'how unlikely it was that a youth with so much to puff him up (not to mention Critias as a guardian) should be moderate in any sense'. Also, van der Ben 1985, 22–3, considers much of the praise ironical.

[131] *Contra* van der Ben 1985, 21–2.   [132] ἐγκεκωμιασμένη παραδέδοται ἡμῖν: 157e7.

[133] Recall that Critias has described Charmides as 'very beautiful and good' (πάνυ καλὸς καὶ ἀγαθός: 154e4).

does not clarify whether these qualifications concern their character or their worldly achievements. Thus, he leaves room for one to wonder whether the beauty of these people or their admirable works need to go together with moral goodness. As Socrates remarks, on the side of Charmides' father, the line of Critias, son of Dropides,[134] is an extremely distinguished one. Not only has the family been praised by many poets, it also counts amongst its members one of the greatest poets of the archaic age: Solon the Athenian,[135] whose patriotic verses defend the reforms that he effected as a statesman and whose laws constitute the foundation of Athenian democracy. Thus, Solon is celebrated as both a statesman and a poet, and his reputation as one of the Seven Sages could intimate that he is a philosopher as well. As on an earlier occasion (154e1–155a1),[136] so at present Socrates points to the fact that the gifts of beauty and virtue are commonly viewed as Charmides' rightful inheritance. And, given the family connection with Solon and other eminent men, Charmides is probably expected to eventually participate in politics and distinguish himself in that domain as well.[137] However, Socrates does not reveal whether he himself admires the house of Critias for the reasons that Anacreon and other poets give. While these latter honour Charmides' paternal ancestors 'as excelling in beauty and virtue and everything else called happiness' (167e7–158a1), we cannot be sure that Socrates agrees that these men were virtuous or happy.

The part of the speech that concerns the maternal side of Charmides' lineage puts us on guard in a similar manner. While 'it is said' (158a3) of Pyrilampes[138] that, whenever he visited the Great King or some other eminent person on the Asian continent,[139] he was universally 'believed

---

[134] This Critias was Critias' grandfather. Both the father and the great-grandfather of Critias the elder (Dropides I and Dropides II, respectively) were archons of Athens. Solon was a near-contemporary of Dropides II (see also next note). Information gathered from a vast variety of sources is found in Nails 2002, 106–13.

[135] While later sources claim that Solon was a brother of Dropides (Critias' great-grandfather) and hence a direct ancestor of Critias and Plato, other sources indicate that, in fact, Solon was a distant relation and a family friend (cf. συγγενείας: *Charm.* 155a3; οἰκεῖος: *Tim.* 20e1).

[136] When Socrates proposed that they strip Charmides' soul in order to examine whether it is beautiful (154e1–7), Critias replied that in respect of his soul too his ward is both beautiful and good (154e4) and, moreover, that he is philosophical and most poetic (154e8–155a1). In reply, Socrates made the comment that, in truth, beauty (*to kalon*) has been present in their family for a long time because of their kinship with Solon (155a2–3).

[137] See Tulli 2000, 260–3.

[138] Pyrilampes was Plato's stepfather and an eminent member of Pericles' circle.

[139] Socrates refers to the Asian continent and in particular to the Persian empire: cf. van den Ben 1985, 22. As the latter remarks, the translations 'de la Grèce' and 'in the country', by Croiset 1921 and Sprague 1973, respectively, do not make sense in the present context.

to' (158a3) excel in beauty and greatness, we are not told whether Socrates too considers Pyrilampes a truly great man. There is no indication that Socrates is speaking ironically in this instance.[140] He truthfully states that Pyrilampes was hugely respected as an envoy and greatly admired for his excellence, and this statement has an obvious psychological and pedagogical function. It simply would not be expedient for his purposes to disclose his own opinion about the value of a worldly reputation or about Pyrilampes' true deserts. Nonetheless, he does flag his reluctance to take anything entirely for granted regarding Charmides' prospects. For he says that, since the youth comes from such stock, 'it is likely' (*eikos*: 158a7) that he will be first in all things. But what is likely need not come to pass.[141]

Subsequently, however, Socrates does allude to his own attitude towards the praise traditionally bestowed upon Charmides' family and the expectations commonly entertained about the youth's future. By implicitly contrasting physical beauty, which Charmides has obviously inherited from his ancestors (158a7–b2), and moral virtue, which the youth may or may not sufficiently possess (158b2–4), Socrates underscores the hereditary character of the former as opposed to the latter. Even assuming that Charmides' forefathers were virtuous, as the tradition wants it, there is no guarantee that Charmides too is sufficiently endowed with virtue and, therefore, this question must be pressed further. Furthermore, consistently with the emphasis that Socrates earlier put on the beauty of the soul vis-à-vis the beauty of the body (154d3–e3) and his expressed desire to strip and examine Charmides' soul (154e5–7), he now discloses to the latter that he considers virtue or, specifically, temperance[142] of supreme importance for happiness (158b2–4) but says nothing about the role of physical beauty in that regard. Then, in the closing sentences of the speech, he presents Charmides with the following challenge:

> The situation is this: if temperance is already present in you, as Critias here asserts, and if you are sufficiently temperate, you would no longer have any need of the incantations of Zalmoxis or of Abaris the Hyperborean,[143] but

---

[140] *Contra* van den Ben 1985, 22–3, who claims that 'there is then strong irony in Socrates' words, in that the Persian king taken as a measure by which to judge a man is at the farthest remove from Platonic standards'.

[141] Compare *Lach.* 179b–d, *Prot.* 319e–320b, *Tht.* 142d.

[142] καὶ πρὸς σωφροσύνην καὶ πρὸς τἆλλα: 158b3.

[143] According to legend, Abaris was a physician, magician, and prophet of Apollo, who visited various parts of Greece sometime in the early eighth century BC carrying a golden arrow, Apollo's gift, curing the sick, foretelling the future, working miracles, and purifying individuals and towns from various kinds of pollution. The golden arrow also gave him the power to fly and to be invisible. Plato is the first known author to use the attribute 'Hyperborean', someone from the far North, the

should be given the headache remedy itself straightaway. But if, on the other hand, you appear to be still lacking in them [sc. temperance and the other such qualities], you must have the incantations sung to you before you are given the drug. So, tell me yourself whether you agree with our friend here and declare that you already participate sufficiently in temperance, or whether you are deficient in it. (158b5–c4)

Like many other passages in the dialogue, this excerpt, taken together with the preceding lines (158a7–b5), is susceptible to a metaphysically neutral or, alternatively, metaphysically laden reading. For it contains words and phrases that Plato's readers may but need not associate with the so-called theory of Forms. On the one hand, Socrates can be taken to say, simply, that Charmides is in no way inferior to his ancestors regarding 'what is visible of the form' (*ta horômena tês ideas*: 158a7–b1), i.e. the perceptible beauty of his bodily appearance as opposed to the imperceptible beauty of his soul. Indeed, nothing further is required in order to make sense of what Socrates tells Charmides in this instance. On the other hand, however, the phrase 'what is visible of the form' can be taken to refer, proleptically, to Charmides' physical beauty as an empirical instantiation of the Form of Beauty or Beauty itself. Defenders of this approach reasonably point out that Socrates does not merely ask the young man whether he is sufficiently temperate, but uses the verb *metechein*, participate – a verb frequently employed by Plato in a technical sense to convey the relation between empirical particulars and the corresponding Forms. This interpretation too is self-standing and receives some support from the text. On either reading, Socrates' challenge to Charmides amounts to this: would he be willing to confirm his guardian's assertion on his behalf, namely that he excels in temperance with regard to all his peers (157d1–4)? Is he in a position to assert that, at this early age,[144] he has a sufficient share in that virtue (158c3–4)?

These are extremely hard questions for Charmides to address: is temperance present in you[145] or not? Do you claim to have enough of it or not?

---

domain beyond, the realm of the North Wind. Abaris figures also in the Neoplatonist tradition, and a connection is drawn between him and Pythagoras insofar as it is said that he eventually gave Apollo's arrow to Pythagoras. According to the Suda, Abaris wrote on Scythian oracles. It is possible that, in the passage cited here, Plato appeals to some kind of mythical connection between Abaris and Zalmoxis, the North, Thrace, and conceivably Scythia as well, and even to a common religious and medical tradition in those areas. Or, one might interpret Socrates' summary reference to both Zalmoxis (whom he has discussed in some detail) and Abaris (whom he mentions here for the first and only time) as an indication that we should disregard the quasi-historical aspects of these legendary characters and focus on the philosophical message that Socrates wishes to convey.

[144] ἤδη: 158c3.

[145] πάρεστιν (158b5) – this is another verb that Plato sometimes uses in a technical sense to indicate the presence of a Form in some way.

Are you really a good person or not? A person so young would be unlikely to have reflected on such matters, let alone have formed settled views about them. In addition, as Charmides will soon confess, he finds himself in a socially awkward situation and cannot see how to get out of it. Furthermore, the way in which Socrates phrases his query and, in particular, the vocabulary that he uses raise complications that Charmides is unable to discern or pursue, e.g. whether there can be different degrees of participation in temperance or what it could mean to have 'sufficient temperance' in oneself. Readers who are interested in such problems are directed towards the *Parmenides*, while Charmides is left to decide how to react to the challenge before him.

8   The Best Method of Enquiry (158c5–159a10)

> First, Charmides blushed at this and looked even more beautiful than before, for his modesty became his youth. Then, he replied in quite a dignified manner. He remarked that it would not be easy at present either to affirm or to deny what he was being asked. – For if, he went on, I deny being temperate, I shall both be doing something absurd in saying that about myself and be showing Critias here and, as he claims, many others who consider me temperate to be liars. If, on the other hand, I affirm that I am temperate and praise myself, perhaps this will appear offensive. So, I cannot decide what answer I should give you. – Charmides, I said, your answer seems to me reasonable. And I think, I continued, that we should examine in common whether or not you already have what I am enquiring about, to save you from being forced to say what you do not wish to say, and me, for my own part, from applying myself to medicine in a thoughtless manner. Thus, if it is agreeable to you, I am willing to pursue the question together with you, but otherwise let us leave it aside. – Nothing, he said, could be more agreeable. To this end, therefore, do proceed with the enquiry in whatever way you think is better. (158c5–e5)

The *aporia*, puzzle, expressed in this passage motivates the method that Socrates will introduce a little later as the 'best method' for the enquiry that is about to begin. The puzzle itself is articulated by Charmides in reaction to the question asked by Socrates, namely whether or not the youth believes himself to be sufficiently temperate. The exchange between these two characters yields further insights into their portrayals, and reveals something about Socrates as narrator as well.

Charmides expresses his perplexity in terms of a classic aporetic dilemma. He can see exactly two alternatives, neither of which appears acceptable. It seems that he should neither assert that he is temperate nor declare that he is not, for, as he believes, highly undesirable consequences are attached to each of these options.[146] What are these consequences? And what may they reveal about the young man's character and values? On the one hand, he considers it improper to say something pejorative about himself or undermine the credibility of his guardian, while, on the other, he wishes to avoid giving the appearance of singing his own praises. Charmides, then, has a keen sense of self-worth, of the behaviour that a youth of his rank is expected to have, and of what he owes to himself and others, including of course his own cousin and guardian. So, he is portrayed as temperate in this traditional sense: he knows who he is and what he owes to himself and others, and behaves accordingly in a decent and composed manner. For his own part, Socrates indicates that he considers the youth's answer appropriate if measured by social standards. In his role as character, he remarks that what Charmides says seems reasonable (*eikota*: 158d7), namely that he ought not to slander himself, expose his guardian, or appear boastful. Moreover, in his capacity as narrator, Socrates comments that, on that occasion, the youth spoke *ouk agennôs* (158c7), i.e. not without dignity or modesty. If either or both of these features capture what temperance really is,[147] it would seem that Charmides has the virtue.

In fact, Socrates confirms that Charmides has at least one of these characteristics, namely a disposition to be modest or feel shame (*to aischyntêlon*: 158c6), for when he asked Charmides if he was sufficiently temperate, the young man blushed.[148] Typically, blushing is taken to be a manifestation of feelings of shame or embarrassment caused by one's perception of oneself as violating some social value that one considers wrong to disregard or transgress.[149] This is precisely the circumstance that Charmides finds himself in.[150] He blushes because he feels ashamed either to call himself intemperate (men of his origins and upbringing would condemn such an act of self-humiliation) or to boast about himself

---

[146] Note that Charmides leaves out the sufficiency requirement, presumably because he is not aware of its possible implications. He does not put to himself the question of whether or not he is sufficiently temperate (or, equivalently, whether or not he sufficiently participates in temperance), but the question of whether or not he is temperate *simpliciter*.

[147] In due course, Charmides will define temperance, first, as a sort of quietness, i.e. doing everything (including *dialegesthai*: 159b4) in a calm and decorous manner (159b2–6), and then as modesty or a sense of shame (160e3–5). See Chapters 3 and 4, respectively.

[148] ἀνερυθριάσας: 158c5.

[149] On the nature of shame and its relation to guilt, see the classic discussion by Williams 1986.

[150] E.g. Benardete 1986, 18, takes the blush on Charmides' cheeks as an outward manifestation of a modest disposition.

(most members of his social milieu would consider this distasteful). At first glance, therefore, Charmides' measured and thoughtful reply to Socrates appears to vindicate Critias' earlier assertion that his ward is both beautiful and good (154e4). The great beauty of his body seems matched by a beautiful soul. Indeed, as Socrates suggests, what appeared like psychic beauty did enhance the beauty of the young man's physical form. The blush on his face made him appear even more beautiful than he did before 'for his modesty became his youth' (158c6).[151]

But is the sort of modesty made manifest on the youth's rosy cheeks the same thing as psychic beauty? Is it the same thing as temperance? Neither the characters of the dialogue nor its readers are presently in a position to give an answer. We need to wait and see and, in fact, we have some reasons to withhold judgement as to whether Charmides is temperate. For, according to the narration, he is not perplexed about the truth of the matter, i.e. whether he really has temperance, but about how to speak and what to say in order to avoid exposing himself and his guardian. He seems to hesitate not because he realises that it is terribly important and terribly difficult to discover the condition of his own soul, but because he wants to observe certain social norms but is not sure as to how to apply them.[152] It is possible, though by no means certain, that the message of the Thracian doctor has been lost on him. Nevertheless, Socrates encourages him to go on.

We should pause for a moment to consider Socrates' double role in that scene. First, there is continuity between Socrates as character and Socrates as narrator insofar as, in both these capacities, he notes the causal effect that a feature of Charmides' soul has on the beauty of his body and thus lends support to the central intuition of Zalmoxian holism. Also, we have had the opportunity to observe Socrates' subtlety as a pedagogue. Even though he must have registered the mundane nature of Charmides' puzzlement, he finds something positive to say, i.e. that the youth's concerns seemed quite reasonable (158d7), and he turns Charmides' perplexity to pedagogical advantage. His message is this: the situation as you describe it, Charmides, is delicate and it is perfectly natural for you to feel at a loss; but perhaps I can help you, so let us make a joint effort to find out whether

---

[151] On this point, see the subtle analysis by Woolf 2019.

[152] Some interpreters claim that Charmides is concealing something, but disagree as to what the concealed element is. McAvoy 1996, 74, suggests that Charmides' blush is an involuntary expression of something kept hidden, namely a kind of bashfulness indicating a tendency towards philosophy. Others, however, contend that the youth shows no inclination to philosophy, but believes himself to be temperate and puzzles over how to say this in a decent manner.

you have temperance. This move is calculated to put the young man at ease: he will probably feel less pressure if he knows that he won't be alone in his search for an answer. Furthermore, Socrates stresses that the success or failure of the investigation crucially depends on the youth's attitude. Only if the youth finds the prospect of a joint endeavour congenial (*philon*: 158e3) will Socrates wish to pursue it (158e3).[153] Recall that Zalmoxian therapy can have an effect only on condition that the patient freely chooses to engage with the doctor. In the opposite case, the doctor's remedies are bound to be ineffective (158e1–2).

For his own part, Charmides reacts in a positive and promising manner. He declares that nothing could be more congenial to him and urges Socrates to use whatever method of enquiry he deems better (158e4–5). Even so, we cannot be sure about his motivation for speaking in that way. On the one hand, his enthusiasm could be sincere and due to a genuine inclination towards philosophy. After all, according to Critias, he regards himself as a philosopher as well as a poet (154e8–155a1). On the other, Charmides is well aware of his guardian's wish to bring him close to Socrates and have him converse with the latter. By showing himself eager to do so, he knows that he is fulfilling Critias' expectations and winning his approval. We cannot exclude either of these options, nor can we rule out the possibility that a combination of these motives is prompting the young man to appear eager to contribute to the investigation. In any event, since he gives Socrates a free hand to proceed as he deems better (*beltion*: 158e5), his interlocutor outlines the following method:

> The best method of enquiry into this matter, I said, seems to me to be the following. It is quite evident that if temperance is present in you, you can express some belief about it. For if it really resides in you, wherever it resides, it must provide a sensation [or an awareness] from which you can hold a belief about it, namely what temperance is and what kind of thing it is. Do you not think so? – Yes, I do, he replied. – And since you know how to speak Greek, I said, you could also, I suppose, express it, saying what it appears to you to be. – Perhaps, he said. – So, in order that we may guess whether it is in you or not, tell me, I said, what you declare temperance to be according to your own belief. (158e6–159a10)[154]

This passage effects the transition from the prologue to the first part of the dialectical investigation constituting the main body of the dialogue, i.e. the

---

[153] εἰ οὖν σοι φίλον, ἐθέλω σκοπεῖν μετὰ σοῦ· εἰ δὲ μή, ἐᾶν: 158e3.

[154] Van der Ben 1985, 23, takes τοῦτό γε ὃ οἴει to be the grammatical object of ἂν εἴποις and maintains that the expression αὐτὸ ὅτι σοι φαίνεται is epexegetic of τοῦτό γε οἴει. See his criticism of Lamb's translation *ad loc.*

round between Socrates and Charmides. For Socrates now suggests that the optimal method for discovering whether the youth has temperance is for them to examine together what Charmides believes to be the answer to the so-called 'what is X?' question: what temperance is and what kind of thing it is. To put it differently, they need to jointly examine what Charmides will propose as the definition of temperance. Nonetheless, the 'best method' (as I shall call it from now onwards) requires clarification regarding its scope and purpose, the argument that it entails, and the psychological and cognitive concepts that it involves. I think that these are the issues that we primarily need to address: is the method supposed to be 'best' without qualification or optimal just for the particular task at hand? What relations obtain between the presence of temperance in oneself, one's *aisthesis* (awareness, sensation, or feeling) of that virtue, and one's *doxa* (belief) about its nature? Why does Socrates mention *hellenizein*, speaking Greek, in this context? In the end, is Socrates' choice of method defensible? Is it really optimal? And if it is, in what way?

Regarding the method's scope and intent, there is no reason to suppose that Socrates proposes it as the 'best method' in every context and circumstance. Rather, he favours it on this particular occasion for a number of different reasons. Psychologically and pedagogically, the path that Socrates proposes answers Charmides' concern to avoid saying something disgraceful or immodest about himself. For the question that Charmides is now asked to address is not whether he is temperate, but rather what he takes temperance to be.[155] He does not feel forced any more to make an evaluative judgement that could expose him or his guardian to derision or ridicule. Instead, he has been offered an alternative and unexceptional way of submitting himself to dialectical scrutiny.[156] Philosophically, despite claims to the contrary, the method under discussion is neither indefensible nor arbitrary.[157] In fact, Socrates' outline of the method implies an argument explaining how the latter is supposed to work. We shall look at this argument immediately below, but it should be mentioned at the outset that Socrates does not justify, severally or jointly, its premises

---

[155] Compare Bruell 1977, 152: 'Charmides apparently would never be required to reveal his belief as to whether he possessed moderation; they would examine only the fact of possession or non-possession'.

[156] Solère-Queval 1993, 12, stresses the pedagogical dimension of Socrates' method as well as its modest epistemological requirements. In her view, Socrates asks Charmides to spell out his δόξα (belief) and not his ἐπιστήμη (expert or scientific knowledge) about the nature of temperance because he assumes that whatever Charmides says will be grounded on αἴσθησις (sensation) and, hence, will not qualify as a knowledge claim.

[157] On the relation between the dramatic and the philosophical elements related to the 'best method', see the brief comments by Bruell 1977, 152–3, Solère-Queval 1993, 12–13, and Taylor 1926, 49–50.

and assumptions. Therefore, the attempt to reconstruct and discuss it must involve a certain degree of speculation.

The argument, I submit, goes as follows. (P1) If one has *sôphrosynê*, one must[158] also have an *aisthêsis*, i.e. some sort of awareness, sensation, or feeling[159] about it: a feeling about what temperance is and what kind of thing it is, i.e. what it is like to have it (159a3). (P2) And if one has such a feeling, one already has formed, or should be able to form, also a belief (*doxa*) about it (159a2).[160] (C) Evidently, then,[161] if temperance is present in Charmides, he should have, or should be expected to have,[162] an opinion about the nature of the virtue and what it is like.[163] It is clear that Socrates does not consider this opinion an autobiographical report: it will not merely relay a feeling that Charmides has about himself, but will purport to capture something objective about the nature of *sôphrosynê* (159a3). In point of fact, the 'best method' requires Charmides to attempt to define the virtue.

Again, in addition to making perfect sense in the immediate context, the 'best method' also directs us outside the frame of this dialogue to Plato's theory of Recollection or to his theory of Forms. Beginning with the object of the 'best method', for the purposes of the investigation underway it presently suffices to assume that temperance is a certain sort of disposition or attitude that Charmides may or may not possess. Or the choice of words in the phrase 'if temperance is present in you,[164] you should be able to hold a belief about it' (158e7–159a1) could be taken to be proleptic. One might

---

[158] ἀνάγκη: 159a1.

[159] So, e.g., Bruell 1977, 152. Solère-Queval 1993, 12, renders 'αἴσθησις' by intuition.

[160] It is not clear to me what the correct modality is here. On the one hand, δῆλον at 158e7 appears to point to some sort of necessity: if temperance is present in you, evidently you will have something to say about it (158e7–159a1). On the other, ἀνάγκη at 159a1 governs the claim that, if one has temperance, one must also have a feeling about it, but, I think, does not govern the further claim that, if one has a feeling about the temperance in oneself, one will be able to form a judgement. The verb in the optative (ἄν . . . εἴη) at 159a3 indicates that this latter claim is rather tentative.

[161] δῆλον γάρ: 158e7.   [162] See note 158 in this chapter.

[163] Stepping back from the framework of the *Charmides*, one might object that (P1) is dubious, since I might have a virtue but not have any sense of it, e.g. I could be brave but have no sense that I am brave or, still less, know that I am brave. However, later in the dialogue, Critias explicitly denies that people could act temperately and be temperate without knowing themselves to be temperate (164c7–d3) and Socrates does not disagree (see Chapter 6, 153–8). This intuition is defensible and perhaps applies to all the virtues and not only to *sôphrosynê*. However, one might object to (P2) as well: supposing that I have some inner perception of bravery, does it follow that I also have a belief about the nature of bravery? Couldn't there be self-perceptions that do not automatically give me corresponding beliefs? I don't think that Socrates is blind to this sort of objection. Rather, he postulates (P2) for protreptic purposes, i.e. to give Charmides enough confidence to say what he thinks about the nature of temperance.

[164] εἴ σοι πάρεστιν: 158e7.

think of the theory of Recollection in this connection, insofar as Recollection is a basic way to gain access to concepts that are 'in us' and begin an enquiry on the basis of them. Moreover, as mentioned, the ordinary expression 'to be present in' (*parestin*)[165] also belongs to the technical vocabulary that Platonic interlocutors sometimes use in order to refer to Forms and their causal relation to particulars. Thus, one might contend that Socrates is not merely saying that if Charmides has temperance, we should expect him to hold some belief about it; he is suggesting that if Temperance somehow inheres in Charmides, it will cause him to have a grasp of its own nature.

Similar observations apply to Socrates' use of the verbs *doxazein*, to believe, and *phainesthai*, to appear, as well as the nouns *doxa* and *aisthêsis*. They are mostly taken to bear, straightforwardly, on Socrates' exhortation[166] that Charmides attend to his awareness of whatever he registers as temperance in his own soul and, on that basis, try to articulate his own belief about that virtue.[167] Alfred Edward Taylor, for instance, interprets *aisthêsis* in such a broad and non-technical sense. 'If a man has this [sc. temperance) or any other character of soul, it must, of course, make its presence felt, and its possessor will therefore have an opinion of some kind about its nature. (It is not meant, of course, that the possessor of the character need have a "clear and distinct idea" of it, but only that he must have some acquaintance with it)'.[168] However, as has been noted in the literature, the perceptual and doxastic vocabulary that Socrates uses in order to outline the 'best method' could be taken to point, proleptically, to the middle books of the *Republic*. Socrates could be suggesting a contrast between *doxa*, belief, and *epistêmê* (scientific) knowledge; between the objects of belief, which are cognisable through *aisthêsis*, and the objects of knowledge, which are apprehended by the mind. Obviously, the former reading is self-standing and

---

[165] πάρεστιν at 158e7 is the third-person singular present indicative of the verb παρεῖναι. Similar uses of the verb occur at 160d7 (ὁποῖόν τινά σε ποιεῖ ἡ σωφροσύνη παροῦσα) and 161a8–9 (σωφροσύνη δέ γε ἀγαθόν, εἴπερ ἀγαθούς ποιεῖ οἶς ἄν παρῇ, κακούς δὲ μή).

[166] Solère-Queval 1993, 12, draws attention to the repeated use of doxastic terms in connection with the 'best method', and she comments on their epistemic implications and pedagogical utility.

[167] Socrates neither says nor implies that the 'best method' intends to provide a grounding relation. Such a claim would be absurd. All that the method implies is that, if one possesses temperance (to an undetermined degree), then one has a sort of dim awareness expressed in a belief. But there is no suggestion that beliefs of that sort can have proper epistemic grounding.

[168] Taylor 1926, 49–50. Compare McCabe 2000, 30: 'the thought here is that self-control in the soul is transparent to the person who has it; so Charmides' accurate reporting of what he sees in himself will be what the inquiry needs (or that would be so, if in fact Charmides turned out to be self-controlled in the right way)'.

does not imply the latter in any way.[169] But it seems part of Plato's strategy to lay the text open to theoretically laden interpretations where he deems it appropriate.

As to the remark that, since Charmides knows how to speak Greek (*hellenizein*), he should be able to say what temperance appears to him to be (159a7),[170] it probably amounts to little more than a platitude which, however, serves a pedagogical purpose. Socrates points out that all that Charmides needs in order to speak his mind is knowledge of Greek, which of course Charmides has. Like the modest epistemic requirements of the 'best method', this comment too seems intended to put the young man at ease, encourage him to say what he believes, and prompt him to engage in the dialectical search. Socrates makes a comparable move in the *Meno* with regard to the slave boy that he is about to question in order to demonstrate that all learning is recollection. 'Is he (sc. the slave boy) a Greek and does he speak Greek (*hellênizei*)? – Very much so, in fact he is born in the house' (82b4–5). In this case too, the boy's mastery of the Greek language is, according to Socrates, all that is required for the interrogation that will follow. On the other hand, several commentators attribute the comment concerning Charmides' ability to speak Greek with theoretical dimensions. For instance, according to one view, '[Plato here] does represent Socrates linking together virtue with knowledge and knowledge with express-ability'.[171] According to another, assuming that Charmides has some acquaintance with temperance, 'language about it [sc. the corresponding belief] will have some meaning for [the young man], exactly as language about sight or hearing will mean something to anyone who can see or hear, though it would be meaningless to beings born blind or deaf'.[172] In my view, the non-theoretical reading of the passage makes excellent dramatic and psychological sense. Nonetheless, it is worth registering that Socrates' remark about *hellênizein*, Charmides' mastery of the Greek language, admits of theoretically informed interpretations as well.

---

[169] Bruell 1977, 152, rightly stresses that Socrates' outline of the 'best method' avoids raising epistemological issues. Notably, Socrates does not explain on what grounds the person experiencing an *aisthêsis* will be able to identify temperance as the cause of this latter. According to Bruell, Charmides accepts the assumption that temperance will always make itself known to its possessor, precisely because he is not alerted to the epistemological problems connected with that assumption.

[170] οὐκοῦν τοῦτό γε, ἔφην, ὃ οἴει, ἐπειδήπερ ἑλληνίζειν ἐπίστασαι, κἂν εἴποις δήπου αὐτὸ ὅ τί σοι φαίνεται: 159a6–7.

[171] Jenks 2008, 30. In fact, however, Socrates does not link together temperance with knowledge but with belief. And ἑλληνίζειν, speaking Greek, is not as broad as 'express-ability'.

[172] Taylor 1926, 50. In fact, Socrates does not say anything explicit about the meaningfulness of sentences concerning temperance.

Socrates' concluding words underscore the relatively low epistemic expectations of the 'best method' and highlight its protreptic and pedagogical function.

> So, in order that we may guess [*topasômen*] whether it is in you or not, tell me, I said, what you declare temperance to be according to your belief. (159a9–10)

Literally, the verb *topazein* means to locate, but its habitual use is metaphorical and carries the connotations of guessing or forming a conjecture. Socrates, then, sets the bar rather low regarding the epistemic status of the 'best method' and its prospective achievements. Assuming that Charmides will be induced to state his belief about what temperance is, all that the interlocutors can reasonably aspire to is to make an informed guess as to whether temperance is present in Charmides or whether the opposite is the case. In addition to the fact that the 'best method' is relatively easy to follow, it is also directed towards a goal that appears not very difficult to attain. Indeed, by indicating that the search will not be too demanding and that the expectations will not be too high,[173] Socrates succeeds in prompting Charmides into action.

---

[173] See Solère-Queval 1993, 12, and also the remarks by Taylor 1926, 50 and Grote 1865, 483.

CHAPTER 3

Charmides' First Definition of Sôphrosynê
Temperance Is a Kind of Quietness (159b1–160d4)

At first he was hesitant and not very willing to answer. But presently he said that it seemed to him that temperance is doing everything in an orderly and quiet manner [*kosmiôs kai hêsychêi*] – walking in the streets, and talking, and doing everything else in a similar way. 'So', he said, 'it seems to me that, in a word, what you are asking about is a sort of quietness or calmness [*hêsychiotês tis*]'. (159b1–6)[1]

Despite the relaxed epistemic conditions of the 'best method' and the encouragement that he has received from Socrates, Charmides remains initially reluctant to state what he believes *sôphrosynê* to be. Another brush-stroke is added to his character, for the narrator makes us wonder why the youth still hesitates to answer. Perhaps he is intellectually idle[2] or thoroughly convinced that he is temperate, and does not really wish to enter the conversation. Or, more likely, he is disposed to react in a quiet and somewhat slow manner to the challenge that lies ahead. We may assume that he is following Socrates' instructions and taking the time to attend to his own awareness of temperance in himself and articulate it in the form of a belief. And we may also assume that, because he perceives temperance as a kind of quiet self-restraint, he is trying to display this specific quality in the way he answers. For, as Socrates has suggested, if he has temperance, he can be expected to have an opinion about what it is, whereas if he has no opinion about the virtue, then it would seem that he does not possess it (158e7–159a4).[3]

---

[1] Καὶ ὅς τὸ μὲν πρῶτον ὤκνει τε καὶ οὐ πάνυ ἤθελεν ἀποκρίνασθαι· ἔπειτα μέντοι εἶπεν ὅτι οἷ δοκοῖ σωφροσύνη εἶναι τὸ κοσμίως πάντα πράττειν καὶ ἡσυχῇ, ἔν τε ταῖς ὁδοῖς βαδίζειν καὶ διαλέγεσθαι, καὶ τὰ ἄλλα πάντα ὡσαύτως ποιεῖν· καὶ μοι δοκεῖν, ἔφη, συλλήβδην ἡσυχιότης τις εἶναι ὃ ἐρωτᾷς (159b1–6).

[2] The narrator says that Charmides ὤκνει (159b1) and the verb ὀκνεῖν can mean 'to be hesitant' but also 'to be lazy'.

[3] The sufficiency condition that Socrates mentioned earlier (158c3) suggests the following qualifications: one's sufficient participation in temperance (158c3–4) entails the ability to express a true belief about its nature, whereas one's inability to express an opinion about temperance will indicate insufficient participation in temperance or the total absence of it. Furthermore, it is possible that

Charmides' answer, that temperance seems to him (*dokei moi*: 159b5) to be a kind of quietness or calmness (*hêsychiotês tis*: 159b5), shows some cleverness and skill. In the first place, taking advantage of the 'best method', he advances that claim as a belief that he holds,[4] not a piece of knowledge that he has. Thus, even if he is refuted, he won't feel terribly embarrassed about it. Furthermore, unlike, for example, Euthyphro or Meno who initially give the wrong kind of answer to the 'what is X?' question, the former by pointing to a particular instance of X and the latter by citing different Xs in different groups of people, Charmides understands at once what sort of answer he is required to give. Formally, his claim concerning the nature of temperance is correct and can become the object of a dialectical investigation.

I

Charmides states his belief about what temperance is in two different ways. The first is, so to speak, substantival: temperance is 'some sort of quietness' (159b5). The second is adverbial: 'temperance is doing everything in an orderly and quiet manner' (*kosmiôs kai hêsychêi*: 159b3). He treats these formulas as nearly equivalent, but suggests that the former may be inferred from the latter on inductive grounds. For first he gives the adverbial definition and illustrates it by means of examples ('walking in the streets, and engaging in dialogue, and doing everything else in a similar way': 159b3–5), and then summarises all this 'in a word' (*syllêbdên*: 159b5) as quietness of some sort (*hêsychiotês tis*: 159b5).[5] Charmides appears to assume that all and only the possessors of temperance have that sort of quietness or the ability to accomplish everything they do (159b4) in an orderly and quiet manner. And he can be taken to refer, more broadly, to a calm, decorous, seemly, tactful, socially appropriate manner of behaving.

Why does Charmides think of *sôphrosynê* in that way? Is he right? And whom does Socrates have in mind when he retorts that people do indeed say that 'quiet persons are temperate' (159b8)? It is a commonplace that the Greeks associate *sôphrosynê* (literally, the possession of a sound and healthy mind)[6] with quiet, calm, decorous behaviour, since sane people are

---

insufficient participation in the virtue (158c4) would cause one to have false beliefs about temperance or beliefs that are not really about temperance at all.

[4] οἳ δοκεῖ: 159b2; μοι δοκεῖ: 159b5.

[5] If Charmides meant that temperance is a species of ἡσυχιότης, this could invite the criticism that the ἡσυχιότης lacking in, for example, running or boxing is a different species than the quietness present in decorous behaviour.

[6] See Chapter 1, 3.

typically in control of themselves and do not behave like maniacs.[7] This association may carry specific political connotations, insofar as it is part of a political and civic ideal advanced in classical Athens especially by the oligarchic faction and frequently related to pro-Spartan tendencies.[8] It is noteworthy that, in addition to the value of *sôphrosynê* itself, the ideas of doing things '*kosmiôs*', in an orderly or decorous way, and *hêsychêî'*, in a quiet, dignified, unobtrusive manner, belong to the repertoire of Athenians engaged in aristocratic and pro-Spartan propaganda. The same holds for the notion of *hêsychiotês*,[9] which became especially popular in the early 380s, close to the likely date of composition of the *Charmides*, at a time of revival of debates concerning the junta of the Thirty.[10] Given Charmides' family environment and his connection with Critias, it is reasonable to suppose that he endorses, if unreflectively, these values of oligarchic ideology and is bringing them to the fore on the present occasion.

However, one need not appeal to such specifically political factors to explain why Charmides believes that temperance amounts to doing things in a certain manner – calmly and decorously. For, regardless of the political affiliations of their families, well-bred Athenian youths were taught to value unobtrusive and decorous behaviour. They were expected to show themselves as dignified and composed and aware of their place in Athenian society; in short, to show themselves to be *sôphrones*, temperate, in a broad and quite ordinary sense of the term.[11] Thus, Charmides' appropriation of the belief that temperance is a kind of quietness derives from his endorsement of a broadly shared social and cultural code rather than any specific political inclinations. If so, when Socrates refers to those who say that quiet men are temperate (159b8), he probably has in mind upper-class Athenians independently of the political party that each of them favours. Within the

---

[7] See Santas 1973, 112. A contrast can be drawn between Chaerephon's behaviour and the behaviour suggested by Charmides' definition. For Chaerephon comports himself in something like a manic manner when he jumps up to greet Socrates upon his entrance into the gymnasium.

[8] See above, 3–4.

[9] See Witte 1970, 44 ff., especially the terminological parallels between the *Charmides* and Lysias, XXVI 3 and 5 (*On the Scrutiny of Evandrus*).

[10] See Dušanić 2000, 60.

[11] E.g. Taylor 1926, 50, explicitly takes ἡσυχιότης in this sense: 'As is natural in a mere lad, Charmides fixes first of all on an external characteristic of *sophrosyne* in the form which would be most familiar to a boy – the form of decent and modest bearing towards one's elders and "good behaviour" generally'. Moreover, he suggests that this aspect of temperance is closely connected with self-control: 'There is a "hurry" which means that one's limbs or one's tongue are not really under control as they should be'. See also Tuckey 1951, 19: 'This is the reply that might be expected from a noble young Athenian, for it describes the sort of conduct required of him by the conventions of Athenian society'.

frame of our dialogue, there is no special reason to tie Charmides' belief that temperance amounts to doing things in a quiet manner specifically with the ideology of the oligarchic party.

Philosophically, the adverbial version of the definition strongly suggests that, even though Charmides' definition of temperance need not entail crude behaviourism,[12] nonetheless it strongly suggests that he conceives of the virtue primarily in terms of a style of behaving.[13] Temperance is not so much a matter of *what* we do as *how* we do it; not something that the temperate man *has* but rather a special feature of his manner of acting.[14] In an important sense, then, Charmides appears to consider what one *does* prior to who one *is*. And (whether or not he realises this) he advances the very strong claim that every temperate action is done with a certain kind of quietness or calmness, and every action performed in that manner is temperate.

What does 'acting *hêsychêi*' actually mean? Both this adverb and the noun, *hêsychiotês*, as well as the verb *hêsychein*, have a vast range of meanings which, nonetheless, share a common semantic core and exhibit family resemblances. Hence these terms are not, strictly speaking, ambiguous in the sense in which, for example, the noun 'cardinal' is ambiguous.[15] In the elenchus that follows, Socrates will use examples that highlight the semantic richness of the adverb '*hêsychêi*' and the noun '*hêsychiotês*', but also raise questions about the legitimacy of certain dialectical moves. For instance, in addition to acting in a quiet or calm or unobtrusive manner, he will assume that acting *hêsychêi* is equivalent to acting in a slow, sluggish, absent-minded way as opposed to acting quickly, briskly, and with total concentration. He stretches semantic boundaries even further, when he contrasts, for example, boxing *hêsychôs*, in a spirit of friendliness and peacefulness, with boxing *oxeôs* or both *oxeôs* and *tacheôs*, in an intense and aggressive way (159d1–2), or when he assumes that performing certain mental activities *hêsychôs* implies intellectual laziness or deficiency or both

---

[12] Many scholars take Charmides' first definition to refer exclusively to behaviour and talk about a gradual movement from the outer to the inner, from behaviour to character or the state of one's soul. For instance, see North 1966, 156; Santas 1973, 112–13; Burnyeat 1971, 111–16; and, most recently, Tuozzo 2011, 157. However, I can find no decisive textual evidence of a consistent line drawn between one's disposition to behave in a certain manner and the corresponding behaviour.

[13] There are no grounds to support the widespread view that Charmides' definition implies that temperance is *exclusively* a matter of behaviour, even though the focus unquestionably is on the behavioural aspects of the virtue.

[14] See Burnyeat 1971, 211–15; Santas 1973, 112–13.

[15] A cardinal is a songbird, but also a dignitary of the Catholic church.

(159e3–160b2). We should keep an eye on these shades of meaning and the ways they are interrelated in the refutation that follows.

2

The elenchus aiming to refute Charmides' first definition of temperance has been reconstructed in different ways and has received mixed reviews. On some accounts the argument is invalid[16] and vitiated by a paralogism,[17] while on others the argument is faulty but nonetheless has some persuasive force.[18] In fact, I submit, the argument is better and more effective than it has widely been judged to be. It exploits the rich semantic nuances of '*hêsychein*' (primarily, to be quiet or calm or unobtrusive) and its cognates, as well as the different connotations of '*kalon*', which, here, I render by 'admirable',[19] in order to draw certain intuitively defensible inferences and reach the right conclusion.

We may begin by looking at two sketches of the logical skeleton of the argument drawn from the secondary literature. First: temperance or acting temperately[20] is always something *kalon*, admirable; temperance cannot be the same as quietness, unless quietness is also always something *kalon*; but it is not the case that quietness is always something *kalon* and, therefore, temperance cannot be the same thing as quietness.[21] Or: all temperance is *kalon*, but some quietness is not *kalon* and, therefore, (some) quietness is not temperance.[22] These sketchy reconstructions correctly suggest that the major premise of the argument does much work, since it attributes to temperance what we might call an essential characteristic (i.e. temperance is *kalon*) that quietness must also have if it is to define temperance. Socrates' counterexamples aim to demonstrate that, in fact, quietness does not have that characteristic: even though quietness may sometimes be *kalon*, it is not always or invariably *kalon*; or, even if some quietness is *kalon*, much of it is not. The above sketches, then, are defensible as far as

---

[16] See, for instance, the scathing assessment by Beversluis 2000, 137–41.

[17] Lutoslawski 1897, 203, attributes to Socrates this paralogism: from the premises 'temperance is *kalon*' and 'quickness is *kalon*', he infers that quickness is temperate. Tuckey 1951, 19, also holds that view.

[18] So Santas 1973, 117: 'And since Socrates cannot perform miracles, his argument may perhaps remain convincing enough for activists, but not so convincing for people who put a high premium on quietness of behavior'.

[19] On the meaning and connotations of καλόν, see below, 113–14.

[20] Henceforth, I treat these expressions interchangeably.

[21] For example, see Santas 1973, 113, who subsequently offers a detailed and sensitive analysis of the comparative judgements constituting many of the premises of the argument.

[22] Kosman 1983, 204.

they go. But they do not capture important features of this elenchus, notably the fact that several premises involve comparative judgements between, for example, acting more quietly and acting less quietly, or acting quietly and acting in an opposite or contrary manner.[23] Nor could schematic outlines convey the range of semantic nuances of '*hêsychiotês*' as well as of its cognates, near-synonyms, and opposites. It will be helpful, therefore, to lay out the argument in full detail and consider how it is supposed to work as a dialectical refutation. I propose the following reconstruction:

(1) Temperance or acting temperately is a sort of quietness or acting quietly (159b2–6).

(2) Temperance is a *kalon*, an admirable thing (159c1, d8, 11; cf. - 160d1–2).[24]

(3) In fact, temperance is the greatest or one of the greatest *kala*, the most admirable things (cf. 157a5–b1).

(4) Quietness or acting quietly[25] must be *kalon*.

(5) Insofar as an action or manner of acting is *kalon*, it must be more or at least no less *kalon* than that same action performed in the contrary manner (e.g. 160d4–11).

(6) Temperance or acting temperately is at least more *kalon* than its contrary.

(7) A sort of quietness or acting quietly should be at least more *kalon* than its contrary.

(8) A sort of quietness or acting quietly should be superlatively *kalon* in comparison to every action performed in a different or contrary manner.

However, Socrates' counterexamples suggest that:

(9) Many types of actions exhibiting quietness are at least less *kala* than those types of actions exhibiting the opposite property.

(10) Some types of actions exhibiting quietness are not *kala* but the opposite, namely *aischra*, disgraceful.[26]

Therefore, 'at least according to this argument' (160b8):

---

[23] Santas 1973, 112–17, is attentive to that feature of the argument. On the other hand, Beversluis 2000, 138–9, views the comparisons as 'bizarre' contrasts and suggests possible reactions to them which, however, could not take place in a dialectical argument.

[24] On the meaning and connotations of '*kalon*', see below, 113–14. All emphases are mine.

[25] That is, the sort of quietness that Charmides deems identical with *sôphrosynê*: see note 5 in this chapter.

[26] See note 23 in this chapter.

(11) It is not the case that temperance is a certain sort of quietness (160b7–8).[27]

(12) By implication, it is not the case that a temperate life is a quiet life (160b7–8).

Summing up the argument, Socrates concludes that, according to the above reasoning, it seems to follow that:

(13) Either in no cases or in very few cases are quiet actions more admirable than their opposites (160b9–c2).

(14) In all events, even assuming that, of the actions that are most admirable, the quiet ones are no fewer than the actions performed in the opposite manner (160c2–4), since temperance is a most admirable thing, it follows that temperance is equivalent, equally, both to acting quietly *and* acting in an opposite manner (160c4–6).

(15) By implication, it follows that the quiet life is no more temperate than the life that is not quiet (160c7–d1).

At the outset, Socrates' claim that temperance is a *kalon* and the use of adjectival and adverbial forms of that word throughout the argument require comment. As has been convincingly shown,[28] '*kalon*' is an evaluative term that can signify something aesthetically beautiful or functionally useful or morally good, and also can carry more than one of these connotations. In the *Charmides*, '*kalos*' and its cognates are used, first, in a visual sense bearing ostensibly on physical beauty. For example, Socrates asks about the *kaloi*, beautiful youths (154a3, b5); Critias describes Charmides as *kallistos*, supremely beautiful (154a5); Chaerephon calls him *pankalos*, adorned with every beauty (154d5); and Socrates relays that when the youth blushed he became *eti kalliôn*, even more beautiful than before (158c5). Moreover, the implicit comparison between Charmides and a statue that everybody gazes at (154c1–8) indicates that the young man is *kalos* in the manner in which an *agalma* or statue (154c8) is *kalon*: admirable on account of his beauty, which has a peculiar sort of value in its own right.

Does Socrates consider temperance *kalon* in that sense? Well, many of the activities of the body and possibly some of the activities of the soul that will be mentioned in the course of the elenchus can be appreciated from an aesthetic point of view. A person who reads beautifully (159c6), plays a musical instrument beautifully (159c8–9), is a beautiful athlete (159c11–d2), or has a beautiful mind (159e1–160a2) may well be a source of aesthetic

---

[27] See notes 5 and 24 in this chapter.   [28] Nehamas 2007.

pleasure. But such activities of the body or of the soul may be *kala*, admirable, in another sense of *kalon* as well: as manifestations of a well-functioning and prudentially useful mechanism, physical or psychic. The student who reads and writes well, the musician who plays well, the athlete who competes well, quick learners, and those endowed with a good memory – all of these are *kaloi* in the sense of being skilful in what they are doing and of acting in a manner well suited to their respective goals. Furthermore, and importantly, the tale of Zalmoxis illustrates that temperance and every temperate action is *kalon* in a moral sense as well: it is a supremely good thing. For, according to the Thracian doctor, temperance is tantamount to the health of the soul, which secures both goods related to the health of the body and moral goods (156e6–157b1). If we suppose, together with Charmides, that temperance essentially consists in a particular manner of doing things, then the claim that temperance is *kalon* entails that deeds accomplished temperately have moral worth. Socrates does not clarify in just what sense he means that temperance is *kalon*, but this is not important for the purposes of the argument. All we need to assume is that *kalon* represents a positive value and an object of praise, whereas something that is not *kalon* or is *aischron*, disgraceful, has negative value and is an object of blame.[29]

We may now turn to the argument. Comparably to Laches' second definition of courage as '*karteria tis*', some sort of endurance (*Lach.* 192b–c), and the specification in the *Meno* that justice is '*aretê tis*', some sort of virtue (*Men.* 73e1), Charmides' definition of temperance is *hêsychiotês tis*: not every sort of quietness but a certain kind of quietness which, however, remains unspecified. We are never told exactly what kind of quietness Charmides has in mind. And although the counterexamples that Socrates brings illustrate different cases of actions which might count as temperate, nonetheless questions can reasonably be raised as to whether the defining concept has unity or the refutation is effective. (More on this later.) Premise (2) is repeated no fewer than five times in the argument[30] and is intended to provide grounding for it.[31] Socrates underscores that (2) is hypothetical (160d1–2). Nonetheless, the contention that temperance (or any virtue for that matter) is a *kalon* receives support from the story of Zalmoxis, is corroborated by other dialogues (e.g. *Lach.* 192d7–8), and has intuitive plausibility in its own right. Socrates appears strongly committed

---

[29] See Nehamas 2007, 98–102. Also, Santas 1973 maintains that, in this argument, *kalon* primarily has the sense of praiseworthy.

[30] As Kosman 1983, 204, points out, the premise is mentioned at 159c1, d8, d11, 160b8, d11.

[31] Santas 1973, 113.

to this view and, as for Charmides, he readily accepts it in this instance[32] and will do so again later (160e8).

We should consider the objection that Charmides could have undercut the argument by raising a methodological problem. 'Asked whether temperance is admirable, (Charmides) should have replied: "I have no way of knowing that, Socrates; for, as you yourself constantly imply, one cannot know what properties are predicable of a virtue until one knows what that virtue is. And we have not yet discovered what temperance is"'.[33] But this reply is completely at odds with Charmides' portrayal and the dramatic representation of his encounter with Socrates. He is terribly young and has never conversed with Socrates before, and while he has probably heard some things about him, he won't have heard something as specific as the issue of the priority of definition. Also, although he has already received sufficient dialectical training to give the right sort of answer to the 'what is X?' question, he does not have nearly as much experience as, for example, Polus (*Gorg.* 448e).[34] In short, Charmides is simply not in a position to challenge Socrates in the way mentioned above.

Another objection also bears on (2), namely that the argument would be valid if (2) stated not merely that temperance is *kalon*, admirable, but that it is the most admirable thing or one of the most admirable things. For, in that case, even if doing things quietly were still admirable, provided that Socrates could prove that doing things quietly is *less* admirable than doing things in the contrary manner, he could validly infer that doing things quietly is not the same thing as temperance.[35] In fact, the story of Zalmoxis provides strong grounds for supplying (3), i.e. the premise that temperance is the greatest or one of the greatest *kala*, admirable things. For, according to the Thracian doctor, temperance amounts to the health of the soul, from which every other good can derive (157a5–b1). It is clear that Socrates assumes (3), for instance at 159c3–d12, where he infers that quickness is more temperate than quietness on the grounds that quickness or nimbleness is *kalliston*, a most admirable thing. For the record, Socrates reasserts this claim towards the end of the dialogue, when he declares that *sôphrosynê* is *kalliston pantôn*, the most admirable thing of all (175b).[36]

The implicit premises (3) and (5), taken together, underpin the comparative judgements that Socrates makes in his counterexamples. It has been objected against (5) that, although Socrates does show that quiet

---

[32] πάνυ γε, ἔφη (159c2).   [33] Beversluis 2000, 140–1.   [34] Compare Beversluis 2000, 141 n. 13.
[35] So Santas 1973, 115.
[36] Santas 1973, 115, mentions this passage but, since it comes much later than the elenchus of the first definition, he considers it irrelevant to the validity of that elenchus.

actions are frequently less admirable than their contraries, he fails to establish that they are not admirable or not temperate at all;[37] in fact, quiet actions can still be temperate, albeit less than their contraries and, therefore, the definition of temperance as some kind of quietness has not really been refuted. However, premise (5) postulates a special relation between the property of being *kalon* and the action bearing that property: minimally, insofar as an action performed in a certain manner is *kalon*, it must be more or at least no less admirable than that same action performed in the contrary manner. This requirement seems to me defensible. It is not unreasonable to assume that an action that is admirable and praiseworthy is a virtuous action. And it is not asking much to infer that any such action will be *more* admirable than its contrary. This minimal concession suffices for present purposes. Of course, one could opt for the stronger thesis that 'if calmness is treated as the essence of σωφροσύνη, it seems legitimate to treat its contrary (e.g. vehemence, in the terms of this argument) as the essence of intemperance'; then, showing that 'intemperate (vehement) actions are sometimes more beautiful than temperate (calm) ones would, indeed, be a decisive refutation of the definition'.[38] Socrates, I think, takes it for granted that premise (5) is implied by (4) and implies (6). But since, according to (6), temperance is at least more admirable than its contrary, and supposing that quietness or acting quietly is equivalent to temperance, it follows (7) that quietness or acting quietly must be at least *more kalon* than its contrary. However, (8) makes a stronger claim on the basis of (3): supposing that quietness or acting quietly is equivalent to temperance, and supposing that temperance is supremely admirable, acting quietly must be supremely admirable as well: it should be more *kalon* than acting in any other manner, let alone in the contrary manner.

We should now examine the counterexamples intended to secure inferences (9) and (10).[39] They fall into two groups explicitly identified by Socrates (160b3–5), one consisting of activities supposed primarily to concern the body (159c3–d12), the other of activities supposed primarily to concern the soul (159e1–160b1). Writing, reading, playing the lyre, and also wrestling, boxing, fighting in the *pankration* (wrestling-and-boxing), running, and long-jumping belong to the first group. Learning, teaching, remembering or recollecting, discernment, learning ability, and also enquiry, deliberation, and discovery belong to the second. This

---

[37] Santas 1973, 114–16.   [38] Tuozzo 2011, 158 n. 6.

[39] Compare Santas' inference (9) in Santas 1973, 114: 'so, in all that concerns either our soul or our body, actions of quickness and nimbleness are found to be *more* praiseworthy than those of slowness and quietness' . Also, compare Benson's inference (7) in Benson 2000, 72.

categorisation may look arbitrary and also misleading. For, on the one hand, activities such as writing, reading aloud, and playing an instrument surely involve the mind as well as the body. On the other hand, the psychic activities mentioned above, arguably, cannot take place without the engagement of the body at some level. However, it seems to me that the distinction can be defended on the grounds that every activity in the first group is centred on some physical adroitness, whereas every activity in the second group crucially is centred on a mental or psychic faculty. Moreover, it may be of significance that the former can be taught and, indeed, Socrates emphasises their educational context,[40] whereas the latter are by and large natural endowments which contribute to a greater or a lesser extent to the acquisition of knowledge or the performance of action. In both categories the examples concern types of activities as well as instances of them: types of activities, e.g. reading, wrestling, and learning, are such that many instances of them are less admirable when they are performed quietly than when they are performed in the contrary manner.[41] Finally, all examples in both lists should be taken in a perfective sense, entailing completion or success.[42] This last point is important for the interpretation of the comparative judgements contained in the counter-examples, and also for the detection of the common theme underlying them, namely that actions that have in any degree the property of being *kalon* are those that exhibit the possession of the relevant expertise or skill (*technê*).[43] We should be especially attentive to the semantic nuances of the adverbs that Socrates employs for purposes of comparison, and also to the uses of *kalon*, 'admirable', in the positive, comparative, and superlative forms.[44] First, let us look at the cases of activities primarily concerning the body.

(a) In the grammar class, writing similar letters[45] quickly (*tachy*) is most admirable (*kalliston*), whereas writing them quietly or in a laidback way (*hêsychêi*) is less admirable (159c3–4). In this example, the

---

[40] See Tuozzo 2011, 158–9.

[41] Van der Ben 1985, 27, discusses this issue specifically with regard to *Charm.* 165c1–2. As he points out, some interpreters assume that οὐδαμοῦ and ὀλιγαχοῦ refer to instances of actions (e.g. Lamb 1927 *ad loc.*), whereas others believe that the terms refer to types of actions (e.g. Croiset 1921 *ad loc.*, and also van der Ben 1985 *ad loc.*).

[42] See van der Ben 1985, 24–5; also Dieterle 1966, 157, cited also by van der Ben.

[43] See also Kosman 1983 and Tuozzo 2011, 157–61.

[44] Santas 1973, 114–16, mentions both these features in relation to two main faults that he finds in the argument: first, the comparisons are unfair; and second, the uses of *kalon* in its different modes render the argument invalid.

[45] That is, letters of the same quality: see the relevant comment in van der Ben 1985, 24–5.

principal factors which determine the admirability of the action are speed and facility: of students copying letters of the same quality, those who copy[46] them quickly and easily deserve *more* praise than those who write them slowly and with difficulty. Taken in that sense, 'quickly' and 'quietly' are contraries: one cannot copy letters both quickly and slowly, both smoothly and cumbersomely, both with ease and with difficulty. The former member of these pairs is supremely *kalon*: it indicates the optimal manner of performing that kind of activity. On the other hand, the latter member is certainly less *kalon* or even not *kalon* at all. A first-grade student who writes with some difficulty is, to be sure, less praiseworthy than a classmate fluent in writing, but still merits some praise. An Economics major who has done nothing to improve his verbal expression and under-performs in all written exams gives no cause for admiration.

(b)   That this is the meaning of 'quietly' above is confirmed by the second counterexample, which is very similar to the first: it is also most admirable (*kalliston*) to read quickly (*tacheôs*) rather than slowly (*bradeôs*). In this case, quickly and slowly are treated as contraries. Moreover, as in the previous case, the claim that reading quickly is *supremely* admirable implies that acting in the contrary manner must be *less* admirable, or indeed not admirable at all.

(c)   Playing the lyre and wrestling are far more admirable (*poly kallion*) when performed quickly (*tacheôs*) or quickly and keenly (*oxeôs*) than when performed quietly and slowly (*hêsychê*) or sluggishly and slowly (*bradeôs*). The same holds for boxing and fighting in the *pankration*. These examples are quite complicated. The contrary of playing an instrument quickly is not playing it quietly but playing it slowly. Yet, the primary sense of '*hêsychê*' is 'quietly' and the reason Socrates uses it, I take it, is to indicate not so much the speed with which the notes are produced as the musician's sedate manner of playing. Something similar holds for wrestling: the contrary of *oxeôs*, 'keenly', is not *bradeôs*, 'slowly', but the relevant contrast is implied in the assumption that, typically, keen wrestling is also quick, while slow wrestling is also sluggish.[47] Once again, the comparisons are supposed to show that acting quietly in the senses specified above is clearly less *kalon*

---

[46] For a different view, see Santas 1973, 115.

[47] In the next set of examples, Socrates draws an explicit contrast between acting keenly and quickly on the one hand, and [slowly and] quietly on the other (159d1–2).

than the contrary manner of acting; but nothing precludes that acting quietly is also *kalon* to some degree.

(d) Running, leaping, and, generally, all such bodily activities belong to the class of admirable things (*tou kalou esti*) if they are accomplished keenly and quickly (*oxeôs kai tachy*), but to the class of disgraceful things (*tou aischrou*) if they are slow and quiet (*[bradea] te kai hêsychia*). The contrast implicit in the previous group of examples here becomes explicit, and the corresponding judgements are not comparative but positive: of such bodily actions, every quick action is a *kalon*; and every quiet action is something *aischron*, i.e. the contrary of *kalon*. Unlike the previous cases, which allow that a quiet action *can* be *kalon* (though less so than its contrary), this set of examples is supposed to demonstrate that certain quiet activities of the body are, in fact, disgraceful. This seems to be a lethal counterexample to Charmides' definition but, nonetheless, in his partial summary of the argument (159b4–5) Socrates chooses to weaken his claim. For, in the first place, he concludes that, regarding activities which have to do with the body, the *most* admirable (*kalliston*) are not the quieter ones but the quickest and keenest (159d4–5). Again, this is comparative: the quickest and keenest actions are incomparably more admirable or praiseworthy than those that are less quick and keen, but, nonetheless, it is possible that certain quieter actions too may deserve lesser praise. In the second place, Socrates appears to reason that, since temperance is *kalon* and since quicker bodily actions are more *kala* than their opposites, it follows that quickness is more temperate than quietness (159d10–11). This is often regarded as a particularly bad mistake on Plato's part: from the claims that temperance is admirable and that quickness is admirable it does not follow that quickness is temperate.[48] But I think that this criticism can be met by paying close attention to the context. Immediately after commenting on the activities of the body, Socrates turns to the activities of the soul and argues that, in these cases too, quickness is more *kalon*, admirable, than slowness. The quickness with which Charmides assents to the aforementioned fallacy, however, undercuts that claim. Had he taken the time to carefully consider the proposed argument and had he been slower in responding, he might not have fallen into the trap. Indeed,

[48] See Lutoslawski 1897, 203, who claims not only that the argument is vitiated by a paralogism, but also that such paralogisms are characteristic of Plato's state of logical development at the time of writing the *Charmides*. Beversluis 2000, 138–9, has a similar approach.

Socrates' methodology is not meant to show that *sôphrosynê* is speed. It is an elenchus aiming to examine whether Charmides doesn't know what he believes he knows.

In the next phase of the argument, Socrates turns to certain activities of the soul or the mind.

(e)   In the cases of learning, teaching, recollecting, and remembering, it is *more* admirable (*kallion*) to function quickly (*tacheôs*) or quickly and intensely (*tacheôs kai sphodra*)[49] than quietly and slowly (*hêsychêi kai bradeôs*).[50] Here 'quickly', I take it, means primarily getting the job done without delay[51] and with mental vigour. On the other hand, 'quietly and slowly' indicates difficulty[52] in accomplishing these types of actions, but also, I think, a sort of mental idleness or haziness or weakness. Although the comparative use of *kalon* leaves open the logical possibility that this latter manner of acting could occasionally attract praise, pragmatically this possibility is almost nil: even when we praise a slow learner, we do not do so because we deem admirable that manner of learning but rather for some other reason, e.g. to encourage the student to try harder.

(f)   *Anchinoia*, readiness or incisiveness of mind, is a sort of nimbleness[53] or sharpness (*oxytês tis*), not quietness (*hêsychia*). In this example, Socrates designates the contrasted manners of acting by using nouns, not adverbs. The suggested conclusion is that responding readily is *kalon*, whereas responding quietly, in the sense of hesitantly or dully, is not *kalon*. It is not clear whether this latter manner of acting is actually the opposite or the contrary of *kalon*. Like the previous group of cases, this case too supports the contention that engaging in such activities quietly (in a broad sense of the term, as indicated above) is at least less admirable than engaging in them in the contrary or opposite manner. Furthermore, like the previous examples, this one lends plausibility to the claim that acting quietly can be downright disgraceful.

(g)   Apprehending what is taught, whether it is writing or music or anything else, is *most* admirable (*kallista*) when it is accomplished *most* quickly (*tachista*), not *most* quietly (*hêsychaitata*). 'Moreover, in enquiries of the soul[54] and especially in deliberation it is not the most

---

[49] In the case of learning, ταχέως alone is used (159e3), whereas both adverbs are used in the cases of teaching, recollection, and remembrance (159e9–10).

[50] Both adverbs are used in varying order in all four cases.

[51] A different reading is proposed by Santas 1973, 114.   [52] Santas 1973, 114.   [53] Santas 1973, 114.

[54] The phrase ἔν γε ταῖς ζητήσεσιν τῆς ψυχῆς can be rendered in different ways, e.g. 'in the operations of thought' (Sprague) or 'in the searchings of the soul' (Lamb). My own translation 'in enquiries of

quiet (*hêsychiôtatos*) person, I think, or he who deliberates and discovers with great difficulty (*mogis*) that is considered praiseworthy (*epainou axios*), but the person who does this most easily and most quickly (*rhaista te kai tachista*)' (160a8–b1). Again, in the case of apprehension, 'most quietly' and 'most quickly' designate contrary ways of acting, and the same holds for the way in which 'the most quiet person' deliberates (i.e. most quietly and with difficulty) which is contrasted with deliberating most quickly and most easily. Both in the educational environment of the classroom and in activities involving deliberation and enquiry, thinking 'most quietly' is a damning description: it points to a weakness of the mind, whether this is a student's slowness to understand and assimilate what he is being taught, or an adult's difficulty to think things through and find the truth or the right course of action. On the other hand, as Socrates suggests, doing these things 'most easily and most quickly' typically exhibits highly valued mental qualities: good mental reflexes as well as intellectual power, thoroughness and incisiveness, an adequate grasp of means and ends related to the process of deliberation, and effectiveness in forming correct judgements or making good decisions. Such features are as praiseworthy as they are rare to find and, on many accounts, they require an optimal understanding of both facts and values. Socrates' repeated use of superlatives is significant: the capabilities under discussion are of the utmost importance. Those who have them and exhibit them in their manner of acting deserve great praise, whereas those who can't act in that manner get no praise. Again, Socrates does not state whether, in the aforementioned cases, acting 'most quietly' is actually disgraceful, but it seems likely that it may be.

So far, different groups of examples have led, on inductive grounds, to three different conclusions. First, quickness of all sorts[55] is *more kalon*, admirable, than quietness of all sorts or, equivalently, quietness of all sorts is *less* admirable than quickness of all sorts. Second, in many cases, quickness is *most* admirable – which leaves open the issue of whether, in these same cases, quietness is *less* admirable than quickness or rather not admirable at all. Third, in some cases, quickness is admirable, whereas

---

the soul' is closer to Lamb's translation. I take καὶ τῷ βουλεύεσθαι as one of the soul's enquiries: the soul is the subject that enquires, deliberates, and discovers.

[55] According to the rules of antilogic, Socrates is entitled to make this generalisation, all the more so because he examined a fairly large number and variety of examples.

quietness is disgraceful. On these counts, I conclude, the counterexamples that Socrates adduces lend considerable support to (8) as well as the tentative inferences (9) and (10).[56]

As many have noted, however, in his final conclusions (13–15), Socrates understates the results of the elenchus. Claim (13) has the form of a dilemma: either in no case or in very few cases have quiet actions appeared to be (*ephanêsan*: 160c) *more* admirable (*kallious*) than their contraries. According to (14), of the more admirable actions (*kallious*), there are no fewer quiet actions than their contraries; that is, quick and forceful ones. While Socrates had earlier concluded that quiet actions are *less* admirable than their contraries and some of them are not admirable at all, he now allows that *some* quiet actions may be *more* admirable than their contraries. A modern critic remarks: 'He [sc. Socrates] is, of course, wrong about this. The foregoing argument did not demonstrate that at all. What it purported to demonstrate was not that quick actions are *no less* admirable, and, therefore, *no less* temperate than quiet ones, but rather that they are *more* admirable, and, therefore, *more* temperate, than quiet ones. In addition to arguing fallaciously, Socrates has misrepresented the conclusion of his own argument'.[57] The structure of Socrates' final claims might appear to play into the critics' hands. For, first, he states that acting quietly is *no more* temperate than acting quickly, whereas the elenchus aimed to show that acting quietly is actually *less* temperate than its contrary; and, second, he declares that the quiet life is *no more* temperate than its opposite,[58] whereas the elenchus suggests that, in fact, it is much *less* temperate.

Nonetheless, it seems to me that Socrates' decision to soften the final claims of the refutation can be justified. In the first place, to refute Charmides' definition, Socrates does not need to establish that quickness (or some other, closely related property) is *more* temperate than quietness. All he needs to show is that, very frequently, quietness is just as admirable as its contrary; therefore, quietness is no better candidate than quickness in order to define temperance. This goal is compatible with Socrates' implicit suggestion that there can be some cases of acting quietly which, coincidentally, may also be cases of acting temperately, just as there can be some cases of acting quickly which, coincidentally, are temperate actions. In

[56] Socrates underscores the dialectical nature of the argument and the provisional or tentative character of the conclusion by noting that the latter follows ἔκ γε τούτου τοῦ λόγου, at least according to this reasoning (160b8). The use of the optative mood both in this instance (ἂν εἴη: 160b7) and throughout the argument may also serve that purpose.
[57] Beversluis 2000, 140.
[58] This is the only time that ἡσύχιος, quiet, is contrasted with μὴ ἡσυχίου, not quiet: 160c7.

the second place, Socrates' strategy is pedagogically very astute. On the one hand, he shows to Charmides that quietness or doing things quietly cannot serve to define temperance, while, on the other, he leaves room for the possibility that, in some cases, acting temperately may exhibit a sort of *hêsychiotês*. Thus, the young man does not feel completely discouraged, but remains willing to pursue the search.

In the end, what are the effects of this elenchus on Charmides? And what effects does it have on ourselves? Charmides seems now quite convinced that temperance is not identical with quietness or any other related manner of acting. However, we cannot be sure whether or to what extent he was able to follow the argument and grasp its central point. As for ourselves, I think that we have gained valuable insights into the relations that might obtain between virtue and some specific manner of acting and, in particular, between temperance and dignified conduct. The take-home lesson is a correct one: such relations are at best contingent and can be deceitful as well. Furthermore, some of Socrates' counterexamples may serve to direct us to other dialogues of the Platonic corpus. For instance, recollection and memory (159e9–10) are topics occurring in the *Meno*, the *Phaedo*, and the *Phaedrus*, while the mental and psychic activities of the second group of Socrates' examples partly overlap with the qualities of the Guardians in the *Republic*. Not only must the Guardians love wisdom, but they also must be good at learning (486c) and remembering (486c), and must excel in practical deliberation as well as theoretical enquiry. In the context of the *Republic*, it would be defensible to claim that the optimal performance of these activities requires a kind of mental quickness: e.g. sharpness, incisiveness, precision, mental agility, intellectual concentration, and the ability to easily spot connections and draw inferences. But this is not our present concern. Rather, we should follow Charmides in his next attempt to determine the nature of temperance.

CHAPTER 4

Charmides' Second Definition
Temperance Is a Sense of Shame (160d5–161b4)

So, Charmides, I said, this time pay closer attention, turn away (from other things) to look into yourself,[1] think about what kind of person temperance by its presence makes you, and what sort of thing temperance would have to be in order to make you that kind of person, and taking all this into account tell me, well and bravely, what it appears to you to be. And he, after holding back a little and after thinking things through to himself very manfully, said: 'Well, it seems to me that temperance makes a person feel ashamed or bashful, and that temperance is the same as a sense of shame'. (160d5–e5)[2]

Socrates' exhortation to Charmides accords with the 'best method' (158e6–7).[3] He asks the youth to attend more carefully to his own sense of himself in order to register the causal effect of temperance in him and hence determine the nature of the virtue (160d5–8). Again, all that Charmides is expected to do is articulate a belief based on direct awareness. As on the previous occasion, so on this one the belief will be submitted to dialectical examination. Now, however, Socrates raises the bar a little higher. He urges Charmides to look *more* carefully into himself (*mallon*: 160d5) and uses the term '*apemblepsas*' (160d6)[4] – literally 'looking away from something and into something else' – to indicate that Charmides should try harder to switch his attention *away* (*apo-*) from external things and *inwards* (*en-*) towards himself.

---

[1] At 160d6, I keep the ms. reading ἀπεμβλέψας instead of Burnet's ἐμβλέψας.

[2] Most translators render αἰδώς by 'modesty': see, for instance, Lamb and Sprague. I prefer 'a sense of shame', because this rendering better conveys that αἰδώς is not merely a matter of modest behaviour but also an inner attitude underpinning modest behaviour. On this point, see Raymond 2018, 23 and n. 1.

[3] Schmid 1998, 28, contends that the first definition merely expresses a common opinion whereas the second expresses Charmides' own perception of himself. However, there is no textual evidence supporting that claim. Charmides is supposed to have reached both definitions by attending to his αἴσθησις, awareness, of himself, as Socrates urged him to do.

[4] ἀπεμβλέψας B sed λεψ in ras. See note 1 in this chapter.

What should Charmides look away from? Given the socio-political connotations of the conception of temperance as a sort of *hêsychiotês*, doing things quietly or unobtrusively, it is probable that Socrates is inviting the youth to put such external considerations aside in order to concentrate solely on his own sense of the virtue. In addition, Socrates is encouraging the young man to try to assess and reflect on his own sense of himself: 'take all this into account [*syllogisamenos*: 160d8] and tell me again, well and bravely, what [temperance] appears to you to be' (160d). Although he does not explain what exactly '*syllogisamenos*', 'taking into account', entails in this context, his earlier outline of the 'best method' suggests that he is asking Charmides to consider together his own sense of temperance in himself, the kind of person that, according to his own belief, temperance turned him into, and, consequently, the kind of thing that temperance is. Hence, Socrates indicates to his young friend that the method that they are following does not merely rely on one's intuitive awareness of oneself, but also crucially involves reflection and reasoning. Whatever belief Charmides ends up expressing about the nature of *sôphrosynê* won't reflect his own awareness of the virtue in an unmediated manner, but will be the outcome of a rational process engaging different aspects of himself.

Socrates stresses this latter element when he tells Charmides that, after he has considered the matter, he should speak *eu*, well, and *andreiôs*, bravely (160d8–e1). Both adverbs are evaluative and require comment. Is Charmides supposed to speak well as opposed to badly, and what might this mean? Also, why is the virtue of *andreia*, courage, evoked at this point? According to Drew Hyland, what Socrates is really inviting Charmides to do is to enter a philosophical life of self-examination; this decision takes courage[5] as well as clarity of thought; in fact, *sôphrosynê* is interconnected with courage, and also self-knowledge and the examined life.[6] It is true, I think, that the passage can be read as containing a hint about the unity of virtue: if Charmides has one virtue, temperance, he can be assumed also to do things bravely (*andreiôs*) and, generally, *kat'aretên*, in accordance with virtue.[7] But Socrates' exhortation can be best understood in a simpler way.[8] Charmides was initially hesitant to answer the question of whether or not he had *sôphrosynê* and, when he finally brought himself to do so, the belief that he expressed about the nature of temperance was refuted. Therefore, Socrates suspects that his young

---

[5] Hyland 1981, 68.   [6] Hyland 1981, 69.
[7] This is precisely the meaning of εὖ in Aristotle, *NE* I.7 and elsewhere in that work.
[8] The exact same expression, εὖ καὶ ἀνδρείως, occurs at *Gorg.* 480c6, *Leg.* 648c3, and *Tht.* 147d4, as well as *Charm.* 160d9–b1. Its use is virtually identical in the latter two dialogues and supports my own reading of the passage in the *Charmides* against Hyland's reading.

partner may now be even more reluctant to speak his mind for fear of defeat. For this reason he urges Charmides to speak 'well and bravely': in earnest, without beating around the bush and without dreading the possibility of being refuted again. Once again, the youth's reaction appears promising. According to the narrator, he withdrew for a moment to think things through[9] and then responded *andrikôs*, manfully, to the question as it had most recently been put to him: temperance, he says, makes the person who has it feel ashamed (*aischynesthai*) or bashful (*aischyntêlon*), and it is this very thing, i.e. a sense of shame (*aidôs*) (160e4–5).[10] Perhaps Charmides took the point: what requires courage is not only the process of introspective examination, but also the decision to make the result of this latter known to others and submit it to critical scrutiny.

I

To begin our discussion, we should note that, on this occasion, the interlocutors spell out an important assumption grounding the 'best method of enquiry': a causal relation holds between the presence of *sôphrosynê* in oneself and the corresponding disposition that one has or, in the end, the sort of person that one is. Specifically, this time Socrates asks Charmides not merely to register his sense of himself and state the belief that this feeling gives rise to, but rather to consider carefully what kind of man *sôphrosynê* causes him to be.[11] Then, in accordance with the principle fully developed in the *Phaedo*, i.e. that like causes like, he suggests that, by looking at the effect of temperance on himself, Charmides will be able to infer the nature of the cause. The young man meets this challenge in a very precise and unambiguous manner: temperance causes one to *aischynesthai*, feel ashamed, and be *aischyntêlos*, have the tendency of feeling ashamed, and, therefore, it seems reasonable to infer[12] that the cause responsible for the inclination to feel *aischynê*, 'shame', as well as the occurrence of actual feelings of *aischynê*, is *aidôs*, 'a sense of shame'. Presumably, given Plato's prevailing view of causation, the cause must be essentially akin to these latter. If so, Charmides' claim can be taken to imply that the *aidôs* present in oneself is a deeply set disposition responsible for the corresponding occurrent feelings and, to a greater or lesser extent, for a certain behavioural pattern as well. There is extensive secondary literature on *aidôs* and its close

---

[9] πρὸς ἑαυτὸν διασκεψάμενος: 160e2–3.
[10] δοκεῖ τοίνυν μοι, ἔφη, αἰσχύνεσθαι ποιεῖν ἡ σωφροσύνη καὶ αἰσχυντηλὸν τὸν ἄνθρωπον, καὶ εἶναι ὅπερ αἰδὼς ἡ σωφροσύνη: 160e4–5.
[11] ὁποῖόν τινά σε ποιεῖ ἡ σωφροσύνη παροῦσα: 160d6–7.   [12] Cf. δοκεῖ μοι at 160e3.

ties to *sôphrosynê*,[13] but nonetheless it will be useful to say a few things about that notion.

Although '*aidôs*' is conventionally rendered as 'shame' or 'a sense of shame', it also captures central aspects of what we call guilt.[14] Primarily, '*aidôs*' is about being exposed, vulnerable, or humiliated, in the eyes of others, especially in the eyes of people whose opinion matters to us.[15] It involves fear not merely of what other people think, but of not living up to our own standards. The other's 'gaze' can be personal or collective, real or imagined. The presence of *aidôs* involves the assumption that there is a set of ethical attitudes whose value one recognises and shares with others.[16] When one violates such ethical values and norms, one experiences feelings of shame and tends to adopt avoidance-behaviour. One desires to hide away, disappear, even die. As for actual or fictional spectators who witness the shameful act, they too tend to avoid the agent or the scene of action, and experience derision and contempt. But also, *aidôs* has to do, so to speak, with an inner voice of judgement that one hears when one perceives oneself as having wronged another. While we feel shame because we have fallen short of a standard that we recognise as our own, typically we feel guilt because we have done something that has had a significantly adverse impact on someone else. In cases where this impact becomes known, the reactions triggered in other members of the community are overtly negative: deep resentment, indignation, rage.

Whether *aidôs* indicates both shame and guilt or shame alone, it was commonly taken to bear crucially on *sôphrosynê*. One's desire to live up to the standard of the 'imagined gaze', which one recognises as one's own, constitutes a strong motive for exercising self-control and refraining from certain sorts of actions, while engaging in others. Generally, temperate actions dictated by *aidôs* involve principles as well as precepts: agents follow what they perceive as requirements of morality, but are also attentive to social rules and matters of etiquette.[17] The heady blend of *sôphrosynê, aidôs*, and manly courage that we find in our passage was also part of the value system of the philo-Laconian aristocracy of fifth-century Athens, to which Plato's family belonged.[18] Such qualities were objects of high praise, and

---

[13] See, notably, Cairns 1993.   [14] See the brilliant discussion by Williams 1993.

[15] Compare Aristotle, *NE* V (4): we do not just desire to be honoured, but rather we want to be honoured by people who really value what we are doing.

[16] Raymond 2018 interestingly suggests that Socrates finds Charmides' blush beautiful precisely because they both share a common ethical ground.

[17] Gottshalk 2001 argues that αἰδώς implies an acknowledgement of limits, of standards, of hierarchy.

[18] All three qualities are attributed to the Spartans: Thucydides, *Hist.* I.84. On this passage, see Schmid 1998, 26.

many believed them to be related to a modest and self-controlled behaviour, respect for the opinions of others,[19] deference to authority, and an unwillingness to expose oneself and risk ridicule. On the downside, these attitudes could be in tension with intellectual initiative, critical spirit, and the desire to determine one's own identity and mode of life. In general, prevailing conceptions of *sôphrosynê* and *aidôs* could act as impediments to the development of one's potential and cause one's character to be formed unreflectively, in accordance with dominant values and norms. In sum, even though Charmides' second definition of temperance in terms of *aidôs* points more deeply to one's inner world than his first definition does, there is continuity between them. Doing things quietly, unobtrusively, decorously is closely related to doing things modestly and in conformity to an internalised social and ethical code. *Aidôs* as well as *hêsychiotês* indicates a distinctive manner of acting, but the former more than the latter chiefly concerns the perceptions, feelings, beliefs, and other attitudes related to shame and, to some extent, guilt as well.

2

> But, I retorted, did you not agree a little while ago that temperance is admirable [*kalon*]? – I certainly did, he answered. – Is it not also the case[20] that the temperate are good [*agathoi*] men? – Yes. – And could anything be good that does not make people good? – Of course not. – Hence, temperance is not only admirable [*kalon*] but also good [*agathon*]. – So at least it seems to me. – But then, I said, don't you believe that Homer speaks correctly, when he says that 'a sense of shame is no good [*agathê*] companion for a man in need'? – I do believe so, he replied. – So, as it seems, a sense of shame is both not good and good. – Apparently. – Temperance, however, is just good, if it makes good those in whom it is present and doesn't make them bad. – It certainly seems to me that things stand exactly as you say. – It follows, then, that temperance could not be a sense of shame, if it is in fact good, while a sense of shame is no more good than bad. – Well, Socrates, he said, I do think that this is correctly stated. (160e6–b4)

The refutation of Charmides' second definition has received remarkably mixed reactions. Regarding its logical structure, for instance, Lutoslawski claims that the argument marks a turning point in the development of Plato's logic and is a correct syllogism of the form Cesare. On the other

---

[19] See Shorey 1933, 102.
[20] οὐκοῦν at 160e9 is not inferential, but indicates an addition to what has already received assent. This observation bears on the reconstruction of the argument (see the analysis below).

hand, John Beversluis describes it as 'one of the lamest arguments in the early dialogues'[21] and suggests ways in which the argument might have been saved. From an ethical point of view, some commentators praise its moral and pedagogical value for a number of reasons: e.g. it impresses upon Charmides the importance of the care of oneself,[22] or extends the limits of the youth's knowledge by exposing inconsistencies in the ethics of shame,[23] or brings Charmides to realise that his virtue is only partially developed.[24] Others, however, highlight the limitations of the young man's conventional thinking,[25] or his dialectical inadequacy, or also the arbitrary character of the distinctions and inferences drawn by Socrates.[26] In particular, the main areas of controversy concern, first, the logic of the argument; second, the counterexample on account of which the definition is abandoned; and third, the lesson that we are to draw.[27]

Let us start with the reconstruction of the argument on account of which Charmides abandons his claim that temperance is *aidôs*. According to Lutoslawski, the argument is the following: temperance is a good; *aidôs* is not a good; hence *aidôs* is not temperance.[28] Tuckey's articulation is closer to the text: *sôphrosynê* is invariably good; *aidôs* is not invariably good; hence *sôphrosynê* is not *aidôs*.[29] In fact, however, this elenchus is considerably more complex and more problematic, and it is important to lay it out in detail in order to assess its faults or merits. I propose the following reconstruction:

(1)   Definition: temperance is *aidôs* (160e4–5).
(2)   Temperance is *kalon*, admirable (160e6–7; cf. 159c1–2).
(3)   In addition,[30] temperate men are *agathoi*, good (160e9).
(4a) If something causes men to be good, it must itself be invariably good (causal assumption).
(4b) Conversely, if something does not have the power to cause men to be *agathoi*, good, it cannot itself be invariably *agathon*, good (160e11).[31]

---

[21] Beversluis 2000, 141.   [22] So Tuozzo 2011, 165.   [23] Schmid 1998, 144.
[24] Gotshalk 2001, 75.
[25] Lampert 2010, 172: the argument reveals that Charmides 'has not escaped the conventional and in all likelihood never will'.
[26] Beversluis 2000, 141.
[27] The fullest discussion of this argument to date is offered by Raymond 2018, and I engage later with certain aspects of Raymond's analysis.
[28] See Lutoslawski 1897, 203. Tuckey 1951, 19–20 and Saunders 1987, 168 also take the argument to be valid.
[29] See Tuckey 1951, 19–20.   [30] See note 19 in this chapter and the discussion below.
[31] I object to the transposition of μή before ἀγαθόν at 160e11 for the reasons given by Murphy 2014. On the other hand, Raymond 2018 seems willing to entertain that option.

(5) Since temperance causes men to be good and doesn't cause them to be bad, it is invariably *agathon*, good (161a8–9).

(6) Hence, temperance is something *kalon*, admirable, and invariably *agathon*, good (160e13).

(7) If temperance is *aidôs*, *aidôs* must be *kalon*, admirable, and invariably *agathon*, good.

(8) But Homer is right that, in at least one type of case, *aidôs* is not *agathon*, good: it is not good for a man in need (161a2–4).

(9) Hence *aidôs* is no more good than not good: it is good in some contexts but not good in others.

(10) So *aidôs* is not invariably good.

(11) Therefore, temperance is not *aidôs*.

As the argument indicates, (1) involves the assumption that *sôphrosynê* and *aidôs* must share their essential characteristics in common, if the latter is to define the former. (2) has been established at 159c1–2 and is reiterated at 160e6–7. I take it that (3) is not an inference[32] but is presented as an additional, self-evident fact.[33] Accordingly, the claim at 160e13 probably means: it has now been shown that temperance is not only *kalon*, admirable (as established at 160e6–7), but also, on new independent grounds, *agathon*, good ((5) below). Even if some might question that temperate people are good people, the tale of Zalmoxis strongly suggests that this is the case, and Charmides could hardly disagree given his values and upbringing. Premises (4a) and (4b) are grounded on a prominent causal assumption of Plato's Socrates: (4a) if something causes something else to be F, it must itself be F. Conversely, (4b), if something does not have the causal power to make another thing F, it cannot itself be F. This assumption is particularly prominent in (5), namely the claim that if temperance makes (*poiei*: 160a8) men good and does not make them bad, then temperance is invariably good (161a8–9).[34] Compare the last argument of the *Phaedo*, where the soul's being essentially alive is linked to the fact that whatever the soul is present in is thereby caused to be alive (*Phd.* 105b–107a). The claim in (6) is an interim conclusion: temperance is invariably good, as well as admirable. It paves the way to (7): if *aidôs* is the same thing as temperance, it must be

---

[32] Contra Raymond 2018 and many others.

[33] Some interpreters take (3) to follow from (2) on the grounds that *kalon* here has a moral sense or that Socrates trades on the ambiguity of the term, taking it in a moral sense in order to infer (3). On this point, see Irwin 1995 *ad loc.* and Benson 2003 *ad loc.*

[34] According to Raymond 2018, 26–7, the refutation as a whole does not depend on what he takes to be a fallacious move from (2) to (4), for at 161b8–19 Socrates reiterates the point of the first part of the argument.

assumed to have the same (essential) properties as this latter. Hence *aidôs* too must be invariably good as well as admirable.[35] However, (8) advances a counterexample intended to establish (9), namely that *aidôs* is no more good than not good and, therefore, (10): unlike *sôphrosynê*, *aidôs* is not invariably good. Most of the dialectical work is done not on the basis of the assumption that temperance and *aidôs* are both good, but on the basis of the contention that, while temperance is invariably good, *aidôs* can also be not good. Since the counterexample in (8) is absolutely pivotal for the refutation of Charmides' definition, and also extremely controversial in the literature, it should receive further attention.

Let us remind ourselves of the specific context in which Homer is brought into the argument. Having established that temperance is not only admirable but also good (160e13), Socrates asks Charmides: 'don't you believe that Homer speaks correctly when he says that "*aidôs* is no good companion for a man in need"?'[36] And the youth confirms, without hesitation, that he does believe this (161a5). The verse that Socrates cites is from the *Odyssey*: Telemachus sends advice to the beggar in the palace hall, who is Odysseus in disguise, to go around and beg the suitors for his meal, for '*aidôs* is no good companion for a man in need' (XVII, 347). Telemachus' message is ambiguous on many levels, since Odysseus is the king and not a beggar, and his real need is to reclaim what belongs to him and not to beg for food. Insofar as Telemachus' message concerns the beggar, it advises him to suppress his sense of shame and beg the suitors to give him something to eat. Insofar as Telemachus is addressing his father, he exhorts him to keep his counsel and not let *aidôs* and, presumably, his love of honour cancel his longer-term plans to retrieve his own. The same holds for Telemachus himself as well: he is reminding himself that he simply cannot afford to heed his sense of shame and honour, but must swallow his pride and allow the suitors to mistreat Odysseus in his own home.[37] Likewise, Socrates' use of the Homeric verse is susceptible to multiple interpretations regarding some hidden message that it is supposed to convey. For example, on one view, the Homeric citation aims to suggest

---

[35] Some commentators view as a problem the fact that Socrates does not defend the claim that *aidôs* is good. On my reading, however, this claim is based on the assumption implied by (1). Since Charmides has defined temperance as *aidôs* and since he has accepted that the former is good, he has also implicitly accepted that the latter is a good. Moreover, even if *aidôs* were considered independently of temperance, it would be commonplace to assume that it is good in so far as it was commonly valued as a positive moral characteristic.

[36] 161a2–4: Ὁμήρῳ οὐ πιστεύεις καλῶς λέγειν, λέγοντι ὅτι "αἰδὼς δ' οὐκ ἀγαθὴ κεχρημένῳ ἀνδρὶ παρεῖναι".

[37] See Raymond 2018, 41–2 and nn. 33 and 34.

that, since Socrates is a man who is needy like the beggar, he must conduct himself like Odysseus, i.e. he must be shameless and stealthy and *polytropos* in order to fulfil his destiny.[38] On another view, as Telemachus, who is in the know regarding the beggar's identity, intends his message to mean that Odysseus should leave *aidôs* aside and take care of his own needs by recovering what is rightfully his own, so Charmides must take the advice to heart and become concerned, in a fundamental way, with the care of himself.[39] Another set of suggestions is that Socrates' return to Athens recalls Odysseus' return to Ithaca,[40] Charmides' character is modelled on the character of Telemachus,[41] and the Homeric citation has the purpose of reminding Charmides that he should struggle to overcome his *aidôs* and achieve the virtues of manhood as Telemachus tells himself he must.[42]

These parallels are interesting and useful. They embed Charmides' conception of temperance as *aidôs* in a rich and layered cultural background and draw connections between the perspectives formed by the latter and the perspective of Socratic philosophy and pedagogy. Nonetheless, worries still remain. First, does a single counterexample constitute adequate grounds for refuting the definition under examination? And, second, does the argument get compromised by Socrates' appeal to the authority of Homer and Charmides' unreflective acceptance of that authority?

Regarding the former of these issues, I believe that Socrates' move is logically justified and dialectically successful. Since Charmides claims that the relation between temperance and *aidôs* is a relation of identity,[43] even a single exception suffices to refute the definition. If *sôphrosynê* were the same as *aidôs*, every property possessed by one of them would also be possessed by the other. Homer's verse, however, suggests that there is at least one property that *sôphrosynê* essentially has but *aidôs* does not: temperance is invariably good, whereas *aidôs* can be not good as well as good. There isn't anything wrong or irregular about the brevity of this refutation.[44] Its point is clear and Charmides grasps it at once.[45]

Regarding the latter charge, i.e. that Socrates appeals to authority or that Charmides relies on it, first of all, it is simply not true that Socrates does

---

[38] Lampert 2010, 173.   [39] Tuozzo 2011, 165.   [40] See Brouwer and Polansky 2004.
[41] Raymond 2018, 40, draws a parallel between the beauty and *aidôs* adorning the adolescent Charmides and the same qualities in the adolescent Telemachus.
[42] Raymond 2018, 40–2.   [43] καὶ εἶναι ὅπερ αἰδὼς ἡ σωφροσύνη: 160e4–5.
[44] E.g. contra Schmid 1998, 27–8.
[45] According to Saunders 1987, 167–8, Socrates 'telescopes the argumentation' on the grounds of the inductive reasoning by which Charmides' earlier definition has been refuted.

anything of the kind. He is not asking Charmides whether he *trusts*[46] Homer to be making an admirable point, nor does he intimate that the young man ought to accept Telemachus' claim on the basis of authority. Rather, he asks the youth whether or not he *believes*[47] that claim to be correct. Hence Socrates is not guilty of a dubious pedagogical strategy, but can be taken to encourage the young man to reconsider his belief.

What about Charmides, however? Does he do as badly as he is accused of doing, notably because he does not challenge Homer,[48] but also because he does not resist the premise that *sôphrosynê* is *kalon* by appealing to the priority of definition?[49] Taking these questions in reverse order, Plato's portrayal of Charmides makes it appear highly unlikely that he would question the claim that temperance is *kalon*. In addition to his noble upbringing and to Critias' description of him as the most temperate of youths, he has tacitly accepted the Zalmoxian contention that temperance is a supremely admirable thing, and has explicitly agreed on an earlier occasion (159c1–2) to the premise that temperance is *kalon*. Overall, it seems clear that the young man truly holds the belief that temperance is an admirable, good, and beneficial thing. If he had refused to concede the premise that temperance is *kalon*, he would have acted disingenuously and in bad faith. Moreover, there is no hint that Charmides is *au courant* with the issue of the priority of definition, and it would be strange if he were. For he is very young, has begun his dialectical training not long ago, and has not been around Socrates since he was a child (so he has not heard him talk about the priority of definition). It is not reasonable to criticise him for failing to object to Socrates that they cannot assert that *sôphrosynê* is *kalon* before they determine what *sôphrosynê* is.[50] An experienced debater could make this move, but not Charmides.

It is more difficult to address the charge that Charmides relies unreflectively on Homer's authority and accepts without proof that *aidôs* is not good for a man in need.[51] On the one hand, we can safely assume that Charmides knows his Homer and finds quite credible the counterexample drawn from the *Odyssey*. His attitude is not unreflective. He can see for himself that, if the beggar/Odysseus had indulged his feelings of shame and honour and had attacked the suitors, he would have risked his own life and the lives of his wife and son, and he would have been morally blameworthy by virtue of doing so. Instead, he let the suitors humiliate him without

---

[46] See the translation by Moore and Raymond 2019, 14, *ad loc.*   [47] Cf. οὐ πιστεύεις: 161a2.
[48] Beversluis 2000, 141, citing also Chambry 1967, 267. On this point, see also the speculations of Schmid 1998, 28, Lampert 2010, 172, and others.
[49] Beversluis 2000, 141.   [50] See previous note.   [51] See note 48 in this chapter.

reacting to the insults and, in doing so, he acted without *aidôs* but, presumably, with *sôphrosynê*. On the other hand, Charmides does not push this matter further. He does not appear to entertain the possibility that Homer may be wrong and *aidôs* may be an admirable thing even for beggars. And even if such a thought had crossed his mind, it seems unlikely that he would have pursued it to the point of openly contradicting Homer.[52] The reason lies, precisely, in his *aidôs*, which gives beauty to his appearance (158c5–6) but, nonetheless, can prevent him from acquiring a beautiful soul. Neither the narrator nor the characters of the narrated episode are yet in a position to know whether Charmides will eventually be able to put aside his *aidôs* and ask the sort of 'shameless' questions that could improve his soul and make it temperate.

To take stock, Charmides' second attempt to define temperance is not implausible; the argument by which the definition is refuted is quite good. Charmides makes considerable progress by defining temperance in terms of *aidôs* – a dispositional characteristic commonly believed to accompany *sôphrosynê* and valued by many in its own right. Moreover, the youth follows the argument with ease and understands the ostensible point of Homer's citation. The fact that he does not try to deny the premise that temperance is *kalon* indicates both decency and a gentle and cooperative spirit regarding the investigation. To be sure, his prompt acceptance of Homer's claim may be due to excessive reverence for the great poet and possibly a tendency to accept authoritative claims. However, it need not be unreflective, and it probably is not. On balance, it seems unfair to conclude that Charmides 'has not escaped the conventional and in all likelihood never will'.[53] Rather, he shows some promise, and we might have had reason to be optimistic about the youth's future, were it not for Critias' imposing figure looming large in the background.

---

[52] See Lampert 2010, 172; Raymond 2018, especially 36–45. Schmid 1998, 28, suggests that Charmides cannot violate his sense of shame because this would entail that he would violate his public identity. And he contends that traditional temperance precludes one from asking specifically moral questions, because of the fact that one's attitudes are determined by social conventions and rules. As my analysis suggests, I think that this view has merits but also oversimplifies the matter.

[53] Lampert 2010, 172 and note 25 above.

CHAPTER 5

Charmides Abandons the 'Best Method'
The Third Definition – Temperance Is 'Doing One's Own'
(161b4–162b11)

Charmides' final attempt to determine the nature of temperance differs from the other two and marks a turning point in the dialogue. Dramatically, it represents both an end and a beginning. For after Charmides is refuted, he withdraws from the front stage of the action and is replaced by Critias, who claims on his own account that temperance is 'doing one's own', undertakes to defend that definition anew (162b12–164d3), and remains Socrates' dialectical partner almost to the end of the dialogue. Philosophically, the two-fold discussion of the third definition of *sôphrosynê* (the round with Charmides, 161b4–161b11, and the round with Critias, 162b12–164d3) links the joint search of Socrates and Charmides aimed at discovering whether there is temperance in Charmides' soul to the investigation jointly conducted by Socrates and Critias and focused on the relation between temperance and self-knowledge. Notably, on the one hand, the conception of temperance as 'doing one's own' provides a platform for integrating the values of acting *hêsychôs*, quietly and unobtrusively, and of acting with *aidôs*, a sense of shame, into a broader socio-political context, while, on the other hand, the debate between Socrates and Critias eventually leads to the realisation that temperance or acting temperately has intrinsic worth and presupposes self-knowledge of some sort.

> But consider the following view about temperance to judge whether you like it. For I just remembered something that I once heard someone say, that temperance might be doing one's own. So I should like you to examine whether you think that the person who said this is right. – You scoundrel, I said, you have heard this from Critias here or some other wise man! – Apparently, said Critias, he heard it from someone else. For he certainly hasn't heard it from me. – But Socrates, said Charmides, what difference does it make whom I heard it from? – None, I replied. For, in any case, we ought to consider not who said it, but whether or not the claim is true. – Now you are speaking correctly, he said. – Yes, by god, I retorted. But

I would be amazed if we are also going to discover the truth of the matter. For it seems to be a sort of riddle. (161b4–c9)

The phrase 'doing one's own' (*ta heautou prattein*: 161b6)[1] sounds odd to the modern ear. Nonetheless, it was widely used in the Periclean age, was part of the vocabulary related to the Athenian ideological debate between the oligarchic faction and the democrats, and had specific political, social, and ethical connotations for Plato's near-contemporaries.[2] Generally, 'doing one's own' was taken to be conceptually related to *apragmosynê*, the reluctance to meddle in things, and *hêsychia*, the unintrusive quietness of citizens who are contented to deal with their own affairs. All three terms indicate a similar attitude and all three are frequently contrasted in the sources with '*polypragmosynê*', which refers to one's tendency to have many different concerns and activities that are not only 'one's own', but also may involve other people or the city as a whole.[3] While the aforementioned phrases could be (and, in the fourth century, had been) used in an increasingly neutral way,[4] in the late fifth century they usually pointed to specific political associations and had an evaluative aspect. It was typical of aristocratic oligarchs to praise *hêsychia* or concentration on one's private affairs as a positive feature of one's character and one's attitude as a citizen. Peaceful inactivity (*hêsychia apragmôn*) was taken to indicate loyalty to the state, obedience to the laws, willingness to live and let live in the *polis*, love of peace, and justice. Also typical of those who had an anti-democratic bent was the tendency to deprecate *polypragmosynê* for causing trouble and chaos, and for leading to aggression and war. From their perspective, *polypragmosynê* or involvement with the affairs of others and not just with one's own often indicated civic restlessness, primitive and destructive instincts, the lust for power, and insatiable greed.

At the opposite end of the spectrum, the democrats and, in particular, Athenian democrats stigmatised *apragmosynê* as a kind of quietism that was useless or even dangerous to the *polis* and unbefitting free men. From the democratic point of view, engagement with the *polis* was considered the hallmark of a distinctly Athenian vitality and optimism that enabled the city to thrive despite various setbacks.[5] As Athenian supremacy approaches its end, however, the ancient sources highlight

---

[1] The phrase τὰ ἑαυτοῦ πράττειν is also rendered by, for example, 'doing one's own things', 'minding one's own business', or 'minding one's own affairs'.

[2] Also, as readers of the *Republic* well know, this phrase takes a special meaning as part of the definition of justice in that work. More on this later.

[3] See the classic study by Erhenberg 1947.   [4] Erhenberg 1947, 47.

[5] Ehrenberg 1947, especially 47–53.

a particular aspect of *apragmosynê* especially relevant to the historical subtext of the *Charmides* and the conception of temperance under consideration. That is, in the last few decades of the fifth century, the attitude of quietism related to 'doing one's own' was frequently interpreted as deliberate defiance of the mob by a person of know-ledge and education, intellectually superior to the many, and fre-quently devoted to theoretical as well as practical pursuits.[6]

As indicated, Charmides' first definition of temperance has been widely interpreted along these lines. For instance, according to Noburu Notomi, 'doing one's own' represents a step in the development by Plato of Critias' elitist ideology;[7] and although Plato takes pains to distinguish Critias' elaboration of that concept from Socrates' ideal of self-sufficiency,[8] none-theless he retains some sympathy for Critias and implicitly acknowledges that 'evil results are not incompatible with a good will'.[9] Or, according to Thomas Tuozzo,

> Plato's portrayal of Critias in the *Charmides* should be seen as, in part, Plato's move in a literary struggle over the meaning of Critias and his activity, a struggle analogous to that waged over the meaning of Socrates and his activity. It goes without saying that Plato does not put Critias on the same level as Socrates, either morally or intellectually. But he does think that Critias represents a positive strand of Greek political and cultural thought, a strand that Plato considers himself as in some measure continuing and deepening.[10]

On such approaches, 'doing one's own' is an expression of the political ideal also expressed in negative terms by *apragmosynê*. Citizens who 'do their own' are not doing nothing but, on the contrary, engage only with things properly concerning themselves. Both the surviving writings[11] and the political trajectory of the historical Critias make it seem likely that he was the originator of the formula '*ta heautou prattein*',[12] or one of the prominent users of that phrase.

One important difference between this definition and the previous ones has to do with its provenance. This time Charmides does not look inside himself but outside. He advances the claim that temperance is 'doing one's own' not as a belief that he has formed on the basis of self-awareness, but as a view that he recollects (*anemnêsthên*: 161b5) someone else having stated.

---

[6] Erhenberg 1947, 53–9, explains how ἀπραγμοσύνη, concentration on one's own affairs, gets to be closer connected with ἡσυχία, quietness, and the private cultivation of one's mind and soul.
[7] Notomi 2000, 246.   [8] Notomi 2003, 250–2.   [9] Notomi 2000, 249. See also Chapter 1, 18.
[10] Tuozzo 2011, 57.   [11] The fragments of Critias' works are found in DK II: 375–99.
[12] See Bultrighini 1999.

Thus, he violates a basic requirement of the 'best method' and makes it impossible for him and Socrates to find out whether temperance is present in his own soul. For the belief under discussion does not derive from Charmides' own sense of himself, but from an external source. Even though Charmides will undertake to defend it, he cannot really claim ownership of it: it is not *his* in the sense in which the first two definitions of temperance undoubtedly are. Why does Charmides proceed in that manner? Perhaps he has become so engrossed in the previous search that he has forgotten the initial purpose of the search. Or perhaps he wants to remove himself from the conversation and, therefore, is trying to provoke Critias to take over.[13]

Another possibility is that he is shocked by the abrupt refutation of his previous definition and feels unable to continue. 'He is shaken by this experience, as well he should be: Socrates has called into question his deepest self-understanding, not only of the pride he takes in himself (a pride reinforced by his many admirers), but also of the values and even the society supporting that pride of self-evaluation.'[14] Also, it is conceivable that the youth understood the point that Socrates made earlier, namely that *sôphrosynê* involves concern with one's own good and not just concern with other people's expectations, and the definition that he now offers gives Socrates the opportunity to clarify the notion of concern for one's own good by focusing first 'on the outward looking, social nature' of the virtue.[15] If so, we may assume that Charmides sincerely endorses on his own account the claim that temperance is 'doing one's own'.[16] The narrator gives us no help in deciding between these competing options. However, it may be helpful to compare Charmides' move of advancing a view derived from someone else to a similar move in the *Euthyphro*. Like Euthyphro, Charmides has run out of suggestions regarding the definition of the virtue under consideration. And as Euthyphro accepts and tries to defend Socrates' suggestion (cf. 11e) that piety is part of justice, so Charmides accepts and undertakes to defend a view that comes from an external source rather than from within himself. In both cases it is clear that Socrates' interlocutor won't be able to contribute to the argument much longer. But in neither case does Plato give decisive indications as to what the feelings of the interlocutor might be.

In any case, Charmides is represented as advancing this third definition in an even and self-controlled manner: he invites Socrates to consider a new response to the 'what is X?' question in case it might be correct. Again,

---

[13] So Bruell 1977, 156–7.   [14] Schmid 1998, 29.   [15] Tuozzo 2011, 166.   [16] See Blyth 2001, 43.

there is no telling what his motives are. He may be entirely sincere or somewhat sly: if the definition holds good, he will get credit for it, but if it is not, someone else will get the blame. Likewise, his attitude to Critias seems ambiguous. Assuming that he wishes Critias to step in, does he try to provoke him to do so because he knows Critias to be a far more experienced debater, or does he merely want to annoy him? It is possible that Charmides' move is motivated by playfulness, mischief, reaction to authority,[17] suppressed anger, or the desire to see his vain guardian refuted by Socrates. But the narrator says nothing explicitly on that score. Philosophically too, the passage under discussion is open to different readings. Charmides' reference to the process of *anamimniskesthai*, remember or recollect,[18] makes complete sense if we take the verb in the ordinary sense of bringing back to mind an experience that one has had in the past, and of making available to oneself in the present the contents of that experience. But it cannot be excluded that '*anamimniskesthai*' is intended to point towards the theory of recollection and the arduous process of recovery of the Forms latent in one's soul.[19]

Other issues debated in the literature need to be addressed as well. It has been contended that when Socrates exclaims 'ô miare!' (161b8), he characterises Charmides by a 'very derisive term';[20] for the latter conveys the idea of *miasma*, pollution, and especially pollution resulting from bloodshed. In fact, Plato's Socrates frequently employs that adjective in a coaxing or playful sense. For instance, when Phaedrus swears an oath that he will never read to Socrates another speech unless Socrates produces his own counter-speech, Socrates retorts: 'Oh! Oh! You wretch (*ô miare*)! How well you discovered how to force a lover of speeches bid your will!' (236e). I think that his exclamation to Charmides should be understood in a similar way. He reacts playfully rather than seriously, for he wishes to encourage Charmides to go on with the conversation as long as he can sustain it. If he feels disappointed in the youth, he does not show it at present.[21] Nor, on the other hand, does he appear pleased at Charmides' move.[22]

---

[17] See the remarks of Blyth 2001, 42. [18] ἄρτι γὰρ ἀνεμνήσθην: 161b5.
[19] See *Men.* 81a–85d, *Phd.* 72e–77a, *Phdr.* 246a–257b. [20] Schmid 1998, 31.
[21] Contra Schmid 1998, 30–1, who takes Socrates' use of μιαρός to indicate that he feels disappointment at the fact that Charmides does not 'do his own': he does not give his own definition and retain his role in the search, but acknowledges the authority of his guardian and is ready to yield his place to him.
[22] Tuozzo 2011, 166, suggests that Socrates feels pleased at the thought that Charmides finally came to realise that temperance involves some sort of concern with one's own good. However, I do not think that the text supports that suggestion.

A more puzzling issue is why Critias so emphatically[23] denies that he is the author of the proposed definition. Does he merely wish to deceive those present?[24] Does he want to give Charmides another chance to show off? Does he take offence at the fact that Socrates lumped him together with 'other wise men' (161b8–c1)? Or is he acting out of fear that he might be refuted by Socrates and thus might be shamed in front of his ward? It is impossible to tell with any degree of certainty, and we must leave our options open. But the thing to register is that, for whatever reason, Critias is lying. It is the second time in the dialogue that he has preferred deception to truth.

For his own part, Socrates too says something perplexing, namely that 'doing one's own' is like a riddle (161c9) and that he would be amazed if they were able to solve it and discover the truth (161c8–9). Thus he implies that the argument to follow will have as a primary aim to try to resolve the enigma. Nonetheless, in the first place, it would seem that the expression 'doing one's own' is far from mysterious: as indicated, fifth-century Athenians knew what it meant. In the second place, many have judged that the cross-examination purporting to clarify the matter defeats this purpose. The elenchus that follows has been considered a joke in bad taste at Charmides' expense,[25] a parody of the proposed definition,[26] an interpretation both literal and pedestrian entailing ridiculous consequences,[27] one that is 'least plausible'[28] or deliberately apolitical,[29] or, alternatively, one that indicates the social and political dimensions of *sôphrosynê* in a bizarre manner.[30] I believe these contentions to be mistaken. Even though the elenchus to follow is one where Socrates probably has a bit of fun, it also offers preliminary clarifications of the meaning of 'doing one's own' by eliminating certain possibilities but allowing for others. Thus, it paves the way to Critias' more sophisticated attempt to defend the claim that temperance is 'to do one's own'.

We should look at the argument aiming to refute Charmides (161d1–162a9). Socrates pretends to be far more literal-minded than he really is, and takes 'doing one's own' to mean, literally, engaging in all sorts of activities, all of which are directed solely towards oneself.[31] To undermine

---

[23] οὐ γὰρ δὴ ἐμοῦ γε: 161c.   [24] Hyland 1981, 76.   [25] Notomi 2000, 251.

[26] Beversluis 2000, 142.   [27] Solère-Queval 1993, 16–17.   [28] Blyth 2001, 43.

[29] Hyland 1981, 73, interprets 'doing one's own' as being 'neither in need of nor a dependable contributor to a healthy *polis*'.

[30] Schmid 1998, 32.

[31] In this sense, therefore, 'doing one's own' can be considered reflexive. If it is read in that way, Socrates' point that, in fact, the experts' activities are not self-directed but other-directed can be taken to foreshadow the Argument from Relatives.

the view that temperance is 'doing one's own' in this latter, very narrow sense, he asks Charmides to entertain several examples of experts in various *technai*, arts and sciences, and consider whether the experts in these *technai* are concerned in truth with 'their own' rather than 'other people's own'. In response, Charmides has to concede that, in fact, experts primarily or exclusively direct their activities towards goals concerning others, not themselves. They do or make 'other people's own' rather than 'their own'. For example, assuming that the teacher of grammar *does* (*prattein*: 161d3) something when he writes or reads or teaches, he does not perform these activities by reproducing, for instance, only his own name, nor does he instruct his pupils to write only their own name but other names too, including the names of people that are not 'their own' but alien or hostile to them (161d8). But even though both the teacher and the pupils (including Charmides himself) do not only 'do their own' but also 'other people's own', they cannot reasonably be considered busybodies (*polypragmones*) or intemperate (161d11–e1). The same observation holds for expert work in medicine, building, weaving, and generally any work (cf. *apergazesthai*: 161e8) done in an artful manner in the domain of first-order arts (161e6–9). Note that Socrates does not draw distinctions between different kinds of arts (productive, performative, etc.) and the works that they do. He intends his point to apply to deeds and productions of all sorts and, therefore, he uses indiscriminately the verbs '*prattein*', to do, and '*ergazesthai*' or '*apergazesthai*' (161e8, 162a2) – a verb designating both actions and productions. His practice will be challenged later on. At present, however, we begin to understand why the definition proposed by Charmides might be riddling. It is not all that clear what 'doing one's own' may mean. But one thing it cannot mean is that the experts must focus their activities solely on themselves on pain of being proclaimed intemperate.

Next, Socrates extends this reasoning to the *polis*, city or state. On the assumption that legislation is an art whose work (*ergon*) consists in making laws able to ensure the well-being of the city, he leads Charmides to concede that, if a city were governed according to a law prescribing that everyone should produce or do (*ergazesthai kai prattein*: 162a2) only 'one's own', e.g. weaving only one's own cloak or making only one's own shoes, the city would not be governed well (*eu oikeisthai*: 161e10). But running a city temperately would be running it well (162a4–5). 'Therefore', Socrates infers, 'temperance would not be "doing one's own" in those kinds of cases or in that way' (162a7–8). The conclusion, then, leaves open the possibility that temperance *might* involve 'doing one's own' in different cases or in a different way. Nonetheless, it is strongly suggested, I think, that even if that were the case, i.e. even if temperance did imply 'doing one's own' in some *other* way, the latter would have to accommodate the intuition that the work of every art and every expert is primarily to benefit other people rather than the experts themselves.

As we shall see, this intuition lies at the core of the debate between Socrates and Critias. But it also governs certain aspects of the argument in the *Republic*. As many have noted,[32] 'doing one's own' has a special meaning as part of the definition of justice in the context of the analogy between the city and the soul. While the meaning and implications of 'doing one's own' differ in these two works,[33] we may now begin to discern some sort of thread linking them. The virtue of justice holding together the tripartite structure of the Callipolis consists in the proper function of each citizen class. Each of the three classes 'does its own' in the sense of doing what its members are naturally best fitted to do. And each of the three classes 'does other people's own' not, of course, in the sense that its members are busybodies, but in the sense that they function with a view to the common good rather than their own.

Towards the end of the Myth of Er concluding the *Republic*, we are told that when the soul of Odysseus came to make its choice of its next life, remembering the former evils that Odysseus had suffered because of his *philotimia*, love of honour, it searched for a long time to find the life of 'a private citizen' minding his own affairs and, upon finding it, declared that this life would have been its first choice in any case (620c–d). The 'quiet solemnity'[34] of the last words of the *Republic* may move us to look back to the *Charmides* and consider how the *Republic* provides an answer to Socrates' query about the meaning of 'doing one's own'. Properly understood, 'doing one's own' entails that every class and every citizen will concentrate on the kind of work that is naturally appropriate for them and will do that work for the good of the whole. The Myth of Er drives home the idea that, by acting in that manner, always pursuing the good and avoiding evil, 'we shall fare well' (*eu prattômen*: *Rep.* 621d). The *Republic*, then, can be taken to provide a fully argued response to the concern highlighted by Socrates in the third elenchus of the *Charmides*: whether a city run according to the principle of 'doing one's own' could be

---

[32] See also note 2 in this chapter.

[33] Solère-Queval 1993, 18, appears to assume that 'doing one's own' has the same meaning in these two dialogues, even though the argumentation differs. 'L'auteur présumé de cette définition, tout aussi bien que Critias, pourrait donc être Socrate!'.

[34] The phrase belongs to Paul Shorey: in his last footnote to the Loeb translation of the *Republic*, he notes the 'quiet solemnity' of the work's last words, 'εὖ πράττωμεν', and compares it to the solemn first word of the *Laws*, 'θεός'.

managed well or, more literally, lived in well[35] by its own citizens, each of them individually and all of them as a whole.

In sum, I hope to have shown that there is more to this elenchus than commentators have allowed for. Once the refutation is completed, however, Socrates and Charmides indulge in what might appear as mere banter.

> So, it seems that the person who claimed that temperance is doing one's own was riddling, as I was saying a moment ago. For he couldn't have been as simple-minded as that. Or was it some idiot that you heard claiming this, Charmides? – Not at all, he said, for he seemed very wise indeed. – Then, in view of the difficulty to understand what doing one's own can mean, it seems to me virtually certain that he was challenging you with a riddle. – Perhaps, he said. – Well, what could it mean 'to do one's own'? Can you say? – By Zeus, he exclaimed, I really have no idea. But it may well be that not even the man who said it had the least idea of what he meant. And as he was saying this, he laughed a little and looked away towards Critias. (162a10–b11)

To be sure, these remarks are presented as a joke at Critias' expense. But the language is unusually strong and even offensive. On the one hand, Socrates concludes that, if 'doing one's own' means what they took it to mean, only a fool (*euêthês*: 162b1) or an idiot (*êlithios*: 162b1) could have believed that it conveys the nature of temperance. On the other hand, even though Charmides has earlier witnessed his guardian's negative reaction to the suggestion that he is a *sophos*, wise man or sophist (161b8–c2), he retorts that the author of the definition did not seem an idiot but *pany sophos*, very wise (162b3). Adding insult to injury, he indicates that, in fact, the man in question was anything but wise, since he probably did not know what he really meant by 'doing one's own' (162b9–10). As if this were not enough, Charmides reveals to everybody present that Critias was, in truth, the source of the claim that had just been refuted: he looks sideways at him and laughs (162b10–11). Clearly, the main purpose of both interlocutors is to prick Critias' *philotimia*, love of honour, and jolt him into action. But the language that they use makes one wonder about Charmides' character and perhaps about Socrates' own feelings as well. The youth appears to have no scruples about ridiculing his guardian and exposing him as a fraud. His smooth manners and deference are momentarily torn asunder by a flash of nasty wit. As for Socrates, one may question whether he really had to call Critias a fool or an idiot in order to draw him into the conversation. In any case, their device succeeds and Critias enters the ring, causing quite a commotion.

---

[35] εὖ οἰκεῖσθαι: 161d10.

CHAPTER 6

Enter Critias

The Third Definition Revisited – Temperance Is the Doing or Making of Good Things (162c1–164d3)

> Well, it was clear that, for some time, Critias had been both anguished and desirous to distinguish himself in the eyes of Charmides and the present company, and having barely contained himself until then, at that point he became unable to do so. For I believe that what I had supposed was entirely true, namely that Charmides had heard this answer concerning temperance from Critias. And because Charmides did not want to explain the answer himself but wanted Critias to, he was trying to stir him up and insinuated that he [sc. Critias] had been refuted. Of course, Critias did not tolerate this, but seemed to me to get angry at Charmides as a poet gets angry at an actor who performs his verses badly on stage. So, he stared hard at Charmides and said: 'do you really think, Charmides that, if you don't know what was the meaning of the man who claimed that temperance is "to do one's own", he did not know it either?' – But my dear Critias, I said, given Charmides' age, his ignorance is no surprise at all. You, on the other hand, can reasonably be expected to know, both because of your age and because of your studies. Thus, if you agree that temperance is what our friend here says it is and you are taking over the argument, I would feel much greater pleasure in examining together with you whether this assertion is true or not. – Indeed, he said, I do agree and am taking it over. – You do well to do so, I said. (162c1–e7)

This is a transitional passage marking the change of interlocutor and raising our expectations about the philosophical quality of the debate to follow. Socrates steps back from the action and, in his role as narrator, shares with us his own thoughts about the behaviour of the protagonists and their respective motives. Earlier intimations are confirmed, new elements are added to the portraits of Charmides and Critias, and tensions in the relation between the two cousins come to the surface. Regarding Charmides, Socrates as narrator confirms a suspicion that we may have had for some time, namely that the young man desired to withdraw from the conversation, either out of intellectual laziness or because he felt unequal to the task at hand. To achieve this end, he deliberately provokes his guardian and expects that Critias will take the bait. Despite his youth, then, Charmides shows himself able to manipulate his cousin's emotions and compel him to react. It appears increasingly clear that, alongside composure and good manners, Charmides can be sly, deceptive, provocative, and perhaps a trifle cruel as well. Critias' portrayal develops along comparable lines. The outburst described in the above passage corroborates a character trait intimated by the opening scene, namely that Critias is prone to very strong emotions and reactions. There, he has appeared immoderate in his praise of Charmides' beauty and gifts. Here, he seems unable to control his frustration and anger. Furthermore, Socrates presently points back to another element of the opening scene, namely the ruse that Critias used in order to summon his ward and the corresponding distribution of roles to the other two characters. For, in the capacity of narrator, Socrates compares Critias' anger at his ward with a poet's anger at an actor's incompetent performance of his lines on stage. In both these instances, Critias is depicted as a *poiêtês*, poet, and Charmides as a *hypocritês*, actor (162d3). The former writes, stages, and directs the script, while the latter is expected to follow the relevant instructions. It is possible that this metaphor captures Critias' dominant influence over Charmides in real life.[1] Nonetheless, within the dialogue, they are represented also as mutually manipulating each other, albeit in different ways. Besides, the cause of Critias' frustration is not entirely evident. Is it merely Charmides' failure to defend a view that Critias holds dear, or does it ultimately lie in the older man's *philotimia*, 'love of honour' or 'competitiveness' (162c2)? And if the latter is the case, what will be the impact of that trait on the investigation?[2]

The elenchus that will follow will be genuine in a way in which the immediately preceding elenchus was not. For while Critias must have a certain degree of commitment to the claim that temperance is 'doing one's own', Charmides did not need to have any. Indeed, the former accuses the latter of being ignorant of the true meaning of the definition, but appears quite certain that he himself knows what 'doing one's own' amounts to and is able to effectively defend it. As I hope to show, the dialectical argument that he will conduct jointly with Socrates is neither

---

[1] Also, the metaphor reflects the relative positions of Critias and Charmides within the Thirty – Critias as the director and Charmides as the directed in the context of the atrocities committed by that regime.

[2] As readers of the *Republic* will remember, in the Myth of Er, the soul of Odysseus chooses the life of a private citizen, flinging away the φιλοτιμία on account of which Odysseus had suffered many misfortunes in his former life (*Rep.* 620c).

self-serving,[3] nor 'ostensibly ludicrous',[4] nor designed to indicate a political shift from the realm of traditional aristocratic values to an axiological system in which *sôphrosynê* appears 'less than a virtue'[5] and may be not even a good.[6] Nor, on my account, does it fail to accomplish its task.[7] The two interlocutors will engage in a successful piece of dialectic that will bring conceptual clarification to the issue at hand, will intimate that temperance must have to do with value, will point to some essential connection between temperance and self-knowledge, and will eventually refute the definition of temperance as 'doing one's own' on defensible grounds. Critias will show himself a responsive and resourceful participant, who has mastered the rules of the game and actively contributes to the advancement of the argument. Although he will eventually decide to abandon the definition, he will in the meantime prove his considerable dialectical skills and give a foretaste of the bras-de-fer to come later.

The argumentative structure of this exchange between Socrates and Critias is complicated and controversial. On my account, the elenctic arguments deployed in the initial phases of the debate (162e2–163a9, 163a10–c8) do not constitute self-standing refutations. Rather, they jointly exert pressure on Critias to disambiguate the meaning of 'doing one's own' and restate his own position in clearer terms. Thus, they pave the way for the final refutation of the claim that temperance is 'doing one's own' (163d7–164d3), but are not, strictly speaking, constituent parts of that refutation.

> Tell me, do you also agree about what I was asking just now, namely, that all craftsmen make [*poiein*] something? – Indeed. – So, do they seem to you to make [*poiein*] only their own things or also other people's things? – Other people's things as well. – So, are they being temperate, even though they do not make [*poiountas*] only their own things? – Why, he said, what is there to prevent that? – Nothing for me at least, I replied; but see whether it may not prevent him who, having posited that temperance is doing [*prattein*] one's own, then goes on to say that nothing prevents those who do [*prattontas*] other people's own from being temperate as well. (162e7–163a9)

---

[3] Contra Schmid 1998, 35.

[4] According to Hyland 1981, 71, the elenchus is not really intended to refute the definition of temperance as 'doing one's own', but rather to highlight the dual aspect of σωφροσύνη as both an apolitical, philosophical stance and a political virtue determining our relations to others. In Hyland's view, the fact that the definition of σωφροσύνη as doing one's own is also (part of) the successful definition of justice in *Republic* IV indicates that these two virtues may amount to one and the same virtue, of which one aspect, σωφροσύνη, concerns primarily oneself, whereas the other, δικαιοσύνη, mainly focuses on our relations to others.

[5] Schmid 1998, 35.   [6] Hyland 1981, 86.

[7] Compare Wolfsdorf 2008 and contrast Brennan 2012.

This first preliminary argument seems deliberately provocative. For it suggests that Critias may have fallen prey to inconsistency. I read it as follows:

(1) Definition: temperance is doing one's own.
(2) Doing (*prattein*) is the same as making (*poiein*).
(3) Hence temperance is also making one's own.
(4) In every art, the craftsmen (*dêmiourgoi*) make something.
(5) In every art, the craftsmen make both their own and other people's own.
(6) In every art, the craftsmen do (*prattein*) both their own and other people's own.
(7) Nonetheless, the craftsmen can be temperate or have temperance.
(8) So, temperance is not doing one's own.

Socrates chooses his words carefully. He refers to *dêmiourgoi*, craftsmen, and this term points principally to experts in productive arts rather than, for example, legislators or mathematicians. The use of the verb *poiein*, to make, and its cognates indicates that Socrates is thinking of the arts or crafts previously mentioned in the round with Charmides: medicine, building, and weaving, as well as scouring coats, cobbling, and making oil-flasks and body-scrapers (161e10–162a2). Premise (5), which states that craftsmen make both their own and not their own, draws support from Charmides' earlier concessions. Namely, craftsmen are principally concerned with making other people's things, not just their own; if they did make only their own things, no society could conduct itself well; but if a society is temperate, it does or must conduct itself well (161e10–162a9). Nonetheless, the present argument is not intended to apply exclusively to the productive arts. For premise (2) equates *poiein*, to make, with *prattein*, to do, and thus extends the claim that experts do 'other people's own as well as their own' to all sorts of arts and disciplines: not only those that produce things, but also those involving non-productive forms of *praxis*.

We should note that, in the immediately preceding debate with Charmides, Socrates used '*poiein*', *prattein*, and *ergazesthai* interchangeably without drawing attention to that fact, whereas on the present occasion he underscores in (2) that he takes '*poiein*' to be the same as '*prattein*'. Evidently, he expects that Critias will take issue with that practice,[8] and this is exactly what happens. Furthermore, we should register a grammatical detail in (7). Socrates' use of the present tense at 163a4[9]

---

[8] See Tuozzo 2011, 172–3.   [9] σωφρονοῦσιν οὖν οὐ τὰ ἑαυτῶν μόνον ποιοῦντες (163a4).

(sc. 'are they being temperate even though they do not make only their own things?') and Critias' emphatically affirmative answer at 163a5 ('why, what is there to prevent that?') might be taken to suggest that Critias endorses the assertion that all craftsmen are temperate. But such a claim would be counterintuitive and incompatible with Critias' aristocratic prejudices. Probably, Critias concedes a weaker claim: not that all craftsmen are temperate, but that nothing obstructs them from being temperate, i.e. they can but need not be temperate. This point will be relevant to a later stage of the refutation.

> Pray, he said, have I agreed to this, that those who do [*prattein*] other people's things are temperate, or[10] was my agreement about those who make [*poiountas*] things?[11] – Tell me, I said, don't you call making [*poiein*] and doing [*prattein*] one and the same? – Certainly not, he replied. Nor do I call working [*ergazesthai*] and making [*poiein*] the same either. For this I learned from Hesiod, who said 'Work [*ergon*] is no disgrace'. Do you suppose, then, that if he called such works as you were mentioning just now workings [*ergazesthai*] and doings [*prattein*], he would have claimed that no disgrace is attached to the shoe-maker or the pickle-seller or the pimp? Of course, Socrates, this is unthinkable. Rather he held, I surmise, that making [*poiêsin*] is something different from doing [*praxeôs*] and working [*ergasias*], and that while something made [*poiêma*] can occasionally become a disgrace, when its production does not involve what is fine [*kalon*],[12] work [*ergon*] can never be shameful. For things made in a good and beneficial manner he called works [*erga*], and such makings [*poiêseis*] he called both workings and doings [*ergasias te kai praxeis*]. Indeed, we should suppose him also to have declared that only things of this sort are our own proper concerns [*oikeia*], whereas all harmful things are other people's concerns [*allotria*].[13] Hence we should conclude that both Hesiod and every other sensible person call temperate the man who does his own [*ta heautou prattonta*]. (163a10–c8)

Critias' reply to Socrates consists, I propose, of two distinct phases. In the first stage, he explicitly rejects the assumption that making and doing are equivalent,[14] and argues that temperance is just this, *doing* one's own. In the second stage, he interprets a claim by Hesiod so as to lend support to the contention that making one's own things *differs* from doing one's own

---

[10] 163a11 ἤ T εἰ Burnet.   [11] I am supplying a question mark at 163a12 (see previous note).
[12] In the present context, '*kalon*' means 'admirable' or even 'good'. See e.g. 163d1–3, and also the discussion below.
[13] I follow Lamb's translation of οἰκεῖα and ἀλλότρια (163c4–5). See the relevant comments below.
[14] See premise (2) above.

deeds or working one's own works and, moreover, that this difference bears on value.

First stage (162e7–163b3):

(1) In every *technê*, the craftsmen (*dêmiourgoi*) make (*poiein*) something.
(2) In every *technê*, the craftsmen make (*poiein*) both their own and other people's own.
(3) Making (*poiein*) and doing (*prattein*) or working (*ergazesthai*) are not the same.
(4) The craftsmen may both do (*prattein* or *ergazesthai*) their own and make (*poiein*) other people's own.
(5) The craftsmen can *both* make other people's own as well as their own *and* be temperate (163a4).
(6) Hence it is not the case that temperance is doing one's own in the sense of *making* one's own.

Second stage (163b3–c8):

(1) Temperance is *doing* one's own, not *making* one's own.
(2) Assumption: temperance is invariably fine (*kalon*) and beneficial.[15]
(3) According to Hesiod, all activities and works (*erga*) that are invariably fine and beneficial are cases of doing (*prattein*) or working (*ergazesthai*).
(4) Making (*poiein*) and what is made (*poiêma*), on the other hand, are not invariably fine and beneficial, but sometimes the opposite.
(5) It follows that doing or working and making are not the same.

Furthermore:

(6) Things made (*poioumena*: 163c3) in an invariably fine and beneficial manner, as well as things done in such manner, are works or deeds (*ergasias te kai praxeis*: 163c4).
(7) Making good and beneficial things is equivalent to doing good deeds or working good works (cf. *agatha*: 163d2).
(8) Only such deeds and works qualify as properly concerning oneself (*oikeia*: 163c5), whereas harmful deeds and works count as alien concerns (*allotria*: 163c6).
(9) Hence temperance is 'doing one's own' in just that sense: doing good deeds and working good works, i.e. doing deeds and works that are one's proper concerns and not other people's proper concerns.

---

[15] Cf. 159c1–2.

On balance, it seems that Critias can defend this definition of temperance better than Charmides. His pivotal move is to reject Socrates' equation of doing (*prattein*) with making (*poiein*) and contend that all activities that are invariably fine and profitable are cases of doing (*prattein*). While craftsmen who *make* other people's things may be 'doing their own' and have temperance,[16] people who *do* 'other people's things' don't 'do their own' and don't possess temperance: they do not focus on affairs that properly concern them, but meddle with the affairs of others. According to Critias, then, the set of temperate people will include all proper doers and may include certain makers as well.

In order to support the aforementioned distinction between doing and making, as well as the claim that deeds are invariably fine but products aren't, Critias appeals to Hesiod. He cites a verse from Hesiod's didactic poem *Works and Days*, namely 'Work is no disgrace' (*WD* 309), whose meaning, as Socrates' and Plato's contemporaries may have known, was debated among the Socratics.[17] On the evidence of Hesiod, he claims that the prima facie trio of synonyms, i.e. doing (*prattein*), working (*ergazesthai*), and making (*poiein*), are not synonyms at all. For, according to Critias, Hesiod clearly assumes that there are cases of *poiein* that are not cases of *ergazesthai* and, therefore, he is likely to make a similar discrimination between cases of *poiein* that are not cases of *prattein*. However, Critias attributes to Hesiod words and tenets absent from the poem. While Hesiod says in the latter that 'work is no disgrace', he does not employ either '*poiein*' or '*prattein*' in that connection. And although he uses '*ergazesthai*' and its cognates, he does not treat that verb as Critias does, i.e. as a near-synonym of *prattein*. Rather, he uses '*ergazesthai*' to cover both works or productions and actions. Furthermore, while Hesiod appears to assume that such works should be honourable, he does not explicitly contrast them with the making of disgraceful products. Given the popularity of Hesiod's poems and the role that they play in the traditional curriculum, it can be taken for granted that the other interlocutors know Hesiod's exact wording and his primary preoccupation: to oppose *ergazesthai* to being idle, and to recommend honest toil over laziness and dissolution. Critias' deviation

---

[16] Compare the options that Socrates outlines in the *Republic* with regard to the first city. Assuming that it consists minimally of a farmer, a builder, a weaver, a cobbler, and a doctor (369d), will each of them spend all his time doing his own work and making it available to all or, alternatively, will he spend part of his time doing his own work, e.g. farming, and the rest of the time building his own house, producing his own clothes, etc., thus minding his own business and not associating with the others (369e–370a)? Adeimantus takes the former option (370a) and this prompts Socrates to talk about natural differences and the so-called principle of specialisation.

[17] See Witte 1970, 81–2; Tuozzo 2011, 174–8.

from Hesiod's text is, I suggest, deliberate. He wants to underline that he is conveying his own understanding of Hesiod's verse, not the poet's *ipsissima verba*. He relays what he *learned*[18] from Hesiod, but does not claim that Hesiod made the assertions that he will attribute to him.

Proceeding in this manner, Critias makes an ingenious move.[19] He pairs *ergazesthai* with *prattein* and contrasts both of them with *poiein*. Thus, he restricts the domain of activities that Hesiod's verse applies to, bringing to the fore a presupposition that Hesiod would acknowledge as well: no work brings disgrace, provided that it is honourable. It is not entirely clear, however, whether, in Critias' eyes, many (or even any) first-order *technai* qualify as such. On the one hand, he evidently thinks that the activities of shoe-makers, pickle-sellers, and pimps or prostitutes cannot count as honourable deeds or works.[20] On the other, we cannot be sure what he thinks about the arts that Socrates has previously mentioned, e.g. medicine, architecture, weaving, and tool-making (161e–162a). One may reasonably object that these arts are perfectly respectable and cannot be compared with pedestrian skills such as cobbling or dishonourable practices like pimping and whoring. Nor is it easy to maintain that the lowly activities mentioned by Critias qualify as makings, as opposed to doings. For while the cobbler does *make* shoes, pickle-sellers don't necessarily make their own preserves, and pimps and prostitutes make nothing at all; if anything, they *do* something shameful. In sum, Critias' choice of examples indicates contempt for lowly occupations such as shoe-making, and also raises questions about Critias' attitude in respect of quite prestigious arts, e.g. medicine and architecture. Would he claim that these latter are not invariably good and beneficial and, therefore, do not invariably qualify as doings but rather as makings?

I believe, however, that these worries can be met to some extent. First, when Critias points out that Hesiod would never deny that there is disgrace in 'such works as you [sc. Socrates] were mentioning just now',[21] he is probably not referring to the works of medicine and architecture, but rather to the string of pedestrian activities that Socrates enumerates in connection to the management of the city: weaving,

---

[18] ἔμαθον: 163b4.
[19] It is possible that Plato had read Xenophon (*Mem.* I.2.56–7): see Tuozzo 2011, 174–8. Nonetheless, I do not think that this hypothesis is necessary to explain Critias' move. In my view, Critias' interpretation of Hesiod's passage is Plato's own invention.
[20] The expression 'ἐπ᾽οἰκήματος καθημένῳ' (163b7–8) can be taken either way. Lamb translates it as 'serving the stews'.
[21] εἰ τὰ τοιαῦτα ἔργα ἐκάλει ... οἷα νῦν δὴ σὺ ἔλεγες: 163b6.

coat-scouring, shoe-making, flask-and-scrape-making, and other similar tasks (161e10–13). Insofar as these latter are 'makings' rather than 'doings', they are indeed comparable to cobbling and perhaps pickle-selling (if the latter involves making the pickles that one sells). Next, while the distinction that Critias draws between *poiein* and *prattein* carries sophistical associations (163d1–e2), it is not entirely untenable. Few would deny that some arts focus on *poiêsis*, the making of self-standing products, while others mainly consist of the artistic activity itself. On the other hand, most of us would resist, for good reason, Critias' devaluation of productive arts, as well as the suggestion that, properly speaking, production need not involve action.

Also, Critias' attitude towards 'makings' and 'productions' derives not only from social prejudice, as interpreters do not tire of remarking, but also from certain intellectualist presuppositions concerning the nature of the good. For in addition to the belief that temperance entails doing something good, Critias appears to assume that the good in question must be sufficiently robust to account for the greatly beneficial character of that virtue and, moreover, must involve some sort of knowledge or understanding. In the light of these assumptions, we can explain (though we need not accept) Critias' hierarchical evaluation of the *technai* as well as the suggestion that, for instance, coat-washing and pickle-making do not qualify as *praxeis*, actions, in the full sense, namely a sense involving a sufficiently rich understanding of value. In sum, while Critias' comparative assessment of the arts is probably biased, his basic intuition is both free of prejudice and philosophically defensible: only certain sorts of actions can be considered good in a way relevant to morality. Finally, it is worth noting that Critias holds a view also attributed to Plato's Socrates with regard to the relative value of the arts and the benefits that they yield. Namely, he seems to think that even the most elevated arts, such as medicine and architecture, do good only if they are practised in the right manner (163b9–c8). Only then does the practice of these arts amount to 'doing one's own', i.e. to focusing on one's proper concerns, which, according to Critias, typically involve benefiting others as well as oneself.[22]

Socrates' response is interesting both dramatically and philosophically. He says that, as soon as Critias began to speak, he immediately realised that the latter would call the actions proper to oneself good, and that he would

[22] In my view, the distinction between making and doing, productions and actions, has precisely the purpose of introducing the idea that temperate activities must essentially involve value. In the next phase of the refutation, as we shall see, that distinction does not play any role at all.

call the productions of good things actions (163d1–3). Moreover, Socrates suggests that Critias' practice is inspired by Prodicus and consists in drawing distinctions that are not substantive but merely verbal (163d3–4). The significance of this remark is, I think, philosophical rather than biographical.[23] Socrates need not reject the use of verbal distinctions as such. Rather, he objects to the assumption, possibly made by Prodicus and others, that verbal distinctions alone can settle the philosophical problem under consideration. In order to ensure that Critias won't operate on that assumption and that the investigation will remain on the right track, he allows Critias to draw the distinctions he wishes to draw but asks him to make clear the meaning of the terms he employs and specify what they refer to. The endeavour to find out 'what *sôphrosynê* is and what kind of thing it is' cannot be conducted solely at the level of language, but must involve consideration of the things that the names apply to (163d1–d7).

> Well, you have my permission to assign to each thing any name you please. Only make clear whenever you say a name what you are applying the name to. So begin now all over again and give a clearer definition. Do you claim that the doing or making, or whatever else you want to call it, of good things is temperance? – Yes, I do, he said. (163d5–e3)

Critias rises to the occasion. He evidently understands Socrates' observation and takes it in good part. And he attempts anew to defend his conception of 'doing one's own' as doing deeds or making things that are good. The argument that follows (163e3–164d3) is complicated and susceptible to different reconstructions and readings. In my own view, it represents an instance of a genuinely cooperative dialectical examination, which ends when Critias realises that the definition of temperance that he is defending is probably inconsistent with one of his most deeply seated beliefs about the nature of virtue. As I understand it, the argument is this:

(1) Temperance is the doing or making of good things.[24]
(2) Hence one is temperate if and only if one does[25] good things and not bad ones.
(3) Per Critias' earlier admission, the experts make[26] other people's things as well as their own, and yet may be temperate.[27]

---

[23] Compare Brennan 2012, 244.
[24] τὴν τῶν ἀγαθῶν πρᾶξιν ἢ ποίησιν ἢ ὅπως σὺ βούλει ὀνομάζειν: 163e1–2.
[25] πράττων (163e4), ποιοῦντα (163e9).   [26] ποιοῦντας: 164a6.
[27] Cf. εἰ σωφρονοῦντας: 164a2.

(4)   The doctor, in making someone healthy,[28] makes[29] something bene-
      ficial happen to both himself and the patient whom he has cured.

(5)   (implicit). Generally, in making the products of their arts, experts
      cause beneficial things to happen to both themselves and others.

(6)   Any expert who does beneficial things does what he/she ought to
      do.[30]

(7)   (implicit). Whenever one does what one ought to do, one does good
      things.

(8)   (implicit). Hence, any expert who does what he/she ought to do
      does good things.

(9)   Any expert who does what he/she ought to do is temperate.[31]

However:

(10) If temperance is the doing or making of good or beneficial things, all
      temperate people must necessarily know themselves in respect of
      knowing that they have done something beneficial for themselves or
      others (cf. 164b8–9).

(11) But, for example, in treating a disease, a doctor does not necessarily
      know whether or not he has acted beneficially (cf. 164b7–8).

(12) Generally, in doing or making things, experts do not necessarily
      know whether the work that they do[32] is beneficial or harmful to
      themselves.

(13) It follows that doctors and, generally, all experts sometimes may act
      temperately and be temperate without knowing themselves to be
      temperate.[33]

(14) But this can never happen. It could never be conceded that people
      ignorant of themselves could be temperate (164c7–d3).

   Allow me to comment briefly on certain features of this argument.
Claim (1) reveals that, after relying on the distinction between doing and
making in order to introduce value, Critias puts it aside. First, he declares
that temperance is 'the doing (*praxin*) or making (*poiêsin*) of good things'
(163e1). Then, he switches to the terminology of *praxis*: 'not he who does
(*prattôn*) bad things but he who does good things is temperate' (163e4).
Next, he elaborates and restates his claim using both verbs and their
cognates: 'I say that he who makes (*poiounta*) bad things is not temperate,

---

[28] ὑγιᾶ τινὰ ποιῶν: 164a9–b1.   [29] ποιεῖν: 164b1.   [30] πράττει ὅ γε ταῦτα πράττων: 164b3.
[31] Ὁ τὰ δέοντα πράττων οὐ σωφρονεῖ: 164b5.   [32] ἔργου οὗ ἂν πράττῃ: 164b9.
[33] οὐκοῦν, ὡς ἔοικεν, ἐνίοτε ὠφελίμως πράξας πράττει μὲν σωφρόνως καὶ σωφρονεῖ, ἀγνοεῖ δ'ἑαυτὸν
ὅτι σωφρονεῖ: 164c5–6.

whereas he who makes good things is temperate. For I plainly define for you temperance as the doing (*praxin*) of good things' (163e8–11).

Moving on, it seems intuitively plausible and philosophically preferable to construe (2) as a biconditional claim. If one makes or does good things (or good works), one has temperance, and if one has temperance, one makes or does good things. The focus is on the goodness of one's achievements, not on whether these achievements are productions or actions. The same observation applies to (4) as well, where the interlocutors twice use '*poiein*' rather than '*prattein*' (cf. 164a–b). Consistently with Critias' interpretation of Hesiod, which left open the question of whether the activities of the doctor qualify as doings or as makings, it is now suggested that, so long as the activities of the doctor and of other craftsmen are *good*, it does not make any difference whether we call them productions or actions. Critias appears to be on the same page as Socrates: he does not seem interested merely in the verbal distinction between doing and making, but concentrates on an essential feature of temperate people, namely that they do good. It is worth noting that (4) refers to the beneficial effects of medical practice not only for others but also for the doctor himself. It is very unusual for Plato's Socrates to highlight the self-regarding aspects alongside the other-regarding aspects of expert activities.[34] Possibly, Socrates draws attention to the self-beneficial results of expertise in order to point forward to the importance of self-care and self-knowledge.[35] Alternatively, the dual nature of expert activity may be intended to capture Critias' belief that an expert can engage with other people's concerns as well as his own. The doctor is in a position to treat himself as well as others; and assuming that his work is beneficial, he manifests his temperance in the former case as much as in the latter. As stated in (5), the same inference can be drawn with regard to other sorts of experts as well.

(6) is a crucial premise, because it attributes what looks like a moral dimension to beneficial actions or productions. Relying on the example of the doctor, Socrates gets Critias to agree that the person who effects some beneficial work for himself or others does what he ought (*ta deonta*: 164b3). Experts who practise their professions successfully can be viewed as fulfilling a sort of ethical requirement. They act as they ought to act insofar as, in the domains of their respective arts, they do good to themselves and others. The idea is not implausible, provided that we keep in mind Socrates' view

---

about the relative value of first-order arts and of their functions and outcomes. The *Apology* is especially pertinent here (*Ap.* 22d–e).[36] As Socrates tells the jury, when he tried to discover whether the craftsmen were wiser than he was, he found out that they had expertise in many fine things and knew things that Socrates did not know. Barring adverse circumstances, they presumably were able to deliver the goods pertaining to their respective arts and, in that obvious sense, did what they ought with regard to themselves and others. Nonetheless, they were both ignorant of 'the most important pursuits' and unaware of that fact (22d–e). The idea that the craftsmen may be incapable of assessing value and may lack self-knowledge will become crucial to the refutation of Critias' definition. For the moment, note that (6) together with (7) and (8) provide grounds for the inference drawn in (9): if doing what one ought amounts to doing good things, and if doing good things is what it is to be temperate, it follows that craftsmen who do what they ought are temperate.

Interpreters disagree about the nature of the experts' shortcomings regarding self-knowledge and, therefore, the claims in (10) to (13) are bound to be controversial. On the hypothesis that temperance is the making or doing of good things, does Socrates suggest that, when the first-order experts practise their professions, they may be unaware of the fact that they are *doing* something? Or, alternatively, does he suggest that, in practising their arts, the experts may be unaware of the fact that they are doing something *good*? The former option seems to me both trivial and irrelevant to the elenchus underway. It does not make much sense to problematise whether the experts are self-aware of their deeds and productions, whereas it makes perfectly good sense to question whether they are always aware of the value of their own achievements. Furthermore, the definition of temperance as articulated in (1) concentrates on the *good* works effected through temperance, not the doings or workings themselves. Accordingly, in the elenchus that follows, the craftsmen's self-knowledge concerns the *value* of what they do rather than the fact that they do it.

On this reading, (10) is pivotal both because it serves as a basis for the final stage of the refutation and because it suggests that there is a necessary connection between temperance and self-knowledge. In particular, (10) posits self-knowledge as a necessary condition of temperance or, also, an essential component of that virtue. If temperance is doing or producing good or beneficial things, and assuming that the experts in various arts and

---

[36] See also *Euthyd.* 279b–280a, *Rep.* 340d–e.

disciplines do or produce such things, it should follow that the experts must be aware of the value of their own deeds or products. However, (11) points out that this is not always or necessarily the case.[37] In fact, in doing his own work, for example, a doctor can do something good and thereby be temperate, without knowing, however, that what he does is actually *good*.[38] The purpose of (11), (12), and (13) is not to contend that first-order experts are *never* aware of the value of their own doings and, therefore, can *never* be temperate. Rather, they jointly suggest a weaker thesis, namely that doctors and the other first-order experts need not always be aware of their temperance, i.e. of the positive or negative value of their actions.[39] At least sometimes (*eniote*: 164b11), they appear to lack self-knowledge in that sense. The implication stated in (13) is, precisely, that according to the above argument one *can* be temperate without knowing oneself to be so (164c1–2). As stated in (14), Critias finds it impossible to accept this conclusion.

> But Socrates, he said, that could never happen. But if you think that this is in any way a necessary consequence [*anankaion*] deriving from the things I previously agreed, I would certainly prefer to withdraw some of them and I would not be ashamed to declare that I have spoken incorrectly, rather than ever agree that a person who is ignorant of himself is temperate. (164c7–d3)

Critias' response is loud and clear: if (13) is a necessary inference, either some of the premises must be withdrawn or the definition must be abandoned. It is remarkable that, in spite of his *philotimia*, love of honour, and his evident attraction to the idea that temperance is equivalent to 'doing one's own' in the sense of doing good works, he finds (13) so absurd as to concede defeat. The reason for this reaction is found in (10): Critias' unreserved commitment to the intellectualist assumption that possession of temperance entails that one knows oneself regarding the value of one's works and deeds. If one is temperate, one must know oneself as temperate. On the hypothesis that temperance is 'doing one's own' in the

---

[37] The counterexample in (11) leaves unclear whether the beneficial or harmful nature of the medicine concerns the patients or the doctor himself. On the other hand, (12) clearly indicates that a craftsman's lack of self-knowledge concerns the benefit or harm that his works or deeds might bring upon himself. As Tuozzo 2011, 183, remarks, the verb ὀνήσεσθαι (164b9), to be benefited, is self-referential.

[38] Compare *Gorg.* 510a–512b.

[39] ἐνίοτε ἄρα, ἦν δ'ἐγώ, ὠφελίμως πράξας ἢ βλαβερῶς ὁ ἰατρὸς οὐ γιγνώσκειν ἑαυτὸν ὡς ἔπραξεν: 164b11–165c1.

aforementioned sense, one must know that the things that one makes and the deeds that one does are good and beneficial for those concerned.

A concluding note: regarding the virtue of the craftsmen, the implications of the above elenchus are arguably consistent with, but also weaker than, comparable views entertained in other Platonic dialogues. First, as mentioned, the craftsmen of the *Apology* are found to be ignorant about 'the most important pursuits' for a human being (22d–e). The producers of the *Republic* 'do their own' by going about their tasks and, presumably, by having awareness of the prudential benefits that they yield. Nonetheless, they are not able to correctly assess these latter with a view to the good, but must defer to the Guardians' judgement. In the *Statesman*, the first-order experts are in a comparable position. The statesman tells them what to do and supervises the successful accomplishment of their work. He, and not the experts themselves, is the one who determines the value and correct use of their works. Second, while the *Apology* does not say anything about the craftsmen's virtue, and the *Republic* reserves no virtue peculiar to the class of producers, the interlocutors of the *Charmides* leave at least formally open the possibility that first-order experts can sometimes be temperate. Contrary to what has often been claimed, Critias does not abandon the definition under discussion because he holds the prejudicial belief that these latter can have no share in virtue. Rather, he finally realises that the conception of temperance he is defending implies an incongruity in respect of the first-order experts. Namely, assuming that temperance necessarily implies self-knowledge bearing on value, it seems that the first-order experts can be both temperate on account of doing good works and not temperate on account of lacking self-knowledge about the value of their accomplishments.[40] In principle, Critias could have chosen to uphold the former of these claims at the cost of denying the relevance of self-knowledge to *sôphrosynê*. As it happens, however, he does not even consider that option. Instead, he insists that temperance must crucially involve self-knowledge, as Plato's Socrates would have done. His next move will be, precisely, to concentrate on what he takes to be the essential feature of temperance: knowing oneself.

---

[40] It is not clear whether Critias is truly convinced by the refutation or has doubts about its validity (164c7–d3).

CHAPTER 7

Critias' Speech
Temperance Is Knowing Oneself (164d4–165c4)

As a matter of fact, I am almost ready to assert that this very thing, to know
oneself, is temperance, and I am of the same mind as the person who put up
an inscription to that effect at Delphi. For it seems to me that this inscription has been put up for the following purpose, to serve as a greeting from
the god to those who enter the temple instead of the usual 'Be Joyful', since
this greeting, 'Be Joyful', is not right nor should people use it to exhort one
another, but rather should use the greeting 'Be Temperate'. Thus, the god
addresses those entering the temple in a manner different in some respects
from that in which men address each other, and it is with that thought in
mind, I believe, that the person who put up the inscription did so. And it is
alleged that he [sc. the god] says to every man who enters the temple nothing
other than 'Be Temperate'. However, he says it in a more enigmatic manner,
as a prophet would. For while 'Know Thyself' and 'Be Temperate' are one
and the same, as the inscription and I assert, perhaps one might think that
they are different – an error that, I believe, has been committed by the
dedicators of the later inscriptions, i.e. 'Nothing too much' and 'A rash
pledge and, immediately, perdition'. For they supposed that 'Know Thyself'
was a piece of advice, not the god's greeting to those who were entering.[1]
And so, in order that their own dedications too would no less contain pieces
of useful advice, they inscribed these words and put them up in the temple.
The purpose for which I say all this, Socrates, is the following: I concede to
you everything that was debated beforehand. For concerning them perhaps
you said something more correct perhaps than I did, but, in any case,
nothing we said was really clear. However, I am now ready to give you an
argument for this, if you don't agree that temperance is to know oneself.
(164d4–165c4)

Critias' speech is not just a rhetorical display. Structurally, it provides
continuity between the intellectualist assumption on account of which
Critias has abandoned the definition of temperance as 'the doing or
making of good things' and the view that *sôphrosynê* is knowledge of

---

[1] I delete ἕνεκεν, following Cobet.

oneself. Thus, the speech links what is commonly considered the first part of the investigation with the second part.[2] Conceptually, Critias' interpretation of the Delphic inscription 'Know Thyself' focuses on the notion of self-knowledge in a new way. His central claim is not merely that knowing oneself is a necessary condition for having temperance, but that knowing oneself is what temperance is in its nature. Dialectically, Critias' move is astute and effective. For, in his speech, he indicates *why* he found unpalatable the implication that the craftsmen may be temperate and yet ignorant of their temperance and, moreover, supports his intuition by appealing to the authority of the god. His opening statement, i.e. that he is *almost* ready to assert that temperance is this very thing, to know oneself, underscores the dialectical context of the discussion. The qualification 'almost' (*schedon*: 164d3) points to the fact that the new definition is not the result of deductive reasoning or of careful consideration of all relevant factors. Rather, Critias has been brought to the point of suggesting that temperance is self-knowledge as a result of the previous argument and, in particular, the stance that he took vis-à-vis the hypothesis that people can be temperate without having knowledge of themselves in that regard. While Critias will appear firmly committed to the view that temperance is knowing oneself, it is worth bearing in mind that he initially proposes that view in a dialectical mode.[3]

A. E. Taylor and others claim that the view that temperance is knowing oneself is 'generally accepted',[4] but this is probably not true. While the contemporaries of Socrates and Plato commonly assume that self-knowledge is an aspect of *sôphrosynê*[5] and acknowledge the value of the precept 'Know Thyself', they would probably deny that *sôphrosynê* is just this, knowing oneself.[6] The former view represents a conventional value, whereas the latter is a philosophical position held by Critias and, at first glance, likely to be attractive to Socrates as well. In fact, Critias appears to

---

[2] According to Schmid 1998, 40, Critias' speech constitutes the high point of the dialogue. As he suggests, the investigation ascends to the definition of temperance as self-knowledge through three prior stages, then descends in three stages in which it is criticised on metaphysical, epistemological, and moral grounds. In fact, however, the target of the elenchus is not the claim that temperance is knowing oneself, but Critias' articulation of self-knowledge in terms of the only science that is of the other sciences and of itself (166c2–3).

[3] In my view, the text does not support the claim by Gotshalk 2001, 82, that the word 'almost' points to an aspect of temperance that Charmides has not yet made his own, i.e. 'the need to assume individual responsibility for his own life and to find that way of taking part in things which is his very own as a human being'.

[4] So Taylor 1926.   [5] See Annas 1985.

[6] While *sôphrosynê* was commonly believed to entail self-control (see North 1966, *passim*), this does not hold for self-knowledge.

hope that Socrates will admit on the spot that temperance is self-knowledge and the argument will end there. He tells Socrates: 'I am now ready to give you an argument for this, if you don't agree that temperance is to know oneself' (165b3–4).

As Tuckey remarks, Critias appears to be thinking: 'Oh, of course! Why didn't I think of that before? Socrates used always to talk about the Delphic precept "Know thyself" and he used to tell us that we must know ourselves if we were to reach true spiritual health.'[7] In the *Laches*, Nicias appears to have a similar reaction. After Laches' definition of courage as wise endurance has been refuted, Nicias is summoned to rescue the argument (*Lach.* 194c). And he wonders why Socrates does not put forward a view that Nicias has heard him express in the past, namely that people are good in respect of that in which they are wise and bad in respect of that in which they are ignorant; from this latter it can be inferred that, if people are courageous, they are wise (194c–d). Socrates takes Nicias to suggest that courage is a sort of wisdom (194d). As in the *Charmides*, so in the *Laches* the definition under consideration equates a virtue with a kind of knowledge. As in the former dialogue, so in the latter Socrates' interlocutor fully expects Socrates to agree with the proposed view. Moreover, in both cases Socrates carefully distances himself from the view expressed by his interlocutor. He refuses to answer Laches' question concerning what sort of wisdom is courage, but invites Nicias to respond: the view is Nicias' own and Nicias should take responsibility for it (194e–195a). Likewise, he refuses to accept outright Critias' claim that temperance is knowing oneself (cf. 165b–c). Rather, he appeals to his own ignorance and expresses his wish to consider the matter further.

> Critias, I said, you treat me as though I claimed to know the things that I ask about, and as though I shall agree with you only if I want to. But this is not so. Rather, you see, I always enquire together with you into whatever claim is put forward, because I myself do not know. Thus, it will be after considering the matter that I am willing to state whether or not I agree. So, please hold back until I have done so. – Do consider then, he said. – I am doing so, I replied. (165b5–c4)

Critias as well as Nicias had hoped that Socrates might accept their respective definitions for a similar reason. Both characters are represented by Plato as being familiar with Socrates' ways of thinking and, therefore, both expect him to be favourable to their intellectualist accounts of,

---

[7] Tuckey 1951, 24.

respectively, courage and temperance. They appear to forget, however, that while Socrates conceives of the virtues as a sort of knowledge or understanding, his disclaimer of expertise in 'the most important things' precludes him from accepting the definition of an ethical concept without argument, and also the rules of his method make it impossible for him to undertake on his own account the defence of a definition put forward by someone else. Neither the *Laches* nor the *Charmides* gives us reason to worry that the elenchus demolishes a conception of courage or of temperance known to lie close to Socrates' own heart. For as in the former case, so in the latter the definition under investigation gets refuted on the basis of premises representing the beliefs of Socrates' interlocutor, not necessarily of Socrates himself.

Nonetheless, I contend, the situation in the *Charmides* is far more complicated than in the *Laches*, insofar as Socrates' known view about self-knowledge has an important dialectical and philosophical function from the beginning of the dialogue to its very end. Critias' speech makes this function prominent by prompting us to compare and contrast the speaker's peculiar interpretation of the Delphic dictum with Socrates' own understanding of the oracle and his lifelong devotion to the task set for him by the god. This suggestion is crucial to my reading of the dialogue and, therefore, it may be useful to summarise some things that I have said earlier as well.

Namely, Critias' appeal to the Delphic inscription 'Know Thyself' cannot fail to evoke the god's verdict about Socrates in the *Apology*, namely that no man was wiser than he was (*Ap.* 21a). After cross-examining various experts about things that they claim to know, Socrates comes to the conclusion that he is wiser than they are because he does not believe that he knows when he doesn't, whereas they believe themselves to be experts in certain 'most important matters' that they are in truth ignorant about (21d). Socrates does not explicitly identify these 'most important matters'. However, it is clear that they do not belong to the domain of any first-order expertise (22d–e), but essentially have to do with truth, virtue, and the health of the soul (30a–31c). Socrates provisionally concludes that the mark of his own wisdom, human wisdom (20d–e), is that he does not think himself wise about these matters, while the people that he has cross-examined believe themselves to possess a wisdom 'more than human' (20e).

Arguably, the story of the oracle in the *Apology* has a normative and paraenetic purpose. For Socrates suggests that the god[8] probably used him

---

[8] Burnyeat 1997, 4, underscores that while Socrates frequently refers to ὁ θεός, 'the god' (e.g. at *Ap.* 20e, 21b), and while the members of the jury assume that he is talking of Apollo, Socrates never mentions Apollo by name.

as an example in order to highlight the disproportion between divine wisdom and human wisdom and show what is involved in the latter (23b). His own labours on behalf of the god illustrate both how we ought to seek human wisdom and what human wisdom consists in: a certain sort of self-knowledge, i.e. one's capacity to assess the limits of knowledge and ignorance in oneself and others in relation to the perfect knowledge of virtue and value that only the gods may possess (23d–e). Socrates' account of his endeavours to gain self-understanding appear intended to serve as a paradigm of the way to acquire human wisdom, namely through the lifelong examination of one's own moral beliefs and of the moral beliefs of others (28e). Importantly, in his defence speech, Socrates stresses that his labours were motivated by his perception of himself as a servant of the god. He appears convinced that the gods exist, are far wiser than we are, and we ought to obey their commands and fight against the tendency to think ourselves their equals in wisdom or anything else (29a).

As I claimed previously,[9] these ideas are present or alluded to in the opening scene of the *Charmides*. Especially relevant to Critias' speech is a contrast intimated in the prologue of the work between the *logoi*, discourses or arguments, intended to engender virtue in the soul and those merely aiming to sharpen one's wits for practical purposes (157a–d). On the one hand, the tale of Zalmoxis is designed to launch Charmides into a journey somewhat comparable to Socrates' own, i.e. a journey during which Charmides will gradually discover the limits of human wisdom and become increasingly aware of what he does not know but may think that he knows. On the other, Critias' clever interpretation of the meaning of 'Know Thyself' points back to his ambiguous remark in the prologue, that his ward's *dianoia* (mind, thinking, wits) will be greatly improved by the conversation with Socrates (157c9–10). It seems that Critias' own engagement in dialectical exercise has enhanced his cleverness and ingenuity. But whether it has also contributed to the cultivation of his soul and the development of his understanding remains to be seen.

It will become apparent that the speech does not in any way relate temperance or self-knowledge to the method of *dialegesthai* or the goal of coming to terms with one's epistemic limitations concerning value. Unquestionably, the speech is an interpretative *tour de force* comparable to Critias' ingenious reading of Hesiod (163b–c), and it highlights and elaborates Critias' explicit commitment to a kind of intellectualism (163e1–164d3).

---

[9] Chapter 1, 23–8.

Nonetheless, as we shall see, no element of the speech indicates that the acquisition or possession of self-knowledge requires the moral and psychological qualities prominent in the Socratic search, such as perseverance, concentration, and courage. I propose that we approach Critias' interpretation and use of the Delphic inscription 'Know Thyself' bearing these reflections in mind.

Let us retrace once more the steps that led Critias to assert, albeit with some hesitation, that *sôphrosynê* is the same thing as knowing oneself (*gignôskein heauton*: 164d3–4). The elenchus immediately preceding the speech showed that, if temperance is the doing or making of something good, the experts in first-order arts or sciences can do temperate deeds and be temperate without necessarily having awareness of their temperance and, therefore, without knowing themselves in respect of the value of their actions or productions. Critias emphatically refused to accept this implication – that a person could be temperate without knowing himself to be (164d2–3). He briefly alluded to the possibility of withdrawing one or more of his earlier concessions (164c7–d2), but in the end chose a different path: capitalise on the belief that he articulated in the aforementioned process, namely that one can have temperance only if one knows oneself. Despite some qualms,[10] he advances the far stronger claim that temperance is just that, knowing oneself.[11]

Given the above train of thought, it is reasonable to infer that Critias' conception of self-knowledge involves some reference to value in a more or a less rigorous sense of that term. Moreover, Critias appears to have in mind some kind of second-order or higher-order knowledge, as opposed to the specialised expertise belonging to the first-order arts and sciences. For it seems that, according to Critias, the temperate person has a kind of knowledge that is both more general and more valuable than any first-order expertise. More general because, as Critias appears to suppose, the domain of temperance or self-knowledge is not restricted to any particular first-order art but ranges over all first-order arts. More elevated, because those endowed with temperance or self-knowledge will always be in a position to make correct value-judgements about the deeds and productions of the first-order experts, whereas, as the preceding elenchus has shown, these latter may not. Even before Critias improvises his speech, then, we have reason to think that his conception of self-knowledge will be markedly different from Socrates' own.

---

[10] σχεδόν: 164d3.   [11] I treat 'self-knowledge' and 'knowing oneself' as equivalent.

We should look at the details of Critias' analysis of the Delphic inscription. Some features of the speech corroborate the suggestion that he thinks of self-knowledge in a way quite different from Socrates. An important difference is that, unlike Plato's Socrates in the *Apology*, he believes that he understands the exact meaning of the god and that he is superior to most men in that regard. First, he states that he fully agrees with the dedicator of the Delphic inscription about its true purpose: the engraved words 'Know Thyself' should be read as the god's greeting (*prosrhêsis*) to the worshippers entering the temple (164d6–e2). Also, he contends that the common greeting 'Be Joyful' is a wrong form of salutation, whereas the right salutation would be 'Know Thyself' (164d7–e2).

Critias sharply distinguishes those who do understand the inscription correctly from those who do not (164e7–165a7) and suggests that the members of the former group are precious few. He appears to assume that, in addition to himself, only the dedicator of the inscription and perhaps a few others understand 'Know Thyself' in the right manner, as the god's greeting to those entering his temple. On the contrary, ordinary people don't understand what the god intends to tell them and make the mistake of taking 'Know Thyself' as a piece of advice. The reason why they fail to grasp the god's riddle is that they are misled by synonymy. While Critias himself realises that, from the god's perspective, 'knowing oneself' and 'being temperate' mean or refer to the same thing, ordinary folk assume, mistakenly, that these two expressions mean or refer to different things. Therefore, they miss the true message of the god, which implies that self-knowledge and temperance entail each other or are identical. And they pass through life without ever understanding that we ought to desire temperance more than we desire joy or health.[12] Thus, Critias presumes to act like the diviners of the Delphic temple: he decodes for the sake of the common men the god's enigmatic speech. He says that the god speaks in riddles, not stating plainly what he means but challenging us to discover his hidden meaning (164e6–7). And he explicitly attributes to the god the thought that he also states on his own behalf, i.e. that 'Know Thyself' really means 'Be Temperate' (164e5–165a1).

It is worth pressing these issues further, because they can be informative about Critias' character, his views, and the direction he is likely to give to the enquiry.

First of all, why does he insist that 'Know Thyself' ought to be interpreted not as a piece of advice, but as a greeting? Philosophically, pieces of

---

[12] Another common form of greeting is 'ἔρρωσο', 'Be Healthy'.

advice and salutations are different sorts of speech act, which imply different sorts of relations between the involved parties and focus on different
kinds of goods. Typically, protreptic or apotreptic advice applies to
a particular action or type of action. In the latter case, advice is frequently
equivalent to a precept, a general rule telling us what we ought or ought not
to do. 'I advise you to avoid foolish risks', 'You do not seem to care for
others but you should', 'If possible, you should avoid telling lies'. In the
former case, the advice may consist in the specific application of a general
rule or may be produced ad hoc. 'Don't dive from such a height, it is risky',
'This time you should think about your sister's feelings', 'In principle it is
bad to lie, but in this case I advise you to do so'. Generally, the purpose of
advice is to help one secure some sort of good – moral or prudential, greater
or lesser, more abstract or more concrete.

Moreover, advice usually implies an asymmetry between someone
who is offering the advice and another who receives it. The advisor is
supposed to know better, see clearer, have more experience, or be in
some other way superior to the advisee. If the Delphic inscription is
understood in the traditional manner, it is a piece of advice given by
the god and presupposes a vastly asymmetrical relationship between
the divine and the human. Just as the god advises his worshippers to
do nothing in excess or to avoid giving rash pledges, so he advises
them also to try to know themselves. On the other hand, if 'Know
Thyself' is read as a greeting, it does not have such an exhortatory
character, and it is questionable whether it entails any asymmetry
between god and man. According to some scholars,[13] Critias leaves
open the possibility that the god may stand on an equal footing with
those whom he greets and who greet him in return[14] – an idea that is
incompatible with traditional religious views regarding the relation
between the divine and the human spheres. Other elements of the
speech can also put strain on the traditional boundary between these
two spheres: the nagging suspicion that Critias is turning the god into
his own mouthpiece; Critias' belief that a few exceptionally intelligent
thinkers, including himself, have access to the god's true meaning;
and his intellectual arrogance vis-à-vis ordinary people unable to
decipher the god's message, which drives a wedge between them and
men like himself rather than between men and gods.

Hence the question arises whether the speech lends support to the
ancient tradition designating Critias, as well as Prodicus and Diagoras, as

---

[13] See Lampert 2010 and note 20 in this chapter.   [14] See Lampert 2010.

atheists,[15] which probably originated in a list composed by Theophrastus[16] and was subsequently used by other ancient authors including Epicurus (Philodemus, *De piet.* col. 19 Obbink) mainly for polemical purposes. The question is especially pressing because Critias' speech appears to be in line with the surviving fragment from the *Sisyphus* (a text fathered on Critias or Euripides, but in fact composed probably by some other author who remained anonymous),[17] according to which the notion of divinity was invented by an exceptionally clever and resourceful man in order to control humans through fear (DK 88 B25). How to answer the aforementioned question, however, is not a straightforward matter.

On the one hand, even though Critias' claims in the speech indicate intellectual pretension and arrogance, they fall short of implying that the gods don't exist.[18] In fact, one might argue that Critias presupposes both the god's existence and his benevolence to those entering his temple. Moreover, if we assume, as some scholars have done, that the object of a greeting is a general and comprehensive good,[19] then Critias' claim that the god intends to greet the worshippers entering his temple by the salutation 'Be Temperate' can be taken to point to an idea agreeable to Socrates as well (156e–157a): no human good is greater than *sôphrosynê* and, therefore, temperance rather than joyfulness[20] ought to be the overarching goal of human life.[21] Furthermore, the fact that Critias interprets the inscription as a greeting addressed by the god to men does not necessarily

---

[15] On the semantic range of ἄθεος, 'atheist', and the cognate name ἀθεότης, 'atheism', see Sedley 2013, 329 and n. 1.

[16] See Sedley 2013, 330.

[17] See Sedley 2013, 337, who makes the case that the *Sisyphus* circulated as an excerpt and was not an entire play.

[18] This is one of the meanings of ἀθεότης, 'atheism', and the sole meaning relevant to our discussion.

[19] On the other hand, the object of a piece of advice is frequently taken to be some specific benefit.

[20] The common greeting 'χαῖρε!' (164d7) means 'Be Joyful!'.

[21] Hyland 1981, 88–93, maintains that Critias' interpretation of the inscription as a greeting indicates the openness and receptivity of the visitor to the temple of Apollo. As Socrates 'greets' the unknown through philosophical questioning, so the visitor 'greets' the god in an open and interrogative, i.e. temperate, manner. According to Hyland, the endorsement of that stance amounts to self-knowledge because it results from the recognition of human incompleteness. On this view, self-knowledge as described by Critias is identical to the Socratic stance: temperate action is the taking of that stance, which Critias renders in terms of a greeting. However, Hyland adds, the irony is that Critias, the dramatic author of the greeting metaphor, does not assume the interrogative stance at all, but rather the opposite. Briefly, I object to Hyland's interpretation for the following reasons. (1) I do not find in Critias' speech anything indicating 'the interrogative stance'. A greeting need not indicate openness and receptivity; it is a complex speech act and, on the present occasion, the god's greeting is best interpreted as pointing to a major, global good, as opposed to a specific and merely prudential one. (2) Critias is not so concerned with the attitude of the visitor entering the temple as with the god's intention with regard to the worshippers. (3) Unlike Hyland, I find nothing inherently wrong in the traditional reading of the inscription as a piece of advice. In particular, I do not see why the

show that he treats these two parties as equal.[22] A salute does not always require that one salutes back, nor is it necessary that the latter person, i.e. the one who returns the salute, perceives the former, i.e. the person who saluted first, as an equal. In these respects, therefore, Critias' speech appears compatible with traditional religion and perhaps Socratic morality as well.

On the other hand, the speech has a whiff of the intellectual climate in Athens in the last decades of the fifth century BC, i.e. the period that the dramatic date of the *Charmides* belongs to. For the Athens of that period provided two crucial necessary conditions for the emergence of atheism as a theoretical stance: the development of the materialist physical system that came to be known as atomism; and the articulation of a social anthropology explaining the origins of religious belief through *nomos*, 'convention'.[23] So far as we can tell, however, atheist authors did not openly assert their beliefs and did not circulate their writings under their own name for fear of persecution. Even if Critias were an atheist, it is unlikely that he would ever have stated his beliefs publicly in speech or in writing. But he could have conveyed them covertly and indirectly, and he could be represented as doing so. I think that his speech in the *Charmides* is sufficiently ambiguous so as to be taken to indicate covert atheism or to be consistent with it. While Critias appears to take for granted the existence of the god, he also may seem irreverent and even blasphemous insofar as he claims to be one of the few who understand the god's true meaning. While he talks about the god's greeting to those who enter his temple, he does not say anything directly bearing on religion or the nature of divinity. As for his ingenious interpretation of the Delphic inscription, he omits a central element of what 'Know Thyself' implies for most Greeks, i.e. the need to become aware of our limitations as human beings and to avoid *hybris* with regard to the gods.

Philosophically, the impact of Critias' speech is clear and important. By interpreting the Delphic inscription in the way he does, he supports and

---

god's advice to the worshippers would preclude them from remaining 'open and aporetic'. The fact that Critias proposes a new interpretation of the inscription does not have to do with the desire to cultivate an 'open and aporetic' attitude, but rather with his desire to stress the great value of temperance or self-knowledge for the good life. On this point, see also the remarks of Tuozzo 2011, 184–8.

[22] Contra Lampert 2010, who contends that greetings must be between equals and that, therefore, by interpreting the inscription as a greeting, Critias treats the god as an equal and winks to other atheists like himself. Worse, according to Lampert, Critias treats Socrates as someone in the know, i.e. as someone who also thinks that there are really no gods.

[23] Sedley 2013 argues convincingly in defence of that claim. As he points out, Plato's *Laws* X 885e–886c and 888b–c present atheism as a widespread current in Athens.

strengthens the intuition motivating the speech, namely that it is impossible for a person to be temperate but be ignorant of himself in respect of his temperance. The speech advances the view that, in truth, 'Know Thyself' means 'Be Temperate', and that knowing oneself and having temperance amount to the same thing. One implication of this definition, which will become crucial later in the argument, is that no one can be temperate on account of their expertise in some particular domain. Rather, if certain first-order experts happen to have temperance, this will be because they possess self-knowledge, not because they have scientific knowledge of their respective fields. Another feature of Critias' conception of temperance has begun to emerge as well. As mentioned, the speech seems to me to intimate that temperance or self-knowledge differs from the other forms of (expert) knowledge in significant ways, notably in respect of being more general and higher-order than they are. Critias has not yet articulated these aspects of his own conception of the virtue, nor has he drawn attention to the peculiarly self-referential character of knowing oneself. He will do so in the debate that follows.

CHAPTER 8

Socrates and Critias Debate the Technê *Analogy*
From 'Knowing Oneself' to 'the Knowledge of Itself'
(165c4–166e3)

As might be expected, Socrates refuses to accept Critias' claim that temperance is knowing oneself for the reason that he believes himself to be ignorant about the topic (165b5–c1), and expresses the wish to consider that definition further in order to decide whether or not it seems acceptable (165c1–2).[1] At the very outset, then, Socrates distances himself from the notion of self-knowledge that Critias has in mind, whatever the latter may be. And he begins the investigation in typical fashion, by asking his interlocutor to clarify exactly what knowing oneself amounts to. To contribute to this task, Socrates will introduce one of the most familiar features of Plato's so-called Socratic dialogues, namely a set of analogies between virtue and *technê* or the *technai*, art or the arts. In the debate that will follow, he will use '*technê*' and '*epistêmê*' interchangeably[2] to refer to all sorts of first-order branches of expertise, including medicine, architecture, mathematics, geometry, and weaving.[3] And assuming, as he often does in

---

[1] As in the *Laches* and the *Euthyphro*, so in the present instance, the search begins when one of the characters puts forward a definition of a virtue in the capacity of an expert, while Socrates denies having expertise regarding the virtue under discussion. Even though Critias does not explicitly state that he is an expert on *sôphrosynê*, his confidence regarding the temperance of his ward as well as his elaborate speech about the meaning of the Delphic inscription strongly suggest that he thinks of himself as one of the very few experts on the topic.

[2] Consider, e.g., the *Gorgias* (500b), where Socrates refers to medicine as a τέχνη, as compared to e.g. *Charm.* 165c, where he calls it an ἐπιστήμη. In the *Republic*, the one family of terms frequently substitutes for the other, especially in contexts involving the use of the art model for virtue: as a craftsman makes mistakes only insofar as he lacks ἐπιστήμη, so the strong ruler makes mistakes in pursuing his own interest only insofar as he lack ἐπιστήμη (340e1–341a3). And like all other τέχναι (342c4–9) or ἐπιστῆμαι (342c11), the art or science of ruling looks after the good of the weaker, i.e. the rulers' subjects, and not the good of the stronger, i.e. the rulers themselves (342c11–12). In the *Statesman*, the Eleatic Stranger calls mathematics and other 'pure' sciences τέχναι (*Plt.* 258d; also *Rep.* 532c4 and elsewhere), whereas one might have expected them to be characterised as ἐπιστῆμαι. And while he initially labels the political art as an ἐπιστήμη (258b), he then classifies it as a τέχνη (258e, 259b). See also the next note.

[3] As I mentioned (Chapter 1, 5 and note 8), I endorse the view that, although in many contexts Plato uses 'τέχνη', art, and ἐπιστήμη, science or (expert) knowledge, interchangeably (Roochnik 1996, 298–9; Woodruff 1992, 66), he does not consider them, strictly speaking, synonyms but treats the

other dialogues, that these forms of expertise are relevantly analogous to virtue (presently, *sôphrosynê*), he will attempt to draw certain implications concerning a particular aspect of *sôphrosynê*, namely what it is *of* and what it may be good *for*. And he will suggest that these implications also concern the people who possess *sôphrosynê* and are temperate. Nonetheless, for the first and only time in Plato's Socratic dialogues, Socrates' reliance on the *technê* analogy will be seriously challenged. Critias will deny that temperance is art-like in respect of its object and function, and eventually will appear to prevail: Socrates will back down and will assist Critias to fully articulate what he takes to be unique about temperance and submit it to dialectical scrutiny. At present, our aim will be to lay out in detail this methodological debate between the two interlocutors, highlight what is involved in their respective stances, and indicate what is at stake. To begin, it seems apposite to say a few things about the nature of the analogy and its philosophical importance.

I

While the Socratic dialogues are interspersed with analogies between the virtues and the *technai*, Socrates rarely suggests an argument in defence of the contention that virtue is a sort of *technê*.[4] Rather, he usually appears to assume that the former is identical to or closely resembles the latter. And he often compares the possessor of virtue or of some particular virtue with an expert in the arts and sciences: a doctor, mathematician, geometer, architect, grammarian, and musical performer, but also a cobbler, weaver, carpenter, or some other lowly artisan. Typically, Socrates draws inferences about the virtuous person on the basis of features exhibited by first-order experts. For instance, he argues against Meletus that, as the horse-trainer is the only person who benefits horses while the many harm them, so he himself may be the only person who benefits the Athenians while the many

τέχνη–ἐπιστήμη relationship as a case of 'interchangeability by synecdoche' (Hulme Kozey 2018). While in many contexts (including the present one) the terms substitute for each other in virtue of their substantial semantic overlap, each term retains its own connotations and these two sets of connotations are not identical. One of the examples that Hulme Kozey discusses is found in *Rep.* I (332d2): there, justice is called a τέχνη analogous to medicine and cooking, presumably because the argument focuses on the notions of function and benefit. I suggest that something similar holds for the passage to be discussed in the present chapter, so long as the debate focuses on the object and function of each art. On the other hand, once the interlocutors agree that henceforth they will take temperance to be a form of knowledge that has the peculiarity of being oriented solely towards knowledge itself, they will consistently call temperance an ἐπιστήμη, not a τέχνη, for they will focus on the rational and cognitive connotations of the virtue.

[4] Exceptions include *Prot.* 352a and *Men.* 86e–89a.

corrupt them (*Ap.* 24e1–25c4). Or he counters Thrasymachus' claim that the true ruler unfailingly operates in his own interest by arguing that, in fact, the true ruler acts like the experts in first-order arts: as doctors, sea-captains, horse-breeders, etc. direct their activities to the good of others, so the ruler, insofar as he is a ruler, seeks what is advantageous to his subjects rather than what is advantageous to himself (*Rep.* 340c–342e). There is vast disagreement about the nature and scope of such arguments and, generally, about what the craft model amounts to and what purpose it serves.[5] But almost everyone agrees on this point: regardless of whether or to what extent the character Socrates is committed to the craft model in the so-called early dialogues of Plato, there comes a time when he subjects it to scrutiny, demonstrates its weaknesses, and abandons it altogether.[6]

Traditional readings frequently suggest the following outline. The early Socrates uses the *technê* model to elucidate the intellectualist thesis that virtue is a kind of knowledge and to lend support to a series of paradoxes related to that thesis: virtue or knowledge is sufficient for happiness, all error is due to ignorance, all desire is for the good, and weakness of the will is impossible. To achieve his goal, Socrates focuses on the intellectual and cognitive elements of *technê*[7] to match his rationalistic conception of virtue. Namely, he suggests that, like every genuine expertise, virtue should be supposed to consist in the expert mastery of a body of knowledge that is governed by rules, uses a particular set of methods and tools, has

---

[5] Scholars who believe that the Socrates of the so-called early Platonic dialogues seeks a model for moral knowledge patterned on the model of first-order *technai* include Gregory Vlastos, Terence Irwin, Paul Woodruff, Martha Nussbaum, Terry Penner, Rosamond Kent Sprague, and many others. However, they differ in their interpretations of what the Platonic Socrates takes a *technê* to be, and they also disagree as to whether Plato eventually abandons that model entirely or, alternatively, retains some variant of it in his middle or late works. Roochnik 1996, on the other hand, argues against all proponents of what he calls SAT (Standard Account of *Technê*), regardless of the differences between their positions. He contends that, in fact, the so-called early dialogues *reject* *technê* as a model of moral knowledge, in favour of the view that moral knowledge is non-technical knowledge. Here, I shall not discuss this matter in any general way. I shall focus exclusively on the *Charmides* and revisit the question of whether this dialogue does in fact reject the *technê* analogy, as it is commonly believed to do.

[6] This assumption is shared by developmentalists and unitarians alike. See also the previous note.

[7] This hypothesis readily explains Plato's interchangeable use of '*technê*' and '*epistêmê*'. According to Emily Hulme Kozey (see note 3 in this chapter), the synecdoche consists precisely in this: in virtue of the fact that *technê* and *epistêmê* overlap in part, i.e. in respect of their cognitive elements, the corresponding terms are frequently employed to substitute each other. Unlike synonyms, however, each of them has its own distinct set of connotations. The latter partially overlap but are not identical. Notably, '*technê*' preserves connotations related to manual work, whereas '*epistêmê*' has prominent connotations of a rule-governed, rationalised, and coherent body of beliefs constituting the cognitive part of an expertise. This fact will become especially important later, when the interlocutors will completely abandon the use of '*technê*' in favour of '*epistêmê*', which they will use to the end of the argument.

a distinctive function or work (*ergon*), and pursues in a systematic manner its own proprietary goal.[8] Importantly, like every other *technê*, virtue is just the sort of knowledge susceptible to giving a *logos* – a rational explanation of its own practices. And because of the latter feature, one might expect that virtue, like every other *technê*, is transmissible from one person to another and can be taught.

Two further features of the *technê* analogy are significant. First, in the same way that every first-order *technê* is set over a distinct domain and governs whatever falls within it, virtue too must be set over a distinct if greatly extended sphere and must be taken to govern everything belonging to that sphere.[9] In other words, just as medicine is *of* health, arithmetic *of* number, divination *of* foretelling the future, and carpentry *of* producing wooden artefacts, and these objects or subject-matters determine the function and goal of the corresponding forms of expertise and experts, so also virtue must be *of something* (*tinos*), i.e. it must govern a domain that determines the *ergon* of virtue and, consequently, of the virtuous agent. Second, in tandem with fifth-century attitudes towards the first-order arts and their products, Plato's Socrates underscores the beneficial character of the *technai* and the difference that they make to the preservation and quality of human life.[10] And he repeatedly suggests that, likewise but much more so, insofar as virtue is an expertise directed towards a certain goal, its possession and achievement must be of the greatest benefit to us. Thus Plato's Socrates develops, many believe, a conception of virtue as the crowning achievement of human rationality and the essential component of the good life: virtue as an expertise whose distinct domain is the realm of value, whose function or work consists in the fulfilment of our peculiarly human capacities, and whose goal is nothing less than happiness for both the individual and society. Indeed, it seems plausible to infer that Plato's Socrates uses the *technê* analogy to pursue and reframe an aspiration initially expressed by the great sophists of the Classical era.[11] That is, he argues, in different dialogues and from different perspectives, that the pursuit of virtue coincides with the exercise of the true political art and that those devoting their lives to it are the only people fit to rule the state.

To complete this fairly traditional scenario of the trajectory of the *technê* model in Plato, we must turn to the dialogues that developmentalists and unitarians treat, for different reasons, as transitional. These dialogues are

[8] The interrelations between the domain, object, *ergon* (function or work), and benefits of a *technê* or *epistêmê* will be clarified and investigated in the Argument from Benefit (see Chapter 11, *passim*).
[9] This feature is rarely discussed in the secondary literature. A notable exception is Barney 2021.
[10] See, for instance, Nussbaum 1986.   [11] See Barney 2021.

taken to show Socrates challenging central features of the *technê* analogy and drastically undermining the idea that virtue is relevantly art-like. The main reason given is that Plato gradually comes to acknowledge that human beings are motivated by non-rational as well as rational forces and that, therefore, virtue cannot be merely a matter of knowledge but also depends on natural inclination, training, and habit. Thus, it has been claimed that the arguments for and against the teachability of virtue in the *Protagoras* and the *Meno*, and the refutation of the hypothesis of a kingly art in the *Euthydemus*, mark Plato's decisive turn away from the Socratic craft analogy and towards his own substantive ethics.[12] The same conclusion has been drawn, with even greater confidence,[13] with regard to the central argument of the *Charmides*. The reason lies in the passage that we shall now discuss: a rare instance of explicit and sustained criticism against a particular aspect of the analogy between the virtue of *sôphrosynê* and various branches of technical expertise. As mentioned, the almost unanimous consensus is that the criticisms exercised by Critias against Socrates' use of the *technê* model are successful[14] and reveal Plato's readiness to shake off the spell of Socrates and open his own wings.[15]

While we must bear in mind that hypothesis, we shan't be able to fully assess its merits until we reach the end of the search. In this chapter, we shall take the first step towards that goal. We shall closely follow the moves that the two interlocutors make in debating the *technê* analogy and determine their respective dialectical positions at the end of this exchange.[16] But, first, let me briefly explain why I believe that it is important to set the record straight regarding the stance of the *Charmides* vis-à-vis the analogy between virtue and the arts. Historically, this question bears on one's overall interpretation of the *Charmides* and its position in the Platonic corpus. If the *Charmides* is a transitional dialogue, it should be classified as such for the right reasons and not for the wrong ones. Exegetically, the

---

[12] The argument advanced by Jones 2013 against the standard reading of *Euthydemus* 279c4–282d3 implies, I believe, that Socrates modifies his attitude with regard to the *technê* analogy without, however, completely abandoning it.

[13] J. I. Beare was perhaps the first to declare that the *Charmides* more than any other early dialogue of Plato distances itself from the Socratic idea that virtue is equivalent to *epistêmê* (see Beare 1914, 43, and also Tuckey 1951, 33 and n. 2).

[14] See e.g. the account of Guthrie 1975, 168, and the reference of the latter to Stenzel 1940, 36.

[15] According to unitarian accounts, the *Charmides* marks a point at which Plato judges it appropriate to represent Socrates as leaving behind the *technê* analogy and coming up with a new set of conceptual tools.

[16] From now on, the threads of Plato's argument become ever more tightly interlaced. Every detail has philosophical significance. To facilitate the reader's task, I shall quote in full each passage under discussion.

widespread assumption that, in the passage to be discussed, Socrates abandons the *technê* analogy is largely responsible for the tendency of many scholars to interpret the elenchus occupying roughly the second half of the dialogue, and notably the Argument from Relatives, in a subversive manner: while the ostensible point of the latter is that there probably cannot be a science that, unlike all other sciences, is orientated solely towards itself, the examples that Socrates brings up in order to defend that contention do in fact undermine it. As I have indicated,[17] I reject that reading because it misconstrues Socrates' own position, violates the principle of charity, and disregards the say-what-you-believe rule of the Socratic method. Therefore, in my view, there is strong motivation for us to reconsider whether it is true that the *Charmides* does imply or strongly suggest the rejection of the *technê* model of virtue.

Philosophically, the ethical intellectualism inherent in that model has, in fact, its own attractions. Not only does it highlight certain structural features of virtue as a sort of knowledge or understanding, but it can also have important implications for politics and society. However, the power and appeal of the *technê* model cannot be properly measured if we do not explore further the issue of what virtue as a *technê* might be really like. In the *Charmides*, Plato's Socrates makes some moves in that direction. He intimates that the *technê* of virtue, if one may call it that, is not merely a matter of cognitive mastery, but also entails that the virtuous people will dedicate themselves to the single-minded, disinterested, and life-long pursuit of their goal in much the same way as that in which the best experts endeavour to fulfil their respective tasks.[18] If we consider virtue in such terms, we need to think about rationality and cognition, functions and norms, systematicity and method, success and failure, and the price-tags attached to each of them. Let us keep these reflections alive as we walk from this point onwards, together with Socrates and Critias, from one passage to another and from one argument to the next until we reach the end of the search.

2

For if in fact temperance is knowing something, then it is obvious that it would be a sort of knowledge or science and, moreover, a science of something. Or not? – Indeed it is, he replied, of oneself. – And isn't medicine the science of health? – Very much so. – So, I said, if you asked

---

[17] Chapter 1, 34–6, 38–40.   [18] Barney 2021 develops this point.

me what use medicine is to us, being the science of health, and what work it achieves, I would answer that it achieves no small benefit. For it produces health, a fine work for us, if you are willing to accept as much. – I am. – And likewise, if you asked me what work is achieved by housebuilding, since it is the science of how to build, I would say houses. And the same holds for the other arts as well. Therefore you too, on behalf of temperance, since you claim that it is a science of oneself, should be able to tell us the answer, if asked 'Critias, given that temperance is the science of oneself, what fine work worthy of the name does it achieve for us? Come, do tell us'. (165c4–e2)

Even though Socrates calls temperance an *epistêmê*,[19] the terms in which he argues belong unmistakably to the *technê* analogy. *If* temperance is knowing something, then it is an *epistêmê*. And *if* it is an *epistêmê*, like every other *epistêmê* or *technê* (*kai tôn allôn technôn*: 165d6), it will have a work or function (*ergon*) and a domain[20] distinct and different from itself.[21] To put it a different way, assuming that temperance is a science and also that it is a relative, it follows that, like all the other sciences and arts, temperance too will be aliorelative: it will be *of* something – i.e., as Socrates seems to think, a correlative other than itself.[22] Socrates takes it that what a science is *of* constitutes the object or subject-matter[23] of that science and determines its own domain and the benefit that it brings.[24] As medicine is *of health* and its beneficial function consists in making us healthy, so temperance must be of *something* other than itself and its beneficial work must be determined by reference to that *something*. On these grounds, Socrates now asks Critias what the proprietary object of temperance might be. The question is far more difficult than it might initially appear. For, according to Critias' definition, temperance is knowing oneself, and the relation between the *epistêmê* responsible for the knowing and the thing known is tricky. Grammatically and

---

[19] Here, the expertise of building is characterised as an *epistêmê*, whereas soon afterwards it will be a *technê* (165e7). On the suggestion that *epistêmê* and *technê* are used interchangeably by *synecdochê* and their use depends largely on their immediate context, i.e. the terms and notions surrounding them, see nn. 2 and 3 in this chapter. Given that the interlocutors never characterise the knowledge of oneself as a *technê* but always as an *epistêmê*, it is natural to expect that first-order forms of expertise mentioned in that context will be frequently (but not always) called *epistêmai* as well. As we shall see, Critias' notion of temperance as a strictly reflexive form of knowledge will always be called an *epistêmê* (not a *technê*), and it will be claimed to govern the other *epistêmai* (not the other *technai*). As mentioned, the interlocutors' choice of terms appears determined by the fact that they focus on the predominantly intellectual and cognitive nature of this expertise.
[20] See note 8 in this chapter.
[21] Note Socrates' use of conditionals: he is appropriately cautious with regard to the identification of, generally, knowing something (γιγνώσκειν: 165c4) with having an *epistêmê* of something.
[22] The object need not be a corresponding *relative*, but Plato seems to think that it is.
[23] A relevant distinction between object and subject-matter will be drawn later (165e3–166a2).
[24] Compare *Rep.* I 341c–342e, 346a–347a.

syntactically, the *epistêmê* under consideration appears to be aliorelative: the phrase '*epistêmê heautou*' appears to imply that this *epistêmê* is of something distinct from itself, namely oneself. Philosophically, however, it would seem that the science doing the knowing and the object of knowledge occur in one and the same person: the temperate knower both is the subject of knowing himself/herself and constitutes the object of that capacity, or, on an alternative reading, it both engages in the activity of knowing himself/herself and constitutes the object of that activity.

Even so, Socrates contends that a distinction needs to be drawn between the science equivalent to temperance and what that science is of. An obvious move would be to claim that temperance is knowledge of the self. For although the self is a notoriously elusive item, it is arguably distinct from the *epistêmê* that knows it. Thus, in the terms of the *technê* analogy, as health is the correlative of medicine and buildings the correlative of the building art, so the self could be posited as the correlative of temperance.[25] It is important to note that Socrates has high expectations regarding the work of temperance and the benefits that it yields. Whatever its *ergon* is, he says that it must be 'worthy of the name' (165e2) – an expectation that Critias probably shares. At present, however, neither interlocutor gives us information about the sorts of benefits he may have in mind.

Critias responds to Socrates as follows:

> But Socrates, he said, you are not conducting the enquiry in the right manner. For this science is not like the other sciences [*epistêmai*], nor indeed are the other sciences like each other. Yet you are conducting the investigation as if they were alike. For tell me, he said, what is the work [*ergon*] of the art [*technê*] of calculation or the art of geometry, comparable to the way a house is the work of the art of building, or a coat is the work of the art of weaving, or many other such works are those of many arts that one might be able to point to? Can you, in your turn, point out to me some work of that kind in those [two] cases? But you cannot. (165e3–166a2)

Dialectically, Critias' move is squarely within the rules. For, as Aristotle would remark (*Top* VIII 157b34–6),[26] in his role as questioner Socrates has every right to demand that Critias should accept the inductive generalisation that every art and science has a distinct object, unless Critias can bring

---

[25] Already at this stage of the debate, the interlocutors appear to rely on a constitutive view of relatives and relations, including the sciences or arts and their relations to their respective proprietary objects. See Duncombe 2012a and 2020 *passim*.

[26] I am grateful to Paul Kalligas for drawing my attention to this passage. According to Aristotle's analysis, when the answerer cannot adduce counterexamples against the questioner's inductive generalisations, then the latter count as a dialectical proof.

some counterexample. And Critias does bring quite effective counterexamples: calculation and geometry are arts which do not have distinct products in the sense in which housebuilding and weaving do. Again, Critias is portrayed as having consummate dialectical skills that find no close parallel in any other character of Plato's Socratic dialogues other than Socrates himself.[27] Also, from an intuitive point of view, Critias' criticism seems eminently plausible.[28] Not all arts and sciences seem to be alike in respect of their function and outcome. The arts of building and weaving aim at the production of ontologically self-standing products, whereas the arts of mathematics and geometry do not have such an aim. Nonetheless, the latter do not for that reason qualify any less as arts or sciences. Critias suggests that temperance is more similar to mathematics and geometry than it is to building and weaving: like the former pair, but unlike the latter, it is not *of* something distinct and separate from itself, such as a cloak or a house. All the same, it qualifies as an expertise at least as much as the so-called productive arts do.

Up to this point, Critias' criticism of the *technê* analogy has a narrow focus. On the one hand, he takes Socrates' use of the *technê* analogy to suggest that temperance must produce some ontologically independent thing and retorts that not all arts and sciences aim at such things. On the other, he has given no indication as yet that he objects to what we may call the requirement of aliorelativity: the idea lying at the core of the *technê* analogy, that every art or science is related to a proprietary object distinct from the art or science itself. Nor does Critias yet challenge an assumption that Socrates builds into the *technê* analogy, namely that whatever benefit derives from the exercise of an art or science has to do with the aliorelative object of this latter. Because medicine has health as its own object, it is beneficial in just that regard. And because the art of weaving aims to produce cloth, it is profitable in exactly that respect. In sum, Critias' initial moves do not affect the art model at its core. Consider Socrates' answer:

> What you say is true, I replied. But what I can point out to you is what thing, different from the science itself, each of these sciences is *of*. For instance, the science of calculation is presumably the science of the even and the odd, how they are quantitatively related to themselves and to each other. Is that right? – Of course, he said. – The odd and the even being different from the art of calculation itself? – How could they not be? – And again, the art of weighing is concerned with weighing heavier and lighter

---

[27] Regarding the mastery of dialectical rules, Protagoras is the only character comparable to Critias.
[28] See Guthrie 1975, 168–9.

weight, and the heavy and the light are different from the art of weighing itself. Do you agree? – I do. – Tell me, then, what is that of which temperance is a science and which is different from temperance itself? (166a3–b6)

Socrates is not concerned with the distinction that Critias introduced between productive and non-productive arts, for it is irrelevant to his point. Clearly, he intends the contention that every form of expertise has an object or governs a domain distinct from itself to be applicable to arts or sciences as different as medicine, housebuilding, weaving, arithmetic, measurement, dancing, boxing, and lyre-playing.[29] And his commitment to the *technê* model of virtue inclines him to infer that temperance too, if it is a kind of knowledge, must have, likewise, an object other than itself and extend over the domain determined by that object. Having thus clarified his meaning, Socrates puts his question to Critias again in clearer terms: assuming, on the grounds of the analogy with the first-order arts, that temperance is of something other than itself, what is this? It does not make any difference whether the latter is an ontologically independent product or a distinct subject-matter. What Socrates is asking Critias to do is identify what temperance is a science *of* in terms that do not comprise reference to that science itself. The following reply by Critias provides the main textual basis for the virtually unanimous agreement that, here, Plato parts company with Socrates by denouncing the flaws of the *technê* model and by suggesting that it should be completely abandoned.

There it is, Socrates, he said. You have reached the real issue of the investigation, namely in what respect temperance differs from all the other sciences. But you are trying to find some similarity between it and them and that is not how things stand. Rather, while all the others are sciences of something other than themselves and not of themselves, this one alone is the science both of all the other sciences and of itself [*epistêmê autê heautês*]. And these matters are far from having escaped your attention. In fact, I believe that you are doing precisely what you just said that you were not doing. For you are trying to refute me, abandoning the topic that the argument is about. (166b7–c6)

At first glance, Critias appears to be on the right track when he contends that Socrates' methodological procedure is at odds with the purpose of the search. His argument is this: since they want to examine what temperance is,

---

[29] Contrast e.g. the view advanced by Nussbaum 1986 and her criticisms of Irwin 1977 (Nussbaum 1986, 73–4) and compare with the cautionary remarks by Vlastos 1978. My own approach is indebted to Vlastos 1978 and implies that Socrates' observation cuts across the distinction between productive and performative arts or other kinds of arts (notably, acquisitive).

they should focus on what is distinctive about it, not on what it shares in common with other sciences; but the *technê* model relies on commonalities, not differences between virtue and the first-order arts; hence, it impedes rather than advances the investigation underway. Worse, Critias appears to think that Socrates' misguided application of the *technê* model is deliberate on his part (166c3–4) and accuses him of intellectual dishonesty: even though Socrates knows that the art model is misleading in this context, he is using it merely in order to win the debate (166c4–6). Critias therefore steers the argument onto what he believes to be the right track, by specifying what he takes to be distinct about temperance in relation to all the other sciences or arts: 'while all the others are sciences of something other than themselves and not of themselves, this one alone is the science both of all the other sciences and of itself (*epistêmê autê heautês*)' (166c1–3).

In the important passage quoted immediately below, Socrates rejects summarily the accusation of contentiousness and explains why he wishes to pursue the investigation. He throws new light on the nature of the elenchus and on his conception of his own self-knowledge.

> If my chief effort is to refute you, I said, how can you possibly think that I do it for any other reason than that for the sake of which I would also investigate what I am saying, i.e. the fear of inadvertently supposing at any time that I knew something while I didn't know it? And so this is what I am now doing: I am examining the argument first and foremost for my own sake, but perhaps also for the sake of my other companions. Or do you not think that the discovery of the nature of each being is a common good for almost all humans? (166c7–d7)

The first thing to note is Socrates' implicit admission that he sometimes thinks he knows something. But he also realises that he has to check again, and he wishes to continue the enquiry precisely because he fears that he might suppose that he knows (*eidenai*: 166d2) something that he doesn't know. Furthermore, he makes the significant remark that he wishes to conduct an investigation primarily for his own sake, but also 'perhaps' (*isôs*: 166d4) for the sake of his friends. This confirms that, although Socratic cross-examinations are typically *ad hominem* and proceed on premises conceded by the interlocutor, they somehow benefit the questioner as well as the answerer: Socrates engages in them primarily in order to gain self-knowledge and only secondarily in order to help his interlocutor scrutinise his own beliefs. Presumably, the converse holds true of the interlocutor, if the latter is a right-thinking person. In this sense, the Socratic elenchus is genuinely a joint search: each of the two participants has something important to gain, even though, formally speaking, the contention under scrutiny as well as the premises of the argument belong to the answerer and not to Socrates himself. Yet another comment by Socrates is revelatory about his own view of the goal of the elenchus, and may tell us something about his relation to Critias as well: he asks Critias, rhetorically, whether he doesn't share with him the conviction that 'the discovery of the truth about everything there is is a common good for almost all men' (166d4–6). His tone seems to me to suggest that he is merely reminding Critias of something that has been commonplace in their conversations, much as in the *Crito* he reminds Crito of their 'serious discussions' regarding the principle of justice and the rejection of retaliation (*Crit.* 49a–b). Socrates appears confident that Critias will readily acknowledge the value of discovering the truth about each of the things there are[30] and, consequently, will withdraw his accusations and agree to continue the conversation. This is exactly what happens (166d7).

On the other hand, Critias appears to have gained the upper hand in the debate. For, as it seems at present, he has successfully met the challenge issued by Socrates that, if temperance is an *epistêmê*, then, like every other science or art, it must be of something other than itself. Critias contends that, on the contrary, temperance differs from the other sciences in just this respect: while these latter are of something other than themselves and not of themselves, temperance alone is of itself and the other sciences and not of any other object. As we shall see later, this amounts to the claim that temperance alone is a science of science (and of its privation) and of nothing else, with the consequence that temperance alone governs the other sciences, whereas each of them governs only its own specific domain. In sum, Critias' position implies that the *technê* model for virtue is misleading: there is really no similarity between temperance and the first-order sciences or arts in respect of their corresponding correlative objects. For his own part, Socrates chooses to put an end to that dispute by conceding his interlocutor's claim and inviting him to attend to its investigation (166e1–2). At this early point, we simply do not have enough information to decide whether Socrates makes this move in earnest, tacitly acknowledging that the *technê* model is flawed and that Critias is right to insist that temperance alone, unlike every other science or art, is directed towards science itself and no other object distinct from itself. I urge that we keep an open mind about this matter and monitor it in the chapters that follow.

Nonetheless, it is worth mentioning at the outset that the *Republic* arguably offers grounds for being cautious about accepting too readily the traditional view according to which, in the *Charmides*, Socrates pushes

---

[30] ἕκαστον τῶν ὄντων ὅπῃ ἔχει: 166d6.

the craft model aside and, in particular, abandons the assumption that virtue has an object or governs a domain distinct from itself. In order to undermine Thrasymachus' claims that justice is the advantage of the stronger (*Rep.* 340c) and, moreover, that the stronger or the ruler, insofar as he is a ruler, does not err about his own advantage (340d–341a), Socrates argues that in fact every *technê* (342c4–6) or *epistêmê* (342c11) is orientated towards the good of the object that it governs and not towards its own good. The doctor's art entails that he governs and seeks the good of his patients and not his own (341c), the art of seamanship entails that the captain rules over and looks after the good of his sailors and not his own (341c–d), and the same holds for all other arts and sciences. No art or science needs the help of another art in order to determine the good of its own proprietary object and no art or science is orientated towards itself (342a–b). Medicine does not judge its own interest but the interest of the human body (342c), the equestrian art does not seek its own interest but the interest of the horses (342c), and, generally, no art aims at its own interest (because it is complete and does not need to) but rather at the interest of what it is an art of (342c). And since each science (*epistêmê*: 342c11) rules over its own object and is stronger in that respect, it follows that the ruler, who possesses the art of ruling and is stronger, looks after the interest of the objects of his art, i.e. his subjects, who are weaker, and not after his own interest (342c).

Notwithstanding the considerable differences between the two dialogues, it is striking that in the *Republic* as well as in the *Charmides* Socrates argues for a very similar view: all the sciences or arts have as their object something distinct from themselves, not (or perhaps not mainly) themselves.[31] Besides, as in the former dialogue, so in the latter (*Rep.* 346a), Socrates argues that every art or science is individuated precisely by reference to its own distinct object. Every time we judge that an art is different from others, we make this judgement in virtue of the fact that it has a different power (*dynamis*). And this power is typically related to the distinct object, work, and benefit peculiar to the art in question and not to any other art (346a).[32] To summarise this point, I suggest that, in the first book of the *Republic* (as well as later in that work) Plato's Socrates argues for a cluster of views about the *technai*, including the *technê* of ruling, which are closely similar to the position that he initially defends vis-à-vis Critias (*Charm.* 165c4–166b6) but eventually appears to give up. In both

---

[31] At *Rep.* 342a–b Socrates goes as far as suggesting that reflexivity implies regress.
[32] See Duncombe 2020, *passim*. Compare Harte 2017.

cases the central idea is that every *technê*,[33] including temperance and ruling, is typically or exclusively[34] related to and directed towards a proprietary object distinct from the art or science itself. This parallel should give us pause regarding the concession that Socrates makes to Critias about temperance, i.e. the concession that the latter is a science directed only towards science (i.e. towards itself and the other sciences) and no other object. We should not assume, without further examination, that the concession in question represents Socrates' better judgement rather than a strategic move on the chessboard.

Moving on, I shall briefly address the vexed issue of the transition effected by Critias from the fairly innocuous claims that temperance is knowing oneself (*gignôskein heauton*: 165b4) and that it is knowledge or science of oneself (*epistêmê heautou*: 165e1) to the peculiar contention that temperance alone is a science of itself (*epistêmê autê heautês*: 166c3), as well as of the other sciences. There is extensive literature on this topic and I shall therefore restrict my comments to the origins of the notion of a 'science of science', the hypothesis that it may reflect a view held by the historical Critias, and some speculations as to how it may be related to Socrates' conception of virtue.

T. G. Tuckey's useful survey of nineteenth- and early twentieth-century scholarship[35] gives a sense of the range and quality of interpretations that have been on offer. For example, according to Grube, Critias posits that temperance is knowledge of the self and problematises the question of how the knowing subject can be the object of his/her own knowledge. Hence, the question of whether a knowledge of itself is possible amounts to the query whether self-knowledge is possible, and Critias' inability to establish the former entails his inability to defend the latter. In a similar vein, von Arnim maintains that the transition under discussion proves that Critias is entirely confused. Worse, Bonitz believes that this transition marks the beginning of a long digression, since, in his view, the investigation concerning the 'science of science' has no relation to the main goal of the dialogue, which is to define *sôphrosynê*. On the other hand, Schirlitz argues that the 'knowledge of oneself' is closely connected with the 'knowledge of knowledge' so that the former notion entails the latter. Likewise, Susemihl suggests that the 'knowledge of itself and everything else that is knowledge' constitutes an explanation of what it is to know oneself. In his view, 'knowledge of knowledge' is equivalent to 'knowledge of oneself', because

[33] The point could be extended, generally, to every power, but this is controversial (see previous note).
[34] Accounts of the *Republic* differ widely regarding this point. The same holds regarding the Argument from Relatives in the *Charmides*: see Chapter 10.
[35] Tuckey 1951, 33–7, who also gives the relevant references.

the true self just *is* knowledge. In sharp contrast, Pohlenz argues that the transition in question is a fallacy and Plato flags that fact. In reality, according to Pohlenz, there are no conceptual links between the 'knowledge of oneself' and the 'knowledge or science of itself and the other sciences'. The latter is merely a theory that Plato wishes to shoot down, whereas the former conception remains intact. On an entirely different wavelength, Taylor maintains that Critias' identification of self-knowledge with the 'science of itself and the other sciences' is an effort to turn moral psychology into epistemology.

Such views have been developed by recent interpretations as well. These dwell also on the question of where the notion of 'a science of itself and all the other sciences' may derive from, and the answer differs according to each author's negative or positive view about Plato's portrayal of Critias. For instance, according to one approach, the 'science of itself and the other sciences' has a sophistic ring[36] and corroborates the picture of Critias as a representative of the new learning taught by the sophists.[37] According to another, the notion of a 'science of itself and the other sciences' derives from the intellectualism detected in the extant remains of Critias' writings and alluded to in the *Charmides* as well.[38] A group of interpretations propose that Critias' final definition of temperance is a competent response to the 'what is X?' question, but also conveys Critias' aristocratic values and attachments – especially, Critias' deep-seated belief that temperance essentially consists in doing noble deeds including, first and foremost, deeds related to the successful governance of the city.[39] Each of these positions

---

[36] For example, Tuckey 1951, 39, claims that Critias proposes 'knowledge of itself and the other sciences' as the definition of temperance because of his sophistic love for antitheses.

[37] As Tuozzo 2011, 66–7, mentions, there are different interpretations of the historical Critias as a sophist. An older strand attributes to him an egoistic hedonism related to the conviction that might is right and to his deeds as the leader of the Thirty, whereas a more recent strand argues that Critias represents a kind of sophistry which professes to have a craftlike knowledge of moral and political matters and which, in virtue of that (so to speak) technological knowledge, claims the right to supreme power. (A notable proponent of this latter view is Schmid 1998: see, for instance, 47–8.) Yet another strand of interpretation, I suggest, adopts a more neutral tone and attempts to draw a connection between the techniques of Critias in the *Charmides* and the sophistic training of his historical counterpart: see, for example, Tuckey 1951.

[38] See Notomi 2000 and 2003, and also Tsouna 1998.

[39] So Tuozzo 2011, 199, who also adds: 'such political management must in some sense control or oversee the activity of the crafts that take place in it, even if that is not its only, or even its most important, concern. Such control may well be expressed by the notion that σωφροσύνη *knows* these crafts, which neither know themselves nor are able to coordinate themselves toward a higher purpose. If indeed that is what σωφροσύνη does, it would also make sense to credit it with knowledge of itself. For it is not something to be controlled for some yet higher purpose but must itself possess the knowledge of the purpose to which it and the other sciences are to be put' (199–200).

has merits, but none of them is founded on firm evidence. Whether or not Plato borrowed the expression 'science of science' or 'science of itself and the other sciences' from somewhere or simply invented it, it is a successful choice. Dramatically, it corroborates Socrates' insinuation that Critias is a *sophos*, wise man or sophist (161b8–c1). Philosophically, there can be no doubt that the elaboration of the notion of a 'science of science' is Plato's own. As has been shown, however, there is no agreement about the philosophical content and implication of the latter.[40] As a preamble to the argument that will soon follow, recall that, on one sort of view, Critias misunderstood Socrates' contention that temperance must be an *epistêmê* of *something*, i.e. it must be a rule-governed form of expert knowledge, and instead took *epistêmê* to be equivalent to *gignôskein*: knowing in a non-expert manner or knowing how.[41] Hence, 'the science of itself and the other sciences' is intended to coincide with Socratic self-knowledge, and the elenchus targets either the 'scientific' body of knowledge identical to temperance,[42] or a 'knowing how the mind knows itself'.[43] On the other hand, many other readings argue, in vastly divergent ways, that the 'science of itself and the other sciences' is different from or even incompatible with Socratic self-knowledge.[44] It should be clear by now that my own

---

[40] See Chapter 1, 17–23, 34–6, 38–40, and Tsouna 2017.

[41] See Tuckey 1951, 38–9, and Wellman, 1964, who, however, differs from Tuckey in that he suggests that, in this context, the term *'epistêmê'* refers to a knowing how.

[42] So Tuckey 1951, 39 and onwards.

[43] See Wellman 1964, who contends that, here, Plato raises the problem of self-consciousness.

[44] Several interpretations of this sort take the 'science of science' to epitomise the theory of some pupil or colleague that Plato is attacking, and also take Socrates' articulation of the 'science of science' at 167a to indicate Plato's own reason for that attack: Plato believed that 'the science of science' could not explain Socrates' peculiar ability to refute people who were supposed to be wise or clever (see Tuckey's discussion of Polhenz's thesis in Tuckey 1951, 40). Or, according to Schmid 1998, Socrates speaks in such a way as to create a twofold ambiguity: whether the temperate man distinguishes between what he knows about technical matters and what he knows about the good life; and whether the temperate man realises what Socrates himself, according to the *Apology*, came to realise, namely that no one possesses moral wisdom of the kind that several people make a claim to (Schmid 1998, 58). While Critias remains oblivious to this ambiguity, Socrates exploits it so as to question whether the alleged object of self-knowledge has in fact any content at all. In the face of Critias' persistent blindness to his own moral condition, Socrates will eventually clarify matters by indicating that the object of self-knowledge is, in the end, the realisation of one's own ignorance concerning the human good (Schmid 1998, 59). Or, on a different approach, Critias' earlier definition of *sôphrosynê* as self-knowledge and Socrates' own development of 'knowledge of itself and the other knowledges' have an important common point: neither contains explicit mention of the value of *sôprosynê* and both indicate by the absence of any such mention that the issue of value will have to be explicitly addressed later in the dialogue (Tuozzo 2011, 206–7). A radically different interpretation that, nonetheless, still belongs to the present group is inspired by Heidegger: Socrates points to a mode of knowledge different from *epistêmê*, which represents an alternative to Critias' mode of cognition and which makes coherent the possibility that there may exist a kind of knowledge which is 'both of itself yet forces itself beyond itself' (Hyland 1981, 106). In a more

interpretation lies closer to this latter camp, since, first, I distinguish the Socratic conception of self-knowledge from the counterpart developed by Critias and, second, I take it that, from this point of the debate onwards, the sole direct target of the elenchus is Critias' 'science of itself and the other sciences'. If the elenchus will also raise problems for Socratic self-knowledge, it will do so in some oblique if significant way.

Ending this chapter, I wish to stress again that what prompted Critias to define *sôphrosynê* in the way he did was his rejection of an assumption central to the *technê* analogy,[45] namely that every *epistêmê* or *technê*, including temperance, is relative to an object other than itself and governs a distinct domain determined by that object. Only because he refused to accept that temperance is thus analogous to the other sciences was he able to come up with the definition of the virtue as 'the only *epistêmê* that is both of the other *epistêmai* and of itself' (166c2–3). Socrates, on the other hand, initially appeared entirely committed to that assumption and defended it, even though he eventually backed down. We cannot know for certain whether he did this for the sake of the argument or because he was persuaded by his interlocutor's criticisms. But we may suspect that he would not abandon his own position so easily. If his retreat is merely strategic, he can't be expected to find congenial the idea of temperance as a unique sort of science solely directed towards science (i.e. itself or any science). Be this as it may, from the moment that he has conceded to Critias his point, he will act as a well-intended, constructive, and superbly skilful debater. At the outset, however, he will take the liberty of articulating Critias' conception of temperance and of the temperate person in his own strikingly Socratic terms.

---

aporetic vein, Bruell (1977, 171) wonders whether Critias does truly accept Socrates' own elaboration of the 'science of science' at 167a. I do not intend to address each of these views (or many others) in detail, but I shall occasionally refer to them when I consider this especially relevant to my analysis.

[45] It is not clear whether Critias rejects the *technê* analogy altogether or maintains it while expunging the assumption of aliorelativity. Philosophically, it does not make much difference which one of these two alternatives one chooses. For if the assumption of aliorelativity is removed, the analogy between virtue and *technê* can do very little work.

CHAPTER 9

Critias' Final Definition
'Temperance Is the Science of Itself and the Other Sciences' or 'the Science of Science' (166e4–167a8) – the Third Offering to Zeus (167a9–c8)

> So tell me, I said, what you mean with regard to temperance. – I mean, he said, that it alone of all of the sciences is a science of both itself and the other sciences. – Then, I said, if indeed it is a science of science or knowledge of knowledge [*epistêmê epistêmês*], will it not be knowledge of non-science or ignorance as well? – Very much so, he said. – So, the temperate man alone will know himself and will be able to examine thoroughly what he really knows and what he does not know, and will be capable of judging others in the same way, namely as to what someone knows and thinks he knows in cases in which he does know and again what someone thinks he knows but in fact does not know, and no one else will be capable of that. And so this is what being temperate and temperance and knowing oneself are, namely to know what one knows and what one does not know. Is that what you are saying? – Indeed, he replied. (166e4–167a8)

This passage brings to the fore the interplay between the two conceptions of self-knowledge that, on my reading, are in evidence in the dialogue.

On the one hand, Critias reasserts the distinctive characteristic of the *epistêmê* that he claims to be equivalent or identical to temperance: it is the only epistêmê of both itself and the other sciences. While he earlier defined temperance as a science both of the other sciences and of itself (166c1–3), he now reverses that order, mentioning first that temperance is a science of itself and, then, that it is also of the other sciences (166e5–6). This shift is not accidental but is, I think, intended to highlight the focus of the elenchus to follow: not so much that Critianic temperance is a higher-order science governing the other sciences as that it is the only science whose sole object is science itself. The shorthand that Socrates uses, with Critias' consent, points in the same direction: '*epistêmê epistêmês*' (166e7–8), a 'science of science', underscores that the feature of primary interest to the interlocutors is the strictly reflexive character of the science in question rather than the fact that it is also set over the other sciences.[1] Furthermore, Socrates obtains from Critias another preliminary admission that will play a fairly important role in the elenchus, namely that, since temperance is supposed to be a 'science of science' (166e7–8), it must also be a science of its contrary: *anepistêmosynê*, the privation of science (166e7). This inference does not mark a turn towards epistemology.[2] Rather, it derives from the application of the familiar Socratic principle that every capacity extends over both its positive object and the privation of the latter.[3] And, crucially, it bears on the idea that the temperate person is in a position to discriminate between knowledge and ignorance.

On the other hand, in elaborating Critianic temperance or self-knowledge, Socrates finds a way of reminding us of his own pursuit of self-knowledge through the cross-examination of himself and others about 'the most important things'. Namely, he uses language strikingly similar to the expressions he uses in his defence speech in the *Apology*, as well as in other dialogues including the *Charmides* itself (166c7–e2), in order to suggest on behalf of Critias that the 'science of science' entails substantive as well as discriminatory knowledge. The temperate person in possession of that science will 'know himself' (*heauton gnôsetai*: 167a1) both in the sense that he will be able to test (*exetasai*: 167a2) the *content* of knowledge claims, i.e. *what* he himself and others know (*eidôs*: 167a2) or do not know even though they think they know, and in the sense that he will thus be able to distinguish knowers from non-knowers. This articulation of Critias' view inevitably brings to mind Socrates' own path to self-knowledge. The sustained *exetasis*, testing (22e), of different groups of citizens revealed to him what he and others knew or did not know but may have thought they knew (*Ap.* 21b–23b), and thus enabled him to understand the true meaning of the oracle, i.e. how he was wiser than other people. On both these occasions, Socrates favours the use of the cognitive verbs '*gignôskein*' or

---

[1] Critias does not object to Socrates' use of this shorthand, and indeed there is nothing puzzling about it (compare, however, Tuozzo 2011, 203–4). For, as the sequel of the dialogue will show, when Critias defines temperance as a 'science of itself and the other sciences', what he means to claim is that temperance is a science of science simpliciter; this scientific knowledge is of itself as well as of all the other sciences *insofar as they are sciences* but, as we shall see, it is not knowledge of the proprietary objects of these latter. Also, the sequel of the debate strongly suggests that temperance governs the other sciences precisely because it is a science of science simpliciter. On my reading, therefore, the higher-order status enjoyed by the 'science of science' depends on what I call the strict reflexivity of the latter.

[2] Contra Taylor 1926 and others.

[3] For instance, see *Rep.* I 333e. However, towards the end of the *Charmides*, Socrates will problematise the idea that there can be a science of ἀνεπιστημοσύνη on the grounds that it is impossible for one to know in any way things that one does not know at all (175c3–8).

'*eidenai*' over '*epistasthai*', even though everywhere else in the *Charmides* the interlocutors almost always employ the latter verb and its cognate noun '*epistêmê*' in order to talk about Critianic temperance. It appears, therefore, that Socrates' present choice of terms is significant,[4] especially because he is supposed to elaborate rather than loosely paraphrase Critias' meaning.[5] Why, then, does Socrates express Critias' conception of temperance in a way that could be misleading? And why does Critias not object?

Given Critias' familiarity with Socrates' views and methods, and also the intimation that he shares with Socrates some common philosophical ground (e.g. at 165b3–4), we are entitled to suppose that he registers the twist that Socrates' gives to the conception of the 'science of science' and approves of it. I think that he has sound philosophical grounds for doing so, which can be related to his presentation by Plato as a Socratic.[6] In the first place, he appears to endorse on his own account the view expressed elsewhere by Plato's Socrates – that every *epistêmê* is both of something and of its opposite (*Rep.* I 333e3–334a10; cf. *HMi* 367c2–4). If temperance is a 'science of science' (*epistêmes*: 166e8), it must also be of the privation of the latter, i.e. of non-science or the privation of science (*anepistêmosynês*: 166e7). Also, Critias seems to find congenial the implication drawn by Socrates that the person who has an *epistêmê* of itself will thereby (*ara*: 167a1) know himself. In fact, he will assert this explicitly later in the argument (169d9–e5). Furthermore, he has every reason to welcome the assumption made explicit by Socrates that the 'science of science' entails *both* the temperate person's capacity to discern knowledge or ignorance *and* the capacity to know content, i.e. *what* oneself and others know or do not know. For, as we shall see, Critias is especially interested in the application of temperance to political rule, and each of these two kinds of knowledge is necessary for that purpose.

In sum, we should appreciate the subtle and effective character of Socrates' intervention. He highlights certain crucial elements of Critias' conception of self-knowledge as a 'science of science' and prepares the ground for problematising each of them in turn in the course of the refutation. But also, he brings his own conception of self-knowledge to the fore, underscores its relevance to the examination that will follow, and alerts us to the possibility that the criticisms that will be levelled against the

---

[4] Consider the following remarks by Tuozzo 2011, 205: 'while I do not think much can be made of different connotations of knowledge terms when those connotations are not explicitly thematized in the text, nonetheless the switch here does indicate how different the Socratic formulation is from the Critian one'.

[5] ἆρα ταῦτά ἐστιν ἃ λέγεις – Ἔγωγε.   [6] See Tsouna 2015.

'science of science' may also affect the Socratic method and its principal goal. One may object that Socrates did not need to follow such an oblique approach. However, the rules of dialectical debate prevent him from doing anything else. The claim under examination is Critias' definition of temperance, not his own. All that Socrates is allowed to do is assist his interlocutor to state adequately his own meaning and then ask questions intended to test the coherence of Critias' view. Of course, in his role as questioner, he can influence the course of the argument considerably. But he may not change its primary target, nor may he propose another view for investigation, while the investigation of Critias' claim is about to begin.

Before turning to this latter, we may recapitulate in contemporary philosophical terms the characteristics that the interlocutors attribute to Critianic temperance.

First, the 'science of science' is unique. It alone (*monê*: 166c2) is of itself and the other sciences, whereas every other science is not of itself but of an object different from itself (166c1–3). Second, it is, as I call it, strictly reflexive: it is *only* of science and the absence of science and of nothing else (166c2–3). Conversely, every other science is *only* of its own distinct object and of nothing else (166c1–2). The supposition that temperance is a science of the other sciences as well as of itself does not make it inclusive with regard to its object.[7] Since it governs the other sciences *only insofar as* they are branches of *science*, reflexivity is preserved throughout.[8] Third, the 'science of science' is non-transparent[9] or intransitive[10] with regard to the proprietary objects of the first-order sciences or arts. Since it is posited as an *epistêmê* only of *epistêmê*, it cannot be (also) of any other object. Importantly, the 'science of science' cannot be related either to tokens or to types or kinds. As will become clear later in the argument (notably at 170a6–171c10), Critianic temperance can know, for example, medicine *qua* science, but cannot know health and disease and cannot know any particular medical treatment.[11] Conversely, medicine knows health and disease and involves knowledge of particular treatments, but cannot know itself *qua* science. Fourth, the 'science of science' is supposed to be higher-order or second- order, formally as well as pragmatically. Formally, because by definition it is set over every other science, *qua* science as well as over itself. Pragmatically, because, according to the argument, it involves the capacity

---

[7] See also Chapter 1, 26, 37–9.
[8] I thank Thomas Tuozzo and David Sedley for their remarks on this point.
[9] So Duncombe 2012a and 2020 *passim*, who also explains why he prefers 'non-transparent' to 'intransitive' (see also the following note).
[10] So McCabe 2007a and 2007b.   [11] See Chapter 11, 240 and note 11.

of delegating and overseeing the execution of tasks and of ruling the state. Fifth, Socrates and Critias agree that the 'science of science' entails both discriminatory and substantive knowledge: the capacity to discern *that* one knows or doesn't know (but may have believed to know), and also the capacity to judge *what* knowledge one has or doesn't have (but may have believed to have). To put it differently, the 'science of science' entails both the power to distinguish a knower from an ignoramus or a fraud and the power to judge what these persons' knowledge or ignorance is about. It is this highly peculiar and highly ambitious conception of temperance championed by Critias that will become, from this point onwards, the direct target of the elenchus. As for Socratic self-knowledge and the method by which it is achieved, we shall have ample opportunity to consider in parallel with the actual debate whether it can resist some of the criticisms directed at the 'science of science'.

> Once more then, I said, as a third offering to the Saviour, let us investigate as if from the beginning, first, whether or not this thing is possible, namely to know of what one knows and does not know that one knows and does not know [it]; and second, however possible this may be, what would be the benefit to us of knowing it. (167a9–b4)

Here, Socrates articulates the twofold question motivating the search.[12] And he suggests that it has a quasi-sacred character by devoting it to Zeus the Saviour. The dedication of the investigation to the supreme deity flags its philosophical importance and is a plea to the god to assist the discussants in their task. For those familiar with the palinode of the *Phaedrus*, it may have dramatic significance as well. According to the myth of the palinode, the souls of people who practise philosophy on earth, when they are in their disembodied state in the heavens, belong to the retinue of Zeus. In their embodied state, these are the only people capable of apprehending Forms and discerning Beauty in the youths of their choice. Every pair consisting of a philosopher-lover and his beloved has Zeus-like characteristics and aims to live a Zeus-like, philosophical life. On the present occasion, Socrates' offering to Zeus of the argument that he will conduct with Critias could point back to the time when the two of them were frequently in each other's company (156a6–8) and Critias was still young and beautiful.[13] It could be a way of alluding to the nature of their past

---

[12] In this instance too, Socrates' ἀπορία does not mark an impasse resulting from the failure of an investigation, but motivates a dialectical search.

[13] As mentioned, Critias' beauty was famous and, therefore, can be considered part of the background information that dramatic aspects of the *Charmides* rely on.

relationship and to the emotional and intellectual bonds that, as Plato's audiences know, will eventually be severed.

Be this as it may, in the above excerpt Socrates specifies the object of the search with remarkable precision. The enquiry will be centred on two problems, one having to do with the possibility (*dynaton*: 167b1) of the 'science of science', the other with the benefit (*ôphelia*: 167b4) that it might bring. Even though Socrates does not explicitly identify them as *aporiai*, puzzles, soon afterwards he employs twice a form of the verb *aporein* (167b7), to puzzle over something, in order to convey his own state of mind. So, first, he asks whether or not 'this thing' (*touto*: 167b1) is possible, namely to know *that* one knows or doesn't know *what*[14] one knows and doesn't know.[15] Perhaps it is needless to stress that 'this thing' is Critias' definition of temperance or self-knowledge as a 'science of science'; it does not concern Socratic self-knowledge in any direct way. Of course, the same holds for the second question, for it depends upon the first: assuming that 'this thing' is entirely possible or that we can possess the aforementioned knowledge, what benefit would it bring to us (167b3–4)?[16] Socrates underscores that the question of benefit can be raised *only if* the argument establishes that a 'science of science' is possible,[17] in some sense of 'possible'.[18] Also, he clearly indicates that, while he is willing to entertain the idea that Critianic temperance may not be possible, he is not willing to assume that it might be possible but not beneficial in any way. On any plausible account, temperance is a cardinal virtue and hence a great good for man. If Critias wants to uphold his conception of what temperance is, and if the latter proves to be coherent, he still will need to explain just how it benefits us.

Next, Socrates openly avows his perplexity and identifies its main source: the strictly reflexive character of Critianic temperance, which appears to him odd or even incoherent.

> Come then Critias, I said, see if you can show yourself more resourceful than I am about it. For I myself am perplexed.[19] Shall I tell you exactly how I am

---

[14] Again, this is ambiguous: 'what' can be an indirect question or it can mean 'that which'. The ambiguity will be clarified in the Argument from Benefit: see Chapter 11, *passim*.
[15] Cf. τὸ ὃ οἶδεν καὶ ἃ μὴ οἶδεν εἰδέναι (ὅτι οἶδε καὶ) ὅτι οὐκ οἶδεν: 167b2–3. Compare the concluding statement of the elaboration of Critias' view by Socrates: καὶ ἔστι δὴ τοῦτο τὸ σωφρονεῖν τε καὶ σωφροσύνη καὶ τὸ ἑαυτὸν αὐτὸν γιγνώσκειν, τὸ εἰδέναι ἅ τε οἶδε καὶ ἃ μὴ οἶδε (167a5–7).
[16] ἔπειτα εἰ ὡς μάλιστα δυνατόν, τίς ἂν εἴη ἡμῖν ὠφελία εἰδόσιν αὐτό: 167b3–4.
[17] εἰ ὅτι μάλιστα δυνατόν: 167b3.
[18] The elenchus will indicate that Socrates is interested primarily in the logical and conceptual possibility of the 'science of science'. Moreover, we shall discover that this issue has metaphysical and psychological aspects, as well as important political implications.
[19] ἐγὼ μὲν γὰρ ἀπορῶ: 167b7.

perplexed? – By all means, do so. – Well, I said, assuming that what you said just now is the case, wouldn't the whole thing amount to this, namely that there is one science which is not of any other thing but only science of itself and the other sciences, and moreover that this same science is also a science of the absence of science as well? – Very much so. – Then look what a strange thing we are trying to say, my friend. For if you consider this very same thing in other cases, you will surely come to think, as I do, that it is impossible. (167b6–c6)

Socrates' *aporia* conveys both the sense that he finds himself at an impasse and the hope that Critias may help him out of it.[20] His puzzlement can be traced back to the debate between him and Critias concerning an aspect of the *technê* analogy, namely the assumption that every art or science is of something distinct and different from that art or science itself. While towards the end of that debate he conceded to Critias that, unlike all the other sciences, temperance is solely and exclusively orientated towards itself, now he avows that he finds that position out of place (*atopon*: 167c4), and the same holds for Critias' more recent admission that temperance is a science also of non-science (166e7).[21] Herein lies the specific source of Socrates' unease (*hêi aporô*: 167b6), which, as he suggests, becomes worse when he considers the above position in the light of other examples. For then it seems to him downright impossible (*adynaton*: 167c6).

We should note that Socrates shows himself aware of the difficulties surrounding the 'science of science' *before* the argument begins. As he indicates, he already foresees 'other cases' of strictly reflexive constructions comparable to *epistêmê* and finds them too strange or incoherent (167c4–5). Rarely does Plato's Socrates anticipate the outcome of the elenchus in that manner, and even more rarely does he intimate that he has gone in advance through the relevant dialectical moves. Perhaps this is Plato's way of flagging his own work on relatives and relations and alerting us to the importance of the Argument from Relatives.

In any case, the passage cited immediately above makes entirely clear that Socrates is not concerned with every kind of reflexivity, but with strict reflexivity alone. What perplexes him is not merely that the *epistêmê* posited by Critias has a self-referential function, but that the object of that *epistêmê* is supposed to be *epistêmê* and nothing else (*ouk allou tinos*: 167b11).[22]

---

[20] See again Politis 2008, which presents a case study of a general interpretation defended in Politis 2006.

[21] On this point, see Wolfsdorf 2004.

[22] So, the elenchus will not concern, for example, the hypothesis that there may be an *epistêmê* of both itself and the other *epistêmai* and *also* of the objects of these latter, or generally the idea of a higher-

Consequently, he will bring the elenchus to bear on just this conception: temperance as a science exclusively and exhaustively directed towards itself. There is no evidence whatsoever that Socrates intends to argue on two sides, i.e. against the 'science of science' insofar as it is directed only towards itself, but *for* it insofar as it is directed towards other things as well.[23] Rather, he appears poised to play his dialectical role as questioner to the end of the debate with only one goal in sight.

As we stand at the threshold of the Argument from Relatives, we should take a moment to appreciate how high the stakes are for both participants. The tensions between them extend beyond the adversarial context of a dialectical argument to their competing conceptions of self-knowledge and, ultimately, to their respective values, characters, and ways of life. On the one hand, Critias has banked his all on the definition of temperance as a 'science of itself and the other sciences': a higher-order form of expertise both reflexive[24] and directive that, he supposes, enables the temperate person to identify the knowers and distinguish them from ignorant people or charlatans, oversee the first-order arts and their experts, and (as we shall see) scientifically govern the state. He obviously finds this intellectualist ideal attractive, and he also loves to win. Therefore, it matters to him enormously to be able to defend his thesis and prevail. On the other hand, Socrates is about to launch an attack on a position that, in the first place, he finds strange and, in the second place, he must view as both competing and incompatible with some of his own intuitions. At the same time, his elaboration of Critias' notion of a 'science of science' (167a1–7) indicates that he is aware of certain features that this latter shares in common with his own notion of knowing himself in the sense of discerning what he himself and others know or don't know but think they know. So, Socrates too is in a tight spot. He intends to scrutinise Critias' position and hopes thus to come closer to the truth regarding the nature of temperance (166c7–d6). He is compelled by the rules of dialectical argumentation to

order *epistêmê* governing the first-order sciences or arts. I shall return to this point in the following two chapters.

[23] Contra Politis 2008. Politis contends that Socrates argues both against and for the 'science of science' without contradiction: he argues *against* it on the assumption that it is both reflexive and restrictive, whereas he argues *for* it in order to suggest that temperance may be both reflexive and non-restrictive. However, I find no textual support for this interpretation. Moreover, while Politis appears to assume that every aporetic formulation of an issue requires argumentation on both sides, a survey of the occurrences of '*aporia*' and its cognates in Plato reveals that this is not the case. Besides, Politis' reading does not do justice to the cumulative force of the Argument from Relatives, nor can it account for the logical and dialectical ties between the Argument from Relatives and the Argument from Benefit.

[24] By 'reflexive' I mean 'strictly reflexive' unless I indicate otherwise.

do his utmost in order to refute his opponent. However, he probably suspects that, if his argument against Critias is successful, it may amount also to criticism of his own conception of self-knowledge and the method by which he tries to attain it. Given the dialectical skill of both interlocutors, neither of them can be confident about the outcome of the argument. Many possibilities are open, suspense is at its peak, and we should get ready to follow Socrates and Critias as they address in turn the two horns of the puzzle.

CHAPTER 10

Can There Be an Epistême of Itself?
The Argument from Relatives (167c8–169c2)

The Argument from Relatives[1] concerns what I take to be the fundamental source of perplexity for Socrates and the primary philosophical challenge for the dialogue's readers: the contention advanced by Critias that, unlike the other arts or sciences, temperance is an *epistêmê*, science, only of *epistêmê* itself[2] and of no other object. While at the previous stage of the conversation Socrates helped Critias articulate that claim, it is now clear that he did so merely for the sake of the argument. In truth, he says, the claim seems to him strange (*atopon*: 167c4) or, in the light of certain cases that serve as counter-examples, impossible (*adynaton*: 167c6). And he urges Critias to consider these examples with the expectation that, when Critias does so, he will come to the same conclusion (167c4–6). The Argument from Relatives consists precisely in this endeavour and has an explicitly stated goal: examine whether or not there can be a 'science of science' (167b1–2) and, on the basis of cases that are supposed to be analogous with *epistêmê*, bring Critias to admit that such a thing, i.e. a strictly reflexive form of science, appears strange or incoherent.

---

[1] Duncombe 2020 gives compelling reasons for calling this argument 'the Relatives Argument' rather than 'the Relations Argument'. These have to do with the conception of relativity operative in this argument, i.e. constitutive relativity (see immediately below).

[2] As suggested, the claim that temperance is a science only of science itself entails that temperance is a science of all the sciences as well as of the corresponding privative state, i.e. non-science. Not only do the interlocutors assume that the strict reflexivity of the 'science of science' is compatible with the postulate that it is higher-order, but also the argument strongly suggests that temperance is higher-order *precisely because* it is strictly reflexive. The root of this assumption lies in Critias' stance vis-à-vis Socrates in the debate concerning the analogy between temperance and the other sciences or arts with regard to the nature of their objects: Critias contended that temperance *alone* is 'of both the other sciences and itself' as opposed to the other sciences, which are 'of something other than themselves and not of themselves' (166b9–c4). The contrast is between the strict reflexivity of temperance and the aliorelativity of the other sciences, and Critias appears to take it for granted that the strict reflexivity of temperance entails that it is higher-order as well: since it governs science simpliciter, *ipso facto* it governs each and every science *insofar as it is science*. Conversely, Critias also assumes that since the other sciences govern only their respective aliorelative objects, they are only first-order and cannot govern themselves in respect of being forms of *science*: only temperance can do this latter. These claims will become explicit in the course of the Argument from Benefit.

Philosophically, this argument is of the first importance. It contains pioneering work on relatives and relations and represents a major break-through in that regard. It raises questions about reflexivity and foreshadows logical conundrums bearing on self-predication. It may cause us to revisit traditional assumptions about the structure and behaviour of different categories of relatives, especially perceptual relatives and quantitative rela-tives. And it conveys valuable insights concerning the role of relatives in epistemic grounding. Historically, the Argument from Relatives represents a landmark in ancient philosophical thinking about these topics. Not only is it a breakthrough for Plato, but also its influence can be traced to Aristotle's conception of relatives and his analysis of second-order perception and, further, to Stoicism and beyond. So far as the interpretation of Plato is concerned, the counterexamples constituting the main body of this argu-ment point unmistakably to the so-called middle dialogues and the theory of Forms, while Socrates' closing remarks reach further to the metaphysics and methods of the *Sophist* and the *Statesman*. Dialectically, the articulation of Socrates' *aporia* underscores that the viability of Critias' definition of tem-perance as a 'science of science' ultimately depends on whether or not this notion is credible or coherent. Since the Argument from Relatives aims to answer just that query, it is decisive for the development of the investigation.

As I said,[3] I believe that the Argument from Relatives has been misun-derstood in various ways and has frequently been taken to undermine the point that it is supposed to make. I shall try to show that, on the contrary, it attains its principal objective, even though it does not purport to settle the issue in a definitive manner. At the outset, I wish to highlight one central assumption that I shall make and that is crucial for that purpose. Namely, both interlocutors operate with a constitutive view of relativity,[4] which begins with relatives rather than relations,[5] and which posits that every

---

[3] Chapter 1, 38–9.

[4] See Duncombe 2012a and especially 2020, 36–48. To my mind, these studies conclusively show that the Argument from Relatives, as well as the main Platonic passages discussing relatives, entail a constitutive conception of relativity. Duncombe 2020 argues that Aristotle, the Stoics, the Sceptics, and other Greek thinkers, including the ancient commentators, all conceive of relativity in constitutive terms. Several of his arguments are compelling, but here I wish to remain neutral regarding this latter general claim (see also the following note).

[5] Duncombe 2020 contrasts this approach with traditional interpretations of relativity in Plato. He argues that, notwithstanding their differences, all ancient philosophical schools adopt an approach according to which one must start from relatives and ask what makes something a relative, i.e. how a relative is constituted. On the other hand, he contends, the traditional approach, which analyses relativity in terms of incomplete predicates (an item x is a relative just in case an incomplete predicate is true of x), usually fares much worse than the constitutive approach in the interpretation of ancient philosophical texts. While Duncombe's argument concerns the entire Platonic corpus, for present

relative is constituted *just* by the relation to a correlative.[6] Or, a relation constitutes a relative if bearing that relation *just is* what it is to be the relative: being a brother *of someone* just is what it is to be a brother.[7]

I submit that the counterexamples entertained by Socrates and Critias exhibit certain formal features that characterise, more generally, constitutive relativity.[8] First, reciprocity. Assuming that a relation constitutes a relative and that every relation has a converse, if X is relative to Y, then Y is relative to X. Sight is related to colour and colour is related to sight; double is related to half and half to double. Next, exclusivity. While on the standard interpretation of ancient relativity in terms of incomplete predicates exclusivity does not hold, on the constitutive interpretation it must. If a relative relates to a correlative, then it relates only to that correlative and no other. As we shall see, Socrates and Critias take for granted that, for example, sight relates only to colour, hearing only to sound, love only to what is beautiful, and the greater only to the smaller. Some of these constructions are *prima facie* more plausible than others, but there are ways in which we can make sense of all of them.[9] Besides, our interlocutors arguably presuppose that the pairs of relatives under discussion are

purposes I refer the readers only to his analysis of the Argument from Relatives, which demonstrates, entirely convincingly to my mind, that the interlocutors do presuppose constitutive relativity.

[6] I shall not be concerned with 'monadic' accounts of relativity, according to which relativity amounts to a relative, 'monadic' feature and a certain sort of 'bare orientation' or 'towardness', for I believe that such accounts do not give us adequate interpretative tools in order to understand the present argument. On the notion of 'bare orientation' see Marmodoro 2016 and the criticism by Duncombe 2020.

[7] The distinction between an extensional view and an intensional view of relatives bears on this point. Roughly speaking, the extensional account treats most items as relatives. For it sets no restriction over which relation is invoked, and it allows the same relative to bear different relations to different things. For instance, in the case of named individuals, Socrates is a relative in virtue of the fact that many different relations are true of him. He is the husband of Xanthippe, the mentor of Plato, uglier than Phaedo, poorer than Critias, less of an ascetic than Antisthenes, less of a hedonist than Aristippus, and smarter than Prodicus. Correspondingly, each of those characters can be treated as a relative in virtue of the relation he/she bears to Socrates and to other people and things as well. On the other hand, the intensional view is considerably more restrictive. Something is a relative if it bears a *constitutive* relation to a given correlative. So, for instance, assuming that the relations of Socrates to different people do not constitute what it is to be Socrates, he is not a relative. On the other hand, a warmer thing is constituted by its relation to something cooler and hence qualifies as a relative. While, according to the extensional approach, the relation between a relative and a correlative is not exclusive, according to the intensional approach it is exclusive as well as constitutive: a relative is what it is just in virtue of its relation to a given correlative and no other. As Duncombe 2012a underscores, the intensional view does not analyse relativity in terms of incomplete predicates, nor does it identify the class of relative items with the class of items of which a relativised predicate is true. It focuses on things that relate rather than predicates that have certain semantic features.

[8] Duncombe 2020 identifies these features and provides extensive discussion of each of them.

[9] See Duncombe 2020 *passim*, and the discussion of Socrates' counterexamples below.

existentially symmetrical and epistemically symmetrical, but these characteristics do not play any significant role in the argument.

The most prominent feature of constitutive relativity, however, is aliorelativity, and matters are complicated in that regard. On the constitutive
view, a relative *just is* the relation to its correlative, and the latter must be
something distinct from the relative itself. Reflexivity, let alone strict reflexivity, is extremely problematic and, on some views, cannot obtain on pain of
incoherence. For constitution is not a reflexive relation: no item can be
constituted just by its relation to itself. Rather, the constitutive relation is
a grounding relation, a fundamental and unitary relation between a relative
and its correlative. And, arguably, grounding relations are irreflexive. In
principle, therefore, if the Argument from Relatives presupposes constitutive
relativity, there are philosophical as well as dialectical reasons for rejecting
strict reflexivity if not reflexivity *tout court*. Nonetheless, since the real
purpose of the argument is controverted, we need to look closely at each
of Socrates' counterexamples in order to judge that issue.

The structure of the Argument from Relatives is as follows. The cases in
question constitute three main groups that the interlocutors consider in
turn: perceptual states, namely sight, hearing, and, generally, the senses
(167c8–d10); certain psychological states irreducible to perception, i.e.
desire, wish, love, fear, and belief (167e1–168b1); and what we may call
quantitative relatives, namely greater and smaller, double and half, more
and less, heavier and lighter, older and younger, and all other cases of that
sort (168b2–d1). Then, Socrates shifts perspective and re-examines the
perceptual cases of hearing and sound from a different angle (168d1–e2).
Also, he briefly mentions the hypotheses of self-moving motion, self-
heating heat, 'and all other such cases' (168e9–10). These may count as
a fourth, separate group, but receive no further attention. After examining
each of the above cases, Critias agrees with Socrates that none of them
appears to make sense if it receives a strictly reflexive construction. Hence,
Critias also agrees with Socrates' tentative conclusion: assuming that the
aforementioned relatives are relevantly analogous to *epistêmê*, and also that
temperance is a form of *epistêmê*, it seems that strict reflexivity is implausible in some cases and entirely impossible in others (168e3–169a1).

Accordingly, sections 1 to 3 of this chapter discuss, respectively, the
groups of perceptual relatives, psychological relatives irreducible to perception, and quantitative relatives. Section 4 is devoted to the re-examination
of perceptual relatives and, specifically, of hearing and sight, in terms of
powers orientated towards their respective proprietary objects or special
sensibles. Section 5 discusses Socrates' provisional conclusions and

comments briefly on the cases of motion and heat. Section 6 is devoted to Socrates' closing remarks.

I

> Reflect on whether it seems to you that there is some sight [*opsis*][10] which is not of the things that the other sights are of, but is a sight of itself and of the other sights and likewise of the absence of sight [literally: non-sights][11] and which, although it is sight, sees no colour but rather sees itself and the other sights. Do you think there is such a sight? – No, by Zeus, I certainly do not. – What about some hearing which hears no sound, but does hear itself and the other hearings and non-hearings? – There isn't such a thing either. – Consider now all the senses taken together, whether it seems to you that there is a sense which is of senses and of itself while perceiving none of the things that the other senses perceive. – No, it does not seem so. (167c8–d10)

This first group of analogues remains very close to his paradigm. Take the example of *opsis*, sight or seeing.[12] Socrates hypothesises that there is a unique sort of sight[13] which, like the 'science of science', is reflexive: it is of sight and its privation, i.e. non-sight (167c9–10). The relation to its reflexive object is supposed to be exclusive and exhaustive. Even though Socrates does not explicitly state that the hypothesised sight is *only* of sight, he clearly implies it. For he says that the sight under consideration does not see what the other sights see (167c8–9), i.e. colour (167d1),[14] but itself and the other sights, i.e. sight simpliciter, as well as the privation of this latter, i.e. non-sights (167c9–10). Hence a contrast can be drawn between the putative second-order sight and all first-order sights, the

---

[10] Or 'seeing': see below, 203–5.   [11] Or 'non-seeings': see below, 203.

[12] It is controversial whether the examples of this group refer to perceptual faculties, or perceptual activities, or some combination of these two. Notably, see the argument in favour of the activity reading developed by Caston 2002, 772–3, as well as the criticisms of this latter by Johansen 2005, 248–9 and n. 23 and by Tuozzo 2011, 218 and n. 18. Even though I mostly use faculty vocabulary, I shall try to remain as neutral as possible with regard to this issue for reasons that I briefly explain below.

[13] While the word μόνη, alone, is repeatedly used for the 'science of science' (166c2, e5), it does not occur in this and other examples of the Argument from Relatives. However, the context strongly suggests that each of the putative second-order items of the counterexamples is unique. Consider, for example, Socrates' careful phrasing at 167c8: ἐννόει γὰρ εἴ σοι δοκεῖ ὄψις τις εἶναι (my emphasis), and also his evident care to pattern each of the counterexamples on the paradigm of 'the science of science'.

[14] Socrates determines the peculiar object of sight first periphrastically, in terms of 'the things that the other sights [sc. first-order sights] are of' (ὧν αἱ μὲν ἄλλαι ὄψεις εἰσίν: 167c8–9), and then substantially as 'colour' (χρῶμα: 167d1).

object of the former and the proprietary object of the latter.[15] Following the paradigm of *epistêmê*, we may infer that the former can perceive only sight and its privation, whereas the latter can see only green, red, and yellow things.[16] If so, then the 'sight of itself and the other sights' is, so to speak, intransitive or intransparent in relation to the coloured things that constitute the objects of first-order sights: it perceives the other sights but not the green, red, and yellow objects that they see. Can there really be a sight with the above characteristics? Critias replies that he does not think so (167d3).

In accordance with a practice that he will follow all the way through, Socrates sketches the other members of the group in similar but more elliptical terms (167d4–5). He asks Critias whether he thinks that there could be a hearing that hears no sound whatsoever, but only hears the other hearings and non-hearings as well as itself. Comparably to the example of sight, the hearing in question is probably unique, strictly reflexive, intransparent (in the sense indicated above), and higher-order: it is exclusively directed towards hearing (itself and the other hearings, as well as the corresponding privation), but not towards the peculiar object of first-order hearing, namely *phonê*, sound (167d4). Comparably to the 'sight of sight', then, the 'hearing of hearing'[17] hears only itself but nothing distinct from itself. In this it differs from every first-order hearing, which is always directed towards its own aliorelative object, sound. The 'sight of sight' is not of anything substantive, whereas the other sights are. Again, Critias denies that there can be such a sense (167d6).

The last case of this group is more difficult to figure out. On the basis of the two previous examples, Socrates now urges his interlocutor to consider 'all the senses taken together' (167d7),[18] i.e. examine the supposition that there may be a sense that perceives itself and other senses[19] but none of their objects (167d8–9). We may assume that, in this example too, the sense

---

[15] I use 'proprietary objects' to refer to the special sensibles, as opposed to common sensibles, some of which may be common objects of all the senses. Socrates conducts the entire discussion of the senses in terms of the *special* objects of the senses. It is questionable whether *common* sensibles like shape and motion could have satisfied the correlativity requirement.

[16] Socrates builds this condition in every example of the first two groups in a similar way. It is entirely clear, I contend, that he intends every one of these cases to be strictly reflexive: the putative item is supposed to be orientated towards itself and the corresponding first-order items, but not towards the objects of these latter.

[17] I use such abbreviations in accordance with the paradigm of a 'science of science'.

[18] συλλήβδην δὴ σκόπει περὶ πασῶν τῶν αἰσθήσεων: 167d7.

[19] Note that there is no definite article before αἰσθήσεων at 167d8.

under consideration is supposed to be strictly reflexive, govern the corresponding first-order senses, and have no access to their proprietary objects. Since it perceives only sense but no sensible, it cannot perceive what the other senses perceive. Some aspects of this example, however, call for further discussion.

In the first place, it is not clear whether the expression 'some sense' (*tis aisthêsis*: 167d7–8) refers to one of the five senses,[20] or one of the three remaining ones,[21] or a sixth sense perceiving the five senses.[22] This indeterminacy could be philosophically significant, for it could bear on the vexed question of how we perceive that we are perceiving. And while the interlocutors of the *Charmides* do not pursue the latter, the idea of a sense sensing itself cannot fail to evoke familiar puzzles in connection to that topic. For instance, is it through one of the five senses that we perceive that we are perceiving, or through some additional sense? Do we do this reflexively, i.e. without also perceiving the object of our first-order perception? Or do we perceive simultaneously both *that* we are perceiving and *what* we are perceiving? And what view of perception would be a better fit for each of these or other options? Regardless of Plato's own intentions, the hypothesis of a higher-order sense directed towards itself is bound to make us think of such questions and look beyond the Argument from Relatives for possible answers.[23] Nonetheless, in the absence of such evidence in the present context, I think that we should read Socrates' reference to 'some sense' in a deflationary manner, namely as an invitation to Critias to apply the rules governing the examples of sight and hearing to each and every one of the five senses. Thus, Socrates points to new considerations that his interlocutor might want to entertain and then perhaps revise his attitude accordingly.[24]

Next, while Socrates identifies the objects of sight and hearing in concrete terms, as colour and sound, he refers to the objects of the 'other senses' in a more abstract manner, as 'the things that the other senses perceive'.[25] Since Socrates uses similar periphrastic expressions in order to refer to the objects of opinion and of knowledge, the difference between 'substantive' and 'formal' designations has been deemed significant: as has been suggested, each periphrastic formula serves as a place-holder for the 'substantive' description of the relevant object, while Socrates postpones

---

[20] This is a fairly natural way of understanding the phrase περὶ πασῶν τῶν αἰσθήσεων: 167d7.
[21] Bloch 1973, 113–14, holds this view.   [22] See Tuozzo 2011, 214–15.
[23] An important passage to turn to is the opening lines of Aristotle's discussion of perceiving that we are perceiving in *De an.* III.2. See below, 203–6 and notes 33–5.
[24] See Tuozzo 2011, 215.   [25] ὧν δὲ δὴ αἱ ἄλλαι αἰσθήσεις αἰσθάνονται: 167d8–9.

the latter for some other occasion.[26] However, it seems to me that this is an over-interpretation. Since Socrates tells Critias to consider 'all the senses taken together', he could hardly give a 'substantive designation' of the object. For there is no proprietary object of 'all the senses taken together', only of each sense taken separately and in relation to its own special sensible. Also, the difference between 'substantive' and 'formal' designations does not seem to matter philosophically when it concerns a specific sense. In fact, Socrates refers to the object of sight both as 'colour' (167d1) and as 'what the other sights are of' (167c8–9), and he substitutes the former for the latter without seeing any need to justify his move. Presumably, he would not object if the same practice were applied to each of the five senses.

Another noteworthy difference between this latter example and the previous ones is the hypothesis that the second-order sight and the second-order hearing under examination extend over their own privations, whereas corresponding second-order sense does not. In fact, from this point onwards, there will be no further mention of privative objects in the argument and one might wonder why. The reason is not, I believe, that privative objects are irrelevant to the logic of the argument.[27] For since the purpose of the counterexamples is to test the plausibility or conceivability of the 'science of science', and since the latter is set over science as well as its privation, it would make sense to craft all the analogues accordingly. One possible explanation is that the examples of sight and hearing suffice to establish the terms in which the analogy with *epistêmê* is supposed to work and, therefore, Socrates sees no need to continue supplying all the details. Another reason may be dialectical. The explicit mention of privative objects works better in some cases than in others. While one might try to entertain the notion of a sight or a seeing that perceives itself as well as the incapacity to see or the absence of such an occurrent act, the idea that there may be, generally, a higher-order sense orientated towards sense and non-sense appears completely incoherent. Yet another possibility to consider is that, by omitting further reference to privative objects, Socrates intends to alert us to the fact that such objects can be especially problematic. In his final summary of the debate, some of his remarks will bear on this point (175c3–8).

A final comment concerns the question of whether the perceptual cases refer to sensory faculties or sensory activities or some combination of these

---

[26] See Tuozzo 2011, 214–19.

[27] Contra Tuozzo 2011, 212 n. 6. See also Dieterle 1966, 250 n. 1 and Martens 1973, 58, cited by Tuozzo in the aforementioned note.

two. Is Socrates asking whether there can be, for example, a faculty of sight whose sole object is itself and every other such capacity or the absence thereof? Or is he asking whether there can be a seeing that perceives itself and other seeings as well as the non-occurrence of the latter? This issue has been debated in the literature[28] and, therefore, I shall merely outline some aspects of the discussion and indicate where I stand. Regarding the faculty reading, its defenders can point out that the terms *opsis* (sight), *akoê* (hearing), and *aisthêsis* usually refer to capacities rather than activities or occurrent acts. Also, since Socrates' perceptual examples are supposed to be analogous to *epistêmê*, and since the latter is arguably conceived as a capacity or a disposition, it seems reasonable to infer that sight, hearing, and every other sense are supposed to be dispositions as well.[29] Furthermore, as the possessor of reflexive science is able to discern what he himself and others know or do not know, so the person endowed with, for example, reflexive sight is capable of perceiving what he and others see or do not see. Again, the analogy between the 'science of science' and reflexive sight or reflexive hearing seems to focus on faculties rather than activities or occurrent acts.

However, the faculty reading has difficulty accounting, for instance, for Socrates' use of the plural in the hypotheses of 'a sight of itself and the other sights and non-sights' (167c10)[30] and a 'hearing of itself and the other hearings'.[31] And even though the nouns '*opsis*' and '*aisthêsis*' are typically reserved for sensory faculties, arguably they can refer to sensory activities as well. On the other hand, the activity reading offers a *prima facie* plausible interpretation of these locutions: a seeing perceives itself and other tokens of the same type, and also registers the non-occurrence of such tokens. The higher-order sight hypothesised by Socrates is not a sense but a sensing. And its activity consists in perceiving itself and other such sensings. Nonetheless, the aforementioned arguments in support of the faculty reading tell against its rival, albeit not in a decisive manner. For example, the activity reading does not suit well the paradigm of *epistêmê*, for, on some views, the latter is primarily understood as a capacity and not as an activity. Also, the activity reading arguably accounts less successfully than the faculty reading for the cases of the second group. Attempts to combine the two readings vary and each has its own problems too. For instance, if one supposes that the higher-order sight under consideration is a faculty of both itself (i.e. the capacity to see) and

---

[28] See note 10 in this chapter.

[29] Tuozzo 2011, 218 n. 18 makes this point against the activity interpretation defended by Caston 2002, 772–3.

[30] ἑαυτῆς δὲ καὶ τῶν ἄλλων ὄψεων ὄψις ἐστὶν καὶ μὴ ὄψεων ὡσαύτως: 167c10.

[31] αὐτῆς δὲ καὶ τῶν ἄλλων ἀκοῶν ἀκούει καὶ τῶν μὴ ἀκοῶν: 167d4–5.

a given seeing, one needs to confront the undesirable consequence that the terms *'opsis'*, *'akoē'*, and *'aisthēsis'* would switch meanings within the context of a single example. A reflexive sight would 'see' both in the sense of being capable of perceiving the faculty of vision and in the sense of actually perceiving an activity of vision.

The above controversy highlights the fact that no reading on offer can fully account for all the elements of Plato's text. This is all the more striking because Plato shows himself to be perfectly aware of the distinction between faculties and activities, capacities and occurrent acts, at many places in the corpus. To my mind, therefore, the fact that the perceptual cases of the Argument from Relatives, as well as the psychological relatives of the second group, are susceptible to a variety of different readings is deliberate on Plato's part. The following consideration may weigh in favour of that suggestion. Methodologically, Socrates constructs his analogues so as to closely match the paradigm: 'a science of itself and the other sciences and of non-science' or, in shorthand, 'a science of science'. Even though *'epistēmē'*, science, and 'the *epistēmai*', the sciences, are more likely to refer to faculties rather than activities, the interlocutors never specify the meaning of these terms. Likewise, even though it seems more natural to take 'sight', 'hearing', and, generally, 'the senses' to refer to faculties rather than activities, Socrates refrains from doing so. In both cases the motivation is philosophical. On the one hand, Critias intends the 'science of science' to be as general and abstract as possible: govern everything that is science and all the sciences, the capacity to know scientifically as well as every application of such knowledge, the absence of *epistēmē* as well as every individual manifestation of it. The all-comprising scope of the 'science of science' is terribly important for Critias, since, as we shall see, he conceives of temperance as a unique higher-order science on the basis of which the temperate rulers will discern experts from non-experts and will delegate and oversee the execution of works in the state. On the other hand, if Socrates is to show the strangeness or impossibility of such a science, he needs to cast his net as wide as possible. He needs to show that strictly reflexive relatives behave very oddly or even incoherently, whether they are senses or sensings, capacities or activities, dispositions or occurrent acts. Even so, the perceptual cases presented by Socrates appear calculated to generate further reflection on these matters. The ongoing debate between the defenders of the two rival readings and their variations attests to Plato's success in that regard.

What is the dialectical value of the perceptual counterexamples discussed above? And what is their philosophical value? I think that they go some way towards justifying Socrates' discomfort regarding the 'science of science' and towards highlighting its main focus. What appears odd about them is not merely that they are reflexive but that they are both reflexive and intransitive, i.e. their relation to themselves or every item of that type is intransparent. Self-sight is of itself and other sights but not of colour, self-hearing is of hearing but not of sound, and so on. While we normally think of the senses as a principal source of information about the world, the 'sight of sight', the 'hearing of hearing', etc. cannot fulfil that function. Generally, the hypothesis of a sense that can perceive no sensible object is hard to envisage.[32] And the same holds for the probable implication that the exercise of such a sense will not give access to any specific content. Moreover, the aforementioned cases prompt us to reflect on second-order perception,[33] the psychological processes involved in perceptual awareness, and the nature of perception itself.[34]

It is important to acknowledge the legitimacy of raising these issues as well as the philosophical interest that they have in their own right. But it is also important, I think, to stress that Socrates does not appear concerned with such matters in the present context. On balance, T. G. Tuckey's conclusion seems exactly right:

> It is of course possible that it was not the problem of self-consciousness which was exercising Plato here. But even if Plato does not discuss it – and certainly the rest of the argument about ἐπιστήμη ἐπιστήμης is concerned with no such thing – there is no reason why it should not have puzzled him; and it is involved in knowing one's own knowledge . . .. For want of further evidence, we can say no more than this.[35]

2

Well then, does there seem to you to be some desire [*epithymia*] which is not desire of any pleasure, but of itself and the other desires? – No, indeed. – Nor again, it seems to me, a will or rational wish [*boulêsis*] which does not will any good, but wills itself and the other wills? – No, there isn't. – And would you say

---

[32] However, Socrates implicitly acknowledges that this hypothesis is not *impossible* to envisage. One may imagine, for instance, a visual capacity which enables me to tell that I am awake and really seeing things, rather than just dreaming that I am seeing them. That capacity is set over itself and over my seeings of the sky as blue, the grass as green, and this apple as red: it judges not what colour these things are, but whether they are real seeings or not.

[33] An especially relevant text is Aristotle's discussion of perceiving that we are perceiving (*De an.* III.2 425b12–25). On the relation between the Argument from Relatives and the *aporia* articulated in *De an.* III.2 425b12–25, see the different views defended by Caston 2002, McCabe 2007a and 2007b, Johansen 2005 and 2012, and Tsouna in press.

[34] Notably, see McCabe 2007a and 2007b.

[35] Tuckey 1951, 47. It should be noted, however, that Tuckey takes the 'science of science' to refer to a particular act of knowledge being its own object, or to the possibility of one act of knowledge being the object of another.

that there is a kind of love [*eros*] of that sort, one that is actually love of nothing beautiful but of itself and the other loves? – No, he replied, I certainly wouldn't. – And have you ever conceived of a fear [*phobos*] which fears itself and the other fears, but fears no fearsome thing? – No, I have not, he said. – Or a belief or opinion [*doxa*] which is a belief of beliefs and of itself, but does not believe any one of the things that the other beliefs believe? – Of course not. (167e1–168a5)

This second group of counterexamples consists of five cases that cover a fairly broad range of psychological phenomena. How to categorise them is controversial and also a matter of philosophical significance, since it bears on the purpose that they are intended to serve. To begin, I shall address this general issue and, moreover, I shall comment on what I believe to be a distinctive characteristic of these examples: they gain plausibility in the light of other relevant Platonic texts.

Despite claims to the contrary, I submit that the cases of desire, will or (rational) wish, love, fear, and belief belong together, and are intended to jointly bolster the point of the perceptual examples.[36] Textually, nothing indicates that they should be divided into subcategories.[37] Rather, Socrates treats them as a single group and demarcates them from both what precedes and what follows. He introduces the first member of the group, desire, with the word '*alla*' (167e1), an adversative conjunction marking the transition from the previous phase of the argument to the present one. Then, after completing the examination of all five cases and drawing an interim conclusion, he flags the move to another group of examples, i.e. quantitative relatives, with the expression '*phere dē*' (168b2) – an invitation to Critias to turn his attention to this new set of cases. Meanwhile, he uses connectives[38] in order to move from one example to another, thus underscoring that there are strong conceptual links between these five cases.

---

[36] See Lampert 2010, 204, and the discussion by Tuozzo 2011, 211–19.

[37] Hyland 1981, 114–18, maintains that the examples 'fall into three clear-cut groups'. One consists of examples from the senses. Another consists of desire, wish or will, and love, and is individuated by the fact that 'the respective objects are not so evident as in the other examples' (115). The third set of examples, which, according to Hyland, is incomplete, consists of fear and opinion, and a missing component, i.e. *epistême*. Hyland argues that, especially, the third set undermines the supposed point of the argument. For different reasons and with a different aim in mind, Schmid 1998, 90, also claims that 'the key to making sense of it [sc. Socrates' entire list of mental acts] is the fact that it breaks up into three groups of three. The first group is concerned with perception, the second with desire, while the third is a mixture of cognition and emotion'. According to Schmid, the three groups correspond to three events that belong to the dramatic context of the dialogue (154b10–c8, 155d3–e3, 166c7–d6) and suggest that reflexivity is indeed possible for all three types of mental acts. However, there is no mark in the text indicating that this group of examples should be subdivided into smaller groups. Nor, as I hope to show, is there any philosophical need to do so.

[38] οὐδὲ μήν (167e4) marks the transition from ἐπιθυμία to βούλησις, δέ (167e7) from the latter to ἔρως, δέ again (167e10) from ἔρως to φόβος, and again δέ (168a3) from φόβος to δόξα. Finally, Socrates uses

Structurally, Socrates takes care to construct these five examples according to the same pattern and to treat them alike. All of them are strictly reflexive. In every case the relation binding the postulated relative to its correlative is exclusive, exhaustive, and intransparent.[39] And in every case Socrates refrains from mentioning a privative object, e.g. the absence of desire or of love. In these ways too, the examples currently under discussion appear to constitute the same group and have the same dialectical function. At the same time, we should note that there is continuity between Socrates' treatment of the perceptual cases and his discussion of this second group. For every example of the two groups suggests a sharp contrast between a hypothetical capacity or activity, which is strictly reflexive and higher-order, and the corresponding conventional capacity or activity, which is first-order and aliorelative. Moreover, as in the former group, so in the latter, Socrates designates the proprietary objects of first-order capacities or activities in two different ways, one 'substantive', the other 'formal'. On the one hand, parallel with sight and hearing whose objects are colour and sound, the characteristic objects of desire, will or rational wish, love, and fear are, respectively, some pleasure, something good, something beautiful, and something dreadful. On the other hand, comparably to the object of 'all the senses in general', i.e. whatever they perceive (167d8–9), Socrates indicates the characteristic object of opinion as whatever is opinable (168a3–4) and the characteristic object of knowledge as whatever can be learned (168a5).[40]

Philosophically, the five cases of this group taken together amplify the scope of the argument and lend cumulative force to it. The interpretation according to which these examples can in fact admit of reflexive constructions and therefore are intended to undermine Socrates' ostensible purpose will be rejected, I hope, as soon as it becomes clear what sort of reflexivity is at stake. In fact, as I shall try to show, Socrates is not guilty of

----

ἀλλά (168a6) in order to underline the tension between Critias' admission that, in each of these five cases, strict reflexivity seems strange, and his assumption that there can be a strictly reflexive ἐπιστήμη.

[39] The order in which Socrates mentions that the hypothetical relative is of itself but not of a proprietary object varies, as it does elsewhere in the argument. For instance, he says, first, that the postulated desire is not of pleasure and then that it is of itself and the other desires; on the other hand, he mentions, first, that the postulated fear is of itself and the other fears and, then, that it is of no dreadful thing. Nothing philosophical appears to hang on that difference. Contrast the view defended by Tuozzo 2011, 213, according to whom the aforementioned order of Socrates' claims suggests that the oddity of the counterexamples derives primarily from the fact that they are not of the relevant proprietary object and only secondarily from their reflexivity. On this point, see also Tuckey 1951, 115–17.

[40] On the meaning of μαθήματα, see Tuozzo 2011, 215–17, and the relevant discussion below.

double-dealing and Plato does not have a hidden agenda in mind.[41] Like
the perceptual analogues, the psychological analogues are meant to be
taken at face value and can be defended within the limits of a dialectical
argument. One of the aims of my analysis will be to highlight an
important and largely neglected feature of the cases under consideration,
namely that they are intensely intertextual. Part of Plato's tactics in this
passage is, I think, to direct the reader both to other passages of the
Charmides and to other dialogues in order to corroborate the seemingly
arbitrary claims that Socrates makes about the characteristic objects of
desire, rational wish, love, fear, and also belief. Even though intertextuality is an integral aspect of Plato's strategy in the *Charmides*,[42] its role
seems exceptionally prominent in the passage that we are about to
discuss. Let us look at it case by case.

The first counterexample is desire (*epithymia*). Critias is asked to consider
a desire whose sole object is desire, not the proprietary object of desire, namely
pleasure.[43] The relation between the aforementioned desire and its object is
constitutive: that desire just consists of its relation to itself or every desire, and
this precludes its being related *also* to pleasure. If constitutive relativity is
operative for the first-order desires as well,[44] the converse holds true of these
latter. Each of them is related to pleasure, and this precludes their being related
also to themselves. Socrates' language underlines the tentative nature of the
argument's premises: he invites Critias to relay what *seems* to him to be the
case (167e1). Nonetheless, one might object that, as Socrates surely knows,
desires can aim at things other than pleasure, such as honour, virtue, or the
good.[45] Pain too can be an object of desire, and the same holds for evil as
well.[46] Is this example designed, then, to undercut Socrates' stated goal?

There is no compelling reason to accept this inference. For the aforementioned objection invites the retort that, strictly speaking, we only

---

[41] Many interpreters object that we can make sense of the ideas of desiring to feel desire, being in love
with love, fearing one's own fear, or, most importantly, having beliefs about beliefs. If so, it would
seem that Socrates engages in some sort of double-dealing. On the one hand, he argues dialectically
that reflexivity is odd or impossible, while, on the other, he presents cases that suggest precisely the
opposite. As mentioned before, the conclusion frequently drawn is that the intent of these examples
is to establish the possibility of reflexive, higher-order knowledge.

[42] See Chapter 1, 40–51.

[43] Socrates refers here to a desire directed towards a particular pleasure or type of pleasure: ἐπιθυμία
τις … ἥτις ἡδονῆς μὲν οὐδεμιᾶς ἐστὶν ἐπιθυμία: 167e1–2.

[44] This hypothesis will receive strong support from the Argument from Benefit.

[45] See, for instance, Hyland 1981, 115.

[46] It is controversial whether it is rationally possible to aim at evil. According to one kind of approach,
this objective can be made to be coherent, whereas according to another, when we pursue the evil,
we pursue it *as good*.

desire the *pleasure* of having honour, virtue, something good, or even something evil. Moreover, if Socrates assumes that relatives have a one-to-one relation to their respective correlatives (and there is strong evidence that he does), he can only pick one object for desire and no more. Given that '*epithymia*' refers, generically, to desire and, specifically, to appetite, pleasure is a plausible choice as the special object of *epithymia*, or at any rate more suitable than, for example, honour or virtue. The chief philosophical point of the counterexample is also defensible. Although we may conceive of a desire for desire, e.g. for having desires or appetites *about* various things, it is very difficult to envisage a desire that would be *only* of desire and *not* of any desirable object. Desire is an intentional disposition or activity, and a desire that has no intentional object other than desire itself would risk having no content.

Readers familiar with Plato's Socrates will recall that the claim under discussion is articulated and debated elsewhere. Notably, in the *Protagoras*, the desire for pleasure and the desire for the good coincide and constitute the basis of the argument purporting to show on hedonistic premises that weakness of will is impossible (*Prot.* 352e–357e). In the *Gorgias*, the assumption that pleasure is the ultimate object of desire is embedded in Callicles' theoretical stance, which combines psychological hedonism, ethical naturalism, and political amoralism. One could pursue the parallel further, enquiring whether there might not be certain significant associations between the brutal ideology of Callicles and the sophisticated position defended by Critias and pointing to his historical counterpart.

The next example is *boulêsis*, will or rational wish. Critias must consider the possibility of a rational wish that would not be directed to the characteristic object of *boulêsis*, which, according to Socrates, is the good (*agathon*),[47] but would only be a rational wish of itself and every other such item or, equivalently, a rational wish only of rational wish and of nothing else. This is constructed, then, as a strictly reflexive item to be contrasted with every first-order *boulêsis*, which is aliorelative. While the former consists solely of its relation to *boulêsis* itself, the latter is related to a proprietary object distinct from itself. And while the former governs every *boulêsis*, it has no access to the good that the *boulêsis* is of or for. In this case too, the common objection that *boulêsis* can be reflexive misfires. For the issue is not whether we can rationally wish to have rational wishes, but whether there can be a rational wish that has this as its sole object. And

---

[47] I take this to mean 'something good' or 'something perceived as a good'. The contradictory of 'ἀγαθὸν οὐδέν', 'no good' (167e4–5), is 'some good'.

I think that Socrates and Critias are right to give, tentatively, a negative answer: it doesn't seem so. One can rationally wish to have rational wishes for good things. But what would it mean to have a rational wish for rational wishing, period?

One might object that if rational wishing is a good thing, we should be able to wish for it. A defensible answer, it seems to me, could be that our wishing for rational wishing is a wish for it *as a good* – an aliorelative object. One might also point out that Socrates' assertion that *boulêsis* is constitutively related to the good is arbitrary and ought to have been challenged. However, '*boulêsis*' is usually related to deliberation and choice, and Plato's Socrates repeatedly attaches this notion to the operations of reason. Since Critias is portrayed as an intellectualist with Socratic leanings, it is not surprising that he too assumes that, when we rationally wish for something, we wish for it as a good. The idea receives also external support from, for example, the *Gorgias* and the *Laws*. In the *Gorgias*, Socrates contends that a just man will never wish[48] to do unjust things (460c); and he argues that, while power may protect a man against suffering injustice, *boulêsis* (509d3) suffices to protect him against doing unjust deeds (509c–511c). The legislators of Magnesia also presuppose the closest connection between reason and *boulêsis*. Prayer ought to be regulated so that the citizens will ask for their prayers to be answered only if they derive from one's *boulêsis*, rational wish, and are in accordance with one's rational judgement. And the same ought to hold for state prayer as well (*Leg.* 687e).

Next, Socrates presents the case of *erôs*, erotic love. Let us suppose, he tells Critias, that there is a sort of love that is of love alone, but not of what all other loves are about, namely *kalon*, beautiful.[49] In accordance with the above pattern, the *erôs* hypothesised by Socrates is not of anything beautiful, but only of itself and 'the other loves' (167e8). On the other hand, each of 'the other loves' is of something beautiful, but not of love itself. While the 'love of itself and the other loves' is strictly reflexive, 'the other loves' are aliorelative.[50] And while the former has no access to the characteristic object of *erôs*, i.e. *kalon*, it remains formally open whether the latter have

---

[48] οὐδέποτε βουλήσεται: 460c.

[49] Cf. 'ὅς τυγχάνει ὢν ἔρως καλοῦ μὲν οὐδενός' (a love of such a sort), that it is actually love of nothing beautiful: 167e7–8. Again, strictly speaking, the designated object is not 'the beautiful' but whatever beautiful thing or type of thing love is orientated towards.

[50] In this as well as in every other example of this group, if constitutive relativity is operative all the way through (as I believe it is), the first-order relatives ('the other desires', 'the other rational wishes', 'the other loves', etc.) consist just of their relation to their proprietary aliorelative objects. They are *strictly* aliorelative in just that sense. As mentioned (note 44 in this chapter), this supposition will receive considerable support from the Argument from Benefit.

any access to *erôs* itself.[51] Like the examples of fear and belief, the example of *erôs* too has been denounced as blatantly false and revelatory of Socrates' or Plato's real purpose. In the first place, why should Critias accept the arbitrary contention that *erôs* is characteristically of something *kalon*, and also why should we accept it? In the second place, it seems evident that there is such a thing as an *erôs* of itself. There are people who love being in love, never mind with whom. We all encounter such characters in literature, cinema, and, usually to one's detriment, real life as well. Doesn't this show that *eros* can be reflexive in just the sense required by the argument? And if so, should we not conclude that this example is chosen in order to falsify Socrates' earlier claim that reflexivity is implausible or impossible?

There are grounds for resisting that conclusion. First, assuming that '*kalon*' here has a predominantly aesthetic meaning, Socrates' claim that *erôs* is characteristically directed towards something beautiful (or something perceived as beautiful) is borne out by the opening scene of the *Charmides*. There, the narrator portrays the beautiful Charmides as the object of *erôs* for almost everyone present. Not only is he preceded and followed by a throng of young *erastai*, lovers (154a5, c4), but also his beauty (*kallos*) appears to have erotic effects on the older men in the gymnasium, including Socrates himself. In the capacity of narrator, the latter tells us more about his own erotic susceptibility to the *kaloi*, beautiful youths (154b9). He declares himself 'a blank ruler' in respect of measuring their beauty, since every one of them appears to him beautiful (154c8–10).[52] He relays that he admired Charmides' wonderful stature and beauty (154c1–2) and experienced the heat of erotic passion when he accidentally glanced into the youth's cloak (155d3–e1). He was mesmerised by Charmides' look (155c8–d1), was charmed by the beauty of the young man's blush (158c5–6), and attempted to find the beauty of the youth's soul (154e1–7), even though he managed to withstand his physical attractions.

For his own part, Critias is portrayed as overly susceptible to the beauty of his ward. In the opening scene, he describes him as 'most beautiful' (*kallistos*: 154a5), and asserts that the youth is 'beautiful and good' (*kalos kai agathos*: 154e4), philosophical, and 'most poetic' (154e8–155a1), as well as excelling in

---

[51] See previous note.
[52] See the comments concerning the *Symposium* immediately below. Relevant to Socrates' description of himself as a 'blank ruler' is Diotima's description of the second step of the ascent towards the Forms, when the lover realises that the beauty of one body is very like the beauty of another, comes to consider the beauty of all bodies as one and the same, and becomes a lover of all beautiful bodies alike (*Symp.* 201a–b).

virtue (157d1–4). Generally, he appears captured by Charmides' beauty and talks as if he were in love with him. Thus, the dramatic frame of the dialogue illustrates the close relation between *erôs* and *kalon*, whether the latter is physical or psychic, and also explains why Critias does not reject the contention that love is characteristically of something beautiful. Besides, in light of the refined aestheticism of fifth-century Athenians, it seems implausible for a man of Critias' origins and sophistication to reject Socrates' claim out of hand.

Both Socrates' claim that *erôs* is of the *kalon* and the suggestion that an *erôs* directed exclusively to *erôs* and never to its characteristic object would be very strange can be re-examined and re-assessed in the light of different Platonic contexts. One such context is Socrates' attempt to convey the nature of *erôs* in the *Symposium*. While his drinking companions propose different objects of *erôs*,[53] he initially describes *erôs* as 'a desire for beauty but never for ugliness' (*Symp.* 201a). Subsequently, he modifies and elaborates his view in the context of Diotima's speech. According to Diotima, *erôs* is really *every* desire for good things and for happiness, and it includes but is not exhausted by the desire for beautiful things alone (204d–205d). Since loving the good entails desiring to possess it forever (206a), it follows that the object of love is precisely this, to live forever in possession of the good and be immortal (205e): to reproduce and 'give birth in beauty' (206b),[54] and thus subsist after death through one's physical descendants or, better, one's virtuous acts (208e–209e). Only when Diotima undertakes to initiate Socrates in 'the rites of love' (210a) does beauty re-emerge explicitly as the object of the lover's devotion (209e–211d) so that, in the end, the lover comes to know 'just what it is to be beautiful' (211d). Diotima's speech, therefore, supplies a metaphysical and ethical dimension to Socrates' assertion in the *Charmides*, that *erôs* is of the *kalon*. And it also provides implicit support to the point of Socrates' counterexample: those initiated to the 'rites of love' understand that *eros* is orientated outwards towards Beauty, not inwards towards itself. The myth of the *Phaedrus* too brings out that point, insofar as it depicts the lover's longing to recollect the 'radiant' form of Beauty and his erotic pursuit of Beauty through its earthly

---

[53] Phaedrus focuses on the connection between love and virtue but says nothing about what the *erôs* is of. Pausanias distinguishes between the vulgar love of the body and the noble love of the beloved's soul but does not say a word about beauty. Aristophanes determines *erôs* as one's desire to recover one's original nature by uniting oneself with the person one loves and thus by becoming whole and complete. As for Agathon, he describes *erôs* as the youngest, most virtuous, and most beautiful of the gods; according to his eulogy, *erôs* is not *of beauty*, but is himself beautiful.

[54] τόκος ἐν καλῷ: see the rendering of that phrase by Nehamas and Woodruff 1989 and also note 79 of that translation.

images.⁵⁵ Again, love is of beautiful things and, ultimately, of Beauty. It is not of itself.⁵⁶

But could Socrates hold his ground vis-à-vis the objection that a lover's love might have solely itself as its own object? Consider for a moment what it would be to be in love with love alone in the absence of any object. You will probably find it difficult if not impossible to envisage what this might be like. An object will always creep into the picture, even on the hypothesis that the lover has no attachment whatsoever to that particular object and would readily replace it with another. Even if the aim of love is merely to perpetuate the disposition or the experience of love, to achieve that aim the lover will always need to love someone or something. If this concession is made, Socrates' point may stand.

The following case is *phobos*, fear. Switching the order that he has followed in the earlier examples of this group,⁵⁷ Socrates asks his interlocutor whether he has ever thought of a fear fearing fear, i.e. itself and the other fears, but nothing fearsome (*deinon*).⁵⁸ In this case too, the psychological state under consideration is higher-order, has a constitutive relation to its reflexive correlative, and governs its first-order counterparts but not their objects. Moreover, a contrast is implied between that hypothetical fear and every other fear. The former is of itself and the other fears but of nothing fearsome, whereas the latter is, characteristically, of something fearsome but presumably not of fear itself. Critias promptly concedes that he has never conceived of fear in these terms.⁵⁹ It is not clear whether he finds Socrates' hypothesis merely strange or unintelligible.

Like the case of *erôs*, the case of fear appears especially liable to criticism. While the implicit claim that fear is typically of fearsome things is unexceptional, one may point out that it is uninformative. More importantly, one

---

⁵⁵ There are good reasons to take the myth seriously, though not, of course, literally: see Tsouna 2012, especially 215–19.

⁵⁶ What to make of these textual references depends on each reader. The *erôs* example in the *Charmides* can be read proleptically (cf. Kahn 1996), as pointing forward to, for example, the *Symposium* and the *Phaedrus*, or it can be read in developmental terms, as representing an earlier example of Plato's thinking about *erôs*. Or one may choose to remain within the confines of the *Charmides* and interpret the example of *erôs* by reference to the dramatic framework of the dialogue as well as on dialectical and philosophical grounds.

⁵⁷ While in the cases of higher-order desire, will, and love he mentions, first, that they are *not* of the corresponding characteristic objects and, then, that they are of themselves, in the case of higher-order fear he mentions, first, that it is of itself and other fears and, subsequently, that it is *not* of some dreadful thing. As mentioned, some commentators consider this difference philosophically significant.

⁵⁸ τῶν δεινῶν δ' οὐδὲ ἕν φοβεῖται' (167a1), a fear which 'does not fear any fearsome thing'. Note that the object of fear is designated as 'some fearsome thing', not 'the fearsome'.

⁵⁹ οὐ κατανενόηκα, ἔφη: 168a2.

may object that a fear of fear is perfectly conceivable and commonly experienced. A soldier may fear his fear rather than the enemy,[60] and phobic passengers often fear their own fearful feelings rather than the possibility of an accident. It would seem that the example completely fails to suggest that reflexivity is problematic; if anything, it suggests the opposite.

Socrates need not be troubled by these objections. First of all, although the dialectical form of the argument prevents him from defending the contention that, characteristically, fear is of fearsome things distinct from the fear itself, two incidents that he relays as narrator illustrate the aliorelative nature of the emotion. When Socrates accidentally glanced into Charmides' cloak and became ablaze, he remembered Cydias' warning to someone infatuated with a handsome youth: 'beware of approaching as a fawn approaches a lion and of being seized as his portion of flesh' (155d6–e1). At the time, Socrates feared that he would be consumed by such a wild beast (155e1–2). His dread was not about fear itself but about something fearsome: the all-consuming power of sexual passion that had him in its grip. Later in the dialogue, Socrates refers to his own fear about a different object. In response to Critias' accusation that he cares for dialectical victory rather than truth (166c3–6), Socrates declares that the only reason why he wishes to pursue the search is his fear that he might suppose he knows what he does not know (166c7–d2). In a way, his fear is self-referential, since it concerns his own ignorance. Nonetheless, it is not reflexive in the sense that the 'fear of itself and the other fears' is reflexive, but has an intentional object distinct from the fear itself.

The idea that fear is typically of fearsome things is presupposed or illustrated in many other Platonic passages. In the *Laches*, for instance, the interlocutors debate the nature of courage on the assumption that courage primarily has to do with fear of fearsome things (*deina*), such as the perils of war and of seafaring (*Lach.* 191d–e, 193a–c).[61] Nicias conceives of courage as a sort of general knowledge of what is to be dreaded and what is to be hoped for,[62] as opposed to the specific knowledge of fearsome or hopeful things in specific fields of expertise (194e–196e). In either of these cases, i.e. the expertise equivalent to courage or the expertise in the *technai* (arts or sciences), the things to be feared or hoped for are distinct from fear or hope itself.

---

[60] Recall Franklin D. Roosevelt's 'The only thing we have to fear is fear itself'.
[61] However, Socrates extends the concept of courage to comprise also pains and pleasures and desires, as well as the moral and psychological strength to conduct properly a philosophical investigation (194a).
[62] δεινῶν καὶ μὴ δεινῶν ἐπιστήμονι: 195d.

The courageous man knows 'which ones of these things' are harmful and fearsome and which ones not (196a). Likewise, doctors know what is to be feared in disease (195b), farmers in farming (195b), seers in the premonitory signs (195e–196a), etc. Not once do the interlocutors of the *Laches* air the possibility that fear may be *also* or *only* of itself. Similar observations apply also to the *Republic*, since in that dialogue too fear is always treated as an aliorelative whose correlative is distinct from fear itself. 'What is fearsome' includes death and Hades (386a–387b), the decimation of one's family and the deprivation of one's possessions (387b–388c), pains and pleasures, and desires (388c ff., 429c–d). Correspondingly, Socrates suggests that the city is courageous by virtue of the superlative ability of the trained guardian-soldiers to thoroughly absorb the laws, just like a dye (430a), and 'to preserve through everything the correct and law-inculcated belief about what is to be feared and what is not' (430b).

Does the suggestion that fear is typically not reflexive but aliorelative have philosophical merit? I suggest that it does, metaphysically and conceptually as well as psychologically. On the constitutive view, fear must be constituted by its relation to something else, since, if there were a fear solely of fear, that fear would be self-constituting and not grounded in anything. Moreover, there is plausibility to the suggestion that people cannot fear fear without there being some content to the first-order fear. While it is unquestionable that there is such a thing as a fear of fear, it seems virtually impossible to defend the idea that the latter is *only* of fear and of nothing else. As in the case of a 'love of itself', so in the case of a 'fear of itself', it seems that one would eventually have to refer to some object, i.e. what the fear that one fears is *about*.[63] This appears to be a fact of proper grammar and a feature of human psychology. Those who wish to deny it bear the onus of proof.

The final and most challenging case of this group is *doxa*, belief or opinion.[64] Conceptually, it lies closest to the paradigm of *epistême* and serves as a springboard from which Socrates reaches a set of interim conclusions.[65] Can there be, Socrates asks, an opinion that is only of

---

[63] I have in mind typical forms of the emotion of fear, not, for example, panic attacks.
[64] In this context I prefer 'opinion' and 'opinable' to 'belief' and 'believable', because 'believable' invites contrast with 'unbelievable'.
[65] According to Benardete 1986, 250–1, opinion should have been placed right after perception. On the other hand, Lampert 2010, 204, retorts that opinion is placed exactly where it should be, i.e. immediately after the examples that are evidently non-reflexive but immediately before *epistême*, which, like opinion, can be reflexive. According to Lampert, Critias is so carried away by his admissions regarding the former cases that he admits, wrongly, that belief too is non-reflexive. Many other interpreters follow this sort of approach.

other opinions[66] and of itself but not of 'what other opinions opine' (168a3–4), i.e. not of anything opinable? Like all preceding hypotheses, this hypothesis entails that the item to be entertained is strictly reflexive and, by virtue of strict reflexivity, governs the other opinions insofar as they are opinions but cannot access or govern their proprietary object. The latter is designated in a formal manner that carries no commitment regarding the particular content of an opinion but nonetheless underscores its aliorelativity: first-order opinions are of whatever it is that they opine,[67] whereas the opinion under consideration is constructed as an opinion of opinion, namely an opinion orientated only towards opinion itself.

As in the other examples, so in the present one Socrates does not state that the hypothesised item is *only* of itself. However, in the case of opinion, as in all other cases, he makes this explicit by contrasting the reflexive item in question with its first-order counterparts: the opinion serving as a counterexample is directed towards itself (X is directed towards each and every X), whereas all other opinions are directed towards opinable things. Conversely, for reasons indicated above, we are to infer that the first-order opinions are *only* of opinables. They are not of themselves as types or instances of *opinion*.[68] If Critias could defend the notion of a strictly reflexive opinion, he would gain considerable support for his contention that temperance is a strictly reflexive form of *epistêmê*.

Does the argument go through for opinion? Many contend that it does not, for it is evident that we can opine about opinion. This is what Socrates and Critias are currently doing, and this is what epistemology is about. More than any other example, then, belief or opinion would seem to undercut Socrates' stated goal, especially because it is the closest analogue to knowledge. If, as the interlocutors agree, there can be no opinion of other opinions and of itself, it seems probable that there also cannot be knowledge of other knowledges and of itself (168a3–a9). If, on the other hand, one accepts the evident truth that opinion can be of opinion, then one should also probably accept that knowledge can be of knowledge. Nonetheless, this objection too derives from a misunderstanding. Socrates constructs his counterexample so as to challenge, precisely, the idea of an opinion that is only of opinion but, most emphatically, of no content.[69] He does not question in the least the possibility of second-order opinions

---

[66] Note the absence of the definite article before the genitive plural δοξῶν (168a3).
[67] ὧν δὲ αἱ ἄλλαι δοξάζουσιν: 168a3–4.
[68] This claim too will be further supported in the next chapter.   [69] See note 67 in this chapter.

or the coherence of epistemological endeavours.[70] Critias understands him correctly and, therefore, emphatically denies that there can be such an opinion: 'Of course not', he says.[71]

Earlier in the *Charmides*, Socrates' sketch of the 'best method of enquiry' (158e6–159a4) provides an opportunity to compare and contrast the latter sort of belief with reflective beliefs about oneself. There is nothing strange about the suggestion that Charmides should attend to his own sense of himself and tell Socrates what he takes temperance to be 'according to [his] own opinion' (159a10). Likewise, there is nothing strange about the beliefs that the youth expresses in turn, namely that temperance is doing things quietly and decorously (159b2–5) or that temperance is *aidôs*, a sense of shame (160e4–5). Both these beliefs are self-referential insofar as they concern qualities that Charmides registers in himself. And both are substantive: they are *about* temperance as well as about Charmides, and say something about a character that Charmides may or may not truly possess. But neither of them is reflexive in the sense specified above. Neither of them is about belief, but rather about the sort of thing that beliefs characteristically are about. My point is this: the target of the counterexample under discussion is not reflexivity or self-referentiality in a broad sense. In fact, 'the best method' makes it clear that the latter can be unexceptional, and the same presumably holds for most kinds of higher-order belief. Socrates aims only at the hypothetical notion of a belief reflexive in such a way as to have no content. If this is correct, he is merely stating the obvious not only about belief, but about *epistême* as well.

It seems worth pressing the point that, consistently with the *Charmides*, Plato standardly treats belief as an aliorelative in other dialogues. In the *Meno*, knowledge and belief have the same object and that object is distinct from either of these capacities. Socrates uses a well-known example in order to suggest that, at least in some cases, knowledge and belief are equally reliable guides to action: whether one knew the road to Larissa or had true belief about the road to Larissa, one would be in a position to lead people correctly to that town (*Men.* 97a–b).[72] As in the *Charmides*, so in *Republic*

---

[70] The interlocutors do not distinguish between types and tokens, but apparently assume that the counterexample under discussion applies to both: whether as type or token, belief probably cannot be *only* of itself and other beliefs, but (also) of something distinct from itself: even when it is about belief, it must have substantive content.

[71] οὐδαμῶς: 168a5.

[72] This example shows that there is *some* object of belief that is not belief. It does not support the stronger thesis that there is *no* object of belief that is belief – a thesis that is untenable.

V knowledge and belief have distinct objects. But although in the Argument from Relatives Socrates appears to leave the door open for the so-called two worlds of the *Republic*, the world of *epistêmê* and that of *doxa*,[73] he is not in a position to do the metaphysical work to explain the respective objects of these two faculties. However, he does this work in the *Republic*. In the argument aiming to convince the lovers of sights and sounds that they have only belief and not knowledge (*Rep.* V 475a–480a), he distinguishes belief from both knowledge and ignorance and identifies their respective objects: while knowledge is of what-is and ignorance is of what-is-not, belief is of what-is-and-is-not (476d–478e). As it turns out, the empirical particulars instantiating a given Form are cases of what-is-and-is-not and, on account of that fact, they are the proprietary object of belief (478e–480a). For all the controversies surrounding this argument, one thing remains uncontested: knowledge and belief are related to their respective objects in an aliorelative manner. What-is is distinct from the knowledge that knows it, and what-is-and-is-not is distinct from the opinion that opines it.

At this point, we should pause with Socrates to assess where matters stand.

> Nonetheless, we apparently do assert, do we not, that there is a science of this kind, which is not a science of any object of learning, but a science of itself and the other sciences. – Indeed, we do. – And would it not be something strange if it really exists? Let us not yet declare that it doesn't, but consider further whether it does. – Quite right. (168a6–b1)

Speaking in the first-person plural,[74] Socrates points out that their assumption that there is a science directed only towards science and not towards any *mathêma*, scientific object or field, is now under severe strain. Clearly, he thinks that the cases examined so far, taken together, provide reasonable grounds for concluding that, even if the aforementioned science is possible, it is entirely atypical.[75] None of the psychological analogues proved to be relevantly similar to it. Rather, these analogues jointly constitute cumulative evidence for Socrates' intuition that a 'science of science' seems strange or even absurd (*atopon*: 168a10).[76] However, Socrates shows himself fully aware of the fact that such evidence is inconclusive. And therefore he proposes that they press on.

---

[73] This can plausibly be considered an instance of *prolêpsis* (on the proleptic reading of Plato see again Kahn 1996).

[74] φαμέν: 168a6.   [75] Note the rhetorical question at 168a10.   [76] See 167c4.

3

> Now, consider the following. This[77] science is a science *of something*, and it
> has a power such as to be *of something*, is that not so? – Indeed. – For we say
> that the greater too has a certain power such as to be greater *than something*,
> right? – Quite so. – Namely, than something smaller, if it is going to be
> greater. – Necessarily. – So if we were to find something greater which is
> greater than both the greater [things] and than itself but not greater than any
> one of the [things] that the other greater [things] are greater than, then, if
> indeed it were greater than itself, that very property would also necessarily
> belong to it somehow, namely it would also be smaller than itself. Or is it
> not so? – It is absolutely necessary, Socrates, he said. – And also, if there is
> a double of both the other doubles and itself, then of course it would be
> double of itself and the other doubles by being half. For there presumably
> isn't a double of anything other than of half. – True. – And if something is
> more than itself it will be also less, if heavier then lighter, if older then
> younger, and likewise for all the other cases. (168b2–d1, emphasis added)

Socrates now returns to the paradigm of *epistême* to discuss it specifically
from the perspective of science as a *dynamis*, power or capacity: a power or
capacity to be *of something* (*tinos*), i.e. of its proper correlative, whatever
this may be. '*Dynamis*' in this context need not be theoretically loaded or
indicate relations of some specific type.[78] Socrates employs this term
merely to underscore the assumption that this third group of analogues,
i.e. comparative quantities such as the greater and the smaller or the more
and the less, are relative to their own correlative objects, just as *epistême* is.
If the quantitative relatives of this group can be strictly reflexive, the same
probably holds for *epistême* as well. If, on the other hand, they do not
tolerate strict reflexivity, it is likely that *epistême* does not tolerate it
either.[79]

Again, Socrates develops fully the first example of this group and goes
more quickly through the others. He supposes that there is a greater
(*meizon*) whose power to be greater than something smaller (168b5–9) is

---

[77] I opt for the reading αὕτη printed by Burnet, as opposed to Shorey's reading αὐτή (Shorey 1907,
endorsed by van der Ben 1985 and Tuozzo 2011, 220 and n. 23). Ebert 1974, 71, argues in favour of
Burnet's reading.

[78] Compare the use of 'δύναμις' in *Rep.* V 476d–480a. Gosling 1968 argues, convincingly I think, that
Socrates' claim that knowledge and belief are δυνάμεις as well as his description of what he takes
δυνάμεις to be (477c1–4) do not necessitate any specialised interpretation of that term. It need not
refer to faculties but merely capacities by which we can do what we can do.

[79] Different interpretations of this third stage of the argument depend on what its focus is taken to be:
mainly reflexivity (Benson 2003; Tuozzo 2011, 221–4; Tsouna forthcoming) or both reflexivity and
higher-order (McCabe 2007a, 2007b).

directed towards itself and other items like itself (168b10–11),[80] but is not greater than the correlative object that every other greater is greater *than* (168b11), i.e. something smaller (*elatton*). And he infers that, in such a case, the higher-order greater would have to be both greater and smaller than itself, since it both consists in the power to be *greater* than something smaller and is determined by hypothesis to be its own correlative, i.e. *smaller* than itself. Critias considers this a necessary inference and assents to it (168c3).[81]

Also, Critias agrees (168c8) that similar inferences would have to be drawn for other quantitative relatives, if they too received reflexive constructions. Socrates presents these constructions in an elliptical manner, and the reasoning he suggests is the following: since the double (*diplasion*) must be always of half (*hêmiseos*),[82] the hypothesis that there is a double 'of both the other doubles and itself' (168c4–5) entails that the former would be both double and half. Since what-is-more (*pleon*) must be[83] of what-is-less (*elatton*), a reflexive construction of what-is-more would entail that it would be both more-than-itself (*pleon hautou*) and less-than-itself (168c9). Since the heavier (*baryteron*) must be of the lighter (*kouphoteron*), something heavier than itself (and whatever else is heavier) would have to be both heavier and lighter (168c9–10). Since whatever is older (*presbyteron*) is necessarily of (i.e. necessarily older than) something younger (*neôteron*), the supposition that there is something older than 'the other olders and itself'[84] entails that the latter is both older and younger (168c10). And, as Socrates contends (168c10–d1), the same holds for every other example of that kind.

These counterexamples make a stronger point than the previous ones. For while the latter show strict reflexivity to be extremely odd, they fall short of establishing, even provisionally, that it amounts to nonsense. And while they offer cumulative evidence against the plausibility of strictly reflexive perceptual and other psychological notions, several of those cases invite us to entertain inclusively reflexive notions, such as a love which is both of itself and of what is beautiful, or a fear which is both of itself and of what is fearsome. The comparative relatives constituting this third group are, on the contrary, irreflexive in every way. Socrates and Critias stress that the greater is related to the smaller by necessity (168b9, c1,

---

[80] τῶν μειζόνων μεῖζον καὶ ἑαυτοῦ: 168b10–11. [81] Πολλὴ ἀνάγκη, ἔφη, ὦ Σώκρατες: 168c3.
[82] οὐ γάρ ἐστίν που ἄλλου διπλάσιον ἢ ἡμίσεος: 168c6–7.
[83] The modality operative in all these claims is necessity: see πάντως at 168c1 and οὐ γάρ ἐστιν at 168c6, as well as ἀνάγκη at 168b9 and 168c3.
[84] Compare 'the other greaters and itself' (168b10–11) and 'both the other doubles and itself' (168c4–5).

c3), the double is necessarily of the half (168c6–7), and the same applies to every other such relative (168c10–d1). Although they do not clarify further the kind of necessity involved in these relations, it is probably logical or conceptual necessity. But if it is logically necessary that the power of every such comparative quantity be directed to its characteristic object, and if the latter is invariably aliorelative, the supposition that the power of a comparative quantity will be directed towards itself will entail inconsistency or contradiction.

The implication concerning *epistêmê* is this: if *epistêmê* behaves, logically or conceptually, in a way comparable to the way that quantitative relatives behave, then, in all probability, Critias' definition of temperance as a 'science of science' ought to be dropped. Socrates' next move will be to apply the notion of *dynamis*, power, to the perceptual cases of hearing and sight and examine these cases again from a new angle.

4

> Whatever has its own power directed towards itself, won't it also have that special nature [*ousian*][85] towards which its power was directed? I mean something like this: hearing, for instance, we say, is hearing of nothing but sound, is it not? – Yes. – So, if it is going to hear itself, it will hear itself as having sound; for there is no other way that it could hear. – Most necessarily. – And I suppose sight too, my excellent friend, if it really is going to see itself, must itself have some colour; for sight will never see anything colourless. – Certainly not. (168d1–e2)

Socrates begins by articulating a principle that he derives from examining the hypothesis that quantitative relatives might be reflexive. Namely, if a relative has a power such as to be of something, i.e. of a certain *ousia*,[86] and if it has that power directed towards itself, it must also possess the aforementioned *ousia* – in other words, it must also be its own characteristic object. A greater has the power of being greater than a smaller, and so, if it is directed towards itself, it must also possess that special nature, i.e. it must also be smaller. A double has the power of being double of half and, therefore, if it is directed towards itself, it must also be half. In such cases the relative both has the power to be *of* a certain *ousia* and possesses that *ousia*. In the preceding stage of the argument, the application of that principle to comparative quantities appeared to result in logical impossibilities. In the present passage, Socrates undertakes to show that, when the

---

[85] So Tuozzo 2011, 222.   [86] On the present use of '*ousia*' see below, 223.

aforementioned principle is applied to the perceptual examples of hearing and sight,[87] these latter do not fare well either.

First, a brief comment on '*ousia*' – a term that can mean 'being', 'special nature', and also 'that which is one's own'. Like '*dynamis*', '*ousia*' can be a metaphysically loaded term: it can refer to a metaphysical essence captured by a definition. But '*ousia*' need not to be used in a metaphysical sense and, in the present case, it is not. The context strongly suggests that '*ousia*' here refers to the special nature of a relative's proprietary correlative. Thus, the term underscores the one-to-one constitutive relation that, as the interlocutors evidently suppose all along, holds between a relative and what that relative is *of*: the former is a relative just in virtue of its power to be directed towards its own correlative *ousia* and no other. Relatives like the greater and the double are clear illustrations of that sort of relation, and perceptual relatives too, as Socrates will now argue, behave in a comparable manner.

Characteristically, hearing is of sound and sight of colour. But let us suppose that there is a hearing of itself and a sight of itself.[88] In the former case, since hearing is directed to itself, hearing itself must have the *ousia* that it is characteristically related to, namely sound. Regardless of whether hearing is reflexive or aliorelative, it can hear only sound. Hence, to hear itself, hearing must be sonorous. Likewise, in the case of sight, supposing that there is a sight that sees itself, it must have the *ousia* that sight is characteristically related to, namely colour. Irrespective of whether sight is directed to itself or to something else, it can only see colour. Therefore, if sight is to see itself, it must be coloured. In these examples, then, the distinction between hearing and sound, sight and colour, or, generally, sense and sensible collapses entirely. *Prima facie* this implication seems unacceptable, even though later on Socrates will intimate that it may be palatable to some people (168e9–169a1).

It is instructive to compare Socrates' earlier treatment of perceptual relatives with the argument under discussion. For we find that, on these two occasions, he follows different dialectical strategies. In the former passage (167c8–d10), he suggests that the hypothetical cases of reflexive sight and reflexive hearing appear strange on account of the fact that each of them is directed *only* towards itself (and the other sights or hearings) and

[87] As mentioned (note 15 of this chapter), Socrates does not consider common sensibles like shape and motion, but conducts the sections of the argument concerning the senses in terms of the special objects of these latter.

[88] Note that, on this occasion, Socrates does not mention that hearing is of 'the other hearings' as well as of itself, or that sight is of 'the other sights' as well as of itself. This confirms that the higher-order aspect of reflexive relatives is not the focus of this argument.

not towards the characteristic object of that sense, i.e. colour or sound. Therefore, the strangeness of these cases chiefly results from the intransparency of the relation between the postulated reflexive sense and the characteristic object of the other sights or hearings that it governs. A sight that sees only sight but no coloured object seems incredible mainly because it sees nothing visible. And a hearing that hears only itself and every hearing but no sound appears odd mainly because it hears nothing audible.

Contrast Socrates' tactics in the latter passage (168d1–e2). Here, reflexive hearing and reflexive sight are shown to be strange not because they don't perceive sound or colour, but because they must. To repeat the reasoning, since hearing hears only sound and sight sees only colour, if either of them is directed to itself, it itself must possess sound or colour.[89] But the idea that hearing hears itself by virtue of being sonorous and sight sees itself by virtue of being coloured strikes one as paradoxical or absurd. These two tracks of argument undermine the notion of a 'science of science' in different ways. According to the first, as it is strange to suppose that there is a sight that sees sight but no colour and a hearing that hears hearing but no sound, so it seems strange to suppose that there is a science or knowledge that knows only knowledge but no discipline. According to the second, the notions of a sonorous hearing and of a coloured sight are extremely odd, and we are prompted to question whether the same holds for the notion of an *epistême* that is simultaneously a *mathêma* (168a7). As for Socrates, he is poised to draw some tentative conclusions.

5

Then do you see, Critias, that, of the cases that we have gone through, some of them appear to us to be entirely impossible, while others utterly defy belief[90] as to whether they could ever have their own power directed towards themselves. For, on the one hand, in the cases of magnitudes and multitudes and the like this seems entirely impossible. Or not? – Very much so. – On the other hand again, hearing and sight, and moreover motion able to[91]

---

[89] Socrates' contention that hearing and sight must perceive their respective proprietary sensibles holds for both first-order sight and hearing and their second-order reflexive counterparts. The strangeness of the latter derives from precisely that fact. However, one may object that, since, for example, first-order sight is of colour and second-order reflexive sight is also of colour, these two levels of sight or seeing collapse into one. The problem is identified and discussed by Duncombe 2012a and others. However, the interlocutors of the *Charmides* do not raise that issue.

[90] Compare Tuozzo 2011, 223 and n. 27, who takes ἡμῖν in 168e4 with both φαίνεται and ἀπιστεῖται.

[91] <δυναμένη> or a word with a similar function seems to have fallen out of the text. The sentence is grammatically irregular, but the meaning is reasonably clear.

move itself and heat able to burn itself and all other such cases may arouse disbelief in some people, but perhaps not in others. (168e3–169a1)

Socrates urges Critias to 'see' (168e3) where the argument has led them. I take it that he uses that form of the verb *horan*, 'to see', not in order to indicate that perception or knowledge or both are reflexive after all (as some scholars maintain), but in an ordinary sense in order to exhort his interlocutor to focus his attention on the inferences to follow.[92] A fair assessment of the latter requires that we take into consideration the following features: the dialectical nature of the argument; its exact purpose and target; and the fact that Socrates ascribes different degrees of credence to different groups of counterexamples. Furthermore, something needs to be said about the reflexive cases of motion and heat as well as the final allusion to those who might remain unconvinced by the argument.

First, then, let us get clear about the sort of warrant that we are entitled to look for. The Argument from Relatives is dialectical and proceeds through analogy and induction. Thus, to judge whether it is successful and whether its conclusion is legitimate, we should not ask whether the premises of the argument demonstrate the conclusion, but whether the former have Critias' consent and convincingly, albeit not decisively, support the conclusion. I submit that the correct answer is affirmative on both these counts.[93]

As noted, Socrates consistently uses the language of belief both to express the puzzle that motivates the Argument from Relatives and to conduct the latter. At the outset, he tells Critias that, if he is willing to consider cases analogous to *epistêmê*, he too will believe, as Socrates himself believes,[94] that 'a science of itself and the other sciences and non-science' (167b10–c2) is impossible. Thus, he clarifies what the analogues are expected to achieve: provide sufficient grounds for belief, not demonstrative knowledge. Accordingly, after presenting

---

[92] While Plato does not choose to vary his words at random, it does not follow that every one of his words has a technical meaning and, in this instance, I deny that there is a reason why ὁρᾷς should. However, interpreters who maintain that the Argument from Relatives is designed to defeat its stated goal claim otherwise. For example, McCabe 2007a (especially 13–15) argues that Socrates' exhortation to Critias to 'see' the results of the argument suggests that he does not consider perception a direct and 'brutish' relation between a perceiver and a physical object, but a complex, 'civilised' relation involving belief as well. Lampert 2010, 205, maintains that the 'seeing' that Critias is required to do is not really 'seeing' but 'reflexive cognition'. Hence, although the argument goes through for perception and for comparative quantities, it does not go through for cognition which, as Socrates' admonition to Critias to 'see' shows, can be reflexive. According to Schmid 1998, 97–9, the argument goes through only for philistines, i.e. those that do not 'see' the possibility of reflexive being.

[93] See, notably, Santas 1973, 129, and also Carone 1998, Benson 2003, and McCabe 2007a and 2007b.

[94] δόξει σοι ὡς ἐγῷμαι: 167b5–6.

each counterexample of the first two groups, he asks Critias what *seems* to him to be the case, or what he would say *might* be the case, or what he *imagines* to be the case (167d1, 6, 8, e1, 7, 10). Likewise, although he treats the comparative quantities of the third group in a more assertive mode, nonetheless he highlights the dialectical standing of the premises by drawing attention to the fact that they have been secured through agreement (e.g. 168b5, c2). He follows the same practice when he revisits the perceptual relatives of hearing and sight (168d3). For instance, he makes clear that the principle that whatever has its own power directed towards itself also must possess the corresponding *ousia* (168d1–3) will be treated as a premise only if Critias endorses it (168d3–4). Finally, in the passage cited above, he invites Critias to contemplate the conclusions that seem to both of them (168e4)[95] to have been reached. And he remarks that these latter may incite *disbelief* in some people,[96] though not necessarily in everyone.

Next, assuming that the premises of the Argument from Relatives bear, specifically, on strictly reflexive relatives and not every kind of reflexive or reflective psychological capacity and/or activity, the same should hold also for its conclusion. On the reading that I defend, the latter does not prejudice issues such as the possibility of higher-order perception and the legitimacy of higher-order belief. Even if Socrates indirectly problematises these higher-order functions, he certainly does not end up precluding them. As I argued, his counterexamples only aim to suggest that as there cannot be a perception only of itself and of no perceptible or an opinion only of opinion and devoid of content, so there cannot be an *epistême*, knowledge, only of knowledge and of no discipline. The conclusions he draws concern just that point. Furthermore, it is important to register that Socrates' concluding inferences ascribe different degrees of credibility to the counterexamples. He appears to think that some of them offer stronger grounds than others for rejecting the assumption that a 'science of science' is possible.

We should bear these observations in mind while we evaluate, together with Critias, the conclusions that Socrates draws for us. On the basis of the different sorts of cases examined above,[97] he infers that, on the one hand, the examples of the third group, namely quantitative relatives of 'magnitudes and multitudes and the like' (168e5–6), appear entirely impossible (168e4),[98] while, on the other, the examples of the first and the second

---

[95] φαίνεται ἡμῖν: 168e4.   [96] τοῖς μὲν ἀπιστίαν <ἂν> παράσχοι: 169a1.

[97] τὰ ὅσα διεληλύθαμεν: 168e3. This is one of the places where Socrates highlights the inductive nature of his method.

[98] ἀδύνατα παντάπασι φαίνεται ἡμῖν: 168e4. The claim is repeated at 168e6.

group[99] cause grave doubts as to whether or not 'they ever have their own power directed towards themselves' (168e5). While this phrase does not specify whether such doubts concern reflexivity in general or strict reflexivity alone, I propose that we read it consistently with the premises of the argument and take disbelief to concern just cases that receive a strictly reflexive construction: not whether, for example, love ever has its power directed towards itself but whether love ever has its power directed *only* towards itself. The philosophical disadvantages of the alternative option are considerable, as I hope to have shown.

Up to this point Socrates' conclusions are defensible. Even his fiercest critics ought to admit that the hypothesis of a sense perceiving itself and no sensible, or generally of a psychological capacity directed towards itself and nothing else, beggars belief. If one does not want to dismiss it out of hand, one has to do conceptual work in order to explain and uphold it. As for comparative relatives involving quantitative measurement, Socrates puts his finger on a genuine logical puzzle and indicates how to avoid it. *If* the cases he has examined are relevantly analogous to *epistêmê*, they support (but do not demonstrate) his original claim that the conception of a 'science of itself and the other sciences and of the absence of science' is strange (167c4) and, in the light of certain cases, the sort of reflexivity that it exhibits seems impossible (167c4–6).

One may reasonably object that this is a big 'if', for it is not *prima facie* plausible to assume that knowledge is analogous to items as different as, for example, sight, love, and double, even though it may be relevantly analogous to belief. Socrates could respond, however, that his examples are so constructed as to mark out a single feature that constitutes the primary object of this argument: a certain sort of reflexivity, the capacity of a relative to have a one-to-one constitutive relation to itself. Since the analogy with *epistêmê* focuses on precisely that feature, it is arguably legitimate. And although the conclusions drawn on the basis of such analogues do not necessarily apply to *epistêmê*, they highlight a truth that the interlocutors of the *Charmides* and its readers ought to take to heart: reflexivity is not a straightforward phenomenon, and one form of it can be extremely problematic or lead to absurdities. In defending reflective, higher-order knowledge, one should be fully aware of the complexities of that task.

---

[99] I take the distinction indicated by τὰ μέν (168e3) ... τὰ δέ (168e4) as exclusive and exhaustive: Socrates distinguishes between the cases of quantitative relatives and all the other cases discussed above. Subsequently, at 168e9–10, he focuses on a subset of the latter group, namely the perceptual relatives of hearing and sight, and he also adds the cases of motion and heat.

In the sequel of our passage, Socrates concentrates his attention on a subset of the cases where reflexivity arouses disbelief, namely the perceptual examples of hearing and sight. Also, he mentions inadvertently the examples of 'a motion moving itself and a heat burning itself, and again all other such cases' (168e9–10) and adds, in the way of an afterthought, that while some people will find such cases unbelievable, others might not (168e10–169a1). Admittedly, there is much here to puzzle us. The latter remark is cryptic, it is not immediately obvious why he singles out hearing and sight again, and the reference to motion and heat appears unmotivated and out of place. I take up these problems in reverse order.

Motion, heat, and 'all other such cases' (168e9–10) can be taken to constitute a fourth, separate group. For they do not have any obvious connection with perception or other psychological phenomena or, of course, with quantitative relatives. They are naturally associated with the domain of nature,[100] not of psychology. These cases too have commonly been taken to suggest the opposite of what the argument purports to show.[101] In fact, the objection runs, Plato does conceive of the soul as a self-mover (*Phdr.* 245c–e) or as self-moving motion (*Leg.* 894e–896a);[102] or, the prologue of the *Charmides*, in particular the arousal that Socrates experienced when he accidentally glanced into Charmides' cloak (155d3–4) and his 'rekindling' back to his senses (156d2–3), is an illustration of self-moving motion and self-kindling heat.[103] However, first, in describing his arousal due to Charmides' charms, Socrates does not talk about a *motion* moving itself, but about something that caused a motion in *him*. Also, when he relays that, after running the risk of falling prey to Charmides' charms, he eventually was 'kindled back to life' (156d2–3) and regained his self-confidence, he alludes to a heat reviving *him*, not a heat reviving *itself*.[104] The same holds for his successful effort to regain control of himself: if it is a motion, it is not orientated towards itself but towards a distinct goal. Hence, no conclusions can be drawn regarding the cases of motion and heat in our passage, either on the basis of the opening scene of the dialogue or on the basis of what Plato writes about self-movers in other works.

I propose that, elliptical as these cases may be, they have exactly the same form as all the others and serve exactly the same purpose. They too have no

---

[100] See Tuozzo 2011, 224.
[101] An exception is Kahn 1996, 195–6, according to whom Socrates makes no decision regarding self-moving and self-heating, but 'only recognizes the magnitude of the problem'.
[102] See Bruell 1977, 177–81; Halper 2000, 311.   [103] So Schmid 1998, 98–9.
[104] Contra Schmid 1998, 98.

context and are constructed in such a way as to exhibit the property that constitutes the main target of the Argument from Relatives: each of them is of itself and of nothing else. Like the examples of the first two groups, a self-moving motion and a self-heating heat may *prima facie* seem odd. Nonetheless, the fact that Socrates mentions them towards the end of the argument and lumps them together with hearing and sight (in that order) seems to me significant. For his allusion to those who perhaps do not find reflexivity incredible (169a1) concerns, first of all, these four examples. The reason lies, I think, in the argument that Socrates advanced earlier in respect of hearing and sight (168d1–e1): if hearing is to hear itself, it must be sonorous, and if sight is to see itself, it must be coloured. As suggested, this argument has a forward-looking function insofar as it points to the issue of second-order perception and prompts us to examine reflexivity from that angle, as Aristotle did. Perhaps Socrates suggests that we may do something similar with motion and heat. Even though, taken *in abstracto* in accordance with the paradigm, the notions of a motion moving itself and a heating burning itself might appear strange, they can make sense if they are appropriately modified and embedded in some specific philosophical context. The argument about the self-moving soul in the *Phaedrus*, the importance of self-moving motion in *Laws* X, and the doctrine of universal conflagration and eternal recurrence in Stoicism illustrate different ways in which that goal could be achieved.

Where does the Argument from Relatives leave the interlocutors? Judging by his reactions, Critias now realises that his conception of temperance as a 'science of itself and the other sciences and the lack of science' is threatened. He has good reason to wonder whether he made the right move when he contended that temperance differs from all the other sciences and arts in that temperance alone is an *epistêmê* only of *epistêmê* and its privation and of nothing else. For his own part, Socrates ended up qualifying his earlier belief that 'a science of itself' is impossible (167c6) – a belief tightly intertwined with his staunch commitment to the *technê* analogy. The examination of different groups of analogues has led him to the tentative conclusion that some relatives are more susceptible to receiving a reflexive construction than others, and that the perceptual cases and the cases of motion and heat are worth re-examining in that regard.

For all its merits, however, the Argument from Relatives is inconclusive. In his final comments, Socrates suggests that its inconclusiveness is a matter of method, outlines what he takes to be the proper way of investigating reflexivity, confesses his inability to undertake such a project, and delegates it to someone else.

6

What is needed in fact, my friend, is some great man who will draw this division [*diairêsetai*] in a satisfactory manner regarding every aspect: whether no being [*ouden tôn ontôn*] is naturally constituted so as to have its own power directed towards itself but [only][105] towards something other than itself,[106] or whether some beings are so constituted whereas others are not; and again, if there are beings which have it towards themselves, whether or not they include the science which we claim to be temperance. For my own part, I do not believe that I am myself able to draw this division. And therefore, neither am I in a position to affirm with confidence whether it is possible that this obtains,[107] namely that there is a science of science, nor, supposing that it is perfectly possible, do I accept that this is temperance before I have examined whether or not something would benefit us in virtue of being of such a sort – for in fact I have the intuition that temperance is something beneficial and good. You therefore, son of Callaeschrus – since you contend that temperance is this very thing, the science of science and moreover of the absence of science – first, prove that this thing I was just mentioning is possible;[108] and second, in addition to being possible, that it is also beneficial. And then perhaps you would satisfy me as well that you are speaking correctly about what temperance is. (169a1–169c2)

While the main body of the Argument from Relatives can be interpreted without importing elements from the metaphysics and epistemology of the *Republic* and beyond, the above passage has an explicitly forward-looking outlook. Socrates outlines a philosophical enterprise to be undertaken at some future time, which will involve the use of *diairesis*, division,[109] – a hallmark of the so-called late Platonic dialogues, in particular the *Sophist* and the *Statesman*. He seems convinced that such an investigation could conclusively settle the issue under debate, but nonetheless believes himself unable to carry it through.[110] Therefore, he expresses his hope that 'some

---

[105] Lamb's translation 'and not only some other object' (Lamb 1955, 65) does not accurately render the Greek text and is misleading about a crucial point: the question that the division is supposed to settle is not whether there is some being which is of itself *as well as* of something other than itself, but whether there is some being which is of itself *but not* of anything other than itself. Consequently, the inference of many commentators that Socrates here removes the exclusive proviso is erroneous.

[106] πλὴν ἐπιστήμης secl. Schleiermacher.   [107] Here, the aorist γενέσθαι is not tensed.

[108] ἀποδεῖξαί σε secl. Heindorf.

[109] I take it that, in this context, 'διαιρήσεται' refers summarily to the method of division and collection.

[110] ἐγὼ μὲν οὐ πιστεύω ἐμαυτῷ ἱκανὸς εἶναι ταῦτα διελέσθαι: 169a7–8. According to certain commentators, here Socrates is insincere. For instance, Lampert 2010, 204, stresses 'Socrates' ostensible perplexity and actual clear-headedness' and contends that 'the intricate argument devised by a Socrates feigning perplexity confirms that Socrates himself sees that there could be knowledge

great man'[111] will take it on. And he sets out the questions that the 'great man' would have to answer in a familiar aporetic form. Does no being have its own power directed only towards itself, or do some beings have that power (169a3–5)? And if the latter is the case, does the *epistêmê* that Socrates and Critias agreed to be identical with temperance belong to their class (169a5–7)? To address these questions, the 'great man' would have to systematically divide into classes the-things-that-are (169a3). Since Socrates has no expertise in that method, he cannot pursue this agenda in any thorough manner. Nonetheless, as we see, he ventures to trace the main axis of the division and indicate the direction that the latter should take.

Socrates seems to presuppose that, initially, the 'great man' will divide the things-that-are (*ta onta*: cf. 169a3) into two classes, beings *per se* and relative beings.[112] He suggests that the 'great man' will subdivide the class of relatives into two classes: beings that have their power directed towards themselves (reflexive beings), and others that have their power directed towards something distinct from themselves (aliorelatives) (169a3–5). He will thus discover whether some beings are reflexive or none is. At this point, the outline traced by Socrates has a gap: while the 'great man' is supposed to settle the question whether there can be an *epistêmê* which is only of *epistêmê* and no other object, we are now told that, if he finds out that there are beings directed towards themselves, he will be in a position to decide 'whether or not they include the science that we claim to be temperance' (169a6–7). But the issue is not whether this latter science is a relative, but whether it is a relative strictly or exclusively of itself (169a5–6). There is no compelling reason to infer that Socrates lifts without warning the proviso that Critias so copiously built into his conception of temperance, namely that it is a science *only* of science and its privation.[113] Rather, Socrates' *faux pas* seems to me intended to illustrate that he is not an expert in the method of division, and also invite the careful reader to correct him. Namely, assuming that the class of reflexive beings does have members (169a5–6), one should follow again the right line of the stemma and subdivide it into a class of relatives directed towards themselves *as well*

---

of knowledge, just as there is opinion of opinion and seeing of seeings' (Lampert 2010, 206). However, I can see no textual support for such claims. Socrates says that he does not believe (οὐ πιστεύω: 169a7) that he would be able to decisively judge the issue. While he does not necessarily consider himself totally incapable of drawing pertinent distinctions, he indicates that he has no real expertise in that task.

[111] μεγάλου δή τινος, ὦ φίλε, ἀνδρὸς δεῖ: 169a1–2.
[112] If so, he is pointing forward to the *Sophist* (255c).   [113] See note 105 in this chapter.

as some other object (inclusively reflexive relatives) and relatives that are directed *only* towards themselves and no other object (strictly or exclusively reflexive relatives). This subdivision is necessary in order to judge whether or not *epistême* belongs to the class of strictly reflexive relatives. If the answer is affirmative, Critias will be vindicated, whereas, if it is negative, the 'great man' can examine whether *epistême* may belong to the class on the left side of the divisional tree, i.e. the class of relative beings that are of themselves and of some other object as well.

A further comment concerns the nature of the project outlined by Socrates as well as the qualifications of the person who would be able to accomplish it. Unlike the main body of the Argument from Relatives, which according to my analysis can be read without importing ontological commitments, the sketch of the above division clearly bears on ontology. For Socrates assigns to some 'great man' the task of dividing *ta onta*, the-things-that-are, into classes and subclasses with the purpose of discovering something essential about their nature (*pephyken*: 169a4).[114] These divisions, therefore, will not be just conceptual and semantic, but will apply to realities. The many divisions in the *Sophist* and the *Statesman* develop and illustrate that view. A division effected correctly cuts nature properly at its joints. Its aim is not to project some conceptual pattern onto the world, but to accurately reflect the structure of reality.

We may want to compare the details of Socrates' sketch with the features of division discussed and illustrated in late Platonic works. The 'great man's' division of the class of relatives into the subclasses of reflexive relatives and aliorelatives (169a3–5) is arguably consistent with the Eleatic stranger's instruction that 'it is safer to proceed by cutting through the middle, for in that way one is more likely to come across genuine classes; this', he says, 'makes all the difference in how one conducts investigations' (*Plt.* 262b). Also, Socrates' sketch indicates some concern for drawing the divisions systematically and in the correct order, preferably keeping to one side of the stemma and advancing step by step until the nature of *epistême* is discovered and the division is complete. It is obvious that the 'great man' will proceed dialectically, not eristically. For a characteristic feature of dialectical divisions, which marks them off with regard to eristic divisions is, precisely, that the former go systematically through the intermediate steps whereas the latter do not (*Phlb.* 16d–17a, 19a–b). Furthermore, the final move that the 'great man' is supposed to make, i.e. deciding whether or not the *epistême* equivalent to temperance belongs to the class of reflexive

---

[114] On this point, see Lampert 2010, 206, and Tuozzo 2011, 225.

beings and classifying it accordingly, points to both the taxonomical and the epistemological value of the method of division. Perhaps its fullest illustration occurs in the *Sophist*: a string of divisions in combination with a long metaphysical detour are drawn by the Eleatic stranger in the hope of capturing the elusive Sophist and of defining him by reference to the divisional tree.

Finally, I should like to say something about the identity of the 'great man' and his expertise. Despite contentions to the contrary, there is no reason to believe that the 'great man' is Socrates: he explicitly says that he is not. The 'great man' could be taken as an anonymous hint at Plato's future role. Namely, Plato may be indicating that the sort of problem posed by relatives in the *Charmides* needs a metaphysical answer that Socrates could not provide but Platonic doctrine can make available.[115] Evidently, Socrates wishes to underscore that an expert in the method of division will be a person of supreme intellectual ability.[116] Whoever the 'great man' may be, he will be able to perform the very demanding mission assigned to him so as to give satisfaction in every respect (169a1–3). Indeed, one might think that the expertise of such a person is almost superhuman. For, in the *Phaedrus*, Socrates confesses that he is 'a lover of divisions and collections' (*Phdr.* 266b) eager to follow anyone capable of drawing them correctly as if he were a god (266b). Moreover, he says that he has always called such people dialecticians, although he is not entirely sure that this is the right name to use (266b–c). And he attributes to these latter the expertise 'to divide everything according to its kinds and to grasp each single thing firmly by means of one form' (273e).[117]

The *Parmenides* may also be relevant here. In concluding his criticisms against the theory of Forms, Parmenides remarks: 'only a very gifted man can come to know that for each thing there is some Form, namely, a Being itself by itself. And only an even more remarkable prodigy will make that discovery and will be able to instruct some other person who has sifted all

---

[115] Sedley 2004 and 2019 reads, respectively, the *Theaetetus* and the opening of the *Timaeus* along such lines. On Plato's self-references see Sedley 2020.

[116] See Tuozzo's interesting proposal that the division assigned to 'some great man' constitutes an Academic project carried out by Aristotle and other members of Plato's school (Tuozzo 2011, 226–35).

[117] Also see *Phlb.* 18e–19b. The interlocutors conduct an investigation of both *epistēmē* and pleasure in order to judge which of the two is preferable (18e). Socrates remarks that, in order to achieve that goal, they need to 'demonstrate how each of them is one and many and how, instead of immediately becoming unlimited, each of them acquires some definite number before it becomes unlimited' (18e–19a). Protarchus retorts that what Socrates seems to be asking is 'whether or not there are (different) kinds of pleasures, and how many there are, and of what sorts there are; and the same type of questions applies to *epistēmē* as well' (19b).

these problems thoroughly and critically for himself' (*Prm.* 135b–c). Like Socrates in our passage, Parmenides asserts that only a miraculous expert would be able to pursue the project that he himself merely outlines: prove the existence of Forms and instruct a few other people. Dialecticians alone have the ability to carry out that task, whereas people who, on account of the problems raised in the early part of the *Parmenides*, deny the existence of Forms and do not try to determine the class to which each thing belongs 'destroy dialectical reasoning altogether' (135b–c). Whether or not Parmenides has in mind some sort of collection and division,[118] he appears to wish for an expert similar to Socrates' 'great man': a dialectician with prodigious skill in the method of division and an understanding of reality that far surpasses one's own.

In the same spirit, and in line with his intimations regarding the 'great man' in the *Charmides*, Socrates wonders in the *Sophist* whether the Eleatic stranger might not be some god (*Soph.* 216a–b). As it turns out, the stranger shows himself an expert in drawing divisions and in investigating his subject through different or complementary divisional paths. Also, he demonstrates his consummate expertise in the *Statesman*, where he also airs a new thought: while divisions serve to define the nature of the item under investigation (in this case, the statesman), the ultimate reason why we should systematically apply that method is that such practice can make us 'better dialecticians in relation to all subjects' (285d) and, perhaps, true experts in dialectic (253d)[119] and, therefore, godlike. The 'great man' of the *Charmides* could be taken to foreshadow that ideal.

At the end of the Argument from Relatives, however, there does not seem to be an obvious way forward, since Socrates believes himself incapable of dividing being and no 'great man' is at hand. Given the inconclusiveness of the Argument from Relatives, he declares that he cannot tell whether a 'science of science' is possible (169a8–b1). Nor can he assert without further proof that, if such a science were possible, it would be equivalent to temperance *unless* he answered to his own satisfaction the second leg of the *aporia*, namely whether or not the science in question would be beneficial (169b1–3). This latter move comes as a surprise, since it detaches the issue of benefit from the issue of possibility, whereas in the initial formulation of the *aporia* the former was dependent upon the latter (167b1–4). Now he appears ready to grant, if only for the sake of the

---

[118] See *Soph.* 253d–e.

[119] Among other things, this implies that one would acquire a clear grasp of intelligible Forms, determine the inter-relations between them, and give and receive accounts of the finest things that are (*Soph.* 253d–254e, *Plt.* 285e).

argument, that Critianic temperance is credible or possible and proceed to investigate whether it is good for us.[120] At the outset, he indicates his own position regarding the issue that will soon be under scrutiny: 'I have the intuition', he says, 'that temperance is something beneficial and good' (169b4–5). Pointing back to the view of Zalmoxis according to which temperance is the cause of everything good for man, Socrates now expresses a weaker formulation of that view on his own account. The verb that he uses seems significant: '*manteuesthai*', 'to have an intuition' or, literally, to prophesise, appears to intimate that Socrates considers temperance good and beneficial because of a presentiment deriving from some sort of *manteia*, prophetic power. If so, Socrates is presupposing that what he intuits is true, even if he cannot explain *why* it is true.[121] And assuming his presentiment has a divine source, he will honour it: perhaps he will accept that temperance is a 'science of science', but only if the argument shows that it is beneficial for mankind.[122] Thus, the issue of benefit moves to centre-stage and becomes the topic of a superbly crafted argument that will take us to the end of the investigation.

[120] *Pace* Bruell 1977, 181, Socrates' reasoning is not circular.

[121] Plato's Socrates often treats divination as a source of truth that requires rational interpretation in order to yield understanding: e.g. *Ap.* 21b, *Symp.* 206b, *Tim.* 71d–e. According to the protagonist of the *Timaeus*, our divine creators took care to redeem even the non-rational parts of humans by making the liver the centre of divination 'so that it might have some grasp of the truth' (71d–e). Generally, Timaeus continues, divination is god's gift to humans (71e). On the one hand, we engage in divination only when our rational powers recede, as they do in sleep, sickness, or trances of being possessed. On the other hand, only reason is able to recall and interpret the contents of divination, and thus 'determine how and for whom they signify some good or evil, past or present or future' (71e).

[122] This condition is necessary but not sufficient. For Socrates indicates that, even if Critias answers the puzzle, he may have further questions to ask: κἀμὲ τάχ᾽ἂν ἀποπληρώσαις ὡς ὀρθῶς λέγεις περὶ σωφροσύνης ὅ ἔστιν (169c1–2). Both the word τάχα, perhaps, and the mode of the verb indicate that, even if the issues of reflexivity and of benefit were resolved, the investigation might remain inconclusive.

CHAPTER II

The Argument from Benefit (169c3–175a8)

The assumption that temperance is the source of very great benefits is found in every section of the *Charmides*. All three interlocutors share it, even though each understands it differently and relies on it in different ways and for different purposes. For instance, in the opening scene, Socrates relates that, according to Zalmoxis, temperance engendered in the soul by means of *logoi* is the source of physical and mental health and, generally, every good for man (156d3–157b6). Next, in the course of the conversation with Charmides, Socrates obtains the youth's assent to the premise that temperance is pre-eminently a *kalon*, one of the most admirable and most beneficial things (159c1–2, 160e6–7). Then, in the debate between Critias and himself involving the *technê* analogy (165c4–166c6), Socrates highlights the intuitive connection between the work of every first-order art and science and the benefits deriving from it,[1] and suggests that, likewise, the science supposed to be equivalent to temperance should have a distinct domain and accomplish a *kalon ergon* (165e1), an admirable and beneficial work worthy of such a cardinal virtue.

Critias too gives proof of his commitment to the idea that temperance is a great *kalon* for both those who possess it and the people governed by temperate rulers. Recall that, when he first crosses swords with Socrates over the definition of the virtue as 'doing one's own',[2] he relies on a view that he ascribes to Hesiod, according to which a temperate person is one who is doing his own deeds in an admirable and beneficial manner (*kalôs kai ôphelimôs*: 163c3). He takes good and benefit to be tied together in the successful performance of such deeds, and also he initially presupposes that agents' awareness of the value of their own actions is an inseparable component of having temperance. In fact, as we have seen, what made

---

[1] For instance, Socrates obtains Critias' ready assent to the claim that medicine is useful (χρησίμη: 165c11) and its achievement very beneficial (οὐ σμικρὰν ὠφελίαν: 165d1) in respect of its distinct object, namely health and disease.

[2] τὸ τὰ ἑαυτοῦ πράττειν: 161b6.

Critias eventually abandon that definition was the implication, pointed out by Socrates, that doctors and other first-order experts may be temperate in the sense of acting well and beneficially without being aware that they are acting in that manner (164c5–d3). It is precisely this consideration that prompted Critias to claim that, in fact, temperance is knowledge of oneself (164d4).

Importantly, the debate over that knowledge and its object (165c4–166e3) revealed that Socrates and Critias began their conversation by making different assumptions about the benefits deriving from temperance and their ultimate source. On the one hand, Socrates' initial inclination was to assume that temperance is analogous to every other *epistêmê* or *technê* insofar as the benefits that it secures derive from a proprietary object and function distinct from that *epistêmê* itself. On the other hand, Critias argued against that assumption and was allowed to prevail. Unlike the other sciences, he contended, the *epistêmê* that is temperance has *epistêmê* as its only object: it is 'a science of itself and the other sciences and the absence of science' or, equivalently, a 'science of science' (166e7–8). This implies, or strongly suggests, that the benefits the latter is expected to yield come from its reflexive object, namely from the aforementioned science itself. In this crucial respect, Critianic temperance sharply differs from every other science or art: it is good for us by virtue of its strictly reflexive character, whereas the other sciences are useful for us by virtue of their aliorelativity, i.e. the property of being directed to objects or governing domains distinct from themselves.

As mentioned, the Argument from Benefit aims to answer the second horn of the puzzle motivating the interlocutors' 'offering to Zeus', namely the question of whether or not a 'science of science' would be good for us, if it is at all possible. Even though it is dialectical and therefore inconclusive, it is a devastating attack against Critias' conception of temperance and, in particular, his assumption that temperance as a 'science of itself and the other sciences and non-science' is supremely beneficial on account of the fact that it is strictly reflexive and directive of the other sciences, though not of their objects. Even though it raises conceptual and psychological issues, its main focus is ethical and political. Notably, it draws out and challenges the assumption of both interlocutors that the 'science of science' has epistemic content, as well as Critias' view that, in virtue of that higher-order content, temperate rulers would be able to distinguish experts from non-experts, correctly delegate tasks, successfully run the state, and secure the happiness of all concerned. According to the reading that I shall develop, this complex and controversial argument has the form of a *reductio* that develops in five successive steps. They correspond to the five sections of this chapter and I shall discuss them in order.[3]

I

> And when Critias heard these things and saw that I was puzzled, he appeared to me to be compelled by my own state of puzzlement to be besieged and captured by puzzlement himself too, just as those who see people yawning in front of them have the very same sensation induced in them. And since he used regularly to make a good impression, he felt ashamed before the company, and did not want to concede to me that he was unable to go through the divisions that I was challenging him to draw, and made a vague comment which concealed his puzzlement. (169c3–d1)

According to the narrator, the effect of the Argument from Relatives on both interlocutors was *aporia*, perplexity. Socrates was perplexed for the reasons that he gave in the course of that argument, while Critias was apparently perplexed by proxy. He perceived Socrates' puzzlement and fell prey to it as well. The narration is strikingly physical and evokes images of compulsion and violence. Critias 'sees' the perplexity of his companion, as if it were something sensible. He 'catches' it from Socrates, as if it were something infectious, like a yawn. He is 'compelled' to surrender to the puzzlement, as a captured city is forced to surrender to the enemy (*halônai*: 169c6). While in the opening scene Socrates felt stalked and captured (*healôkenai*: 155e2) by the fearsome beast of sexual passion, on the present occasion the fearsome creature is the argument and the interlocutors have been caught by it. One wonders whether they will manage to save themselves or for how long.

The narrator relates something else as well, namely that when Critias found himself reduced to perplexity, he felt shame (169c7) and tried to hide from the audience the fact that he was unable to rise to the task assigned by Socrates to some 'great man': he was unable to draw the divisions necessary in order to settle the issue of whether there can be an *epistêmê* of itself.

Since Critias presumably used to emerge victorious in dialectical encounters, he felt embarrassed to concede defeat in this debate. On the one hand, this does not show that he is entirely indifferent to the truth[4] or completely lacks *sôphrosynê*.[5] Even though his perplexity is second-hand in

---

[3] To help the reader follow the argument and check the interpretation that I defend against Plato's text, I will quote the relevant passages in their entirety as I discuss them.
[4] So Schmid 1998, 101.
[5] So Hyland 1981, 122–3. The remarks by Tuozzo 2011, 237 and n. 1 are, I think, on the right track.

a way,[6] in another way it is not. For he has followed the Argument from Relatives in earnest and has conceded its conclusions. He has shown himself to have some degree of commitment to the epistemic objective of the search and, insofar as he has become aware of the difficulties surrounding the notion of a 'science of science', he has gained some self-awareness. He realises now, as he did not before, that there are problems with his definition of temperance, even though he does not want to acknowledge it in public. On the other hand, there is no doubt that Critias' *philotimia*, his love of honour and victory, is counterproductive with regard to the task at hand. Unlike Socrates, whose open acknowledgement of his perplexity motivates him to continue the search, Critias' sense of shame (*aischynê* or *aidôs*) causes him to hide rather than confront his *aporia*. Looking back to Charmides' second definition of temperance as *aidôs*, one appreciates the wisdom of the Homeric counterexample with which that definition was refuted: 'shame is not a good companion for a man in need' (161a4). Critias would have done well to heed Homer's advice. Once again, then, Critias is portrayed as a complex character, whose urbane appearance conceals a tense psychological reality: an exceptionally intelligent but also proud man, who does not tolerate being exposed or misunderstood. For his own part, Socrates neither indulges nor condemns him. Rather, he finds a way to circumvent Critias' feelings of shame and pursue the investigation.

> And so, in order for our argument to go forward, I said: 'alternatively, Critias, if it seems to you a good idea, let us for now make the following concession, that there may possibly be a science of science, but we shall investigate whether or not this is so some other time. Come then, consider: assuming that this science is perfectly possible, why or how does it make it any more possible for one to know what one knows and what one doesn't? For this is exactly what we said is to know oneself or[7] be temperate. Did we not?' (169d2–8)

Socrates' initial move is to propose that they concede the possibility of reflexive knowledge[8] and, on the basis of that concession, try to answer the

---

[6] Schmid 1998, 101, denies that Critias' perplexity is genuine: 'the narrative is potentially misleading, for it is evident that Critias was not "caught by perplexity" in the full sense of the phrase. Critias' perplexity was … like that of someone whose sneeze is derived: he experienced an imitation perplexity, not a real one'.

[7] I take the καί as epexegetic.

[8] By proposing a concession, Socrates does not step out of his role as a questioner, nor does he compromise the dialectical character of the investigation. The argument will proceed only if and only if after Critias agrees, as indeed he does. A comparable situation occurs in the *Euthyphro*, when Socrates propels the argument forward by asking his baffled interlocutor to consider the idea that piety is part of justice (11e–12e). In this case too, the enquiry begins only after Euthyphro endorses that view as his own. 'This is the kind of thing I was asking before, whether where there is piety there is also justice,

question why that sort of knowledge would make it *any more* possible (*mallon*: 169d6) for its possessors to know what they know and what they don't.[9] Given that he intends to address the second leg of the *aporia* (167a9–b4), i.e. whether Critianic temperance would be beneficial, the way in which he phrases his proposal shows that he intends to problematise an assumption that both he and Critias have shared up to this point, namely that the benefits of the 'science of science', whatever they may be, depend primarily on its substantive content: not merely knowing *that* one knows and doesn't,[10] but chiefly knowing *what* one knows and doesn't.[11] Granting that the 'science of science' is possible, the question he wishes to ask is this: why or how does Critias' temperate man, who is the only kind of person endowed with the 'science of science', have *more* or *greater* substantive knowledge, i.e. knowledge of *what* he knows and doesn't know, than other people have?

This question brings again to the fore the debate between Socrates and Critias in respect of the analogy between the *epistêmê* equivalent to temperance and the other *epistêmai* or *technai*, and also the implications of the positions held respectively by the two interlocutors (165c4–167a8). As we recall, there Socrates had defended the view that a science or art is beneficial in respect of its proprietary object or domain or function, which is distinct from the science or art itself. According to Socrates, the benefit of every *epistêmê* or *technê* has to do with its aliorelative character: the fact that it is directed to an object or subject-matter distinct from itself. Moreover, we may infer that, on that view, the constitutive relation of a science to its own aliorelative object determines *what* experts are supposed to know and *how* they differ from non-experts with regard to their science. The doctor knows about health and disease and, by virtue of that knowledge, he is able to treat

---

but where there is justice there is not always piety, since the pious is a part of justice. Shall we say that or do you think otherwise? – No, I think like that, because what you suggest seems to be right' (12e–d).

[9] Here, Socrates respects Critias' sensitivities and allows him to save face. For he leaves it up to Critias to decide whether or not to make the aforementioned concession: they will take that option only if Critias thinks it is a good idea (εἰ δοκεῖ: 169d1), otherwise not. Also, Socrates suggests that they leave aside the issue of the possibility of a 'science of science' for reasons of argumentative strategy, without referring to Critias' evident incompetence to draw the necessary divisions as a 'great man' would. As he puts the matter, they may want to consider making the proposed concession at present (νῦν: 169d3) and revisit the issue of possibility some other time (169d4–5).

[10] For reasons that will become clear, I call this discriminatory knowledge or knowledge-that.

[11] I call this substantive knowledge or knowledge-what. As mentioned, the expression 'what one knows and doesn't know' is ambiguous between (a) the indirect question 'what it is that one knows and what it is that one doesn't know' and (b) the relative clause 'those things of which one has knowledge and those things of which one does not'. On my reading, the Argument from Benefit concerns both (a) and (b).

patients and, when possible, cure them. As Socrates had suggested, something similar ought to hold for the *epistêmê* equivalent to temperance as well.

In the passage quoted immediately above, Socrates' use of the comparative term '*mallon*', more (169d6), highlights a point of particular interest: he and Critias need to determine not only the content of the temperate person's knowledge, but also, importantly, the extent to which this latter is cognitively superior to other people. For his own part, Critias does not object. Even though, in the aforementioned debate, he has maintained that temperance is unlike the other sciences in respect of having a reflexive and not an aliorelative object, nonetheless he too has taken it for granted that, if temperance or the 'science of science' is to be profitable, it must have substantive content. Therefore, at the present stage of the enquiry, he too wishes to examine just how the temperate man is better equipped than other people with regard to scientific understanding. However, Critias does realise at first that, at this point, Socrates intends to question the assumption that they both have made about the substantive content of the 'science of science' and, notably, his (sc. Socrates') own articulation of that notion in terms of 'knowing *what* oneself and others know or do not know' (cf. 167a1–7).[12] Therefore, he attempts to address Socrates' query as follows:

> Very much so, he said.[13] And indeed, Socrates, this must surely follow. For if someone has a knowledge or science which knows itself, he himself would be of the same kind as that which he has. Just as whenever someone has swiftness he is swift, and whenever someone has beauty he is beautiful, and whenever someone has knowledge he is knowing, so whenever someone has knowledge that is of itself, he will then, surely, be knowledgeable of himself. (169d9–e5)

While, earlier in the dialogue, Critias assumed without argument that knowledge or science of oneself (*to gignôskein heauton*: 165b4) implies knowledge or science which is of itself and every science (cf. *epistêmê heautês*: 166c3), now he claims that the entailment holds in the opposite direction: knowing itself entails its possessor knowing himself.[14] He

[12] On this point, see the excellent discussion by Tuozzo 2011, 239.
[13] Thus, Critias emphatically confirms their agreement that to know oneself and/or be temperate is equivalent to knowing *what* one knows and doesn't.
[14] This passage does not provide justification for Critias' controversial transition from γιγνώσκειν αὐτὸν ἑαυτόν, knowing oneself (165b4), to αὐτή τε αὐτῆς ἐστιν καὶ τῶν ἄλλων ἐπιστημῶν ἐπιστήμη, a science of both itself and the other sciences (166e6). (On this point, see also Tuozzo 2011, 240.) We should note that Critias appears to oscillate regarding the nature of the relation between knowing oneself and the 'knowledge of knowledge'. While he occasionally suggests that the relation is an identity, in the present passage he treats this relation as an implication: knowledge of itself entails knowledge of oneself. In most instances, he appears to assume that the 'knowledge of

suggests that if a person has quickness, he is quick; if he has beauty, he is beautiful; if he has knowledge, he is knowing; and if he has knowledge which is of itself, he will know himself.[15] This reply can be considered a logical truism, but other readings are available as well. On the one hand, Critias may be pointing to a physical or psychological fact: to have a certain physical or psychological character Fness entails being that sort of person, i.e. a person marked by Fness.[16] On the other hand, his response can be read in metaphysical terms: as an individual participating in the Form of Quickness will be quick, and in the Form of Beauty beautiful, and in the Form of Knowledge knowing, so a person participating in the Form of Reflexive Knowledge will be reflexively knowing: he will be knowing the knowing thing, i.e. himself.[17] Whatever we take to be Critias' meaning, Socrates sets the record straight.

> I do not dispute this point, I said, namely that when someone has the very thing which knows itself he will know himself. However, what sort of necessity is there for the person who has it [sc. that which knows itself] to know *what* he knows and *what* he does not know? – Because, Socrates, this knowledge is the same as the other. – Perhaps, I said. But I am afraid I am always in a similar condition. For I still do not understand how knowing *what* one knows and doesn't is the same (as that other knowledge). (169e6–170a4, emphasis added)

The issue that Socrates wants to raise is not how the man who has reflexive knowledge reflexively knows himself. For it seems fair to say that if you have self-knowing knowledge, then, since self-knowing knowledge is in you, in knowing *it*self it also knows an aspect of *you*.[18]

Rather, Socrates is asking how knowing knowledge entails knowing a specific content. Earlier in the argument, in elaborating Critias' position at 167a1–8, he treated knowledge of oneself and 'knowledge of knowledge' as mutually entailing or as amounting to the same thing; and both he and Critias took it for granted that knowledge of itself is equivalent to or entails knowing-what. Now, however, he questions that move. Why assume, as both he and his interlocutor have assumed, that the possessor of reflexive

---

oneself' and the 'knowledge of knowledge' are biconditionally related: knowledge of oneself obtains if and only if 'knowledge of knowledge' obtains. The fact that he saw no need to defend the transition from knowledge of oneself to knowledge of itself (cf. 165b4–166c3), taken together with his current claim that whoever has knowledge of itself is bound to know himself, supports that suggestion.

[15] On this point, see Tuozzo 2011, 240–1.

[16] The point could be extended to inanimate beings as well.   [17] See Kahn 1996, 192–4.

[18] Even so, however, it is not clear how we get from that to full self-knowledge.

knowledge must also, by some sort of necessity, know *what* oneself and others know or do not know? Or supposing, as Critias momentarily does (170a1), that reflexive knowledge is identical to knowing-*what* (*tauton*: 170a1), on what grounds can one defend that assumption? To put the point in a different way, Socrates does not contest the principle according to which whoever possesses the property of reflexive knowledge will also acquire the character distinctive of that property. He problematises the assumption that the 'science of science' better enables its possessor to judge what his knowledge or ignorance is *about*.[19] Like the Argument from Relatives, the elenchus that will follow will be adversarial in form. It will not examine whether knowing oneself enables one to judge what one knows and doesn't, but whether the 'science of itself and the other sciences' entails knowing what one knows and doesn't. Far from 'fading into insignificance',[20] the strictly reflexive nature of Critianic temperance remains central to the dialectical debate between Critias and Socrates. Does Critias' 'science of science' entail substantive knowledge? If it does not, in what way is it good for us? Or, if it does, what benefit do we derive from it?

2

The core of the Argument from Benefit occupies approximately five Stephanus pages (170a6–175a8) and constitutes a paradigmatic case of dialectical reasoning. As we walk through it, it may be useful to keep in mind certain preliminary remarks bearing on the interpretation that I propose.

First, the interlocutors consistently treat the 'science of science' as strictly reflexive, but all the other sciences as strictly aliorelative. The former is only of itself and every other *epistêmê* insofar as it is *epistêmê*, whereas the latter are only of their own proprietary objects, which are

---

[19] Socrates puts his query in two different ways which are determined in part by his interlocutor's reactions. First, he asks, assuming that one can have that which knows itself, what sort of necessity is there for that person to have also knowledge-what, namely knowledge of what he knows and doesn't (169e6–8)? Then, in response to Critias' contention that 'knowledge of knowledge' and knowledge-what are the same (*tauton*: 170a1), Socrates asks just how they are the same (170a2–4). Possibly, the former formulation of the question corresponds to Critias' initial suggestion that knowing-itself *entails* knowing-what, whereas the latter formulation corresponds to Critias' claim that knowing itself is *the same thing as* knowing-what. If the elenchus shows that reflexive knowledge does not entail knowledge-what, there will be no need to examine separately the question of whether they are the same.

[20] See Tuozzo 2011, 243.

invariably distinct from the corresponding sciences themselves. Neither Socrates nor Critias ever oscillates in this respect: they are concerned exclusively with what we may call strict reflexivity and strict aliorelativity, and do not examine the possibility that a science may be both of some distinct object and of itself. Second, the interlocutors sometimes designate temperance by 'epistêmê epistêmês' (genitive singular: science of science), but other times they use the expression 'epistêmê epistêmôn' (genitive plural: science of sciences). We shall not linger over their choice of formula, for, as we shall see, it is not philosophically significant.[21] Third, it will become clear that the distinction that the interlocutors draw between knowing *that* one knows and knowing *what* one knows, which is pivotal to the Argument from Benefit, does not correspond to modern distinctions between propositional and non-propositional knowledge, knowing *that* and knowing *how*, knowledge by description and knowledge by acquaintance.[22] Rather, as we shall see, Socrates contrasts the power to recognise *that* someone is knowledgeable with the capacity to identify *what* particular sort of knowledge one's knowledge is: medicine and not architecture, architecture and not navigation, and so on. However, although this latter distinction plays a crucial dialectical role in the argument, it does not necessarily follow that Socrates or Plato would endorse it in its own right.[23]

Fourth, as in the previous argument, so in this one, Socrates draws attention to the doxastic nature of the premises and the essentially dialectical nature of the investigation. For instance, not only does he repeatedly stress the hypothetical standing of the 'science of science' and of Critias' definition of temperance in these terms, he also appeals to the plausibility of certain premises (e.g. *eikotôs*: 170b9) rather than their necessary truth,

---

[21] While certain interpreters do attribute philosophical significance to Socrates' choice of formula, others do not. For instance, Schmid 1998, 111–12, is puzzled by the fact that Socrates refers to temperance in different ways and suggests that ἐπιστήμη τῆς ἐπιστήμης at 170a6 picks out a feature associated with Critian self-certainty: 'a claim to knowledge of knowledge which, however, ignores the fearful, self-critical element, the knowledge of ignorance'. As for ἐπιστήμη ἐπιστημῶν at 170c6, according to Schmid, it picks out another element especially associated with the Critianic model, namely the hegemony of the 'science of science' over the other sciences. On the other hand, although Tuckey 1951, 58–9, registers these variations, he does not regard them as philosophically important.

[22] See the relevant remarks by Tuozzo 2011, 245.

[23] A related remark concerns the cognitive vocabulary of the Argument from Benefit. While in the earlier stages of the debate the interlocutors mostly use ἐπίστασθαι and its cognates in order to refer to the 'science of science', in the Argument from Benefit Socrates sometimes uses indiscriminately ἐπίστασθαι, γιγνώσκειν, εἰδέναι, and their cognates. The reason could be that, in this argument, the interplay between Critias' conception of a 'science of science' and the Socratic conception of self-knowledge becomes subtler and blurrier. Notably, as we shall see (Chapter 12, 273–86), some of the objections that Socrates raises in his final summary of the argument also affect, albeit obliquely, his own philosophy and method.

and infers what *seems* to him to be the case (e.g. *hôs eoiken*: 170d2, 7) rather than what *is* the case. Although his hand becomes increasingly firmer as the argument develops, he remains epistemically cautious regarding both the interim and the final conclusions to be drawn. Fifth, the Argument from Benefit exposes the implications of the stance that Critias defended vis-à-vis Socrates in the debate about a crucial aspect of the *technê* analogy, i.e. the issue of whether or not temperance is analogous to the other arts and sciences in respect of having an object distinct from itself (165c4–166e3). We should keep that question alive in our mind until the end of the argument, when we shall be in a position to judge whether or not it is true that, in the *Charmides*, Socrates (as well as Plato) rejects the analogy between virtue and the arts once and for all. Let us now switch our attention to the text.

> How do you mean? he asked. – I mean this, I said. Supposing that perhaps there is a science of science, will it really be able to distinguish anything more than that, namely that of two things, the one is science but the other is not? – No, just that much. – Then, is the science or lack of science of health the same thing as the science or lack of science of justice? – Certainly not. – Rather, I think, the one is the science of medicine, the other is the science of politics, and the science we are talking about is of nothing but science. – It must be so. – And if a person does not have additional knowledge of health and justice but knows only knowledge because he has knowledge of only that thing, namely *that* [*hoti*] he knows something and that he has some knowledge, he would also probably know that he has some knowledge both about himself and about others. Isn't that so? – Yes. – But how will he know *what* [*ho ti*][24] he knows by virtue of that knowledge? For he knows, of course, health by virtue of medicine and not of temperance, harmony by virtue of music and not of temperance, building by virtue of the art of building and not of temperance, and the same holds for all cases. Or not? – It seems so. – But if temperance is indeed a science only of sciences, how will [the temperate person] know that he knows health or that he knows building? – He won't know it in any way. (170a5–c8, emphasis added)

Socrates explains why he finds himself in an aporetic state and argues dialectically towards the conclusion that, in fact, the 'science of science' cannot be knowledge of a specific content. He relies on his initial intuition concerning the aliorelative nature of all arts and sciences (165c4–166c3) in order to reason as follows: every science is identical to itself and different

---

[24] Contra van der Ben 1985, 64, there is no reason to emend the mss. reading ὅ τι. Nor, as I hope to show, are there any grounds for accepting the claim by Rosenmayer 1957, 89, i.e. that Plato's treatment of knowing-what and knowing-that is chaotic and that, in fact, he cannot make up his mind as to whether temperance is equivalent to the former or the latter.

from every other science on account of its proprietary object, which is typically distinct from that science itself. Medicine is the science it is in virtue of knowing health, and politics is the science it is in virtue of knowing justice. Also, medicine is the science of health and not of justice, while politics is the science of justice and not of health. Furthermore, every science involves expert understanding of both its proprietary object and the negative object corresponding to this latter: e.g. medicine knows health and disease, politics knows justice and injustice.[25] Hence, every first-order science is able to distinguish both expertise and the lack of expertise regarding its own domain, and to assess what does qualify as scientific knowledge of its own subject-matter and what does not (170a10–b11).

We should note that, here, Socrates reintroduces into the discussion the privations or negative objects of *epistêmê* and the *epistêmai*. He does so in order to emphasise that every science, insofar as it is a science, must define its realm and its limits.[26] Also, he strongly suggests that the first-order sciences can do so precisely because they are aliorelative. Both the domain of a given science and the substantive claims belonging to that domain are determined by what that science is a science *of*: something distinct from the science itself. Health and disease determine what medicine is and what it consists of. And number determines arithmetic and the constituents of that art. Similar observations hold for the first-order experts, in accordance with the principle that, if a person has a property Y possessing a certain character F, then that person will possess the character F just in virtue of possessing Y (169d9–e8). For instance, if the science of medicine can *only* distinguish expertise or the absence of expertise regarding health and disease, the person who possesses that science, i.e. the medical doctor, will *only* be able to judge whether a claim qualifies as a medical claim, whether it is a correct medical claim, and whether the person who makes it is a true doctor. He won't be able to judge expertly or scientifically anything else, although he will of course make all sorts of non-expert judgements about many things.

On the other hand, according to Critias, temperance differs from every other *epistêmê* precisely on account of the fact that its proprietary object is not distinct from *epistêmê* but the same as *epistêmê* itself. Because

---

[25] Note that, earlier in the dialogue, Socrates uses the term '*anepistêmosynê*', non-science or absence of science, to articulate Critianic temperance as 'a science of itself and the other sciences as well as of non-science' (166e7–8, 167b11–c2), but on the present occasion he employs '*anepistêmosynê*' to designate the negative objects of first-order sciences.

[26] Socrates does not distinguish between ways of knowing the object of a science and ways of knowing its privation. However, in the present context, there is no philosophical need to do so.

temperance is a science only of science, it can discern only science simpliciter from non-science simpliciter, but can make no expert judgement
about anything else. As Socrates puts it, temperance entails only knowing-
that: it can only tell that someone knows something or has some sort of
knowledge. But temperance cannot disclose anything more about *what*
someone knows: e.g. it cannot tell you that the knowledge that one has is
medical knowledge, nor can it tell you how to treat a disease and restore
health (170b6–d4).[27] Thus, the distinction between temperance and the
first-order sciences becomes sharper and more extreme. While the 'science
of science' is discriminatory knowledge (knowledge-that) by virtue of
which the temperate person can tell *only* that there is a knower of some
sort, each of the first-order sciences is substantive knowledge by virtue of
which an expert can discern other experts in his own discipline and can
attend in a scientific manner to the object of this latter.

Consider now what this view entails for the temperate person as opposed
to the first-order experts. Assuming that what holds for temperance or for
the first-order sciences also holds for the corresponding experts, on the one
hand, first-order experts can discern *only* scientific knowledge or ignorance
of their own objects, and they differ from experts in the other sciences just
in virtue of that capacity. Doctors have scientific knowledge of health and
disease and, just in virtue of that knowledge, they differ from statesmen,
who have expert knowledge of justice. On the other hand, in virtue of
possessing temperance, the temperate person will be able to identify experts
and distinguish them from non-experts. But he won't be able to tell *what*
experts are experts *in*, unless he himself happens to be an expert in
a particular field *in addition to* being an expert in temperance (170b6–
10). He will be able to judge what someone knows or doesn't know about
health and disease only if, *in addition to* having 'knowledge-of-knowledge',
he *also* has medical knowledge (*prosepistêtai*: 170b6).[28] And he will be
capable of assessing what a person knows or doesn't know about justice
only if, *in addition to* being temperate, he *also* masters the art of politics.

It follows that, contrary to what Critias and Socrates had supposed,[29] the
temperate man would not be able to do (except accidentally) the work
previously assigned to him, namely to test people's claims to expertise and
judge scientifically whether such claims are true or false of the people who

---

[27] Especially, see the following lines: οὐκ ἄρα εἴσεται ὃ οἶδεν ὁ τοῦτο ἀγνοῶν, ἀλλ᾽ ὅτι οἶδεν μόνον
(170b9–10, my emphasis).
[28] On the interpretation of προσεπίστηται, see the comments by Dyson 1974, 108, and van der Ben
1985, 69 n. 8.
[29] See again Socrates' elaboration of Critias' definition of temperance at 167a1–7.

make them. For since he won't have substantive knowledge of the object of
each science,[30] he won't be able to reliably distinguish genuine experts from
those that merely play the part. If we glance back to the opening scene of
the dialogue, we may be tempted to read this as a joke at Critias' expense.
There, Critias thought he was using a ruse when he told Charmides that
Socrates was a doctor. But, according to the present argument, he really
could not have known whether his claim was false or true. In the sequel of
the investigation (170e3–171c10), Socrates slightly changes perspective[31] in
order to explain further the implication that, since the temperate person
has no access to substantive content,[32] he/she is unable to distinguish in an
expert manner between real and fraudulent claims to knowledge.[33]

> Let us consider the matter from a different starting point. If the
> temperate man or anyone else is going to discriminate between the
> person who is truly a doctor and the one who is not, won't he behave
> as follows? Surely, he will not discuss with him about medicine – for, as
> we have said, the doctor has knowledge of nothing other than health
> and disease. Isn't that so? – It is. – But he knows nothing of science;
> instead we have assigned that to temperance alone. – Yes. – Therefore,
> the medical man knows nothing of medicine either, since medicine is in
> fact a science. – True. – Thus, the temperate man will know that the
> doctor possesses a certain science. But when he has to test which one it
> is, will he consider anything other than what things it is a science of? Or
> is it not the case that each science is defined not merely as a science but
> also as a particular one,[34] by virtue of this, namely its being of certain
> specific objects? – Surely it is. – And medicine was defined as being
> different from the other sciences by virtue of the fact that it was the
> science of health and disease, right?[35] – Yes. – So, mustn't anyone
> wishing to enquire into medicine enquire into what domain [*en toutois*]
> medicine is found in [*en ois*]? For he would presumably not enquire into
> domains external to these in which it is not found. – Of course not. –
> Hence it is in the domain of health and disease that the person who
> enquires in the correct manner will enquire into the doctor *qua* doctor. –
> It seems so. – Won't he enquire as to whether, in things either thus said
> or thus done, what is said is said truly and what is done is done
> correctly? – Necessarily. – Now, could a person pursue either of these
> lines of enquiry without the art of medicine? – Surely not. – Nor, it

---

[30] ἐπίστασθαί τι: 170d6 (my emphasis).   [31] σκεψώμεθα δὲ ἐκ τῶνδε: 170e3.
[32] On this point, see the comments by Schofield 1973.
[33] Clearly, Socrates is not concerned with ordinary, haphazard distinctions between experts and
charlatans, but rather with the ability to distinguish between these two in an expert, scientific
manner.
[34] I change τίς, the interrogative printed by Burnet at 171a6, to the indefinite pronoun τις.
[35] I end the Greek sentence at 171a9 with a question mark, where Burnet has a full stop.

seems, could anyone else, except a doctor, nor indeed could the temperate man. For otherwise he would have to be a doctor in addition to his temperance. – That is true. (170e3–171c3)

As I understand the argument, it runs as follows: to expertly judge (*diagnôsesthai*: 170e5)[36] whether someone is, for example, a doctor, the temperate man would have to debate (*dialexetai*: 170e6) with the latter about medical matters. To be able to do so, the temperate person would need to have knowledge-what: substantive knowledge of medicine and of the matters falling within that sphere (*en toutois*: 171a11).[37] No expertise outside that sphere (*tois exô*: 171b2) would be relevant to the task at hand. However, assuming that the temperate man doesn't happen to also be a doctor, he will have no science of medicine, but only 'science of science'. So, he will be able to discern only whether one has or doesn't have science, but won't be capable of discerning whether the person who claims to be a doctor is a real doctor or a fraud. Conversely, the doctor who is to be tested is not an expert in *epistêmê*, but only in medicine. Assuming that he/she is a true doctor, he/she will have scientific understanding of health and disease, but not of *epistêmê* (or anything else). And he/she will be the only type of expert possessing the science of medicine. No other expert or layperson will possess the science of medicine, although some may pretend that they do.

> Hence, Socrates concludes, it is very probable that, if temperance is only a science of science and of the lack of science, it[38] will not be able to distinguish either a doctor who knows [*epistamenon*] the subjects pertaining to his art [*technês*] from a man who does not know them but pretends or believes that he does, or any other expert of those knowledgeable in anything at all, except for the one who happens to have the same art as the temperate man himself [*hometechnon*: 171c8], as is the case with all other specialists as well. – So it seems, he said. (171c4–171c10)[39]

The upshot is, then, that the temperate person and, for example, the doctor have absolutely nothing in common. Both are subject to severe

---

[36] The choice of word seems deliberate: διάγνωσις and its cognates technically refer to the physician's diagnosis of the symptoms of a disease. On the basis of the diagnosis, the physician is able to tell whether or not one has a disease and what particular disease it is.

[37] Socrates' use of ἐν +dative (ἐν τούτοις: 171a11, ἐν οἷς: 171b1) is one way of indicating the subject-matter of a science (compare van der Ben 1985, 70). An expert's knowledge will fall within a certain sphere, as opposed to whatever knowledge lies outside it (ἐν τοῖς ἔξω: 171b1–2).

[38] Unlike Sprague *ad loc.*, I take σωφροσύνη to be the subject of διακρῖναι. On this point, see van der Ben 1985, 71–2, and Lamb's translation *ad loc.*

[39] A particularly noteworthy feature of this passage is the interchangeable use of 'ἐπιστήμη' and 'τέχνη', and their cognates. Clearly, Socrates intends to cover expertise of all sorts, from temperance to medicine to the manual arts (cf. δημιουργοί: 171c9).

cognitive restrictions and neither can trespass into the other's territory. The former knows only about science itself and can make judgements only about science itself and its contenders. The latter knows about health and disease and distinguishes real medicine from fake medicine and real doctors from frauds. However, he knows nothing about medicine as a science, nor, probably, would he be able to tell *that* medicine is a science; for, as it seems, this latter is the privilege of the temperate man alone. The gap between the *epistêmê* equivalent to *sôphrosynê* and the first-order sciences and arts appears unbridgeable and its implications preposterous. The factor primarily responsible for this situation is the strict reflexivity of the 'science of science', i.e. the fact that the latter is supposed to relate only to science, which appears to prevent the 'science of science' from doing any specific work and from yielding any specific benefit.[40] However, in addition to the formal target of the elenchus, this stretch of argument provides grounds for challenging Plato's Socrates as well. If testing one's claim to expertise in medicine requires that the person who is doing the testing should have substantive knowledge of medicine, might it not be the case that the same holds about value? And if it does, how can Plato's Socrates cross-examine self-styled experts in the virtues even though he believes that he has no expertise in these latter? We shall return to this topic in connection with Socrates' final assessment of the search (175a9–d5).

How plausible is the thesis that only a true doctor can distinguish between a real doctor and a charlatan? On the one hand, laypeople or experts in other fields may judge a physician's competence merely on empirical grounds. On the other hand, the interlocutors of the *Charmides* are not concerned with this sort of judgement, but with reliable discriminatory judgements made on the basis of expertise. Hence, the claim that only his *homotechnoi* (171c8), fellow-experts, can discern a true expert from a charlatan is defensible and may well be true. We all have opinions about doctors, diseases, methods of treatment, and drugs. We may be right or wrong about them and we may have better or worse reasons for holding such beliefs. But we have no scientific understanding of these matters, unless we happen to be competent physicians ourselves.

In any case, the argument discussed in this section suggests that, contrary to what Critias expected, the sphere of temperance is not vast, but vastly restricted. Consequently, he faces a tall challenge regarding the

---

[40] Also responsible, to some extent, for the aforementioned absurdities is an assumption that plays a fairly important role in this stage of the argument, namely that the first-order arts or sciences are strictly aliorelative: they are only of their distinct proprietary objects but cannot ground any claims about science in general.

question of benefit. He needs to show that temperance is greatly profitable, even if the temperate person cannot access the content of the sciences and cannot reliably distinguish between genuine experts and their fraudulent counterparts. In the next stage of the elenchus, Socrates raises just this issue.

3

> What benefit then, Critias, I asked, may we still derive from temperance, if it is of such kind? For if, as we supposed from the beginning, the temperate person knew *what* he knew and *what* he did not know, *that* he knows the former but *that* he does not know the latter, and if he were able to recognise another man who has found himself in this same condition, we agree that it would be greatly to our benefit to be temperate. For we would live our life free of error, both we ourselves[41] who would have temperance and all the others who would be governed by us. For neither would we ourselves try to do *what* we did not know, but rather would find those who do know and would hand the matter over to them, nor would we allow the other people governed by us to do anything different from *what* they would be bound to do correctly; and this would be what they would have knowledge or science of.[42] In just this way, then, a house administered by temperance would be well administered, a state would be well ruled, and the same holds for everything else governed by temperance. For, with error removed and correctness leading, it is necessary that the people who are in such condition will act in their every action in a fine and good manner, and that those who do act well will be happy. (171d1–172a3, emphasis added)

This is the first of the fictional societies sketched out by Socrates for the needs of the investigation. It is a society in which temperance reigns supreme. Strictly speaking, it is not a utopia, i.e. an ideal to which we ought to try to approximate.[43] It is best to interpret it, more broadly, as a thought-experiment: an imaginary construct that serves to isolate one or more features of temperance and study them separately from the others.[44] Significantly, Socrates chooses to examine Critianic temperance and those who have it in the context of the household and the state. Thus he brings to the fore a dimension of the 'science of science' which, up to this point, has

---

[41] I preserve the ms. reading καί deleted by Heindorf.
[42] Following van der Ben 1985, 72, at 171e5 I put a full stop after εἶχον.
[43] On the nature of political utopias in Plato, see Schofield 2006, 194–249.
[44] The notion of thought-experiment is broader than that of utopia. Every utopia is a thought-experiment, but not every thought-experiment qualifies as a utopia. For instance, although Hobbes' *Leviathan* is unquestionably a thought-experiment, its author denies that it is a utopia but presents it as a proposal that, in principle, can be materialised.

mostly remained in the background:[45] it is conceived as an architectonic science conferring upon its possessor the exclusive privilege of delegating tasks, overseeing the activities of first-order experts, and thereby ruling the state.

In the fictional society of the thought-experiment, everyone enjoys freedom from error (*hamartia*) (171d7–8). Both the temperate rulers and their subjects act knowledgeably and are guided by *orthotês*, correctness, albeit for different proximate reasons and in different ways. On the one hand, as Socrates puts it, 'we ourselves who would have temperance'[46] would be in a position to know what we don't know[47] and, therefore, would abstain from such tasks and delegate them to experts (171d8–e2). According to his sketch, the scientific execution of the rulers' work would be effected in three distinct temporal stages. First, the rulers would discover the experts in a certain field (*exeuriskontes*: 171e2). Next, they would delegate to each expert whatever task he/she is knowledgeable about (*paredidomen*: 171e2). And, finally, they would ensure that each expert would bring his/her work to successful completion (171e2–172a3).[48] No specifications are given about the implementation of temperance among the ruled. However, Socrates says that 'we', the rulers, would not permit our subjects to do anything different from what they are able to do expertly and correctly (171e3–5), and this suggests that the rulers of the imaginary society would use compulsion as well as persuasion to achieve the desired result.

These hypothetical rulers, then, govern in a way faintly reminiscent of the Guardians' governance in the *Republic*, and they apply a principle that reminds us somewhat of the principle of specialisation in that dialogue. Notably, they don't allow their subjects to do anything other than what they are competent in and can accomplish in the correct manner (171e3–5) and, in that sense, they compel them to 'do their own'.[49] As for the subjects, it seems that they have as little choice regarding their professions as the producers of the *Republic*. But whether they do their jobs willingly or unwillingly, according to Socrates' sketch, the benefit to be gained by the rule of temperance is no less than this: everyone, ruler or subject, will act finely and well in every case (*kalôs kai eu prattein*: 172a1–2) and will be

---

[45] See Rowe in press.

[46] We should note Socrates' use of the first-person plural. He and Critias will examine the fictional society sketched above from the point of view of the temperate people who are supposed to govern it.

[47] ἃ μὴ ἐπιστάμεθα: 171e1.   [48] On the temporality of the passage, see van der Ben 1985, 73.

[49] See also *Charm.* 162c1–164d3.

happy. Thus, Socrates' thought-experiment has political implications,[50] for it intimates that the citizens' happiness is the outcome of good government.[51] Only if Critianic temperance can achieve that result can it qualify as good rule. And only if the temperate rulers can ensure that their subjects will act well and be happy can they be deemed good rulers.

However, Socrates' sketch leaves unclear whether 'acting finely' and 'acting well' have specifically moral connotations, and hence it is difficult to figure out how 'acting well' (*eu prattein*: 172a2) necessarily[52] would make people happy (*eudaimonas*: 172a3).[53] In any case, it seems unlikely that temperance, as Critias defines it, could be responsible for bringing about happiness. For, as the immediately preceding phase of the elenchus has indicated, temperance as the 'science of science' does not entail knowing *what* one knows or doesn't know but only knowing *that* one knows or doesn't know: the 'science of science' is not substantive knowledge, but only discriminatory knowledge. It seems fairly clear that, in the thought-experiment under consideration, the knowledge enabling the temperate rulers to refrain from acting out of ignorance is, on the contrary, primarily substantive: they are cognisant of *what* they do not know and, on that basis, they avoid acting disgracefully and badly (171d2–e5). Compare the previous stage of the Argument from Benefit, according to which the temperate rulers would probably need to have substantive knowledge, if they were to delegate tasks to true experts and hinder non-experts from meddling with matters that they are ignorant about.

Therefore, the present thought-experiment is, I submit, counterfactual[54] and implies the following reasoning: if, against what has been shown, temperance were substantive knowledge (knowledge-what) as well as discriminatory knowledge (knowledge-that), and assuming that those who possessed it ruled the state according to that knowledge, both the rulers and

---

[50] See Schmid 1998, chapter 7, and Schofield 2006, 146–8.   [51] See Schofield 2006, 148.

[52] I take it that the infinitives εὖ πράττειν at 172a2 and εἶναι at 172a3 both depend on ἀναγκαῖον at 172a2.

[53] Acting well (εὖ πράττειν) and faring well (attaining εὐδαιμονία) are very different things in English, but Greek tends to bring them closer together. Notably, Aristotle remarks that both the many (οἱ πολλοί) and intellectuals (οἱ χαρίεντες) speak of the supreme good as happiness and consider living well (εὖ ζῆν) and acting well (εὖ πράττειν) to be the same thing as being happy (εὐδαιμονεῖν) (*EN* 1095a19). Aristotle also remarks that his own definition of happiness, according to which happiness consists not just in being good but in acting well, accords with the common conception of the happy man as one who lives well and acts well (*EN* 1098b21).

[54] Socrates draws attention to the counterfactual function of this sketch, at the grammatical level, by the counterfactual use of the imperfect + ἄν and, at the conceptual level, by explicitly referring to what 'we supposed from the beginning' (171d2–3). He retains the imperfect tense through his summary description of that society and occasionally uses the so-called philosophic imperfect in order to point back to the earlier passages. On this point, see van der Ben 1985, 72 and 75 n. 4.

their subjects would act faultlessly and correctly. If they acted faultlessly and correctly, they would necessarily act well. If they acted well, they would be happy. And if temperance (understood as a 'science of science' involving both substantive and discriminatory knowledge) secured happiness, then it would be a very great good. However, since both Socrates' sketch and the reasoning that it involves rely on an assumption that has already been refuted (i.e. that temperance involves knowing-what: 172a3–5), its point is moot. Thus, Socrates proposes the following alternative:

> But now you see, I said, that such a science has appeared nowhere. – I do, he said. – And so, said I, it may be that the science that we now find to be temperance, namely to know science and the lack of science, has this good attached to it: the person who possesses it will learn more easily whatever else he learns and will perceive everything more clearly, since, in addition to every particular thing that he learns, he also has science in view. And moreover, he will test others more reliably about whatever subjects he also has learnt himself, whereas those who test without having this advantage will do so in a weaker and worse manner. (172b1–8)

Drawing again on perceptual terminology, Socrates prompts Critias to confirm that, nonetheless, he does not see anywhere the appearance of the aforementioned science,[55] i.e. a strictly reflexive science involving substantive knowledge. Clearly, Socrates intends 'nowhere' (*oudamou*: 172a7) to mean 'nowhere in the present investigation', rather than 'nowhere in the scientific objects or fields referred to earlier, namely justice, health, harmony, building, and medicine'.[56] For these latter do not constitute an exhaustive list, but serve as illustrations for the contentions that Socrates wanted to defend. In any case, now Socrates leaves aside the counterfactual hypothesis that temperance involves knowledge-what as well as knowledge-that (both substantive and discriminatory knowledge), makes the assumption that temperance is mere knowledge-that (discriminatory knowledge), and invites Critias to entertain the suggestion that the latter benefits the temperate person in three ways: he will have greater facility in learning subject-matters other than knowledge itself (172b3); things will present themselves to him in a clearer and more vivid manner (*enargestera*: 172b4) than to other people; and he will be a better judge of the expertise of others in respect of whatever field he too happens to be an expert in.

---

[55] νῦν δέ, ἦν δ'ἐγώ, ὁρᾷς ὅτι οὐδαμοῦ ἐπιστήμη οὐδεμία τοιαύτη οὖσα πέφανται; – Ὁρῶ, ἔφη (173a7–9).
[56] A different interpretation is proposed by van der Ben 1985, 77. As he notes, several translators, including Croiset and Sprague, leave οὐδαμοῦ untranslated.

Socrates does not indicate how these capacities might be related to each other. Perhaps the capacity of the temperate person to easily learn things depends on his prior understanding of what a science is. Alternatively, perhaps it depends on the exceptional clarity and vividness of his impressions, and perhaps both these features could account for the reliability of his judgements regarding the expertise of others.

I submit that, on this hypothesis, temperance or the 'science of science' plays a secondary and parasitic role with regard to the first-order sciences. It is an auxiliary *epistêmê* whose presence merely enhances the temperate person's performance in whatever first-order expertise he/she happens to have. In the first place, it is supposed to be beneficial not in its own right, but because it makes its possessor a better learner in *whatever else* he learns[57] other than science itself (172b3). In the second place, the temperate person's clearer and more vivid perceptions are not about 'the science of science' (which, as has been shown, probably has no substantive content), but about 'every particular thing that the temperate person learns *in addition to* his prior understanding of science as such'[58] (172b5–6, my emphasis). In the third place, the temperate man is capable of testing experts in a particular field more thoroughly and more reliably than others *only if* he too happens to have expertise in that same field. His judgements will be better than those of other experts only insofar as they concern 'things that he has also learned himself' (172b6–8). In short, the intellectual advantages secured through temperance can manifest themselves *only if* those who have temperance *also* master some other, first-order science. Otherwise, these gifts are useless.

Socrates' idea seems to be this. If temperance is merely discriminatory knowledge, it cannot provide a substantive domain of application for learning, perceiving, or judging. Rather, these capacities and the corresponding activities need to be situated within the realm of some substantive, first-order expertise. For instance, if the temperate man is also a doctor, he can understand medical matters more easily than other doctors, because he also has temperance. He can remember the symptoms and therapies for each disease more clearly than other doctors, because he also has temperance. And he can test other people's claims to medical expertise in a firmer and surer manner than other doctors, because he also has temperance. But whatever cognitive superiority he enjoys with regard to his fellow-experts is just a matter of degree. While temperance enables him to be a better doctor in the aforementioned respects, it does not suffice to confer upon him the

---

[57] ὅ τι ἂν ἄλλο μανθάνῃ: 172b3.   [58] προσκαθορῶντι τὴν ἐπιστήμην: 172b5.

authority to judge doctors *as doctors* (or any other experts *as experts in their own fields*) without belonging to their ranks. On the face of it, this does not seem an unreasonable suggestion.

In principle, the intellectual advantages secured through temperance as knowledge-that are not negligible. The elenchus of Charmides' first definition of temperance as a sort of quietness (159b5) suggests that *eumathia*, learning quickly, is better than *dysmathia*, learning quietly and slowly (159e1–5). And if we look beyond the *Charmides* to the *Republic*, we find that facility in learning and a good memory bear on other mental and psychological features and jointly constitute the natural equipment that eventually enables the Guardians to contemplate the Forms and rule the state with a view to the Good. One might even be inclined to read the 'lesser advantages' of the 'science of science' in the *Charmides* as pointing deliberately to the intellectual qualities adorning the rulers of the Callipolis. For the latter share with the temperate man the capacities of learning easily and of thinking clearly. Also, it is tempting to compare the philosopher-ruler's twofold capacity to contemplate Forms and pay attention to the corresponding particulars with the temperate man's capacity both to understand science as such and to acquire expertise in some particular discipline.

Such associations, however, cannot be pushed too far for many reasons. Notably, while the understanding of the Guardians is fully substantive, the *epistêmê* of Critias' temperate person is not substantive at all. This is why, according to the argument, the advantages it procures are of small significance, if any.[59] Again, the root of this absurdity can be traced far back to the debate over the relation between temperance and the other sciences in respect of the nature of their objects and, specifically, the concession that while all the other sciences are of something distinct from themselves, temperance alone is a science only of science and of no distinct object. Precisely because the 'science of science' governs only science, it has been shown to entail only the discriminatory capacity to distinguish science from non-science. And precisely because it seemingly entails only that

---

[59] According to Tuozzo 2011, 263–4, Socrates contrasts the great benefits illustrated by the thought-experiment with the lesser ones concerning the mental capacities of the temperate man in such a way as to raise doubts in Critias' mind about the results achieved so far by the investigation. A different interpretation is proposed by van der Ben 1985, 78–9, who claims that the grammatical subject of ἔχοι at 172c3 is σωφροσύνη, while οὕτως at 173c3 refers back to the moderate gains mentioned at 172b3–8 and taken up by τοιαῦτα at 172b8. On the other hand, in my view, Socrates' remark at 172c4–5 indicates that, at 173c3, Critias has agreed, albeit hesitantly, that the 'science of science' appears to offer only the lesser benefits, not the greater ones illustrated by Socrates' counterfactual thought-experiment at 171d2–172a3.

restricted capacity, it can function only in an auxiliary manner and benefit temperate people only in lesser ways. As one might expect, Socrates is strongly inclined to reject this conclusion and the argument reaches an impasse. In the interest of the investigation, he will propose another concession and a new start.

4

> Perhaps, I said. But also, perhaps, we were enquiring about nothing of value.[60] My evidence is that certain strange things seem to me true of temperance, if it is such a thing. For let us examine the matter, if you wish, conceding that it is possible to know knowledge or science and, moreover, let us not withdraw but grant that temperance is what we said from the beginning it is, to know both *what* one knows and *what* one does not know. And having granted all this let us yet better investigate whether something, if it is of that sort, will also be of benefit to us. For what we were saying just now, that if temperance were such a thing, it would be a great good as our guide in the administration of both the household and city, we have not, I think, done well to agree to, Critias. (172c4–d5)

While in the previous phase of the elenchus Socrates points to the absurdity of the idea that temperance as mere knowledge-that brings only lesser benefits, he now concedes that temperance is also knowledge-what and expresses a far more serious doubt: that even if temperance as a 'science of science' has substantive content, it might do no good at all. 'Really, Socrates', replies Critias, 'you are saying strange things' (172e3). Critias' reaction is especially revealing. For, in the first place, it intimates that he did not expect Socrates to question the relevance of scientific understanding to happiness: he considers Socrates an intellectualist, as other Platonic characters do. In the second place, Critias' incredulity discloses his own commitment to the view that acting scientifically brings happiness and his reluctance to question that idea. Both interlocutors appear true to character. Critias reacts in accordance with the intellectualist inclinations that he has shown all along. As for Socrates, he points to the theme of self-care[61] and to his concern about carelessly supposing that he knows something that he in fact doesn't know (166c7–d2). Even at the risk

---

[60] οὐδὲν χρηστὸν ἐζητήσαμεν: 172c4–5. As Tuozzo 2011, 264 n. 17, remarks, some translators render the phrase in the way in which it is translated here, while others, e.g. Jowett, take χρηστόν as an internal accusative and render it accordingly (Jowett translates: 'we have been inquiring to no purpose').

[61] On this point, see Tuozzo 2011, 266.

of appearing to talk nonsense, he is determined to examine what seems to him problematic, as one should do 'if one has even a small concern for oneself' (173a4–5). Here too, the two conceptions of self-knowledge at play are poised against each other. And we have reason to suspect that, although the argument formally aims at a hypothetical feature of Critias' 'science of science', insofar as it questions the value of knowing what oneself and others know or don't know it can also imply a criticism against the Socratic mission and method.

The feature of Critianic temperance currently under scrutiny is, as indicated, the common assumption of both interlocutors that the 'science of science' involves both knowing *that* one knows or doesn't and knowing *what* one knows or doesn't (167a1–8).[62] Socrates now concedes that assumption and, subsequently, tries to explain the source of his worry by narrating to Critias what he calls a 'dream' (*onar*: 173a7). It is another thought-experiment depicting in some detail a society that is governed by one or more temperate rulers and that operates faultlessly under their guidance. The 'dream' is absolutely central to the Argument from Benefit and therefore deserves our attention.

> Listen then, I said, to my dream, whether it has come through the gate of horn or through the gate of ivory. For supposing that temperance were as we now define it and completely governed us, absolutely everything would be done according to the sciences, and neither would anyone deceive us by claiming to be a navigator when he was not, or a doctor, or a general, nor would anyone else remain undetected if he pretended to know what he did not know. And from things being that way nothing else could result for us than that our bodies would be healthier than they are now, and that we would be safe when facing the dangers of sea-travel and war, and that all our vessels or utensils and clothes and footwear and all other things would be expertly made for us because we would use true craftsmen. And moreover, if you would like, let us concede that divination is the science of what is to be in the future, and that temperance, which oversees it, will turn away charlatans and establish for us[63] the true diviners as prophets of what is to be. I do admit that, if mankind were organised in that way, it would act and live scientifically. For temperance, being on guard, would not allow the lack of science to burst in and take part in our deeds. But that by acting scientifically we would also do well and be happy, this, my dear Critias, we cannot know as yet. – However, he retorted,

---

[62] This is the assumption that Socrates must have in mind when he expresses his fear that the enquiry has gone astray 'if temperance is such a thing' (τοιοῦτον: 172c6), as is evident from the passage that immediately follows (172c6–d1).

[63] I take ἡμῖν to be a dative of advantage, while most translators take it together with 'prophets' as a possessive dative and render the phrase by 'our prophets' (see, for instance, Lamb 1927, 79; Tuozzo 2011, 268).

if you discredit acting scientifically, you will not easily find some other goal of acting well. (173a7–d7)

This is an intensely intertextual passage, whose ethical importance is underscored by a uniquely early reference to the moral *telos* (173d6–7). On the one hand, it stretches back to earlier sections of the *Charmides* and, on the other, it looks forward to other dialogues, notably the *Republic*, the *Theaetetus*, and the *Statesman*. Presently, Socrates sketches out another fictional society which, like its earlier counterpart, is intended to single out certain features that are especially relevant to the issue under consideration. However, unlike Socrates' earlier thought-experiment (171d2–172a3), the 'dream' is not grounded on a counterfactual hypothesis, but on the interlocutors' recent concession that temperance entails knowledge-what as well as knowledge-that, substantive as well as discriminatory knowledge. Once they agreed that temperance involves substantive knowledge, Socrates went on to sketch an imaginary society in conformity with that idea: a society governed by temperate rulers who have the requisite expertise in order to judge correctly *what* they themselves and others know or do not know and delegate tasks accordingly.

Socrates repeatedly draws attention to the imaginary nature of that society. He calls it a 'dream' and, grammatically, alludes to its fictional standing by repeatedly using the remote future construction (optative + ἄν). Neither Critias nor we, the readers, are ever allowed to forget that the 'dream' illustrates something *atopon*, a strange idea, and moreover that a certain strangeness characterises the 'dream' itself. Borrowing a metaphor from the *Odyssey* (19.564–7),[64] Socrates invites Critias to consider whether his 'dream' has come through the gate of horn, in which case it is veridical, or through the gate of ivory, in which case it is not.[65] Like the 'dream' of the *Theaetetus* (201d–202c), this 'dream' too constitutes a natural image for inspiration – 'an idea coming to mind, not as something one asserts as definitely true on one's behalf and as a conclusion of a process of reasoning, but more as something which gets said in one's mind, as if by an alien voice, so that one may wonder at first whether to accept it as true'.[66]

---

[64] The metaphor is used by Penelope when she describes her dream to Odysseus disguised as a beggar (*Od.* 564–7). According to Tuozzo 2011, 266–7, as Penelope's dream represents something bad but prophesises something good, so Socrates' dream appears to effect something bad, i.e. undermine the possibility of a knowledgeably run city, but leads to something good, namely a better understanding of the nature of temperance. While I agree that the 'dream' contributes to our understanding of temperance, I doubt that it prophesises anything good. More on this below.

[65] According to Burnyeat 1970, *Rep.* 443b with 432d–433a and *Leg.* 969b illustrate 'a dream coming true', whereas *Lys.* 218c, *Pol.* 290b, and *Tht.* 208b refer to cases in which the dream was 'only a dream'.

[66] Burnyeat 1970.

In both the *Charmides* and the *Theaetetus* the image of the 'dream' aptly conveys the condition of epistemological insecurity that the interlocutors find themselves in. And in both these dialogues the views exhibited by the 'dream' are deemed worthy of consideration, regardless of whether they will eventually prove to be true or false. While the 'dream' is being entertained the discussants are in the eerie realm of belief, as opposed to the firm ground of knowledge.[67] It remains open whether, in their wake, they will discover that their dream was true or, alternatively, that it was only a dream and truth still escapes them (*Plt.* 277d). There is another aspect of the 'dream' as well, which has to do with the subtext of the *Charmides*. 'Telling someone his own dream' was a proverbial expression for telling a person something he is already familiar with in his own experience.[68] In depicting a society ruled by a higher-order knowledge on the basis of which the temperate ruler delegates and oversees the execution of tasks, Socrates may be telling Critias something that Critias has already envisaged. He may be 'telling Critias his own dream'. The historical record suggests that the contents of the dream find a parallel in the ideology of political elitism that Critias pursued as leader of the Thirty.[69] If this is correct, Socrates' 'dream' is not only a dream. It could be read as a nightmare foretelling the future.

Turning to the contents of the 'dream', the first thing to note is that the imaginary society it depicts is not located in time or place. Unlike the ideal city of the *Republic*, which is unquestionably Greek, there is no indication that the city of the 'dream' is Greek or anything else. Nor is there any other element identifying a particular group of citizens or the city as a whole. Rather, Socrates singles out only the features relevant to the point that his thought-experiment is intended to make: the temperate rulers' scientific knowledge of what each person knows or doesn't; their capacity to distinguish experts from non-experts on the basis of that knowledge, and to delegate tasks only to the former and never to the latter; the experts' successful execution of these tasks; and, most importantly, the implications of the rule of temperance for the happiness of all concerned. In the society of the 'dream', everything is done 'according to the sciences' (*kata tas epistêmas*: 173a9–b1)[70] and no error or deception is possible (173b1–4).

The aforementioned sciences are of all sorts, some more prestigious and others less, some more theoretical but others involving greater practical

---

[67] See Burnyeat 1970, who also gives relevant references: *Men.* 85c, *Rep.* 476c, 520c, 533b.
[68] Burnyeat 1970, 106.   [69] See Dušanić 2000.
[70] The accusative plural ἐπιστήμας clearly refers to the first-order sciences or arts. Implicitly, it points to the contrast between the first-order sciences and temperance or the 'science of science', which governs itself and generally every science.

experience, some productive, others acquisitive, others performative, and so on. The first group mentioned by Socrates includes sciences of considerable prestige and prudential importance: navigation, the military art, and medicine, which secure, respectively, safety and health. The next group consists of crafts whose products contribute to our physical sustenance and comfort, and whose artisans (*dêmiourgoi*: 273c2) are valued by every organised society: pottery-making and metallurgy, weaving, and cobbling. The 'dream' does not preclude that, in the society it represents, there is an axiological hierarchy among these arts and that they enjoy different degrees of social recognition.[71] Nonetheless, it is clear that all of them are lower-level occupations in relation to temperance, which presides over them. In just this respect the society of the 'dream' could be compared with the rigidly hierarchical structure of the Callipolis and, specifically, the Guardians' rule over the Producers.

In the fictional society of the 'dream', divination (*mantikê*) is a special case. Socrates seems hesitant to call it a science (173c3–4) or to acknowledge that the seers' practices are beneficial for us.[72] He introduces divination into the 'dream' in a manner that is tentative and entirely dependent on Critias' assent: 'and moreover, if you would like, let us concede that divination is the science of what it is to be in the future' (173c3–4).[73] Within the 'dream', divination is treated just as all the other first-order sciences are treated. It is supervised by temperance[74] and acts together with temperance in order to successfully distinguish true prophets from charlatans. As for the benefits that divination was expected to bring, the argument does not challenge the common assumption that true diviners can secure material prosperity or avert material disasters for the individual or for the city by correctly foretelling the future, and by ensuring that appropriate steps will be taken to gain the good will of the gods.

Despite suggestions to the contrary,[75] there is no indication in the text that Socrates takes the benefits of institutionalised divination to be psychic rather than material. Plato's readers are bound to remember, for instance, that Calchas' prophecy to Agamemnon was not sought for the purposes of psychic benefit, nor, heaven knows, did it offer any. The dubious benefit of its outcome was material: the Greeks were able to sail for Troy and eventually win the war. Also, the Pythian oracle was typically consulted

---

[71] Remember that Critias appears to despise cobblers and their like (163b7), whereas he seems to have more respect, for example, for doctors (164a9–c4).

[72] In this context 'μαντική' refers to institutionalised divination, not to occurrences such as Socrates' divinatory dreams or his δαιμόνιον.

[73] ἐπιστήμη τοῦ μέλλοντος ἔσεσθαι: 173c4.

[74] καὶ τὴν σωφροσύνην αὐτῆς ἐπιστατοῦσαν: 273c4–5.   [75] See Tuozzo 2011, 268–78.

about practical decisions and its famously ambiguous sayings were supposed to give guidance aimed at material safety and prosperity, not at the
good of people's souls. Nor were the prophecies of the diviners always
successful. Far from it. Recall Nicias' catastrophic decision to follow the
omens and delay the departure of the Athenian navy from Syracuse, which
led to the demolition of the naval power of the city and the end of the
Athenian hegemony. This background makes understandable Socrates'
reluctance to brand divination as a science. And in light of Critias' character, it is plausible to surmise that he too may entertain doubts about its
scientific credentials.

For all its scientific organisation, which extends to the whole of mankind
(173c7), the society of the 'dream' conveys no sense of unity or community.
Significantly, Socrates does not say that the city governed by temperate
rulers will itself be temperate, and he does not tell us anything about the
other inhabitants' attitude towards these latter. While in the ideal city of
the *Republic* temperance binds together the three classes through their
agreement as to who should rule, in the imaginary city of the 'dream'
there is no intimation that the subjects accept (or that they don't) the
temperate ruler's authority and respect his judgement concerning the
distribution of tasks. Nor is there any indication that the subjects share
the governors' criteria and objectives. Instead, the 'dream' represents the
subjects of the imaginary city as mere instruments of scientific achievement, vessels of specialised knowledge, makers but not users of the products of their arts.[76] Worse, their actions seem to have no direction. They do
things correctly, but what for? For what purpose? While the Guardians in
the Callipolis pursue the good of the city and guide everyone to do the
same in his/her own way, it is impossible to gather what the temperate
rulers of the 'dream' might aim to attain. Such a way of life appears
disconnected from the intuitive goal of humans: happiness (173d4).

The thought-experiment of the 'dream' brings matters to a head. From our
perspective, it now becomes evident that Critias is faced with two mutually
exclusive alternatives: either temperance is *not* strictly reflexive knowledge, or
it *is* strictly reflexive knowledge but cannot secure our happiness. In either

---

[76] This problem is not unrelated to the problem on account of which Critias dropped the definition of
temperance as 'doing one's own' in the sense of 'doing or making good things': while the experts
might 'do their own' and be temperate on that account, nonetheless they might be unaware of the
goodness of their deeds and therefore of their own temperance (164a1–d3). Likewise, while the
people populating the 'dream' are supposed to act in accordance with temperance and hence act
correctly, there is no indication that they are aware of the correctness of their actions, let alone the
goodness of these.

case, we surmise that he will be compelled to abandon his definition of temperance as a 'science of science', i.e. a science directed only towards science itself and the other sciences. And in either case, the factor responsible for his failure is, it seems, the strictly reflexive character of the *epistêmê* that he takes to be equivalent to temperance. Critias does not yet realise the dialectical impasse he is in, but expresses his profound perplexity about the intimation of the 'dream' that it may be possible to live knowledgeably without living happily. If acting on the basis of scientific knowledge does not secure happiness, he wonders, what does (173d6–7)? In the final stage of the search, Socrates will suggest an answer to that question[77] and will rely on his initial intuition regarding the *technê* analogy in order to do so.

5

> Instruct me, then, about one more small detail, I said. You mean acting scientifically or knowledgeably in respect of what? Of cutting the leather for shoe-making? – By Zeus, certainly not. – Of the working of brass? – Not at all. – Of wool, or of wood, or of any other such thing? – Of course not. – Therefore, I said, we are no longer abiding by the claim that he who lives scientifically is happy. For although these experts live scientifically, you do not acknowledge that they are happy, but rather you seem to me to demarcate the happy person as someone who lives scientifically in respect of certain things. (173d8–e9)

In response to Critias' comment that it would be difficult to find a *telos*, goal or end, of acting well other than acting scientifically (173d6–7), Socrates brings back the *technê* analogy in full force. He appears prepared to consider Critias' intuition that acting scientifically amounts to acting well and being happy, provided that Critias can determine the domain of such actions. Acting scientifically in respect of what and for what purpose? As in his debate with Critias regarding the object of temperance (165c4– 166c6), so in the present instance Socrates ties the function and benefit of the science equivalent to temperance to the proprietary object of the latter. And as in the former passage, so in the latter he treats temperance as analogous to the other arts or sciences, insofar as he appears to assume that the correlative object of temperance should be distinct from temper- ance itself. In both cases, Socrates defends these assumptions on the basis of analogies between temperance or 'the science of science' and first-order arts. And on both occasions, he appears to strongly favour the view that

---

[77] Whether or to what extent Socrates endorses this answer remains controversial. As I shall indicate, in my view, he does not settle that issue.

every *epistêmê*, including temperance, is mainly orientated outwards: it not (or not only) of itself, but of something distinct from itself. However, while in the earlier debate (165c4–166c6) he eventually allowed Critias to have his own way, now he shows himself committed to his original position, i.e. that if temperance is an *epistêmê*, it must have an aliorelative object. As for Critias, one wonders whether he has changed his mind in respect of this topic, for he now does not raise any objection to Socrates. Has he come to tacitly accept that, in order to maintain that acting scientifically secures well-being, one needs to specify what acting in that manner is scientific *about* and what it is good *for*?

To direct Critias to specify the proprietary object of temperance, Socrates asks successive questions that aim to narrow down the relevant options. First, Critias eliminates crafts that consist in the working of various materials: cobbling, metallurgy, and weaving. Since he holds the belief that cobbling and other such crafts cannot be considered *good* doings or makings (163b7–8), he also believes that these arts must differ from the science aiming at happiness (173d9–e5). Thus he clarifies his stance: happy are not the persons who act scientifically without qualification, but those who act scientifically in respect of certain things (173e9). Think of the craftsmen in the *Apology*, who were found to have expert understanding of their particular fields, but no expertise in things that really matter, i.e. things distinctly pertaining to happiness and the proper care of one's soul. Next, Socrates asks Critias to entertain an apparently more promising candidate.

> Perhaps you mean the man I [sc. Socrates] was just referring to, namely the one who knows everything that is to be, the seer. Do you mean him or someone else? – Well, he replied, both him and someone else. Whom? I asked. Is it the sort of person who might know, in addition to what is to be, both everything that has been and everything that now is and might be ignorant of nothing? Let us assume that there is such a person. I won't say, I imagine, that there is anyone alive that knows more than he does. – Certainly not. (173e10–174a9)

The seer might appear a better bet. Some might think that, since he can foretell the future, he can plan better and more effectively than anyone else for the well-being of individuals and of the city. However, Critias' cautious answer ('Well, both him and someone else': 174a3) indicates that, like Socrates (173c2–7), he has reservations about the wisdom of diviners and their contribution to human happiness. While he does not overtly challenge the epistemic authority of seers, he makes clear that he is thinking primarily of someone else. His attitude is consistent with other features of his character. As a conservative aristocrat, he does not wish to undermine the traditional belief in diviners and divination. As a representative of the 'new learning', however,[78] he is likely to be sceptical about the role of seers and, as an intellectualist advocating the rule of those endowed with a higher form of understanding, he is probably inclined to place the seers under the governance of such men. In his speech about the meaning of the Delphic inscription, he has artfully presented himself as one of the privileged few that could read the mind of Apollo and explain his sayings to the populace. And he has indicated that the authoritative men in question have self-knowledge, not expertise in prophecy.

Hence, Critias is likely to be sincere when he states that the person he primarily has in mind is not the diviner, but someone else. According to Socrates, this is an omniscient person whose knowledge extends over all temporal modes and therefore is superior to the seer's knowledge. Then Socrates raises the following question: if there were someone knowledgeable of everything and ignorant of nothing, he would be bound to be happy; but *which bit* of his total knowledge would have caused his happiness?

> There is still one more thing I desire to know in addition: which one of the sciences makes him happy? Or do all of them do so in the same way? – Not at all in the same way, he said. – But what sort of science makes him supremely happy? The science by which he knows one of the things that are or have been or will be in the future? Is it perhaps the science by which he knows how to play draughts? – What are you talking about! he said. Draughts indeed! – What about the science by which he knows how to calculate? – Not in the least. – Well, is it the one by which he knows what is healthy? – More so, he said. – But that one which I mean makes him happy most of all, said I, is the science by which he knows what kind of thing? – That, he replied, by which he knows good and evil. (174a10–b10)

To help Critias articulate his thought, Socrates pursues a new line of questioning. He is not asking what the omniscient man is knowledgeable *of* or *about*, but which one of the sciences that he possesses is chiefly responsible for his happiness. Implicitly allowing that certain sciences may bear contingently on one's well-being, he presents Critias with two alternatives: either all the sciences contribute to one's happiness in the same manner (*homoiôs*: 174a11), or a single science contributes supremely to it (*malista*: 174b1).[79]

---

[78] See Socrates' suggestion that Critias is one of the σοφοί, 'wise men' (161b9–c1).

[79] In the passage that follows, happiness is taken to be uniquely and exclusively related to a single science. Hence the term μάλιστα is not intended to indicate that different sciences contribute to happiness in different degrees, but rather to suggest that a single science is essentially responsible for happiness whereas the other sciences may bear on happiness in some contingent way.

A third possibility is conspicuous by its absence: that all of the sciences contribute to happiness in different ways and possibly to different degrees as well. While the interlocutors of the *Charmides* do not engage with this option, Plato's readers may do so in connection with the hierarchical structure of the ideal state in the *Republic* or the scientific orchestration of the sciences effected by the wise ruler in the *Statesman*. In any case, assuming that the 'dream' illustrates Critias' idea of the rule of temperance, one could hardly expect him to choose the former alternative, i.e. that all the sciences contribute to happiness in the same manner. For, in the 'dream', temperance is the only science responsible for the expert delegation of tasks and hence for acting well and being happy, whereas the first-order arts contribute to the well-being of that society in a conditional and contingent way. Moreover, there is a logical constraint that appears to preclude the possibility that all the arts aim at happiness in the same manner. If the interlocutors endorse a constitutive conception of relatives and relations,[80] they are committed to the view that happiness must be the object of a single science.

Indeed, Critias emphatically rejects the suggestion that all the sciences contribute to the attainment of happiness in the same way (174a12) and proceeds with the assistance of Socrates to identify the science principally and essentially aiming at human flourishing. Some candidates are immediately eliminated, starting with the least plausible, then proceeding to a better option, then finally to a seemingly Socratic answer. First, the interlocutors eliminate draughts-playing (174b2–4) – a provocative suggestion made by Socrates and dismissed vehemently by Critias – and also the science of calculation (174b5–6). Then they consider medicine, which comes closer to what they are looking for (174b7–8) and which brings about the good, but only that of the body. All along, Socrates appears quite confident that Critias does have the answer to the question of which science is responsible for making us happy. And he obtains it in due course.

For Critias finally answers that the science chiefly responsible for happiness is 'the science by which one knows good and evil' (174b10). Critias' statement does not surprise Socrates and should not surprise us. For he is portrayed as someone familiar with Socrates' ideas and way of thinking and, therefore, he acts in a way true to his character when he asserts that temperance is knowledge of good and evil – a view closely associated with Plato's Socrates and the so-called minor Socratics as well. In the present context, however, it is not clear whether Critias truly endorses the latter

---

[80] See Chapter 10, 197–9 and notes 4 to 9.

view,[81] and whether he has truly abandoned his claim that the science securing well-being is a 'science of science' that governs every art and every expert in the state. This ambiguity pertains to the assessment of Critias' character, motives, and affinity to Socrates, and it will be clarified soon. For the moment, it is important to emphasise, as does Socrates (174b11–c3), that the relation between the science of good and evil and happiness is one to one. Happiness is the only object of the science of good and evil, and the latter is the only science that can make us happy. Socrates illustrates the constitutive relation between the science of good and evil and its object using yet another thought-experiment.[82]

> You wretch! I said. All this time you have been dragging me around in a circle, while you were concealing the fact that what made a person do well and be happy was not living scientifically, not even if this were science of all the other sciences together, but only if it were science of this one science alone, namely the science concerning good and evil. Because, Critias, if you choose to remove this science from the set of other sciences, will medicine any the less produce health, or cobbling shoes, or weaving clothes? Or will the art of navigation any the less prevent passengers from dying at sea, or the military art from dying in war? – No less at all, he said. – However, my dear Critias, if this science [sc. the science of good and evil] is lacking, the good and beneficial execution of each of these tasks will be gone out of our reach. – This is true. – And this science, it seems, is not temperance but a science whose function is to benefit us. For it is not a science of the sciences and the lack of the sciences, but of good and evil, so that, if this is beneficial, temperance would be something else for us. (174b11–d7)[83]

We should pause to consider Socrates' uneasy feelings, especially if we are experiencing them as well: a sense of running around in circles as if on a merry-go-round, a sensation of dizziness deriving from the illusion that everything is moving and nothing is stable. Personally, I have struggled with such feelings for a long time, while working through the second half of the dialogue and trying to make sense of it. And I have wondered what precisely may be the cause of them. I have come to the conclusion that the root of the problem is the strict reflexivity of Critias' notion of

---

[81] Tuckey 1951, 78, contends that the knowledge producing happiness is not the knowledge of good and evil but the second-order knowledge of the knowledge of good and evil. See, however, Tuozzo 2011, 278 and n. 42, which contains a reference to the decisive objections against Tuckey by Dieterle 1966.

[82] The sketch can be considered a separate thought-experiment or, alternatively, a follow-up to the 'dream'.

[83] I follow Burnet in excising ἡ ὠφελίμη present in B and T. On the textual difficulties of this passage see Murphy 2007, 228–30, and Tuozzo 2011, 279 n. 44.

temperance – the totally abstract, entirely uninformative conception of a 'science of science' but of no scientific object. Socrates and Critias have gone through many twists and turns in order to keep the argument going, but no move that they have made has yet managed to dispel the ambiguities surrounding that notion, prove the coherence of a 'science of science', and show how the latter might be relevant to our well-being. Rather, both the interlocutors and we ourselves experience a lingering sense of disorientation. We have become entangled in the labyrinthine problems of the 'science of science', losing sight of the main objective of the search: the element on account of which a person can live well and be happy. Socrates accuses Critias of having deliberately concealed his view that the happiness-producing science is the science of good and evil. This may be a playful remark, or it may suggest that Critias' love of victory has been greater than his concern for the truth.

Be this as it may, Socrates' latter thought-experiment (174c3–d1) has affinities with the 'dream' and proposes the following moves: first, remove the science of good and evil from the other sciences that are expertly practised in an imaginary society reminiscent of the society of the 'dream'. Then, consider whether these remaining sciences are any less successful in achieving their respective goals: you will find that they are not. Next, ask yourself whether, in the absence of the science of good and evil, the other experts' successful engagement in their respective domains is likely to yield any true benefit. You will find that it does not seem so. If the science of good and evil is removed, happiness is removed as well.

As with the previous thought-experiments, so the present one points to an argument implicit in the story. Assuming that the sciences differ on account of their respective objects, since the object of the science equivalent to temperance is solely science (and its privation) but the object of the science of good and evil is happiness, temperance must differ from the science of good and evil. 'It would be something other for us' (174d6–7) but, whatever this might be, it would not be the science aimed at securing happiness. The upshot is that the 'science of science' is formally distinct from the only science aiming to procure happiness, i.e. the only science truly beneficial for us. The inference to draw is that, if ethical knowledge were taken away from us, even the most significant technological and scientific achievements would be useless.

Even though the above thought-experiment is sketchy, it contributes significantly to the Argument from Benefit by drawing attention to certain crucial features. First, it highlights an assumption to be built into the 'dream' in retrospect, namely that the society of the 'dream' contained all the sciences *including* the science of good and evil. On the other hand, in Socrates' latter scenario, the science of good and evil is hypothetically removed. As a result, Socrates' latter construct achieves what the 'dream' did not fully achieve, namely it prompts us to draw a sharper contrast between the first-order arts and sciences, which are orientated towards their respective prudential goods, and the science of good and evil, which is directed uniquely and exclusively towards happiness. Second, the scenario presently under discussion indicates that the knowledge of good and evil can benefit us in different or complementary ways, i.e. by its very presence in us, or by ensuring that we use the first-order arts and sciences in a truly profitable manner, or both. Third, the suggested conclusion, i.e. that Critianic temperance does not bring genuine benefit because it does not have happiness as its own peculiar object, affects the 'science of science' whether we take it to be discriminatory knowledge (knowledge-that) or substantive knowledge (knowledge-what) or both. If the removal of the science of good and evil renders substantive technological knowledge useless, the same evidently holds for discriminatory knowledge too. A question can be raised, however. Since Critias now admits that the only science that truly benefits us is the science of good and evil, why does he not change direction? Why does he not abandon his earlier definition of temperance as 'science of itself and every other science' and propose instead that, in truth, temperance is the science of good and evil?[84] The reason is, as we shall see immediately below, that Critias has a last arrow in his quiver.

> But why, he said, should it [sc. the science of science] not be beneficial? For if temperance is above all a science of the sciences and presides too over the other sciences, then, in virtue of ruling over this one, i.e. the science of the good, surely it would benefit us. (174d8–e2)

This is Critias' final attempt to defend the idea that temperance or 'the science of itself and the other sciences' brings great benefit. He relies, I submit, on the assumption that temperance is higher-order *because* it is strictly reflexive: it governs the other sciences *because* it is only of science and no other object.[85] Accordingly, Critias argues that, since 'the science of

---

[84] Many commentators wonder why Socrates does not make that move himself. In my view, both epistemic and formal reasons prevent him from doing so. Epistemically, he does not claim to *know* that temperance is the science of good and evil. Formally, the dialectical rules do not allow the questioner to put forward a definition other than hypothetically (e.g. *Euthyph.* 11e–12d, *Gorg.* 453a).
[85] This could explain why Critias is unwilling to give up the idea that temperance is strictly reflexive. Although the elenchus has done much to undermine that idea, Critias appears still to cling to the intuition that, if temperance is to enjoy a privileged second-order status, it must be reflexive and not tied to any particular field.

science' rules all the first-order sciences, and assuming that the science of good and evil is one of them,[86] the 'science of science' must also rule the science of good and evil. Furthermore, Critias seems to assume that, when one science governs another, it also appropriates the function of this latter; on this assumption, since temperance or the 'science of science' rules the science of good and evil, it also appropriates the work that the science of good and evil is supposed to do, namely make us happy. The 'science of science' is greatly beneficial on account of that fact.

This is a brilliant move. And it might have been successful, if Critias' conception of temperance were such as to allow that temperance or 'the science of science' rules over the other sciences *as well as* their proprietary objects. This is not the case, however. For the relation of Critianic temperance to the objects of the first-order sciences is intransitive or intransparent: while the 'science of science' is set over the first-order sciences, it has no access to the objects that these sciences are of. Temperance is a science only of science and no other thing. Socrates draws the implications of that thesis as follows:

> And, I replied, would this science, and not medicine, also make people healthy? Moreover, would it be the one to bring about the works of the other arts, and the other arts not have each its own work? Or have we not been protesting for some time that it is only a science of science and the lack of science, but of nothing else? Is that not so? – Indeed, it appears to be. – So, it will not be a producer of health? – No, it will not. – For health is the object of another art, is it not? – Yes, of another. – Therefore, my friend, it [sc. the science of science] will not be a producer of benefit either. For, again, we just now attributed this function to another art, did we not? – Very much so. (174e3–175a5)

Socrates refutes Critias outright. He argues that since, according to Critias, every first-order art or science is only of its own peculiar object and has only its own peculiar function, and since temperance is a science only of science, it cannot do any specific work or make any specific thing. Consequently, the temperate person cannot fulfil any specific function and, *a fortiori*, cannot do anything beneficial. In sum, no crossing of boundaries is possible between the 'science of science' and the other arts and sciences with regard to their respective objects or domains. And insofar as their respective functions and goals are determined by their proprietary objects, no crossing of boundaries seems possible with regard to the work

---

[86] Critias is entitled to make that assumption, because the aforementioned science does have a specific aliorelative object, namely good and evil.

that they, respectively, do or the benefits that they yield. It follows that the 'science of science' cannot appropriate the work peculiar to the science of good and evil. Even supposing that the former governs the latter, it cannot make its own the work that the science of good and evil does or the happiness that it brings. The conclusion that the interlocutors reach is immensely disappointing. 'In what way, then, will temperance be beneficial since it is not the producer of any benefit? – In no way at all, Socrates, it seems' (175a6–8).

In the end, Socrates seems vindicated regarding the society of the 'dream'. The temperate rulers can make the state run scientifically; but it appears that they cannot make it run beneficially and make the citizens happy. Recall, however, that the scientific governance of the state depends on the rulers' ability to successfully discern experts from non-experts in particular fields and delegate tasks to the former but not the latter. In turn, the correct delegation of tasks depends on the shaky premise that temperate rulers have knowledge-what as well as knowledge-that – substantive as well as discriminatory knowledge. If that premise were revoked, the temperate rulers' capacity for identifying experts in particular fields and distinguishing them from non-experts would be debatable. In particular, one might question how these rulers can tell *that* there is scientific knowledge, if they don't know anything about its content. Pushing the matter further, one might wonder whether the temperate rulers of the 'dream' are experts in anything or mere frauds.

Why did things go so wrong for Critias? As I have repeatedly indicated, I think that the main reason is that he rejected a central feature of the *technê* analogy, namely the view that every art or science is constitutively related to a proprietary object, which determines the domain of that science as well as its function and benefit. By forcing Socrates to concede, if only for the sake of the argument, that temperance is a strictly reflexive *epistêmê*, Critias narrowed down the domain of the latter to such a degree as arguably to deprive it of substantive content. He placed an insurmountable wedge between temperance and every other science, and he segregated the temperate person's discriminatory activities from the activities of the first-order experts, which aim to improve and enrich many aspects of our lives. Comparably to the Greek doctors who were accused of treating the part but neglecting the whole (156d6–e6), Critias' temperate men could be blamed for focusing exclusively on science as such and disregarding the contribution of virtue and scientific knowledge to the well-being of mankind.

Thus emerged the incongruous picture of a society whose unity under the guidance of the 'science of science' seems artificial and forced, and whose promise of happiness appears empty. There is something quite frightening about the thought-experiments that Socrates sketched out in close succession and, especially, about the thought-experiment of the 'dream'. It depicts a society run by managers rather than statesmen, on the basis of a science revolving solely around itself, obsessed with specialisation and productivity but oblivious to individual or communal welfare. To this all-too-familiar threat the Argument from Benefit suggests the hope of a remedy: a science of value, whose goal would be the well-being of all concerned and whose function would consist in coordinating our various activities and integrating them into an organic whole. The main features of that science are foreshadowed by Socrates in the prologue of the *Charmides* (156d1–157c6). Like Zalmoxian medicine, it charms the soul by means of philosophical discourses, with a view to the whole and not just the part, so that virtue prevails and every good follows.

CHAPTER 12

The Epilogue (175a9–176d5)

1 Pulling Strings Together (175a9–d5)

At this point, Socrates undertakes to summarise the key moves of the investigation dedicated to Zeus in a manner that has no exact parallel in any other Socratic dialogue of Plato. He assesses the current *status quaestionis*, indicates where the enquiry has gone wrong, identifies the main reasons why it went wrong, and assumes partial responsibility for that failure. Once again, we shall have the opportunity to entertain side by side the two competing conceptions of self-knowledge at work in the dialogue: on the one hand, Critias' conception of knowing oneself in the sense of having a 'science of science' that confers on the temperate person a higher-order cognitive capacity both substantive and directive and, on the other, Socrates' conception of temperance as one of the greatest goods that one can acquire through a certain kind of *logoi*, arguments, and as involving the capacity to discover what oneself and others know or do not know. Dialectically, Socrates' critical observations concern the preceding argument and target the 'science of science' alone. Philosophically, however, as I shall argue, some of these observations also raise problems for the Socratic method as a way of judging knowledge and ignorance in oneself and others. If this is correct, the passage quoted below constitutes a unique instance of sustained self-criticism on Socrates' part. While he preserves the intuition that temperance is a form of *epistêmê* and has a distinct object, and while he implicitly acknowledges that his method has a certain use, he also points to the weaknesses of the latter and directs us to new ways of gaining understanding.

> Do you see, then, Critias, that my earlier fears were reasonable and that I was rightly accusing myself of failing to bring under scrutiny anything worthwhile about temperance? For if I had been of any use for conducting a good

search, it wouldn't have been the case that what is agreed to be the finest of all things would somehow have appeared to us to be of no benefit. And now, you see, we are vanquished on all fronts, and are unable to discover to which one of the things there are the lawgiver attached this name, temperance. Nonetheless we have made many concessions which were not forced upon us[1] by the argument. For, as a matter of fact, we conceded that there is a science of science, even though the argument neither allowed nor asserted that there is. Again, although the argument did not allow this, we conceded that the temperate man knows through this science the functions of the other sciences as well, so that we would find him knowledgeable both of knowing *what* things he knows *that* he knows them and of knowing *what* things he does not know *that* he doesn't know them. And we granted this in the most bountiful manner, without examining the impossibility of some-how knowing things that one doesn't know in any way at all; for the concession we agreed on amounts to saying that one knows about them that one doesn't know them. And yet, as I think, this might appear more irrational than anything. However, although the enquiry has shown us to be so soft and lacking in rigour, it cannot do any better in finding the truth, but derided it [sc. the truth] to such an extent that the very thing which, by agreeing with each other and by moulding it together, we earlier posited to be temperance the enquiry has with the utmost contempt shown to be useless. (175a9–d5, emphasis added)

Socrates now steps back from the rigid framework of dialectical exchange and speaks his own mind: the search has failed and he primarily blames himself, but also Critias, for that result. First, he accuses himself of failing to contribute anything valuable to the enquiry about *sôphrosynê* and gives an argument to support that claim (175a9–b2). Then, he specifies the ultimate consequence of their defeat (175b2–4). Next, he identifies the elements of the investigation that he considers particularly problematic and indicates why they are objectionable (175b4–c8). Finally, he criticises the enquiry as well as the enquirers, i.e. himself and Critias, for reaching an absurd conclusion about temperance and for heaping ridicule on the truth (175c8–d5). We shall discuss these charges in succession, first, in respect of the dialectical argument concerning the 'science of science' and, subsequently, in respect of Socrates' own method for attaining self-knowledge.

Again using the vocabulary of vision, Socrates wonders whether Critias can 'see' (175a9)[2] that Socrates has been vindicated regarding the fear that

---

[1] Although the dative plural ἡμῖν goes with συμβαίνοντα, it is difficult to render this phrase. Literally, Socrates refers to concessions that 'were not encountered by us [ἡμῖν] in the course of the argument [ἐν τῷ λόγῳ: 175b5]'. I take this to mean that the concessions that he and Critias made did not follow from or were not entailed by the argument. I shall say more about this point below.

[2] On the significance of this usage of the verb, see Chapter 10, note 92.

he expressed sometime in the past (*palai*: 175a9), when he blamed himself, rightly as it turned out, 'for failing to bring under scrutiny anything worthwhile about temperance' (175a9–11). This earlier point in time does not lie outside the dialogue,[3] nor is Socrates insincere when he says that he was right to inculpate himself.[4] The contrast that he draws between *palai*, some time back (when he experienced the aforementioned fear), and *nyn* (175b2), 'now', i.e. now that his suspicion has been confirmed, is situated within the dialogue and points to an earlier passage where Socrates expressed his own unease, using the same words as he is using here too. That is, in addressing the question of whether temperance as 'science of science' is beneficial, the Argument from Benefit suggests that it might be beneficial if it involved substantive knowledge or knowledge-what (171d1–172a3); as things stand, however, it seems that the 'science of science' does not entail knowledge-what but only knowledge-that (170a6–171c10); therefore, it cannot produce beneficial results on its own, but can only enhance one's performance in learning or practising some first-order art (172b1–8). Having reached that interim conclusion, Socrates remarked that 'perhaps we did not enquire about anything worthwhile' (172c4–5),[5] but that he and Critias have carelessly agreed that knowledge-*what* would be beneficial for mankind. Moreover, he confessed his fear (*phoboimên*: 172e6) that he and his interlocutor were not conducting the examination correctly (172e4–6).

Now, in the close of the investigation, he refers to the content of that fear[6] in a strikingly similar manner: 'I was rightly accusing myself', he says, 'of failing to bring under scrutiny anything worthwhile[7] about temperance' (175a10–11). Note that, in the earlier instance, Socrates did not necessarily imply that he is incompetent, whereas in the later instance he does. In the former case the search was still underway, whereas in the latter the investigation has been completed and he is in a position to assess it. Also notice that earlier (*palai*) Socrates appeared to hold both himself and Critias responsible for the absurd idea that temperance or the 'science of

---

[3] Lampert 2010, 226, takes πάλαι (175a9) to indicate a time before the battle of Potidaea, during which, as Socrates now realises, he was talking about philosophy in the wrong way. 'Failure and blame are altogether fitting; he [sc. Socrates] is right to fear that he did nothing useful in presenting *sôphrosynê* as he did. Socrates justly accuses himself long before anyone else accuses him'.

[4] According to Lampert 2010, Socrates is deliberately lying here, for he has not failed but succeeded in his purpose, i.e. to discover the state of philosophy in Athens and render Critias aware of his own perplexity.

[5] οὐδὲν χρηστόν: 172c4–5.

[6] Compare Tuozzo 2011, 288. Schmid 1998, 148, claims that Socrates' fear was expressed in 166c–d, where he says that he might not know how to investigate beautifully.

[7] οὐδὲν χρηστόν: 175a10.

science' brings only lesser benefits (172c4–5), whereas now, in referring to that earlier occasion, he focuses on his own inadequacy as an enquirer (175a9–11).[8] On what grounds does Socrates infer that, in the end, he has been unable to entertain anything pertinent or valuable regarding the nature of temperance? His reasoning is this: if the enquiry had been conducted correctly, its outcome would have been consistent with (or would have confirmed) the commonly shared belief[9] that temperance is the finest of all things.[10] However, the investigation indicated that temperance is useless and hence not fine at all. Therefore, Socrates concludes that something went seriously wrong with the search and, furthermore, that, for his own part, he failed to contribute anything useful so as to ensure the quality[11] of the enquiry (175a11–b2). In this way he underscores the strength of his conviction that *sôphrosynê* is among the greatest goods and his affinity with the Zalmoxian view that temperance in the soul is the source of every good for man (156e–157a), while he decisively distances himself from the Critianic conception of temperance as a strictly reflexive, higher-order science.

Turning to the criticisms that he levels in retrospect against the search, we find that they stretch back to Socrates' two-pronged *aporia* and the two arguments motivated, respectively, by each of the questions constituting that puzzle: whether or not a 'science of science' is possible, and whether or not, assuming that it is possible, it is good for us (167b1–4). Recall that, in order to keep the investigation alive, the interlocutors agreed to make certain concessions concerning the possibility as well as the content of the science under debate. Summing up the latter, Socrates challenges the legitimacy of these moves and thus fires a final shot at Critianic temperance.

At the outset, he indicates that the failure to conduct the search properly is not merely axiological and epistemic, but has ontological and semantic aspects as well. When he had to defend himself against Critias' imputation that he only cared for victory over his dialectical opponent rather than truth (166c3–6), he said that his sole motivation in cross-examining Critias was to ensure that he did not believe he knew something that he did not know (166c7–d2) and that he engaged in this questioning primarily for his

---

[8] δικαίως ἐμαυτὸν ᾐτιώμην: 175b10.

[9] ὁμολογεῖται at 175b1 may concern either the agreement of most people that temperance is κάλλιστον πάντων (175a11), the finest of all things, or the agreement of Socrates and Critias on that point.

[10] κάλλιστον πάντων: 175a11. See Tuckey 1951, 88.

[11] εἴ τι ἐμοῦ ὄφελος ἦν πρὸς τὸ καλῶς ζητεῖν: 175b1–2.

own sake but also, to some extent, for the sake of his friends (166d2–4). Subsequently, he briefly explained his meaning: he, as well as Critias, assumes that it is good for almost everybody to acquire epistemic clarity regarding the nature of each being (166d4–7).[12] Now that the enquiry has reached its end, he realises that he and Critias were unsuccessful in their efforts to identify and individuate the entity that the name '*sôphrosynê*' was assigned to (175b3–4). Socrates does not disclose who is the lawgiver that attached this word to the corresponding thing (175b3–4). It could be the aforementioned 'great man' (169a1–7), or an expert who would act under the direction of a dialectician,[13] or a divinity. In any case, Socrates' judgement that they have been defeated in every way (175b2–3) has to do with being as well as knowledge, correct naming as well as truth.

The first concession that he targets is that 'there is a "science of science"' (175b6). He and Critias made that concession[14] even though, as he points out, it was neither allowed nor asserted by the argument.[15] Is this criticism justified? And can it be laid at Socrates' own door? The answer, I suggest, is affirmative on both counts. Recall the conclusion of the Argument from Relatives, which addresses the question whether a science solely directed towards itself and no other object is credible or possible. There, after examining different groups of analogues, the interlocutors agree that strictly reflexive constructions of relatives appear in some cases strange and in others impossible (168e3–7). And Socrates adds that, even if some people find such constructions credible (169a1), only an expert in division would be capable of settling the issue in a definitive manner (169a1–7). But although, according to my analysis, the Argument from Relatives does provide adequate grounds for its tentative conclusion, and although Socrates appears quite convinced that strict reflexivity is problematic or incoherent, nonetheless he subsequently proposes to his interlocutor the following move: 'if it seems right, Critias, he said, let us now grant this view, that it is possible that there is a "science of science" – we can investigate on another occasion whether or not this is the case' (169d2–5). Critias consents and thus they proceed to investigate the second part of the *aporia*, i.e. how temperance is beneficial for us. Socrates, then, is the interlocutor who took the initiative of introducing that concession into the enquiry and, therefore, is primarily responsible for it. Is he to blame? He is,

---

[12] γίγνεσθαι καταφανὲς ἕκαστον τῶν ὄντων ὅπῃ ἔχει: 166d5–6.
[13] Compare the 'lawgiver' in the *Cratylus*, who assigned (and continues to assign) names to things. According to Sedley 2003, the 'lawgiver' is not a dialectician, although to accomplish his task well he ought to follow the instructions of a dialectician.
[14] συνεχωρήσαμεν: 175b6.   [15] οὐκ ἐόντος τοῦ λόγου οὐδὲ φάσκοντος εἶναι: 175b7.

278 12 The Epilogue (175a9–176d5)

because, as he suggests in his summary, the concession under consideration has no appropriate warrant. While it serves a dialectical purpose, it lacks epistemic justification. It is neither stated nor implied by the Argument from Relatives. Worse, the concession grants what the Argument from Relatives denies, i.e. that there can be such a thing as a science of itself (175b6–7).

The next concession that Socrates now denounces as arbitrary is that the person endowed with the 'science of science', i.e. the temperate person, would have substantive knowledge: he would expertly know through the 'science of science' the respective functions or works (*erga*) of the other sciences (175b7–c1). Socrates and Critias assumed that the temperate person's knowledge is 'of both *what* things he knows *that* he knows them and *what* things he doesn't know *that* he doesn't know them' (175c2–3, emphasis added). However, Socrates now declares, the argument did not allow this concession (175c1),[16] or indeed contradicted it. Again, it seems to me, Socrates is absolutely right. And again, the blame must be placed primarily on himself. Consider: early in their conversation, Socrates and Critias debated the issue of whether or not the *epistêmê* supposed to be equivalent to temperance is comparable to the other sciences and arts regarding the nature of its object. Socrates maintained that the science in question must be craftlike: like the other arts and sciences, it must be of an object or subject-matter distinct from temperance itself. On the other hand, Critias contended that temperance is unlike the other arts or sciences in this respect: while the latter are aliorelative, temperance is strictly reflexive: it is a science only of science (i.e. of itself and the other sciences) and of no other object. As we saw, Socrates allowed Critias to get his own way and, from that point onwards, helped him fully articulate the notion of a 'science of science' before submitting it for investigation. Then the interlocutors came to agree that temperance is a science of science and non-science (166e7–9) and that, therefore (167a1), the temperate man alone will be able to judge *what* himself and others know and do not know (167a1–5). Thanks to Socrates' interventions, it became clear that Critias understood temperance as an *epistêmê* that is both strictly reflexive and substantive: a science of nothing but science, which, however, involves access to substantive content. 'This', Socrates concluded on Critias' behalf, 'is what being temperate or temperance or knowing oneself is, to know both what one knows and what one doesn't' (167a5–8).

---

[16] οὐδὲ τοῦτ᾿ ἐῶντος τοῦ λόγου: 175c1.

The idea that Critias' 'science of science' entails both knowledge-that (discriminatory knowledge) and knowledge-what (substantive knowledge) was initially taken for granted. However, in the early stages of the Argument from Benefit (170a6–171c10), Socrates' questioning led Critias to admit that, while the temperate man can discern *epistêmê* from the absence of *epistêmê* and the expert from the charlatan, he cannot identify any given science as the science it is or any given expert as the expert he/she is. Conversely, the argument ran, while the first-order experts know what their scientific knowledge is *of*, they cannot tell that what they have is *epistêmê*, i.e. scientific knowledge. Subsequently, the two interlocutors briefly entertained the possibility that temperance as solely discriminatory knowledge (knowledge-that) might bring certain lesser advantages to those who have it (172b1–8) but found that hypothesis unacceptable. For, as Socrates pointed out, it appeared to imply that temperance is virtually worthless (172c4–6). And yet, immediately afterwards, Socrates suggested to Critias the following course of action:

> Suppose that we grant that it is possible to know scientific knowledge and, moreover, we do not withdraw but concede that temperance is what we said from the beginning it is, to know both *what* one knows and *what* one does not know. And having conceded all this let us yet better investigate whether something, if it is of that sort, will also be of benefit to us. (172c7–d1, emphasis added)

In addition to granting the possibility of a 'science of science', here Socrates proposes that they also grant that the latter would have substantive content. Dialectically, this is a shrewd suggestion. For it offers an alternative to the absurd idea that temperance as knowledge-that brings only lesser benefits; and it makes the 'science of science' appear less strange and less thin than it otherwise would. Philosophically, however, the concession that temperance involves knowledge-what as well as knowledge-that seems inconsistent with the reasoning outlined above (170a6–171c10), which points in exactly the opposite direction. Moreover, it does not receive support or justification from any other element of the text. So long as Socrates was engaged in the dialectical debate, he had to rely on it. Now that the debate is over and he is passing judgement on its quality, he deprecates that move.

A third, related objection is this: according to Socrates, the latter concession that he and Critias agreed on[17] appears to entail

---

[17] ὁμολογία: 175c7.

a contradiction. It is equivalent to claiming that one can know *somehow* what one does not know *in any way at all* (175c5–7)[18] or, in short, that one knows what one does not know (175c6–7). This time Socrates and Critias are equally to blame, since neither of them thought of examining the paradoxical nature of that claim, while, as Socrates points out, it might seem totally incoherent.[19] Leaving aside for the moment Socrates' own vulnerability to that criticism, we should concentrate on its direct target: the 'science of science'. The interlocutors have agreed, first, that it is science of *anepistêmosynê* (the absence of science) as well as of *epistêmê* (167c1–3) and, second, that the person who possesses it has knowledge of what things he knows that he knows them and what things he doesn't know that he doesn't know them (167a1–8, 172c7–d1). At first glance, does either of these views appear paradoxical or self-contradictory? I think that Socrates is right: both do, even though, as Socrates observes with biting irony, he and Critias granted them as premises 'in the most bountiful manner' (175c4).[20] There is something distinctly odd in the idea that one can have *epistêmê* of the privation of *epistêmê*, although that idea admits of different elaborations that can render it comprehensible or acceptable. Likewise, the assumption that one can know, in a robust epistemic sense of 'know', *what* one does not know sounds self-contradictory and therefore requires explanation and defence. The absurdity arises when 'what' is read as a relative pronoun, 'that which', but not when it is read as introducing an indirect question. Socrates probably realises that the absurdity turns on something like this, which would explain why he sets the issue aside as too diversionary to pursue here.[21]

Jointly as well as severally, the three criticisms discussed above lend additional support to the conclusions reached, respectively, by the Argument from Relatives and the Argument from Benefit. Socrates highlights the fact that, despite the unwarranted concessions that he and Critias made in the course of the enquiry, they have been unable to defend either the possibility of a 'science of science' or the idea that the latter would bring any substantial benefit. In truth, if these concessions had not been granted, the argument would have ended long ago. Critianic temperance proved to be too problematic to survive dialectical scrutiny, mainly because it was

---

[18] οὐδ'ἐπισκεψάμενοι τὸ ἀδύνατον εἶναι ἅ τις μὴ οἶδεν μηδαμῶς ταῦτα εἰδέναι ἁμῶς γέ πως: 175c4–5.

[19] Cf. οὐδενὸς ὅτου οὐχὶ ἀλογώτερον τοῦτ'ἂν φανείη: 175c7–8.

[20] This use of παντάπασι μεγαλοπρεπῶς (175c3–4) is ironic. Socrates' point is that he and Critias have been excessively generous in granting all these concessions. It is worth noting that the concessionary method is a well-known rhetorical device: see Gorgias' *Encomium of Helen* and *On Not-Being*.

[21] It is a kind of issue that belongs to the *Euthydemus*.

constructed as a science both strictly reflexive and intransparent with regard to the objects of science or the sciences. While we may choose to revisit, modify, and defend it anew, the interlocutors of the *Charmides* must leave it behind. Socratic self-knowledge, however, remains on offer and it is important to examine whether the aforementioned criticisms affect it or in what way.

In outline, the stance that I wish to take is as follows. Socratic self-criticism can be interpreted in many ways and, as mentioned, the consensus of interpreters of the *Charmides* is that, in this work, Plato's Socrates criticises central features of his own philosophical outlook (notably the views that virtue is relevantly analogous to the arts, that virtue is a form of knowledge, and that that kind of knowledge is necessary and sufficient for happiness), highlights the paradox lying at the heart of his principal method, and suggests that the latter should be abandoned in favour of other methods of philosophical investigation. In the present monograph I have challenged this sort of approach and argued for a more complex and nuanced account of what is going on in the dialogue. On my view, while the debate between Socrates and Critias does problematise key elements of the Socratic philosophy and method, it invites us to rethink rather than reject the latter and to erect rather than sever bridges between the so-called Socratic and the so-called Platonic writings of Plato. I propose that Socrates' final summary of the debate be read in the same spirit. Although, as I shall maintain, some of his criticisms against the 'science of science' can also raise problems for the Socratic method of questioning and the conception of self-knowledge associated with it, they are not entirely decisive, and they serve a constructive rather than a destructive purpose. On the one side, Socrates points to the limitations of the dialectical method and his own weaknesses as a questioner. On the other, his final observations do not imply that dialectical questioning is useless but rather that it is insufficient. Cross-examining oneself and others regarding what one knows and what one does not know can take us only part of the way towards virtue and truth. Much more is needed in order to pursue the goal that Critianic temperance blatantly failed to claim for itself, but also that the Socratic search for self-knowledge could never attain on its own: the happiness of both the individual and the state. I wish to elaborate and defend these suggestions.

In the *Apology* and other Socratic dialogues Socrates professes to be ignorant about 'the most important things' but, nonetheless, cross-examines his interlocutors about such subjects with the explicit purpose of judging what he himself and others know or do not know but believe

they know. The latter two criticisms that he raises against the argument
with Critias, then, can be addressed to him as well: first, is it not arbitrary to
assume that he can make substantive judgements about epistemic content,
if he is ignorant of that content? And second, doesn't his method of cross-
examination imply a paradox, namely that one can be in a position to know
what one does not know? Both objections appear *prima facie* plausible, but
neither, I submit, is conclusive. Let me briefly explain why. Regarding the
former issue, one might point out that, despite their obvious differences,
Critias' temperate man and Plato's Socrates find themselves in
a comparable epistemic predicament: they have no expert understanding
of the objects that they are, respectively, supposed to judge. The former has
only knowledge-that, but nonetheless passes judgement on *what* people
know and do not know and distinguishes accordingly between experts and
laypeople. The latter disavows having knowledge, but nonetheless claims
that he is able to tell *what* he himself and others know or do not know. As
for the temperate man, so for Socrates it would seem that the challenge
consists in establishing the legitimacy of such judgements. Can Socrates do
any better than Critias in this regard? I suggest that he can, by appealing to
the dialectical nature of his method. That is, he can plausibly contend that,
insofar as he limits himself to the role of the questioner and the argument
proceeds by means of premises or concessions endorsed by the interlocutor,
he does not necessarily need to have expertise in the subject under discussion. It is the interlocutor who is represented as an expert, not Socrates
himself.[22]

Regarding the charge that it seems irrational to claim that one can
know in some way what one doesn't know in any way at all (175c5–6),
Socrates' phrasing appears calculated to bring to mind Meno's paradox
(*Men.* 80d5–e5).[23] Plato's purpose, I suggest, is to point to the theory of
recollection that constitutes his own answer to that paradox, and also
allude to a contrast drawn in the *Meno* between different types of

[22] This does not entail that Socrates needs no knowledge at all in order to cross-examine his
interlocutors – it only entails that he needs no *expert* or *scientific* knowledge in order to do so.
Arguably, Socrates still needs knowledge of how to conduct a dialectical investigation, how to use
the principle of non-contradiction, how to recognise absurdities, etc. Whether or not these latter
amount to or involve substantive knowledge claims is a matter of debate.
[23] Compare Tuckey 1951, 89: 'this is clearly a reference to the expression εἰδέναι ἃ τις οἶδεν καὶ ἃ μὴ
οἶδεν'. Tuckey contends that, if knowing in some way what one does not know were impossible,
Socrates' claim to know that he doesn't know would be invalidated (Tuckey 1951, 90). However,
Tuckey does not pay attention to the exact way in which Socrates phrases this criticism: he does not
reject the idea that one knows *in some way* things that one does not know (as Tuckey claims), but
challenges the assumption that one can know *in some way* (175c5–6) what one does not know *in any
way* (175b5).

searchers. On the one hand, people who are affected by Meno's paradox turn into lazy, fainthearted, soft investigators (*malakois*: 81d7), while, on the other, enquirers who engage in recollection work hard and energetically in order to achieve their goal (81d5–e1). Recollection, however, is not available to the interlocutors of the *Charmides*. For in the *Charmides* Plato has not (yet) put the theory on the table and, moreover, Socrates and Critias are arguing in a way that does not favour recollection. Therefore, Socrates is in no better position than Critias to respond to the charge of incoherence. His observations concerning their performance in the search closely parallel the remarks concerning enquirers in the *Meno*. Namely, like the slow and soft searchers of the *Meno*,[24] the senior searchers of the *Charmides* have been shown to be mild and not hard, pliable and not firm.[25] Socrates describes himself and Critias as *euêthêkoi*, gentle but also simple-minded, where they should have been *sklêroi*, unyielding. Presumably, he refers to the fact that they made concessions that they should not have made. Instead, they ought to have followed the logical implications of their argument, as the brave enquirers of the *Meno* follow assiduously and energetically the path to knowledge (*Men.* 81e1).[26]

So, viewed from the perspective of Plato's Socrates, his denunciation of the concessions arbitrarily granted in the debate has a self-critical but also a protreptic and forward-looking function. He guides us to reassess his own assumptions, look for solutions to our perplexities in other Platonic texts, and entertain alternative or complementary options. Nonetheless, there is no indication that he definitely rejects his favourite method of investigation or the conception of self-knowledge attached to it. Even when he comments ironically on the paradoxical nature of the admission that one can know what one does not know, he chooses his words carefully. He does not assert that the aforementioned admission *is* irrational, but only that it *might seem* irrational (*Charm.* 175c8)[27] and, therefore, ought to have been examined during the debate (175c4).

---

[24] Cf. ἀργούς (*Men.* 81d6), μαλακοῖς (81d7).   [25] εὐηθικῶν καὶ οὐ σκληρῶν (175e8–d1).

[26] Compare and contrast the interpretation offered by Lampert 2010, 229–30. Lampert maintains that Socrates' judgement that they have been 'simple and not hard' is obviously false, as is the judgement that the enquiry is 'no more able to discover the truth' (cf. 229 and n. 111). 'The enquiry laughs neither at them nor at itself but at the very truth it made apparent to them: that sophrosyne is unbeneficial when understood as what they agreed to and fabricated together "then"' (229), i.e. before Potidaea. Indeed, Lampert continues, it was ridiculously unprofitable 'to attempt to transmit the true understanding of sophrosyne to Critias in the way [Socrates] did' (229). The enquiry narrated in the *Charmides* has been successful because it has forced Socrates 'to view the unbeneficial character of his pre-Potidaean teaching' and to realise that 'his attempt to transmit his philosophy to Critias in fact helped corrupt him' (229).

[27] Contra Tuckey 1951, 89–90.

Socrates' most revealing comments, however, concern his own inadequacy as a participant in the debate and the failure of his method to effectively pursue the truth. For they indicate his attitude as well as Plato's vis-à-vis the Socratic method and, moreover, give us grounds in order to determine our own stance on this matter.

As we saw, while Socrates considers Critias partly responsible[28] for the absurd conclusion of their investigation,[29] nonetheless he primarily blames himself.[30] This is the only occasion in Plato's Socratic dialogues where the principal character accuses himself in that manner or explains why he feels obliged to do so. Moreover, his negative self-assessment concerns his overall performance as a searcher, not merely some point of detail. As we saw, he holds himself accountable for failing 'to bring under scrutiny anything useful about *sôphrosynê*' (175a10–11) or contribute in any significant way to the effort of conducting a proper investigation (175b1–2). In the light of the above discussion, we should take him at his word. He really believes (and is right to believe) that he is blameworthy, first of all, for proposing to grant premises already refuted in argument and for leaving unquestioned an assumption that appears incoherent.[31]

This is a breakthrough for Plato's Socrates. It is the only instance in Plato's Socratic dialogues in which he openly acknowledges that he has played a leading role in the elenchus and holds himself accountable for the shape, quality, and outcome of the latter. Thus he underscores the paramount influence he has exercised as questioner in a dialectical setting. Not only have his questions elicited from the interlocutor the premises of the argument and determined its form and direction, he has also made proposals and taken initiatives that have kept the argument going for a while. These include the controversial concessions mentioned above and many other elements as well; for example, the counterexamples examined by the Argument from Relatives and the fictional societies entertained by the Argument from Benefit. Socrates' self-criticism has, I suggest, an

---

[28] See Socrates' use of the first-person plural at, for example, 175b3–7, c1, c4, d4.

[29] Contrast Schmid 1998, 148: 'Socrates assumes complete personal responsibility for the inquiry' and 'this absolves Critias'. But this needn't be the case. The fact that Socrates focuses on his own deficiencies does not preclude Critias being to blame as well. And there is strong indication that Socrates holds the two of them jointly responsible for the outcome of the debate (see previous note).

[30] Socrates' attitude appears all the more puzzling because, at different points of the dialogue, he repeatedly stressed that the investigation was a joint concern of Critias and himself (e.g. 162e2–5, 166d8–e2, 169d2–5, 172c4–173a1).

[31] There are no grounds for surmising that Socrates is being ironical here. Nor is there any reason to think that he takes 'complete personal responsibility for the inquiry' merely in order to protect Critias' pride (see Schmid 1998, 148).

important implication, namely that he partly appropriates the arguments constituting the preceding debate. He claims them as *his* arguments as well as Critias' own.[32]

Towards the end of his account, however, Socrates indicates that the failure of both of them to determine the nature of *sôphrosynê* has been caused not only by their incompetence as debaters but also, importantly, by the method they have used. For he remarks that the *zêtêsis* (enquiry or method of enquiry) has not fared better than themselves (175c8–d5). While it has made manifest the clumsiness of Socrates and Critias, the *zêtêsis* itself has not been abler than they have been to discover the truth.[33] It has only managed to make a monstrous joke at the truth's expense[34] by reaching the hybristic conclusion[35] that temperance, as the interlocutors conceived of it, is totally worthless.

This is not the only time in Plato's Socratic dialogues that the participants in a debate are ridiculed by a personified element of the investigation. For instance, Socrates urges Laches to show endurance, as the *logos* (argument) commands, and to continue the search so that courage will not laugh at them for failing to search for it courageously (*Lach.* 194a1–5). Nor is it the only time in the *Charmides* that *logos* appears endowed with some kind of agency. For example, in the opening scene, Socrates claims that the *kaloi logoi*, beautiful arguments, constituting the charm of Zalmoxis have the power to cure the soul (157a3–5). Also, when Socrates summarises the unacceptable concessions that he and Critias made, he uses metaphorical language to personify the *logos*: it did not allow the possibility of strictly reflexive knowledge (175b6–7) or the assumption that the 'science of science' entails knowing-what (175c1); nonetheless, the interlocutors slighted the *logos* and were duly defeated. We were not told by whom, but the obvious victor is the *logos*.[36] He has been stronger where they have been weaker, crafty where they have been simpletons, more resourceful than them in finding the means to prevail.

---

[32] Frede 1992 questions whether or how a dialectical argument can reasonably be considered to belong to the questioner. I submit that the passage of the *Charmides* under discussion sheds light on that question.

[33] οὐδέν τι μᾶλλον εὑρεῖν δύναται τὴν ἀλήθειαν: 175d1–2.   [34] Cf. καταγέλασεν: 175d2.

[35] πάνυ ὑβριστικῶς (175d4), rendered 'with the utmost contempt'. As has been noted in the literature, the verb ὑβρίζω and its cognates typically have negative connotations. Mainly, it occurs 'in contexts of emphatic denial, objection, or rejection, often coupled with derision' (van der Ben 1985, 96 n. 5).

[36] Most commentators attribute this claim to Socrates but, in truth, it can only be inferred. All that Socrates says is: νῦν δὲ πανταχῇ ἡττώμεθα (175b2–3), we are now defeated on all fronts, without, however, identifying who came out victorious.

However, the final lines of Socrates' summary stand out. For there, he distinguishes the *zêtêsis* from those who conducted it, censures the *zêtêsis* itself for its incapacity to discover the truth and for turning it into a laughingstock (175d1–2),[37] and suggests that his method of investigation proved unequal to the task at hand. Indeed, while in the conversation between Socrates and Charmides the elenchus worked reasonably well for pedagogical and protreptic purposes, in the debate between Socrates and Critias it proved incapable of pursuing effectively 'a good common to almost all men' (166d5): to illuminate the nature of each being (166d5–6) including, specifically, the nature of temperance. Instead, by following the rules of the Socratic method and making unwarranted concessions as they went along, the interlocutors brought forth something not real but fictional, an offspring of cooperative dialectical activity and consensus: a science of science, i.e. 'the very thing that, by agreeing with each other and by moulding it together, we earlier posited to be temperance' (175d3–4).[38] For all its shortcomings, the *zêtêsis* has succeeded in showing that, in all probability, the 'science of science' is not a reality but only a likeness both artificial and unattractive. On the positive side, it has yielded rich philosophical insights and a deeper understanding of both its central topic, temperance, and related issues in ethics and politics as well as logic and semantics. Nonetheless, Socrates' critical remarks expose the limitations of the elenchus as a method of enquiry and make evident the need for alternative or complementary philosophical methods aiming at the truth. In this respect, as in many others, the *Charmides* is a forward-looking dialogue, since it points to the innovations of the *Meno*, the breakthrough of the *Republic*, and the methodological and systematic achievements of the *Sophist* and the *Statesman*.

2   Socrates' Last Address to Charmides (175d5–176a5)

So far as I am concerned, I am not so upset. However, I said, I am very upset indeed on your own account, if it turns out that, although you have an appearance like yours and moreover are perfectly temperate in your soul, you will draw no profit from this temperance, nor will it by its presence in any way benefit you in your life. And I feel still more upset on account of the charm which I learnt from the Thracian, if I have taken so much trouble to learn it while it has no worth at all. As a matter of fact, I really do not think

---

[37] I disagree with Tuozzo 2011, 290, who takes Socrates' claim that the enquiry has turned hybristic as a piece of irony.

[38] ὃ ἡμεῖς πάλαι συνομολογοῦντες καὶ συμπλάττοντες ἐτιθέμεθα σωφροσύνην εἶναι: 175d3–4.

that this is the case. Rather, I am a bad enquirer. For temperance is surely a great good and, if you do possess it, you are blessed. So, see[39] whether you have it and stand in no need of the charm. For if you have it, I would rather advise you to consider me to be a fool unable to investigate anything whatsoever by means of argument, but yourself to be as happy as you are temperate. (175d5–176a5)

Charmides has been completely silent during the conversation between the two older men. However, Socrates indicates that the youth has been present and has been following the debate. There is no way to tell whether he has paid attention or how much he has really taken in. Nonetheless, he has certainly registered that temperance as a 'science of science' would probably bring no benefit, and he has listened to Socrates' disparaging remarks concerning the quality of both enquirers and of the enquiry itself. Evidently, Socrates worries about this and, therefore, he switches his attention from Critias to the youth and addresses him with a short protreptic speech brilliantly illustrating Socratic pedagogy.

By way of ring composition, he alludes to the dominant themes of the prologue: physical beauty and psychic beauty (175d7–e2), the charm of Zalmoxis and the *logoi* that constitute it, the power of these latter to engender temperance in one's soul, the idea that temperance is one of the greatest goods that essentially contributes to happiness (175e6–176a1), and his own capacity to use the charm as a Zalmoxian physician would (175e3–5). He expresses his frustration at the result of the investigation, not so much on his own behalf as on behalf of Charmides (175d5–e2) and also of the charm (175e2–5). He urges Charmides to disbelieve the absurd conclusion that temperance is useless (175e5–176a1), blames himself again for being a poor searcher (175e6), states his conviction that temperance has very great value (175e7), and exhorts the youth to continue his self-examination in order to find out whether he possesses it (176a1–5). To impress upon Charmides the urgency of that task, he suggests to him that temperance and happiness are interlaced and that the youth should consider himself as happy as he is temperate (176a4–5). Again, he may appear to intimate that temperance is scalar and one may have it to a greater or lesser degree (cf. 158c1–4). While he gives no further indication about this matter, there are other aspects of his address that call for comment.

To begin, it is worth noting the seamless manner in which Socrates reassumes his relation with Charmides precisely from where he left it some time ago. As in the prologue of the dialogue so in the epilogue, his interest

---

[39] Cf. note 3 in this chapter.

in the beautiful youth appears sincere and his objective clear and firm. Namely, he wants to encourage the young man to engage systematically in dialectical *logoi*, follow the path of self-examination and self-discovery, and persevere despite the difficulties of this enterprise. We should take him seriously when he says that the conclusion of the search makes him feel more resentful with regard to Charmides than with regard to himself (175d5–6). His vexation is not empty talk,[40] but derives from his experience as an educator of young people and his understanding of their psychological vulnerabilities and needs.

While he himself disavowed knowing what temperance is (165b5–c3), Charmides appears to initially have deceived himself in that respect. As we saw, his guardian asserted that the youth is more temperate than all his peers (157d6–8) and, moreover, looking into himself, Charmides found that he possessed features that he took to belong essentially to temperance, i.e. decorum and a sense of shame. Nonetheless, his efforts to articulate what temperance is have been refuted and, as if that were not enough to discourage him, he has also witnessed a debate between two people that he considers authoritative, i.e. Critias and Socrates, suggesting that temperance is probably incoherent or, at any rate, useless. At this point, therefore, he probably feels confused and dismayed. Consequently, as Socrates well knows, he may feel inclined to withdraw his trust in argument and abandon philosophy altogether. It is just this reaction, I think, that Socrates' brief speech aims to forestall.

In order to do so, Socrates makes two complementary moves: he blames himself rather than the Zalmoxian incantation for the failure of the search (175e5–7, 176a2–5); and he emphatically reiterates his belief that temperance has paramount value for human happiness (175e7–176a1, 4–5). Consistently with his earlier remarks to Critias, he tells Charmides that he is an incompetent enquirer (*zêtêtês*: 175e6) but, importantly, does not repeat any one of his earlier criticisms concerning the search (*zêtêsis*). Such criticisms would not do Charmides any good, and he would most probably misunderstand them. On the other hand, if his confidence in the value of temperance were bolstered, and if he could be made to see that the collapse of the investigation was due to the incompetence of those who conducted it[41] and not the enquiry itself, this would be a net gain. Thus, Socrates' exhortation to Charmides seems to

---

[40] Contrast Lampert 2010, 230, according to whom 'there's no reason to believe that Socrates is at all annoyed, for his inquiry fulfilled his intentions completely'.

[41] By denouncing himself as a bad enquirer, Socrates implicitly undermines the authority of Critias as well. For both of them are responsible for the poor result of the argument, and Charmides is prompted to register that fact.

amount to this: dismiss what you have heard during the last hour or so; uphold the Zalmoxian conviction, which is also my (sc. Socrates') own conviction, that temperance is one of the greatest goods and its possession secures one's happiness; and, motivated by this belief, continue to examine yourself to discern the truth of the matter, namely whether your soul does have temperance or, alternatively, needs to be treated and healed. From the pedagogical point of view, then, Socrates' principal concern is to make sure that Charmides will not lose his faith in the power of philosophical arguments, for his happiness depends on them.

In the famous passage against misology in the *Phaedo*, Socrates exhibits a similar concern and makes a comparable move. According to the narration, when he realised that the arguments of Simmias and Cebes had spread among those present confusion and doubt 'not only about what had already been said but also about what was going to be said about the soul's immortality' (*Phd.* 88c), he tried to heal their sense of defeat, reinforce their confidence, and encourage them to join him in pursuing the enquiry (88e–89c). Then, caressing Phaedo's beautiful curls, he gently warned him as well as his other companions against becoming a misologue, hater of *logoi* (89b–e), for, as he claimed, no greater misfortune could happen to anyone than that of developing a dislike for argument (89d). Just as some men become misanthropes, haters of people, because they try to form human relations without having a critical understanding of human nature and consequently become disappointed (89d–e), so others become misologues, haters of *logoi*, because they engage in arguments without having the requisite skill and thus form the impression that no argument is trustworthy and every argument fluctuates between truth and untruth (90b–c). This attitude, Socrates contends, is 'a pitiable affection' (90c8) and one must guard against it. 'We should not allow into our soul the belief that *logoi* have nothing sound about them. Instead, we should greatly prefer to believe that it is we ourselves who are not yet sound, and we should pursue with courage and eagerness the goal of becoming sound, you and the others for the sake of your whole life still lying ahead and I for the sake of death itself' (90d9–91a1).

Naturally, Socrates' exhortation to Charmides does not have the poignancy of the aforementioned scene in the *Phaedo*. Nor does Charmides have many common points with Phaedo, since one character represents a privileged aristocrat while, according to certain doxographers, the other portrays a captive of war compelled to work for a while as a male prostitute and eventually freed by Crito at Socrates' request. Nevertheless, both these personages are young and inexperienced in argument, both attend the greatest part of the conversation as listeners rather than talkers, and both experience confusion or worse. We are told that Phaedo silently follows the conversation between Socrates and his interlocutors and becomes depressed. Similarly, after being thrice refuted by Socrates and after witnessing his guardian's refutation as well, Charmides probably feels incredulous and overwhelmed. Therefore, Socrates applies closely resembling therapeutic strategies in these two cases. He blames the arguers rather than the argument for being inadequate, and he urges his addressee to remain hopeful and press on.

As in the *Phaedo*, so in the *Charmides* Socrates attempts to imprint on the mind of his young interlocutors the great value of philosophical discourses and the cardinal role of philosophical argument in order to both seek truth and attain well-being. And as in the former dialogue, so in the latter he closely relates the practice of such *logoi* to the attainment of psychic health. In the *Phaedo*, he suggests that the pursuit of 'healthy *logoi*' results in becoming healthy oneself (90d9–91a1). The *Charmides* can reasonably be taken to advocate a similar approach. For, here, Socrates appears to endorse on his own account the Zalmoxian view that temperance is the source of holistic health and grows in one's soul by means of *kaloi logoi*, beautiful arguments. I suggest that this deeply held belief lies at the basis of Socrates' exhortation to young Charmides, and also of much else.

3 The Final Scene (176a6–d5)

> Then Charmides retorted: 'by Zeus, Socrates, I really do not know whether I have temperance or whether I don't. For how could I know something regarding which, as you yourself say, not even you and Critias[42] are able to discover what on earth it is? However, I do not entirely believe you, and I think, Socrates, that I am much in need of the charm. And, so far as I am concerned, there is no obstacle to my being charmed by you for as many days as it takes, until you say that it is enough'. (176a6–b4)

Charmides' reaction seems predictably modest and recalls the early stages of his encounter with Socrates. There, he was asked by Socrates whether or not he sufficiently partook of temperance (158c1–4) and was reluctant to answer that question. For if he denied having temperance, he would expose both himself and his guardian, whereas if he admitted possessing the virtue, he might appear to brag (158c5–d6). Even after agreeing to submit himself

---

[42] Cf. ὑμεῖς: 176a8.

to scrutiny, he was initially hesitant to say what temperance seemed to him to be (159b1–2). Here, he appears completely at a loss as to whether or not he has temperance, because, as he indicates, he finds it discouraging that people as intelligent and experienced as Socrates and Critias have been unsuccessful in the search for the nature of *sôphrosynê*. In both instances, the youth appeals to the story of Zalmoxis in order to seek remedy for his ignorance (158e2, 176b2–4). And in both instances, he shows himself eager to submit to the charm of *kaloi logoi*, beautiful arguments, in whatever manner (158e4–5) and for as long as (176b3–4) Socrates considers necessary.

Nonetheless, Charmides has made some progress. On the one hand, according to his own admission, his initial reluctance to say whether or not he was temperate was due to modesty and a sense of decorum: he probably believed that he was temperate but did not judge it appropriate to say so. On the other hand, having being examined by Socrates and having subsequently followed the debate between the latter and Critias, he now appears genuinely convinced that he does not know what temperance is or whether he himself has it. In this way, then, the elenchus has had a beneficial effect on the young man. We may infer that, precisely because Charmides has acquired that piece of self-knowledge, he is now asking for Socrates' assistance in order to examine himself further.

Questions can be raised, however, about Charmides' real motivation. Does it spring from self-understanding or from emotion, from the drive to find the truth or from the need to rely on authority and the ministrations of a conventional teacher? Has Charmides been able to follow the arguments by which the successive definitions of temperance proposed in the dialogue have been refuted? Or does he simply feel baffled by the debate between the two older men and conclude that he can never succeed on his own where they have failed? Plato does not settle these questions within the dialogue, but they are legitimate and deserve to be pursued. In the current situation, we can say at least that Charmides' attitude is positive and gives reason for hope. For he recognises that he needs the charm and turns himself over to Socrates for treatment. He shows trust in Socrates, much as a patient shows trust in a competent doctor. As the patient will not refuse treatment and will not press the doctor to end it prematurely, so Charmides says that he will not refuse the charm of Zalmoxis but will take it as long as it is necessary according to Socrates' judgement. The characters play to the end of the dialogue the roles assigned to them by Critias in the opening scene. Socrates plays the doctor and Charmides the patient. As for Critias, he takes his ward's decision to be proof of his virtue and admonishes him to remain close to Socrates and never leave his side (176b5–8). In the immediate sequel, however, the ambience changes abruptly and a threatening cloud hangs over the characters. The tensions and ambiguities of the cousins come into the open, and the words that they exchange with each other as well as with Socrates point to the grim reality of their historical counterparts.

> Well, Charmides, said Critias, it will be proof for me that you are temperate if you do this: if you turn yourself over to Socrates to be charmed and do not leave his side much or little. – Be sure, he said, that I shall follow him and shall not leave his side. For I would be doing something bad if I didn't obey you, my guardian, and if I did not do what you order. – Indeed, he said, I do so order. – I shall do it, then, he said, beginning this very day. – You two, I said, what are you planning [*bouleuesthon*] to do? – Nothing, Charmides replied, we have already made a plan [*bebouleumetha*]. – Will you use force then, I said, and won't you give me preliminary hearing [*anakrisis*]? – Be sure that I shall use force, he answered, since this man here gives the command. Consider again [*bouleuou*] what you will do about this. – But there is nothing left to consider [*boulê*], I said. For when you attempt any operation [*epicheirounti*] and use force, no human being will be able to oppose you. – Well then, he replied, do not oppose me either. – Very well, I said, I shall not. (176b5–d5)

The structure of the dialogue's last scene is comparable to that of the prologue. All three main characters are on stage and have specific roles to play. Critias decides what these roles will be and distributes them to the other two personages. Charmides obediently follows his guardian's instructions. And Socrates appears to comply as well. In the opening scene, he agrees to participate in Critias' ruse and present himself as a doctor able to treat the youth's headache. In the final act, he comes under pressure from the two cousins to keep Charmides by his side and treat him with *logoi* for the foreseeable future. However, the relations between the protagonists are markedly different on these two occasions. While the prologue represents the two older men conspiring together in order to attract Charmides and submit him to Socratic interrogation, the last part of the epilogue portrays the two cousins in cahoots with each other in order to bring Socrates to heel. Relations have shifted, an allegiance has been formed, and the cousins appear determined to work together towards a common end.

The narrator highlights these new dynamics to maximal effect. His directions to the audience are subtle and layered, presuppose knowledge of the relevant historical facts, and suggest different perspectives from which we can contemplate the characters and their interactions.[43] On the one hand, he guides us to look back to the earlier stages of the dialogue with sharpened sensibility and enhanced hindsight. We can do so either from the vantage point of an external observer or from the position of one of the characters in the narrated dialogue or from the standpoint of the narrator and his anonymous friend. On the other hand, Socrates' narration of the last episode points beyond the frame of the *Charmides* to the future events involving Critias, Charmides, and also Socrates. Indeed, the apparently playful banter between these personages foreshadows the relations of power that will bind the cousins to each other, their autocratic and violent rule over Athens, and Socrates' calm resistance to their unjust commands. Nonetheless, as Plato's audiences know, Socrates will not be absolved from the taint of association with Critias and, as many plausibly believe, will be condemned to death in part because of it.

It is impossible to be sure about Plato's intentions in composing this scene. Its consummate artistry tempts one to speculate about his considered view regarding his relatives and their political deeds. I am inclined to think that he wants to highlight the violent streak in the characters of his cousins and express his abhorrence at their methods of exercising political power. The account that I give below is consistent with that assumption, but of course other interpretations of this remarkable passage are defensible as well.

In the first place, Charmides (176a6–b4) and then Critias (176b5–8) return to the issue explicitly raised in the prologue: the question of whether Charmides has *sôphrosynê* or needs to be treated by beautiful *logoi* in order to acquire it. Their initial reactions are in line with their characters. As we saw, Charmides appears confused and at a loss, admits that he doesn't know whether he is temperate, acknowledges his need for the charm of Zalmoxis, and expresses his desire to receive treatment from Socrates. As in the opening scene, so here he speaks in a manner befitting his age, education, and rank: with modesty and decorum, and not without charm. To the very end of the encounter, then, he exhibits the features that he believed to be distinguishing marks of temperance (159b5–6, 160e4–5).

---

[43] There is no consensus concerning the interactions between the characters in the final scene. Many consider the latter crucially important and interpret the words exchanged between the three protagonists in different ways in order to corroborate radically different accounts of the dialogue and its main purpose. Tsouna 2017 offers a selective survey of such views. Others, however, consider the scene unimportant: for example, Tuckey 1951, 89, believes that 'this concluding section of the dialogue requires but little comment'.

Critias' initial reaction also conforms to his character sketch. He takes the youth's desire to associate with Socrates to be proof of his temperance, presumably because it seems motivated by a sort of self-knowledge and a tendency to 'mind one's own'. By submitting himself to Socratic dialectic, Charmides does exactly what his guardian considers appropriate for him to do: sharpen his mind and develop his skills in debate (157c7–d1). According to Critias' own lights, if Socrates agrees to train the young man, he too will 'do his own': he will do something that is good. At the dramatic level, therefore, the conceptions of temperance proposed by Charmides and Critias in the first half of the dialogue remain alive to the very end. If this is correct, it implies that neither of these personages has abandoned his beliefs about temperance, even though they have been refuted by the elenchus. Nor has Critias changed his mind in respect of his claim that Charmides is temperate (157d6–8), despite the fact that the elenchus indicated that he is not. In short, we have reason to suspect that the elenchus did not manage to convince the two cousins that they were mistaken in their views. Perhaps they did not participate in the investigation with the right spirit. Or perhaps they were not able to follow the argument or some part of it.

Their next exchange is especially revelatory. Charmides emphatically repeats that he will follow Socrates and will not leave his side, but also discloses his main motivation for doing so. He will frequent Socrates less because he wants to discover something important about himself and more because (*gar*: 176c1) he wishes to obey Critias' orders (176c1–2). We should focus on the newly introduced concepts of obedience and command. From this point onwards, they will dominate the interactions between the personages, and they will constitute the principal vehicle by which Plato will bring the historical context to bear on the resolution of the dialogue's plot. Indeed, Critias hastens to adopt this vocabulary. He tells Charmides that these indeed are his orders (*keleuô*: 176c3) and, sure enough, Charmides responds that he shall immediately put them into effect (176c4). The playful tone of the exchange does not conceal the serious nature of what is being conveyed. Critias is the leader and Charmides the follower, and the latter does everything he can to please the former. He endeavours to associate with Socrates chiefly because he anticipates his guardian's wishes. But it is doubtful that he values Socrates' company and conversation in its own right.

At this point, Socrates intervenes to ask his companions what they have been planning (*bouleuesthon*: 176c5). We should pause to consider his choice of this word. The verb *bouleuesthai* ('to plan', 'to deliberate') and its cognates are frequently used in judicial and forensic contexts and often refer to both the process of a jury's deliberation and the decision resulting from it. Charmides too employs this verb when he responds in a terse and decisive manner to Socrates' query: '*bebouleumetha*', he says (176c6), 'we have already made a plan', or alternatively 'we have deliberated and have reached a verdict'. Socrates highlights the inappropriateness of this statement when he incredulously asks whether the cousins intend to use force without according him an *anakrisis*, preliminary hearing (167c7). The latter noun too carries forensic connotations, since it can refer, technically, to the preliminary interrogation that precedes the trial of a case at court. Socrates, then, places himself in the position of a defendant who will not be given the opportunity to speak before his case is tried; rather, he will be compelled (*biasêi*: 176c7) to submit to a verdict about which there is no possibility of appeal. No one familiar with the summary executions ordered by the Thirty can fail to think of them in this connection. In the fictional microcosm of the dialogue the cousins' conduct conforms to the same authoritarian pattern as they will later enact on the stage of history.

The sequel of the passage makes clear that these gruesome associations are deliberately woven into the narrative. For, suddenly, the character of Charmides undergoes a radical change. His earlier reticence disappears together with his modesty and deference. He addresses Socrates as if he were his subordinate and issues a threat: Socrates should carefully consider what to do (176c9) for he, Charmides, is prepared to use force against him in accordance with Critias' orders (176c8–9). Nothing within the dialogue justifies that conduct, but everything we know about Charmides' time in power is consistent with it. As Critias' right-hand man in the military junta of the Thirty, the golden youth of our dialogue will put aside his velvet gloves to show his iron fists.

Consider how Socrates' reaction orientates the readers towards a future unknown to the protagonists of the dialogue but very present in the minds of its readers. There is really no point for him, he says, in deliberating about anything (cf. *boulê*), since his young friend has already decided to attempt such an operation (*epicheirein*: 176d2)[44] and to make use of force

---

[44] I render ἐπιχειροῦντι by 'when you attempt any operation' in order to preserve the military nuance that the verb may have. Compare Tuozzo 2011, 300: 'when you set your hand to something'. According to Lampert 2010, 232–4, this verb points to the first and the last recognition scenes of Odysseus' return to Ithaca. In the cases of both Socrates' return to Athens from Potidaea and Odysseus' return to Ithaca, those who recognise the heroes do not really know them. Both Socrates and Odysseus come in order to bring a new order, 'an order that sees to its successful succession by transmitting its core only to its like', 'a new politics' (232).

(*biazomenôi*: 176d1). The general point is correct: deliberation can take place only if one has the possibility of choice. But why does Socrates suggest that he has no choice? Surely it is entirely up to him whether he accepts or refuses the cousins' request. And it is not plausible to surmise that any violence could be exercised against him in the safety of the gymnasium and by his own friends. In brief, nothing in the dialogue can explain Socrates' statement. Plato directs the readers, however, to think of a future time, when nobody will be safe from the cousins' reach and Charmides will be in a position to lay his hands on[45] Socrates and every other Athenian that might oppose him.

It is not accidental that Socrates uses a future-tensed verb to refer to the time when Charmides will be irresistible. 'No human being *will be able* to oppose you' (176d2–3, my emphasis),[46] he tells the youth prophetically, speaking both as the relevant character of the dialogue and as an authorial voice that, from within the dialogue, points to what will come to be. Also, at the very end of the scene, Socrates indulges in a characteristic piece of irony when he refers implicitly to an event that he relays in the *Apology* and that can be confirmed by other sources as well. Namely, while Charmides warns him not to oppose him on the present occasion (176d4),[47] Socrates replies that he won't oppose him *in the future* (176d5)[48] but will follow his orders. In fact, when the Thirty commanded Socrates to arrest Leon of Salamis and bring him in to be summarily executed, Socrates disobeyed them and went home (*Ap.* 32c4–e1).

To end this study, let us look again at the portraits of the protagonists, taking into consideration the dialogue's final scene.

Both as a narrator and as a discussant, Socrates remains the same familiar figure from the opening scene to his critical summary of the argument. He cares for philosophy and beautiful youths, privileges the soul over the body, identifies virtue and, specifically, temperance with psychic health, uses the elenchus for protreptic and pedagogic purposes as well as for the purpose of conducting a serious dialectical investigation, and claims to be indifferent to dialectical victory but wholly committed to the search for truth. In the second part of the investigation he often transcends the limits of the dialogue frame by pointing to views developed in other dialogues. Dramatically, he remains firmly located in the spatio-temporal context of the *Charmides* and makes no overt allusions to future historical events.

---

[45] This is the literal meaning of ἐπιχειροῦντι at 176d2.
[46] οὐδεὶς οἷός τ' ἔσται ἐναντιοῦσθαι ἀνθρώπων: 176d3.   [47] μηδὲ σὺ ἐναντιοῦ: 176d4.
[48] οὐκ ἐναντιώσομαι: 176d5.

However, in the final lines of the *Charmides*, Socrates' personality and manner alter.[49] He seems distanced from the other two characters, not very concerned with the decision that they reached on his account, and indifferent to the prospect of keeping Charmides close to him and enchanting him with *logoi*. He acts as if he were not fully present, as if his mind has wandered somewhere else. His replies to Charmides become increasingly ambiguous and metaphorical, turning away from the present and pointing towards a distant future. On the one hand, in the opening scene of the dialogue, Socrates is depicted as a rather earthly man, while Charmides is portrayed as a distant young god. On the other hand, in the epilogue's last scene, these elements of their respective portraits get reversed. Charmides comes across as unreflective and brutal, whereas Socrates seems detached from his surroundings and the threats that they might pose. It is as if he belonged to a different sphere, not entirely human. Those familiar with the historical facts are bound to remember that Socrates will eventually oppose those that 'no human being will be able to oppose' (176d2–3).

Critias' portrait retains its carefully calculated ambiguity through most of the conversation. On the one hand, as we have seen, Critias appears appreciative of Socrates, proud of his ward and wishing him to receive a good education, cognisant of the value of dialectical conversation, an experienced and ingenious interlocutor, and a person of considerable intelligence and some intellectual integrity as well. On the other hand, the narrator represents him as a man disposed towards irascibility and exaggeration, excessively mindful of his reputation, and intensely interested in politics and one's entitlement to rule. Socrates' successive thought-experiments, and especially the 'dream', intimate that Critias is more interested in power and effectiveness than in the well-being of the citizens and the state. Both in the opening and in the closing scenes of the dialogue he assumes leadership by giving directions to the other two personages as to what they should do. But while on the former occasion he proposes a ruse and asks for Socrates' cooperation, on the latter he merely issues his orders and expects to be obeyed. His use of military vocabulary (176c3) suggests that manipulation will eventually give way to naked force. Looking at the development of Critias' character from the perspective of the final scene, we can see that his sense of privilege and his ambitions and passions await the appropriate opportunity to express themselves in action.

Charmides is the character that the dialogue is named after. This is chiefly because of the exceptional promise he appears to hold for his own

---

[49] See also Hyland 1981, 146, who interprets Charmides' transformation in a different way than I do.

future and the future of Athens itself. Nonetheless, as I have argued, his gifts appear partly offset by the negative elements of his character. On the one hand, he is depicted in the course of the dialogue as a youth of great beauty and some promise, talented in poetry and with a penchant for philosophy, well born and traditionally educated, familiar with dialectical debate and ready to engage in it, and endowed with modesty and commendable decorum. Both his beliefs about temperance and his own demeanour may seem consistent with these features. On the other hand, Charmides' portrait exhibits less reassuring elements too. He appears to be coy, occasionally sly, somewhat spoilt by his guardian's flattery and the admiration of his peers, a little roguish, frequently passive, and always eager to please Critias. His evident reverence for authority is not helpful for philosophy, and his response to the Socratic method leaves something to be desired. In the dialogue's prologue, he asks Socrates to write down for him the charm of Zalmoxis, thus intimating that he does not really want to bother with it. In the epilogue, he acknowledges his need to be charmed by Socrates, but seems clueless as to what this might entail. Generally, he does not really seem to have a philosophical nature. In that respect he fares badly if compared with Theaetetus, a youth of physical ugliness but exceptional philosophical gifts. All the same, he does retain his boyish charm until the dialogue's final scene.

At that point, however, Charmides' character undergoes a transformation. His respect for Critias' authority and his desire to please his guardian motivate his submission to the latter's wishes. He speaks like a soldier sworn to obey his general, a militant who considers his orders adequate justification for his deeds. Humorously, he tells Socrates in so many words that he will use force against him if needed. He seems to have no qualms about threatening, however playfully, the man that he has earlier approached with trust and respect. In the end, then, Charmides is portrayed as a bully and his youthful grace is lost. Like the other two characters, but in a more spectacular manner, Charmides suffers a change that points far beyond the frame of the dialogue. We are guided to look at him telescopically, from the vantage point of his own maturity, in the setting of Athens after its defeat in the Great War and the establishment of the Thirty. We are in a position to know that the cousins' grand plan of compelling Socrates to undertake Charmides' education came to nothing and that, in the course of time, Charmides' physical beauty came to be coupled with a deformed soul. We can also better understand Socrates' quiet and distant manner in the final scene. Even though he agrees not to oppose the cousins' orders, he appears to realise that his association with the young man will not last long. To borrow a famous metaphor from the *Theaetetus*, Socrates can discern that Charmides is not likely to carry any real offspring that Socrates could assist him to deliver.[50] Instead, Charmides will have to be paired with a partner more suitable to his own nature: a wise man such as Prodicus or, more likely, Critias himself.[51]

---

[50] See the discussion by Burnyeat 1977.

[51] In the *Theaetetus*, Socrates describes himself as a matchmaker concluding suitable matches between young men who have no need of his midwifery and *sophoi* such as Prodicus (*Tht.* 151b1–6).

Charmides, or On Temperance: A Peirastic Dialogue[1]

The Prologue (153a1–159a10)

We had arrived the previous evening from the camp at Potidaea and, having arrived after a long absence, I gladly headed for my regular haunts. And so it was that I went into the gymnasium of Taureas opposite the temple of Basile and came upon a great many people there, some of whom were actually unknown to me but most of whom I knew. And as soon as they saw me unexpectedly entering the wrestling-school, they greeted me from a distance from wherever each of them was. Chaerephon, however, acting like the madman that he is, jumped up from the middle of the crowd, ran towards me, and, taking hold of my hand, asked, 'Socrates, how did you survive the battle?'. True, shortly before we came away, there had been a battle at Potidaea that the people here had only just got news of. – Just as you see me, I said in reply. – Well, he said, it has been announced here that the battle has been very severe and many of our acquaintance were killed in it. – In that case, I said, the report is fairly near the truth. – Were you actually present at the battle? he asked. – I was. – Then come and sit down here, he said, and tell us the full story, for we have not had a thorough and clear report as yet. And as he was speaking, he brought me over to a seat near Critias, son of Callaeschrus. So I sat down, greeted Critias and the others, and related in detail the news from the camp, whatever anyone asked about, with different men asking different things.

When we had enough of these things, I turned to questioning them about affairs at home, namely about philosophy, how it was doing at present, and about the young men, whether any among them had become distinguished for wisdom or beauty or both. And Critias, looking away towards the door and seeing some young men who were coming in railing at each other followed by another crowd of people behind them, said, 'As

---

[1] The term 'πειραστικός' characterises dialogues purporting to test a given view or set of views. This is one of several different categories into which Plato's dialogues have been classified.

for the beautiful youths, Socrates, I expect that you will get to know at once; for these who are coming in happen to be the entourage and lovers of the youth who, at least for the moment, is believed to be the most beautiful; and I imagine that he himself is already on his way and somewhere close by'. – Who is he, I enquired, and whose son is he? – You certainly know him, he said, but he was not yet of age before you left: Charmides, son of our uncle Glaucon and my own cousin. – By Zeus, of course I know him, I said. For he was not bad-looking even then, when he was still a child. But now, I would imagine, he has already become quite the young man! – You will know immediately, he [sc. Critias] said, both how much and in what way he [sc. Charmides] has grown. And as he was speaking these words, Charmides came in.

Now truly, my friend, I cannot measure anything. So far as beautiful youths are concerned I am merely a blank ruler. For, somehow, almost all youths who have just come of age appear to me beautiful. Indeed this is so, and especially on that occasion the youth appeared to me marvellous in stature and beauty. As for all the others, they were so astonished and confused when he entered that they seemed to me to be in love with him. Moreover, many more lovers were following in his train as well. Of course, this was not so surprising on the part of men like ourselves. However, I was also observing the boys and noticed that not a single one of them, even the youngest, was looking elsewhere but all gazed at him as if he were a statue.

Then Chaerephon called me and asked, Socrates, how does the youth seem to you? Does he not have a beautiful face? – Very much so, I replied. – And yet, he said, if he were willing to take his clothes off, it would seem to you that he has no face, so great is the beauty of his bodily form. All the other men too agreed with Chaerephon's claim. – By Hercules, I said, you make the man seem irresistible, if indeed he has in him one more advantage – a small one. – What? asked Critias. – If he happens to be beautiful with regard to his soul, I replied. But somehow he ought to be of such sort, Critias, since he belongs to your family. – Well, he [sc. Critias] said, he is very beautiful and good in this respect too. – Why then, I said, did we not strip that very part of him and view it first, before his bodily form? For, in any case, at his age, he surely will be willing to engage in dialogue. – Very much so, said Critias, since in fact he is a philosopher and also, as it seems to both himself and others, he is quite a poet. – That fine gift, I said, my dear Critias, exists in your family from a long time back and derives from your kinship with Solon. – But why haven't you called the young man here and shown him off to me? For even if he were still younger than he actually is, there could be nothing shameful in talking with him when you are here, since you are both his guardian and his cousin. – You are right, he said, and we will call him. And turning at once to his servant he commanded, 'Boy, call Charmides and tell him that I want to introduce him to a doctor with regard to the ailment that he told me this morning he was suffering from'. Then Critias turned to me and added: 'You know, he has complained lately that he feels his head somewhat heavy when he gets up in the morning. Why should you not pretend to him that you know a remedy for his headache?' – No reason why not, I replied, provided that he comes. – Oh, he will, said Critias.

This is exactly what happened. Indeed he did come, and he gave rise to much laughter. For each of us who were seated tried to make room for him by pushing hard at his neighbour so as to have him sitting next to oneself, with the result that the man sitting at one end of the bench was forced to get up, whereas the man sitting at the other end was tumbled off sideways. In the end, Charmides came and sat down between me and Critias.

By that time, my friend, I already began to feel perplexed, and the confidence that I had possessed earlier, because I had anticipated that it would be very easy to talk with him, was quite gone. And when Critias said that I was the person who knew the remedy, and he looked me straight in the eyes in an indescribable manner, and seemed ready to ask a question, and all the people in the gymnasium surged around us in a circle, then, my noble friend, I both saw what was inside his cloak and caught fire and was quite beside myself. And I thought that nobody was as wise in matters of love as Cydias, who, referring to a handsome boy and giving advice to someone else, said, 'The fawn should beware lest, by coming before the lion, he should be seized as a portion of meat'. For I felt that I myself had been seized by such a creature.

Nonetheless, when he asked me if I knew the remedy for the headache, I somehow managed to answer that I did. – So, he said, what is it? – I replied that the remedy itself was a certain leaf, but that there was a charm or incantation to go with the remedy. And if one both sang the charm and used the remedy, the medicine would bring about perfect health. Without the charm, however, the leaf would be completely useless. – Then, he said, I shall take down the charm from you in writing. – Will you do it, I said, if you obtain my consent or even if you don't? – He laughed and said, 'if I do have your consent, Socrates'. – So be it, I said. And are you quite certain about my name? – Yes, if I am not mistaken, he replied. For there is much talk about you among the boys of my age, and I also remember you in the company of Critias here when I was a child.

– Well done, I said. For it means I shall speak to you more freely about the incantation and what its nature is, whereas just now I was perplexed as to how to indicate its power to you. For, Charmides, it is of such a nature that it cannot bring health only to the head, but, as perhaps you too have already heard the good doctors mention, when a patient comes to them with a pain in his eyes, they say something like this: that it is not possible for them to attempt to heal the eyes alone, but that it would be necessary that they treat the head along with them, if the condition of the eyes were going to be in good order too. Moreover, they say, it is utter folly to believe that one could ever cure the head on its own apart from the whole body. Following this principle, they apply regimens to the body in its entirety, trying to treat and heal the part together with the whole. Or have you not been aware of the fact that this is how they talk and how things are done? – Very much so, he said. – And do you believe that this principle is a good one and do you accept it? – More than anything, he said.

When I heard his approval, I regained my courage, my confidence gradually started to rise up again, and I began to feel rekindled. Thus, I said: – Such, then, Charmides, is the nature of this incantation [or charm]. I learnt it over there, on campaign, from one of the Thracian doctors of Zalmoxis, who are said even to aim at immortality. This Thracian said that the Greeks spoke well when they stated the doctrine that I have just mentioned. However, he said, Zalmoxis our king, who is a god, declares that, just as one should not attempt to treat the eyes without treating the head or to treat the head without treating the body, so one should not treat the body without treating the soul. In fact, he said this was even the reason why most diseases evaded treatment by the Greek doctors, namely that they neglected the whole that they should have attended to, since when this does not fare well it is impossible for the part to fare well. For all evils and goods for the body and for the entire human being, he said, spring from the soul and flow from it, just as they flow from the head to the eyes. Hence this [sc. the soul] is what one ought to treat first and foremost, if the condition of the head and that of the rest of the body are going to be good as well. And the soul, my good friend, he said, is treated by means of certain charms or incantations, and these incantations are beautiful [or fine] discourses. Temperance derives from such discourses and is engendered in the soul, and once it has been engendered and is present, one can easily supply health to the head and to the rest of the body as well. So, as he was teaching me both the remedy and the incantations, he said, 'Let nobody persuade you to treat his own head with this remedy who has not first submitted his soul to be treated by you with the incantation'. For at present, he said, this is the error besetting men, that certain doctors attempt to manage without each of the two – that is, without both temperance and bodily health. And he very strongly instructed me not to allow anyone to convince me that I should act in a different way, regardless of how wealthy, brave, or handsome that person might be. As for myself, therefore, I shall do as he bids, since I have sworn an oath to him and must obey him. And if you decide, in accordance with the stranger's instructions, to submit your soul to be charmed first by means of the Thracian's incantations, I shall apply the remedy to your head. Otherwise, my dear Charmides, we would be at a loss as to what to do to help you.

When Critias heard me saying this, he said: Socrates, if on account of his head Charmides will also be forced to improve his mind, then the malady of the head would turn out to have been for the young man a gift of Hermes [sc. an unexpected stroke of good luck]. But let me tell you that Charmides is believed to surpass his peers not only in bodily looks, but also in the very thing that you claim to have the incantation for – you say it is temperance, do you not? – I do indeed, I said. – Well then, you must know that he is believed to be by far the most temperate youth of the day, while, considering his age, in every other respect too he is second to none.

Of course, I said, it is only right, Charmides, that you should surpass the others in all such things. For I don't suppose that anyone else here could easily point to a case of two such Athenian families united together and likely to produce offspring more beautiful or nobler than those you have sprung from. For your father's family, the house of Critias son of Dropides, has been praised for us according to tradition by Anacreon, Solon, and many other poets for excelling in both beauty and virtue and everything else called happiness. Again, your mother's family is also praised in the same way. For it is said of your uncle Pyrilampes that no one in the entire continent[2] was believed to be superior in beauty or influence, whenever he came as an ambassador to the Great King or anyone else in the continent, and this whole side of the family is viewed as not in the least inferior to the other side. Since you have sprung from such ancestors, it seems likely that you will be first in all things. And indeed, dear son of Glaucon, you seem to me not to have fallen behind any of your ancestors in any respect with regard to your looks. But if, in addition, you have sufficiently grown in respect of temperance and those other qualities as your guardian here says, then, I said, dear Charmides, your mother gave birth to a blessed son. The situation is this: if

---

[2] Ast 1819–32 followed by Croiset 1921 and Sprague 1973 remove the phrase τῷ ἐν τῇ ἠπείρῳ in 158a5, while I follow the manuscript reading as does Lamb 1927.

temperance is already present in you, as Critias here asserts, and if you are
sufficiently temperate, you would no longer have any need of the incantations
of Zalmoxis or of Abaris the Hyperborean, but should be given the headache
remedy itself straightaway. But if, on the other hand, you appear to be still
lacking in them [sc. temperance and the other such qualities], you must have
the incantations sung to you before you are given the drug. So, tell me
yourself whether you agree with our friend here and declare that you already
participate sufficiently in temperance, or whether you are deficient in it.

First, Charmides blushed at this and looked even more beautiful than
before, for his modesty became his youth. Then, he replied in quite
a dignified manner. He remarked that it would not be easy at present either
to affirm or to deny what he was being asked. – For if, he went on, I deny being
temperate, I shall both be doing something absurd in saying that about myself
and be showing Critias here and, as he claims, many others who consider me
temperate to be liars. If, on the other hand, I affirm that I am temperate and
praise myself, perhaps this will appear offensive. So, I cannot decide what
answer I should give you. – Charmides, I said, your answer seems to me to
reasonable. And I think, I continued, that we should examine in common
whether or not you already have what I am enquiring about, to save you from
being forced to say what you do not wish to say, and me, for my own part, from
applying myself to medicine in a thoughtless manner. Thus, if it is agreeable to
you, I am willing to pursue the question together with you, but otherwise let us
leave it aside. – Nothing, he said, could be more agreeable. To this end,
therefore, do proceed with the enquiry in whatever way you think is better.

The best method of enquiry into this matter, I said, seems to me to be
the following. It is quite evident that, if temperance is present in you, you
can express some belief about it. For if it really resides in you, wherever it
resides, it must provide a sensation [or an awareness] from which you can
hold a belief about it, namely what temperance is and what kind of thing it
is. Do you not think so? – Yes, I do, he replied. – And since you know how
to speak Greek, I said, you could also, I suppose, express it, saying what it
appears to you to be. – Perhaps, he said. – So, in order that we may guess
whether it is in you or not, tell me, I said, what you declare temperance to
be according to your own belief.

Charmides' First Definition of *Sôphrosynê*: Temperance Is a Kind of Quietness (159b1–160d4)

At first he was hesitant and not very willing to answer. But presently he said
that it seemed to him that temperance is doing everything in an orderly and

quiet manner – walking in the streets, and talking, and doing everything else in a similar way. 'So', he said, 'it seems to me that, in a word, what you are asking about is a sort of quietness or calmness'. – I wonder whether you are right. In any case, they do say, Charmides, that those who are quiet are temperate. So let us see if there is anything in it. Tell me, isn't temperance among the beautiful or admirable things? – Yes indeed, he said. – Well, when you are at the writing-master's, which is the most admirable way to write the same letters, quickly or quietly? – Quickly. – What about reading? Is it most admirable to read quickly or slowly? – Quickly. – And of course it is not far more admirable to play the cithara quickly and to wrestle nimbly than to do so quietly and slowly? – Yes, it is. – What about boxing alone or in combination with other forms of fighting? Doesn't the same thing hold true? – Certainly. – And in the cases of running and leaping and all the other activities of the body, aren't the ones effected nimbly and quickly believed to be admirable, but those effected with considerable effort and sluggishly deemed shameful? – Apparently so. – Then it appears to us, I said, that at least so far as the body is concerned, it is not the more quiet but the quickest and nimblest that is the most admirable. Is this not the case? – Very much so. – Temperance, however, was something admirable. – Yes. – Then, since temperance is admirable, at least insofar as the body is concerned, it is not quietness but quickness that would be the most admirable thing. – So it seems, he said. – What about this? I continued. Is it more admirable to have facility or difficulty in learning? – Facility. – And is it true, I said, that facility in learning amounts to learning quickly, whereas difficulty in learning is learning quietly and slowly? – Yes. – And when one is teaching someone else, is it not more admirable to teach him with quickness and intensity rather than quietly and slowly? – It is. – What about this too? Is it more admirable to recollect and remember quietly and slowly or in a quick and concentrated manner? – In a quick and concentrated manner, he said. – And isn't readiness of mind a kind of nimbleness of the soul, not quietness? – True. – Moreover, is it not the case that to understand what is said, whether at the writing- master's or the cithara-master's or anywhere else, is most admirable not when it is achieved as quietly as possible but when it is achieved as quickly as possible? – Yes. – Besides, when it comes to the soul's investigations and deliberations, I would suppose that it is not the quietest thinker and the one who deliberates and discovers with difficulty that seems worthy of praise, but the one who does this in the easiest and quickest manner. – Just so, he said. – Then, Charmides, I said, in everything that concerns both our soul and our body, activities occurring with quickness and nimbleness appear more admirable than those effected with slowness and quietness. – It seems so, he replied. Therefore, so far as this argument goes at least, temperance would not be a kind of quietness, nor would the temperate life be quiet, since the temperate life must be an admirable life. For there are really these two alternatives: either in no case did the quiet actions in life appear to us to be more admirable than the quick and forceful ones or in very few cases this happened. Or if, my friend, of the more admirable actions the quiet ones turn out to be just as many as the vigorous and quick ones, not even so would temperance be acting quietly more than acting vigorously and quickly, neither in walking nor in talking nor in anything else. Nor would the quiet life be more temperate than its opposite, since in our argument we made the hypothesis that temperance is an admirable thing but we have concluded that quick actions are no less admirable than quiet ones. – What you say, Socrates, he replied, seems to me correct.

Charmides' Second Definition: Temperance Is a Sense of Shame (160d5–161b4)

– So, Charmides, I said, this time pay closer attention, turn away (from other things) to look into yourself,[3] think about what kind of person temperance by its presence makes you, and what sort of thing temperance would have to be in order to make you that kind of person, and taking all this into account tell me, well and bravely, what it appears to you to be. And he, after holding back a little and after thinking things through to himself very manfully, said: 'Well, it seems to me that temperance makes a person feel ashamed or bashful, and that temperance is the same as a sense of shame. – But, I retorted, did you not agree a little while ago that temperance is admirable? – I certainly did, he answered. – Is it not also the case that the temperate are good men? – Yes. – And could anything be good that does not make people good? – Of course not. – Hence, temperance is not only admirable but also good. – So at least it seems to me. – But then, I said, don't you believe that Homer speaks correctly, when he says that 'a sense of shame is no good companion for a man in need'? – I do believe so, he replied. – So, as it seems, a sense of shame is both not good and good. – Apparently. – Temperance, however, is just good, if it makes good those in whom it is present and doesn't make them bad. – It certainly seems to me that things stand exactly as you say. – It follows, then, that

---

[3] At 160d6, I keep the ms. reading ἀπεμβλέψας instead of Burnet's ἐμβλέψας.

temperance could not be a sense of shame, if it is in fact good, while a sense of shame is no more good than bad. – Well, Socrates, he said, I do think that this is correctly stated.

Charmides Abandons the 'Best Method': The Third Definition – Temperance Is 'Doing One's Own' (161b4–162b11)

Consider, however, the following view about temperance to judge whether you like it. For I just remembered something that I once heard someone say, that temperance might be doing one's own. So I should like you to examine whether you think that the person who said this is right.

– You scoundrel, I said, you have heard this from Critias here or some other wise man! – Apparently, said Critias, he heard it from someone else. For he certainly hasn't heard it from me. – But Socrates, said Charmides, what difference does it make whom I heard it from? – None, I replied. For, in any case, we ought to consider not who said it, but whether or not the claim is true. – Now you are speaking correctly, he said. – Yes, by god, I retorted. But I would be amazed if we are also going to discover the truth of the matter. For it seems to be a sort of riddle.

– For what reason? he asked. – Because, I replied, I presume that the person who said that temperance is 'doing one's own' did not mean these words exactly as he spoke them. Or do you believe that the writing-master does nothing when he writes or reads? – Of course I believe that he does something, he answered. – And do you think that the writing-master writes and reads only his own name or teaches you boys to write and read only your own names? Or rather did you write the names of your enemies no less than your own names and the names of your friends? – Just as much. – In doing so, were you meddling in other people's own affairs, then, and being intemperate? – Not at all. – And yet you were not really doing your own things, if writing and reading are really doing something. – Well, they really are. – Besides, my friend, I presume that treating patients, building houses, weaving clothes, and producing any product whatsoever that is the work of any art are cases of doing something. – They certainly are. – Well then, do you think that a city would be well governed by this law that orders that each person should weave and wash their own cloak and make their own shoes, flask scraper, and everything else according to the same principle that one should not touch other people's things but make and do one's own things for oneself? – I don't think so, he replied. – Nonetheless, I said, if a city were to be governed temperately, it would be governed well. – Of course, he said. – Then, I said, temperance would not be 'doing one's own' in those kinds of cases or in that way. – It seems that it would not.

– So, it seems that the person who claimed that temperance is doing one's own was riddling, as I was saying a moment ago. For he couldn't have been as simple-minded as that. Or was it some idiot that you heard claiming this, Charmides? – Not at all, he said, for he seemed very wise indeed. – Then, in view of the difficulty to understand what doing one's own can mean, it seems to me virtually certain that he was challenging you with a riddle. – Perhaps, he said. – Well, what could it mean 'to do one's own'? Can you say? – By Zeus, he exclaimed, I really have no idea. But it may well be that not even the man who said it had the least idea of what he meant. And as he was saying this, he laughed a little and looked away towards Critias.

Enter Critias: The Third Definition Revisited –Temperance Is the Doing or Making of Good Things (162c1–164d3)

Well, it was clear that, for some time, Critias had been both anguished and desirous to distinguish himself in the eyes of Charmides and the present company, and having barely contained himself until then, at that point he became unable to do so. For I believe that what I had supposed was entirely true, namely that Charmides had heard this answer concerning temperance from Critias. And because Charmides did not want to explain the answer himself but wanted Critias to, he was trying to stir him up and insinuated that he [sc. Critias] had been refuted. Of course, Critias did not tolerate this, but seemed to me to get angry at Charmides as a poet gets angry at an actor who performs his verses badly on stage. So, he stared hard at Charmides and said: 'do you really think, Charmides, that, if you don't know what was the meaning of the man who claimed that temperance is "to do own's own", he did not know it either?' – But my dear Critias, I said, given Charmides' age, his ignorance is no surprise at all. You, on the other hand, can reasonably be expected to know, both because of your age and because of your studies. Thus, if you agree that temperance is what our friend here says it is and you are taking over the argument, I would feel much greater pleasure in examining together with you whether this assertion is true or not. – Indeed, he said, I do agree and am taking it over.

– You do well to do so, I said.

– Tell me, do you also agree about what I was asking just now, namely that all craftsmen make something? – Indeed. – So, do they seem to you to make only their own things or also other people's things? – Other people's things as well. – So, are they being temperate, even though they do not make only their own things? – Why, he said, what is there to prevent that? – Nothing for me at least, I replied; but see whether it may not prevent him who, having posited that temperance is doing one's own, then goes on to say that nothing prevents those who do other people's own from being temperate as well.

– Pray, he said, have I agreed to this, that those who do other people's things are temperate, or[4] was my agreement about those who make things?[5] – Tell me, I said, don't you call making and doing one and the same? – Certainly not, he replied. Nor do I call working and making the same either. For this I learned from Hesiod, who said, 'Work is no disgrace'. Do you suppose, then, that if he called such works as you were mentioning just now workings and doings, he would have claimed that no disgrace is attached to the shoe-maker or the pickle-seller or the pimp? Of course, Socrates, this is unthinkable. Rather he held, I surmise, that making is something different from doing and working, and that while something made can occasionally become a disgrace, when its production does not involve what is fine, work can never be shameful. For things made in a good and beneficial manner he called works, and such makings he called both workings and doings. Indeed, we should suppose him also to have declared that only things of this sort are our own proper concerns, whereas all harmful things are other people's concerns. Hence we should conclude that both Hesiod and every other sensible person call temperate the man who does his own.

– Ah, Critias, I said, as soon as you began to talk I pretty much grasped your meaning, namely that the things that are proper to oneself or one's own you called good and the makings of good things you called doings. For in fact I have heard Prodicus drawing countless distinctions concerning names. Well, you have my permission to assign to each thing any name you please. Only make clear whenever you say a name what you are applying the name to. So begin now all over again and give a clearer definition.

Do you claim that the doing or making, or whatever else you want to call it, of good things is temperance? – Yes, I do, he said. – Then, it is not the person who does evil actions but the person who does good actions that is temperate, right? – Don't you <yourself> think so, my excellent friend? he said. – Leave that aside, I replied. For let's not yet examine what I think, but what you are saying now. – All right then, he said. I claim that the

---

[4] 163a11 ἤ T εἰ Burnet.   [5] I am supplying a question mark at 163a12.

person who is not making good things but bad things is not temperate, whereas the person who is making good things and not bad things is temperate. For I give you as a straightforward definition of temperance the doing of good things. – Perhaps there is no reason why your claim should not be true. But, I continued, I am surprised that you believe people who are being temperate do not know that they are being temperate. – But I don't believe that, he said. – Didn't you say a little while ago, I said, that nothing prevents the craftsmen from being temperate when they make other people's things as well [as their own]? – I did say it, he answered. But what of it? – Nothing. Tell me, however, whether you think that some doctor, when he makes someone healthy, makes something beneficial both for himself and for the person whom he heals. – I do think that. – And the person who does this does what he ought? – Yes. – Is not the person who does what he ought temperate? – Certainly he is. – Well, and does the doctor necessarily know when his cure is beneficial and when it is not? What is more, does every craftsman necessarily know when he will benefit from the work that he is doing and when he won't? – Perhaps not. – So, sometimes, I said, the doctor may have acted beneficially or harmfully but fail to know himself in respect of how he has acted. And yet, according to your account, in acting beneficially he has acted temperately. Or is this not what you said? – It is. – Then, it seems, on some occasions the doctor acts beneficially and thereby acts temperately and is temperate, but nonetheless is ignorant of himself, namely of the fact that he is being temperate.

– But Socrates, he said, that could never happen. But if you think that this is in any way a necessary consequence deriving from the things I previously agreed, I would certainly prefer to withdraw some of them and I would not be ashamed to declare that I have spoken incorrectly, rather than ever agree that a person who is ignorant of himself is temperate.

Critias' Speech: Temperance Is Knowing Oneself (164d4–165c4)

As a matter of fact, I am almost ready to assert that this very thing, to know oneself, is temperance, and I am of the same mind as the person who put up an inscription to that effect at Delphi. For it seems to me that this inscription has been put up for the following purpose, to serve as a greeting from the god to those who enter the temple instead of the usual 'Be Joyful', since this greeting, 'Be Joyful', is not right, nor should people use it to exhort one another, but rather they should use the greeting 'Be Temperate'. Thus, the god addresses those entering the temple in a manner different in some respects from that in which men address each other, and it is with that thought in mind, I believe, that the person who put up the inscription did so. And it is alleged that he [sc. the god] says to every man who enters the temple nothing other than 'Be Temperate'. However, he says it in a more enigmatic manner, as a prophet would. For while 'Know Thyself' and 'Be Temperate' are one and the same, as the inscription and I assert, perhaps one might think that they are different – an error that, I believe, has been committed by the dedicators of the later inscriptions, i.e. 'Nothing too much' and 'A rash pledge and, immediately, perdition'. For they supposed that 'Know Thyself' was a piece of advice, not the god's greeting to those who were entering.[6] And so, in order that their own dedications too would no less contain pieces of useful advice, they inscribed these words and put them up in the temple. The purpose for which I say all this, Socrates, is the following: I concede to you everything that was debated beforehand. For concerning them perhaps you said something more correct than I did, but, in any case, nothing we said was really clear. However, I am now ready to give you an argument for this, if you don't agree that temperance is to know oneself.

  - Critias, I said, you treat me as though I claimed to know the things that I ask about, and as though I shall agree with you if only I want to. But this is not so. Rather, you see, I always enquire together with you into whatever claim is put forward, because I myself do not know. Thus, it will be after considering the matter that I am willing to state whether or not I agree. So, please hold back until I have done so. – Do consider then, he said. – I am doing so, I replied.

Socrates and Critias Debate the *Technê* Analogy: From 'Knowing Oneself' to 'the Knowledge of Itself' (165c4–166e3)

For if in fact temperance is knowing something, then it is obvious that it would be a sort of knowledge or science and, moreover, a science of something. Or not? – Indeed it is, he replied, of oneself. – And isn't medicine the science of health? – Very much so. – So, I said, if you asked me what use medicine is to us, being the science of health, and what work it achieves, I would answer that it achieves no small benefit. For it produces health, a fine work for us, if you are willing to accept as much. – I am. – And likewise, if you asked me what work is achieved by housebuilding, since it is the science of how to build, I would say houses. And the same holds for the other arts as well. Therefore you too, on behalf of temperance, since you claim that it is a science of oneself, should be able to tell us the answer, if asked, 'Critias, given that temperance is the science of oneself, what fine work worthy of the name does it achieve for us? Come, do tell us'.

– But Socrates, he said, you are not conducting the enquiry in the right manner. For this science is not like the other sciences, nor indeed are the other sciences like each other. Yet you are conducting the investigation as if they were alike. For tell me, he said, what is the work of the art of calculation or the art of geometry, comparable to the way a house is the work of the art of building, or a coat is the work of the art of weaving, or many other such works are those of many arts that one might be able to point to? Can you, in your turn, point out to me some work of that kind in those (two) cases? But you cannot.

– What you say is true, I replied. But what I can point out to you is what thing, different from the science itself, each of these sciences is *of*.[7] For instance, the science of calculation is presumably the science of the even and the odd, how they are quantitatively related to themselves and to each other. Is that right? – Of course, he said. – The odd and the even being different from the art of calculation itself? – How could they not be? – And again, the art of weighing is concerned with weighing heavier and lighter weight, and the heavy and the light are different from the art of weighing itself. Do you agree? – I do. – Tell me, then, what is that of which temperance is a science and which is different from temperance itself?

– There it is, Socrates, he said. You have reached the real issue of the investigation, namely in what respect temperance differs from all the other sciences. But you are trying to find some similarity between it and them and that is not how things stand. Rather, while all the others are sciences of something other than themselves and not of themselves, this one alone is the science both of all the other sciences and of itself [*epistêmê autê heautês*]. And these matters are far from having escaped your attention. In fact, I believe that you are doing precisely what you just said that you were not doing. For you are trying to refute me, abandoning the topic that the argument is about. – If my chief effort is to refute you, I said, how can you possibly think that I do it for any other reason than that for the sake of which I would also investigate what I am saying, i.e. the fear of inadvertently supposing at any time that I knew something while I didn't know it? And so this is what I am now doing: I am examining the argument first and foremost for my own sake, but perhaps also for the sake of my other companions. Or do you not think that the discovery of the nature of

---

[7] Emphasis added here and everywhere else in the translation.

each being is a common good for almost all humans? – Indeed I do, Socrates, he replied. – Be brave then, I said, my dear friend, and answer the question put to you according to what seems to you to be the case, without caring whether it is Critias or Socrates who is being cross-examined. Rather focus your attention on the argument and examine what the outcome will be of its being cross-examined. – Fine, I shall do so. For I think that what you say makes sense.

Critias' Final Definition: Temperance Is 'the Science of Itself and the Other Sciences' or 'the Science of Science' (166e4–167a8) – The Third Offering to Zeus (167a9–c8)

– So tell me, I said, what you mean with regard to temperance. – I mean, he said, that it alone of all of the sciences is a science of both itself and the other sciences. – Then, I said, if indeed it is a science of science or knowledge of knowledge, will it not be knowledge of non-science or ignorance as well? – Very much so, he said. – So, the temperate man alone will know himself and will be able to examine thoroughly what he really knows and what he does not know, and will be capable of judging others in the same way, namely as to what someone knows and thinks he knows in cases in which he does know and again what someone thinks he knows but in fact does not know, and no one else will be capable of that. And so this is what being temperate and temperance and knowing oneself are, namely to know what one knows and what one does not know. Is that what you are saying? – Indeed, he replied.

– Once more then, I said, as a third offering to the Saviour, let us investigate as if from the beginning, first, whether or not this thing is possible, namely to know of what one knows and does not know that one knows and does not know it; and second, however possible this may be, what would be the benefit to us of knowing it. – True, he said, we must examine this.

– Come then, Critias, I said, see if you can show yourself more resourceful than I am about it. For I myself am perplexed. Shall I tell you exactly how I am perplexed? – By all means, do so. – Well, I said, assuming that what you said just now is the case, wouldn't the whole thing amount to this, namely that there is one science which is not of any other thing but only science of itself and the other sciences, and moreover that this same science is also a science of the absence of science as well? – Very much so. – Then look what a strange thing we are trying to say, my friend. For if you consider this very same thing in other cases, you will surely come to think, as I do, that it is impossible. – How so and in what cases? – These ones.

Can There Be an *Epistêmê* of Itself? The Argument from Relatives (167c8–169c2)

Reflect on whether it seems to you that there is some sight which is not of the things that the other sights are of, but is a sight of itself and of the other sights and likewise of the absence of sight [literally: non-sights] and which, although it is sight, sees no colour but rather sees itself and the other sights. Do you think there is such a sight? – No, by Zeus, I certainly do not. – What about some hearing which hears no sound, but does hear itself and the other hearings and non-hearings? – There isn't such a thing either. – Consider now all the senses taken together, whether it seems to you that there is a sense which is of senses and of itself while perceiving none of the things that the other senses perceive. – No, it does not seem so.

– Well then, does there seem to you to be some desire which is not desire of any pleasure, but of itself and the other desires? – No, indeed. – Nor again, it seems to me, a will or rational wish which does not will any good, but wills itself and the other wills? – No, there isn't. – And would you say that there is a kind of love of that sort, one that is actually love of nothing beautiful but of itself and the other loves? – No, he replied, I certainly wouldn't. – And have you ever conceived of a fear which fears itself and the other fears, but fears no fearsome thing? – No, I have not, he said. – Or a belief or opinion which is a belief of beliefs and of itself, but does not believe any one of the things that the other beliefs believe? – Of course not.

– Nonetheless, we apparently do assert, do we not, that there is a science of this kind, which is not a science of any object of learning, but a science of itself and the other sciences. – Indeed, we do. – And would it not be something strange if it really exists? Let us not yet declare that it doesn't, but consider further whether it does. – Quite right.

– Now, consider the following. This science is a science *of something*, and it has a power such as to be *of something*, is that not so? – Indeed. – For we say that the greater too has a certain power such as to be greater *than something*, right? – Quite so. – Namely, than something smaller, if it is going to be greater. – Necessarily. – So if we were to find something greater which is greater than both the greater [things] and than itself but not greater than any one of the [things] that the other greater [things] are greater than, then, if indeed it were greater than itself, that very property would also necessarily belong to it somehow, namely it would also be smaller than itself. Or is it not so? – It is absolutely necessary, Socrates, he said. – And also, if there is a double of both the other doubles and itself, then of course it would be double of itself and the other doubles by being half. For there presumably isn't a double of anything other than of half. – True. – And if something is more than itself it will also be less, if heavier then lighter, if older then younger, and likewise for all the other cases. Whatever has its own power directed towards itself, won't it also have that special nature towards which its power was directed? I mean something like this: hearing, for instance, we say, is hearing of nothing but sound, is it not? – Yes. – So, if it is going to hear itself, it will hear itself as having sound; for there is no other way that it could hear. – Most necessarily. – And I suppose sight too, my excellent friend, if it really is going to see itself, must itself have some colour; for sight will never see anything colourless. – Certainly not.

– Then do you see, Critias, that, of the cases that we have gone through, some of them appear to us to be entirely impossible, while others utterly defy belief as to whether they could ever have their own power directed towards themselves? For, on the one hand, in the cases of magnitudes and multitudes and the like this seems entirely impossible. Or not? – Very much so. – On the other hand again, hearing and sight, and moreover motion moving itself and heat burning itself and all other such cases, may arouse disbelief in some people, but perhaps not in others.

What is needed in fact, my friend, is some great man who will draw this division in a satisfactory manner regarding every aspect: whether no being is naturally constituted so as to have its own power directed towards itself but [only] towards something other than itself,[8] or whether some beings are so constituted whereas others are not; and again, if there are beings which have it towards themselves, whether or not they include the science which we claim to be temperance. For my own part, I do not believe that I am myself able to draw this division. And therefore, neither am I in a position to affirm with confidence whether it is possible that this obtains, namely that there is a science of science, nor, supposing that it is perfectly possible, do I accept that this is temperance before I have examined whether or not something would benefit us in virtue of being of such a sort – for, in fact, I have the intuition that temperance is something beneficial and good. You therefore, son of Callaeschrus – since you contend that temperance is this very thing, the science of science and moreover of the absence of science – first, prove that this thing I was just

---

[8] πλὴν ἐπιστήμης secl. Schleiermacher.

mentioning is possible;[9] and second, in addition to being possible, that it is also beneficial. And then perhaps you would satisfy me as well that you are speaking correctly about what temperance is.

The Argument from Benefit (169c3–175a8)

Stage 1 (169c3–170a4)

And when Critias heard these things and saw that I was puzzled, he appeared to me to be compelled by my own state of puzzlement to be besieged and captured by puzzlement himself too, just as those who see people yawning in front of them have the very same sensation induced in them. And since he used regularly to make a good impression, he felt ashamed before the company, and did not want to concede to me that he was unable to go through the divisions that I was challenging him to draw, and made a vague comment which concealed his puzzlement And so, in order for our argument to go forward, I said: 'alternatively, Critias, if it seems to you a good idea, let us for now make the following concession, that there may possibly be a science of science, but we shall investigate whether or not this is so some other time. Come then, consider: assuming that this science is perfectly possible, why or how does it make it any more possible for one to know what one knows and what one doesn't? For this is exactly what we said is to know oneself or be temperate. Did we not?' – Very much so, he said. And indeed, Socrates, this must surely follow. For if someone has a knowledge or science which knows itself, he himself would be of the same kind as that which he has. Just as whenever someone has swiftness, he is swift, and whenever someone has beauty, he is beautiful, and whenever someone has knowledge, he is knowing, so whenever someone has knowledge that is of itself, he will then, surely, be knowledgeable of himself. – I do not dispute this point, I said, namely that when someone has the very thing which knows itself, he will know himself. However, what sort of necessity is there for the person who has it [sc. that which knows itself] to know *what* he knows and *what* he does not know? – Because, Socrates, this knowledge is the same as the other. – Perhaps, I said. But I am afraid I am always in a similar condition. For I still do not understand how knowing *what* one knows and doesn't is the same [as that other knowledge].

---

[9] ἀποδεῖξαί σε secl. Heindorf.

Stage 2 (170a5–171c10)

– How do you mean? he asked. – I mean this, I said. Supposing that perhaps there is a science of science, will it really be able to distinguish anything more than that, namely that of two things, the one is science but the other is not? – No, just that much. – Then, is the science or lack of science of health the same thing as the science or lack of science of justice? – Certainly not. – Rather, I think, the one is the science of medicine, the other is the science of politics, and the science we are talking about is of nothing but science. – It must be so. – And if a person does not have additional knowledge of health and justice but knows only knowledge because he has knowledge of only that thing, namely *that* [*hoti*] he knows something and that he has some knowledge, he would also probably know that he has some knowledge both about himself and about others. Isn't that so? – Yes. – But how will he know *what* [*ho ti*] he knows by virtue of that knowledge? For he knows, of course, health by virtue of medicine and not of temperance, harmony by virtue of music and not of temperance, building by virtue of the art of building and not of temperance, and the same holds for all cases. Or not? – It seems so. – But if temperance is indeed a science only of sciences, how will [the temperate person] know that he knows health or that he knows building? – He won't know it in any way.

– Hence, the person who is ignorant of this [sc. health or building] will not know *what* he knows but only *that* he knows. – It seems so. – Therefore, being temperate and temperance would not be this, i.e. knowing *what* one knows and *what* one doesn't know, but, it seems, knowing only *that* one knows and *that* one doesn't know. – Maybe. – And so such a person will not be able to examine another man claiming to know something as to whether he does or doesn't know *what* he claims to know. But, as it seems, he will know only this much, *that* he has some science; however, temperance will not make him know *what* that science is *of*. – Apparently not. – Consequently, he will not be able either to distinguish from the real doctor the person who pretends to be a doctor without being one, or any other knowledgeable expert from a non-expert.

Let us consider the matter from a different starting point. If the temperate man or anyone else is going to discriminate between the person who is truly a doctor and the one who is not, won't he behave as follows? Surely, he will not discuss with him about medicine – for, as we have said, the doctor has knowledge of nothing other than health and disease. Isn't that so? – It is. – But he knows nothing of science; instead we have assigned that to temperance alone. – Yes. – Therefore, the medical man knows nothing of medicine either, since medicine is in fact a science. – True. – Thus, the temperate man will know that the doctor possesses a certain science. But when he has to test which one it is, will he consider anything other than what things it is a science of? Or is it not the case that each science is defined not merely as a science but also as a particular one,[10] by virtue of this, namely its being of certain specific objects? – Surely it is. – And medicine was defined as being different from the other sciences by virtue of the fact that it was the science of health and disease, right?[11] – Yes. – So, mustn't anyone wishing to enquire into medicine enquire into what domain medicine is found in? For he would presumably not enquire into domains external to these in which it is not found. – Of course not. – Hence it is in the domain of health and disease that the person who enquires in the correct manner will enquire into the doctor *qua* doctor. – It seems so. – Won't he enquire as to whether, in things either thus said or thus done, what is said is said truly and what is done is done correctly? – Necessarily. – Now, could a person pursue either of these lines of enquiry without the art of medicine? – Surely not. – Nor, it seems, could anyone else, except a doctor, nor indeed could the temperate man. For otherwise he would have to be a doctor in addition to his temperance. – That is true.

– Hence it is very probable that, if temperance is only a science of science and of the lack of science, it will not be able to distinguish either a doctor who knows the subjects pertaining to his art from a man who does not know them but pretends or believes that he does, or any other expert of those knowledgeable in anything at all, except for the one who happens to have the same art as the temperate man himself, as is the case with all other specialists as well. – So it seems, he said.

Stage 3 (171d1–172c3)

– What benefit then, Critias, I asked, may we still derive from temperance, if it is of such kind? For if, as we supposed from the beginning, the temperate person knew *what* he knew and *what* he did not know, *that* he knows the former but *that* he does not know the latter, and if he were able to recognise another man who has found himself in this same condition, we agree that it would be greatly to our benefit to be temperate. For we would live our life free of error, both we ourselves[12] who would have

---

[10] I change τίς, the interrogative printed by Burnet at 171a6, to the indefinite pronoun τις.
[11] I end the Greek sentence at 171a9 with a question mark, where Burnet has a full stop.
[12] I preserve the ms. reading καί deleted by Heindorf.

temperance and all the others who would be governed by us. For neither would we ourselves try to do *what* we did not know, but rather would find those who do know and would hand the matter over to them, nor would we allow the other people governed by us to do anything different from *what* they would be bound to do correctly; and this would be what they would have knowledge or science of.[13] In just this way, then, a house administered by temperance would be well administered, a state would be well ruled, and the same holds for everything else governed by temperance. For, with error removed and correctness leading, it is necessary that the people who are in such condition will act in their every action in a fine and good manner, and that those who do act well will be happy. Did we not, Critias, speak of temperance in that manner, I said, when we were saying what a great good it was to know both what one knows and does not know? – Very much so, he replied. – But now you see, I said, that such a science has appeared nowhere. – I do, he said.

– And so, said I, it may be that the science that we now find to be temperance, namely to know science and the lack of science, has this good attached to it: the person who possesses it will learn more easily whatever else he learns and will perceive everything more clearly, since, in addition to every particular thing that he learns, he also has science in view. And moreover, he will test others more reliably about whatever subjects he also has learnt himself, whereas those who test without having this advantage will do so in a weaker and worse manner. Are these perhaps, my friend, the sorts of benefit that we shall derive from temperance, and are we picturing something greater, and asking for it to be something greater than it really is? – Perhaps, he replied, this may be so.

Stage 4 (172c4–173d7)

– Perhaps, I said. But also, perhaps, we were enquiring about nothing of value. My evidence is that certain strange things seem to me true of temperance, if it is such a thing. For let us examine the matter, if you wish, conceding that it is possible to know knowledge or science and, moreover, let us not withdraw but grant that temperance is what we said from the beginning it is, to know both *what* one knows and *what* one does not know. And having granted all this, let us yet better investigate whether something, if it is of that sort, will also be of benefit to us. For what we were saying just now, that if temperance

[13] I put a full stop after εἶχον.

were such a thing, it would be a great good as our guide in the administration of both the household and city, we have not, I think, done well to agree to, Critias.

– How so? he asked. – Because, I answered, we conceded easily that it is a great good for men if each one of us did *what* he knew but delegated to other people, namely the experts, what he did not expertly know. – And were we not right to concede this? he asked. – I think not, I said. – You're really talking nonsense Socrates, he said. – Yes, I said, by the Dog, I too have the same impression. And, indeed, it is precisely in view of that that I said just now that certain conclusions strike me as strange and that I feared that we were not conducting the investigation in the right way. For, in truth, even if temperance is very much the sort of thing we said it is, it does not seem at all clear to me that it achieves something good for us. – How do you mean? he asked. Tell us, so that we too can know what you mean. – I think I am talking nonsense, I said. But all the same, it is necessary to examine what appears before one's eyes and not let it idly go by, if one has even a little care for oneself. – Well said, he responded.

– Listen then, I said, to my dream, whether it has come through the gate of horn or through the gate of ivory. For supposing that temperance were as we now define it and completely governed us, absolutely everything would be done according to the sciences, and neither would anyone deceive us by claiming to be a navigator when he was not, or a doctor, or a general, nor would anyone else remain undetected if he pretended to know what he did not know. And from things being that way nothing else could result for us than that our bodies would be healthier than they are now, and that we would be safe when facing the dangers of sea-travel and war, and that all our vessels or utensils and clothes and footwear and all other things would be expertly made for us because we would use true craftsmen. And moreover, if you would like, let us concede that divination is the science of what is to be in the future, and that temperance, which oversees it, will turn away charlatans and establish for us the true diviners as prophets of what is to be. I do admit that, if mankind were organised in that way, it would act and live scientifically. For temperance, being on guard, would not allow the lack of science to burst in and take part in our deeds. But that by acting scientifically we would also do well and be happy, this, my dear Critias, we cannot know as yet. – However, he retorted, if you discredit acting scientifically, you will not easily find some other goal of acting well.

Stage 5 (173d8–175a8)

– Instruct me, then, about one more small detail, I said. You mean acting scientifically or knowledgeably in respect of what? Of cutting the leather for shoe-making? – By Zeus, certainly not. – Of the working of brass? – Not at all. – Of wool, or of wood, or of any other such thing? – Of course not. – Therefore, I said, we are no longer abiding by the claim that he who lives scientifically is happy. For although these experts live scientifically, you do not acknowledge that they are happy, but rather you seem to me to demarcate the happy person as someone who lives scientifically in respect of certain things. Perhaps you mean the man I was just referring to, namely the one who knows everything that is to be, the seer. Do you mean him or someone else? – Well, he replied, both him and someone else. Whom? I asked. Is it the sort of person who might know, in addition to what is to be, both everything that has been and everything that now is and might be ignorant of nothing? Let us assume that there is such a person. I won't say, I imagine, that there is anyone alive that knows more than he does. – Certainly not.

– There is still one more thing I desire to know in addition: which one of the sciences makes him happy? Or do all of them do so in the same way? – Not at all in the same way, he said. – But what sort of science makes him supremely happy? The science by which he knows one of the things that are or have been or will be in the future? Is it perhaps the science by which he knows how to play draughts? – What are you talking about! he said. Draughts indeed!

– What about the science by which he knows how to calculate? – Not in the least. – Well, is it the one by which he knows what is healthy? – More so, he said. – But that one which I mean makes him happy most of all, said I, is the science by which he knows what kind of thing? – That, he replied, by which he knows good and evil.

– You wretch! I said. All this time you have been dragging me around in a circle, while you were concealing the fact that what made a person do well and be happy was not living scientifically, not even if this were science of all the other sciences together, but only if it were science of this one science alone, namely the science concerning good and evil. Because, Critias, if you choose to remove this science from the set of other sciences, will medicine any the less produce health, or cobbling shoes, or weaving clothes? Or will the art of navigation any the less prevent passengers from dying at sea, or the military art from dying in war? – No less at all, he said. – However, my dear Critias, if this science [sc. the science of good and evil] is lacking, the good and beneficial execution of each of these tasks will be gone out of our reach. – This is true. – And this science, it seems, is not temperance but a science whose function is to benefit us. For it is not a science of the sciences and the lack of the sciences, but of good and evil, so that, if this is beneficial, temperance would be something else for us.[14]

– But why, he said, should it [sc. the science of science] not be beneficial? For if temperance is above all a science of the sciences and presides too over the other sciences, then, in virtue of ruling over this one, i.e. the science of the good, surely it would benefit us.

– And, I replied, would this science, and not medicine, also make people healthy? Moreover, would it be the one to bring about the works of the other arts, and the other arts not have each its own work? Or have we not been protesting for some time that it is only a science of science and the lack of science, but of nothing else? Is that not so? – Indeed, it appears to be. – So, it will not be a producer of health? – No, it will not. – For health is the object of another art, is it not? – Yes, of another. – Therefore, my friend, it [sc. the science of science] will not be a producer of benefit either. For, again, we just now attributed this function to another art, did we not? – Very much so. – In what way, then, will temperance be beneficial since it is not the producer of any benefit? – In no way at all, Socrates, it seems.

The Epilogue: Philosophical Conclusions and Dramatic Closure (175a9–176d5)

Pulling Strings Together (175a9–d5)

– Do you see, then, Critias, that my earlier fears were reasonable and that I was rightly accusing myself of failing to bring under scrutiny anything worthwhile about temperance? For if I had been of any use for conducting a good search, it wouldn't have been the case that what is agreed to be the finest of all things would somehow have appeared to us to be of no benefit. And now, you see, we are vanquished on all fronts, and are unable to discover to which one of the things there are the lawgiver attached this name, temperance. Nonetheless we have made many concessions which were not forced upon us by the argument. For, as a matter of fact, we conceded that there is a science of science, even though the argument

---

[14] Following Burnet I excise ἡ ὠφελίμη present in B and T.

neither allowed nor asserted that there is. Again, although the argument did not allow this, we conceded in our favour that the temperate man knows through this science the functions of the other sciences as well, so that we would find him knowledgeable both of knowing *what* things he knows *that* he knows them and of knowing *what* things he does not know *that* he doesn't know them. And we granted this in the most bountiful manner, without examining the impossibility of somehow knowing things that one doesn't know in any way at all; for the concession we agreed on amounts to saying that one knows about them that one doesn't know them. And yet, as I think, this might appear more irrational than anything. However, although the enquiry has shown us to be so soft and lacking in rigour, it cannot do any better in finding the truth, but derided it [sc. the truth] to such an extent that the very thing which, by agreeing with each other and by moulding it together, we earlier posited to be temperance the enquiry has with the utmost contempt shown to be useless.

Socrates' Last Address to Charmides (175d5–176a5)

So far as I am concerned, I am not so upset. However, I said, I am very upset indeed on your own account, if it turns out that, although you have an appearance like yours and moreover are perfectly temperate in your soul, you will draw no profit from this temperance nor will it by its presence in any way benefit you in your life. And I feel still more upset on account of the charm which I learnt from the Thracian, if I have taken so much trouble to learn it while it has no worth at all. As a matter of fact, I really do not think that this is the case. Rather, I am a bad enquirer. For temperance is surely a great good and, if you do possess it, you are blessed. So, see whether you have it and stand in no need of the charm. For if you have it, I would rather advise you to consider me to be a fool unable to investigate anything whatsoever by means of argument, but yourself to be as happy as you are temperate.

The Final Scene (176a6–d5)

Then Charmides retorted: 'by Zeus, Socrates, I really do not know whether I have temperance or whether I don't. For how could I know something regarding which, as you yourself say, not even you and Critias are able to discover what on earth it is? However, I do not entirely believe you, and I think, Socrates, that I am much in need of the charm. And, so far as I am concerned, there is no obstacle to my being charmed by you for as many days as it takes, until you say that it is enough'.

– Well, Charmides, said Critias, it will be proof for me that you are temperate if you do this: if you turn yourself over to Socrates to be charmed and do not leave his side much or little. – Be sure, he said, that I shall follow him and shall not leave his side. For I would be doing something bad if I didn't obey you, my guardian, and if I did not do what you order. – Indeed, he said, I do so order. – I shall do it, then, he said, beginning this very day. – You two, I said, what are you planning to do? – Nothing, Charmides replied, we have already made a plan. – Will you use force then, I said, and won't you give me preliminary hearing? – Be sure that I shall use force, he answered, since this man here gives the command. Consider again what you will do about this. – But there is nothing left to consider, I said. For when you attempt any operation and use force, no human being will be able to oppose you. – Well then, he replied, do not oppose me either. – Very well, I said, I shall not.

Bibliography

Adam, J. (1902) *The Republic of Plato*, 2 vols., Cambridge.

Adamietz, J. (1969) 'Zur Erklärung des Hauptteils von Platons *Charmides* (164a–175d)', *Hermes* 97: 37–57.

Adkins, A. W. H. (1976) '*Polupragmosune* and "Minding One's Own Business": A Study in Greek Social and Political Values', *Classical Philology* 71: 301–27.

Altman, W. H. F. (2010) '*Laches* before *Charmides*: Fictive Chronology and Platonic Pedagogy', *Plato Journal* 10: 1–28.

Anagnostopoulos, G. (1972) 'Review of Robinson 1970', *Journal for the History of Philosophy* 10: 217–21.

Annas, J. (1985) 'Self-Knowledge in Early Plato', in D. J. O'Meara (ed.), *Platonic Investigations*, Washington, DC: 111–38.

(1993) *The Morality of Happiness*, Oxford.

(1999) *Platonic Ethics, Old and New*, Ithaca, NY.

Anscombe, E. (1957) *Intention*, Oxford.

Ast, F. (1819–32) *Platonis quae extant opera*, Leipzig.

Ayalong, N. (2018) '"Exactly as you see me" (*Charmides* 153b8): The Function of Narration in Plato's *Charmides*', *Journal of Ancient Philosophy* 12: 179–91.

Baltzly, D. (1997) 'Plato, Aristotle and the ΛΟΓΟΣ ΕΚ ΤΩΝ ΠΡΟΣ ΤΙ', *Oxford Studies in Ancient Philosophy* 15: 177–206.

Barker, A. (1995) 'Problems in the *Charmides*', *Prudentia* 27: 18–31.

Barnes, J. (1988a) 'Bits and Pieces', in J. Barnes and M. Mignucci (eds.), *Matter and Metaphysics*, Naples: 223–94.

(1988b) 'Scepticism and Relativity', *Philosophical Studies* 32: 1–31.

(2007) *Truth, Etc.*, Oxford.

Barney, R. (2021) 'Technê as a Model for Virtue', in T. K. Johansen (ed.), *Productive Knowledge in Ancient Philosophy: The Concept of Technê*, Cambridge: 62–85.

Beare, J. I. (1914) 'A New Clue to the Order of the Platonic Dialogues', in *Essays Presented to Sir W. Ridgeway*, Cambridge: 27–61.

Benardete, S. (1986) 'On Interpreting Plato's *Charmides*', *Graduate Faculty Philosophy Journal* 11: 9–36.

Benson, H. H. (2000) *Socratic Wisdom: The Model of Knowledge in Plato's Early Dialogues*, New York.

(2003) 'A Note on Socratic Self-Knowledge in the *Charmides*', *Ancient Philosophy* 23: 31–47.

Beversluis, J. (2000) *Cross-Examining Socrates: A Defense of the Interlocutors in Plato's Early Dialogues*, Cambridge.

Bloch, G. (1973) *Platons Charmides: Die Erscheinung des Seins im Gespräch*, Tübingen.

Blondell, R. (2002) *The Play of Character in Plato's Dialogues*, Cambridge.

Blyth, D. (2001) 'Tyrannical Power in Plato's *Charmides*', in D. Baltzly, D. Blyth, and H. Tarrant (eds.), *Power and Pleasure, Virtues and Vices*, Prudentia Suppl., Auckland: 35–53.

Bonitz, H. (1886) *Platonische Studien*, 3rd ed., Berlin.

Boyancé, P. (1937) *Le culte des Muses chez les philosophes grecs*, Paris.

Boys-Stones. G. R. and Haubold, J. H. (2010) *Plato and Hesiod*, Oxford.

Brann, E. (2004) 'The Tyrant's Temperance: *Charmides*', in *The Music of the Republic: Essays on Socrates' Conversations and Plato's Writings*, Philadelphia, PA: 66–87.

Brennan, T. (2012) 'The Implicit Refutation of Critias', *Phronesis* 57: 240–50.

Brickhouse, T. C. and Smith, N. D. (1994) *Plato's Socrates*, New York and Oxford.

Brisson, L. (2000) 'L'incantation de Zalmoxis dans le *Charmide* (156d–157c)', in T. M. Robinson and L. Brisson (eds.), *Proceedings of the V Symposium Platonicum, Selected Papers, IPS Series* vol. 13, Sankt Augustin: 278–86.

Brouwer, M. and Polansky, R. (2004) 'The Logic of Socratic Inquiry: Illustrated by Plato's *Charmides*', in V. Karasmanis (ed.), *Socrates: 2400 Years Since His Death (399 BC–2001 AD)*, Delphi: 233–45.

Bruell, C. (1977) 'Socratic Politics and Self-Knowledge: An Interpretation of Plato's *Charmides*', *Interpretation: A Journal of Political Philosophy* 6: 141–203.

Brunschwig, J. (2003) 'Revisiting Plato's Cave', *Boston Area Colloquium in Ancient Philosophy* 19: 145–74.

Bultrighini, U. (1999) *'Maledetta democrazia': studi su Crizia*, Alessandria.

Burger, R. (2013) 'Socrates' Odyssean Return: On Plato's *Charmides*', in C. Dusting and D. Schaeffer (eds.), *Socratic Philosophy and Its Others*, Lanham, MD: 217–35.

Burnet, J. (1903) Πλάτωνος Χαρμίδης, in *Scriptorum Classicorum Bibliotheca Oxoniensis, Platonis Opera Tomus III*, Oxford.

Burnyeat, M. F. (1970) 'The Material and Sources of Plato's Dream', *Phronesis* 15/1: 101–22.

   (1971) 'Virtues in Action', in G. Vlastos (ed.), *The Philosophy of Socrates: A Collection of Critical Essays*, Garden City, NY: 209–34.

   (1977) 'Socratic Midwifery, Platonic Inspiration', *Bulletin of the Institute of Classical Studies* 24: 7–16.

   (1990) *The Theaetetus of Plato*, translation by M. J. Levett, Indianapolis, IN.

   (1992) 'Is an Aristotelian Philosophy of Mind Still Credible? A Draft', in M. C. Nussbaum and A. Rorty (eds.), *Essays on Aristotle's De anima*, Oxford: 15–26.

(1997) 'The Impiety of Socrates', *Ancient Philosophy* 17/1: 1–14.

(2003) '"By the Dog"'. Review of Ruby Blondell', *The Play of Characters in Plato's Dialogues* (Cambridge 2002), *London Review of Books* vol. 25 No 15: 23–4.

Cairns, D. L. (1993) *Aidôs: The Psychology and Ethics of Honour and Shame in Ancient Greek Literature*, Oxford.

Carone, G. R. (1998) 'Socrates' Human Wisdom and *Sophrosune* in *Charmides* 164ff.', *Ancient Philosophy* 18: 267–86.

Carter, L. B. (1986) *The Quiet Athenian*, Oxford.

Castañeda, H. (1972) 'Plato's *Phaedo* Theory of Relations', *Journal of Philosophical Logic* 1/3: 467–80.

(1978) 'Plato's Relations, Not Essences or Accidents, at *Phaedo* 102b2–d2', *Canadian Journal of Philosophy* 8/1: 39–53.

(1982) 'Leibniz and Plato's *Phaedo* Theory of Relations and Predication', in M. Hooker (ed.), *Leibniz Critical and Interpretative Essays*, Minneapolis, MN: 124–59.

Caston, V. (1998) 'Aristotle and the Problem of Intentionality', *Philosophy and Phenomenological Research* 58/2: 249–98.

(2002) 'Aristotle on Consciousness', *Mind* 111: 751–815.

(2004) 'More on Aristotle on Consciousness: Reply to Sisko', *Mind* 113: 523–33.

Caujolle-Zaslawsky, F. (1980) 'Les Relatifs Dans Les Catégories', in P. Aubenque (ed.), *Concepts et Catégories Dans La Pensée Antique*, Paris: 167–95.

Centanni, M. (1997) *Atene assoluta. Crizia della tragedia alla storia*, Padua.

Chambry, P. (1967) *Platon: Premiers Dialogues*, Paris.

Charalabopoulos, N. G. (2008) 'Πρόσωπο, σῶμα καὶ ψυχὴ στὸν Χαρμίδη τοῦ Πλάτωνος', in Μ. Α. Πουρκός (ed.), *Πλαισιοθετημένη γνώση και εκπαίδευση*, Athens: 509–42.

(2014) 'Πρόσωπο, σῶμα καὶ ψυχὴ στὸν Χαρμίδη του Πλάτωνος', in *Τὸ πλατωνικὸ δρᾶμα καὶ ἡ διαδρομὴ του στὴν Ἀρχαιότητα*, Patras: 47–103.

(in press) 'Plato and the Elusive Satyr (Meta)drama', in A. P. Antonopoulos, M. M. Christopoulos, and W. W. Harrison (eds.), *Brill's Companion to Satyr Drama*, London and Boston, MA.

Chen, C.-H. (1978) 'On Plato's *Charmides* 165c4–175d5', *Apeiron* 12/1: 13–28.

Cherniss, H. (1936) 'The Philosophical Economy of the Theory of Ideas', *American Journal of Philology* 57: 445–56.

(1944) *Aristotle's Criticism of Plato and the Academy*, Baltimore, MD.

(1945) *The Riddle of the Early Academy*, Berkeley, CA.

Clark, J. (2018) 'Knowledge and Temperance in Plato's *Charmides*', *Pacific Philosophical Quarterly* 99/2: 763–89.

Clarke, T. (2012) 'The Argument from Relatives', *Oxford Studies in Ancient Philosophy* 42: 151–77.

Coolidge, F. P. (1993) 'The Relation of Philosophy to Σωφροσύνη: Zalmoxian Medicine in Plato's *Charmides*', *Ancient Philosophy* 13: 1–23.

Cooper, J. M. (ed.) (1997) *Plato: Complete Works*, Indianapolis, IN.

Corkum, P. (2008) 'Aristotle on Ontological Dependence', *Phronesis* 53/1: 65–92.

Crane, T. (1998) 'Intentionality as the Mark of the Mental', *Royal Institute of Philosophy Supplements* 43: 229–51.

Croiset, A. (1921) *Platon. Oeuvres complètes*, vol. 2, Les Belles Lettres, Paris.

Danzig, G. (2013) 'Plato's *Charmides* as a Political Act: Apologetics and the Promotion of Ideology', *Greek, Roman, and Byzantine Studies* 53: 486–519.

(2014) 'The Use and Abuse of Critias: Conflicting Portraits in Plato and Xenophon', *Classical Quarterly* 64: 507–24.

Davidson, D. (2005) 'The Socratic Concept of Truth', in *Truth, Language, and History*, Oxford: 241–50.

Desjardins, R. (1988) 'Why Dialogues? Plato's Serious Play', in *Platonic Writings/Platonic Readings*, New York.

De Vries, G. J. (1973) '*Sôphrosynê* en grec classique', *Mnemosyne* 3/11: 81–101.

Dieterle, R. (1966) *Platons Laches und Charmides. Untersuchungen zur elenktisch-aporetischen Struktur der platonischen Frühdialoge*, Freiburg: 142–312.

Dodds, E. R. (1951) *The Greeks and the Irrational*, Berkeley and Los Angeles, CA.

Dorion, L.-A. (2004) *Platon: Charmide, Lysis*, Paris.

Duncombe, M. (2012a) *The Nature and Purpose of Relative Terms in Plato*, PhD dissertation, Faculty of Classics, University of Cambridge, UK.

(2012b) 'Plato's Absolute and Relative Categories at *Sophist* 255c14', *Ancient Philosophy* 32/1: 77–86.

(2013) 'The Greatest Difficulty at *Parmenides* 133c–134e and Plato's Relative Terms', *Oxford Studies in Ancient Philosophy* 45: 43–62.

(2015a) 'Aristotle's Two Accounts of Relatives in *Categories* 7', *Phronesis* 60: 436–61.

(2015b) 'The Role of Relatives in Plato's Partition Argument, *Republic* 4, 436b9–439c9', *Oxford Studies in Ancient Philosophy* 48: 37–60.

(2020) *Ancient Relativity*, Oxford.

Dušanić, S. (2000) 'Critias in the *Charmides*', *Aevum* 74: 53–63.

Dyson, M. (1974) 'Some Problems Concerning Knowledge in Plato's *Charmides*', *Phronesis* 19: 102–11.

Ebert, T. (1974) *Meinung und Wissen in der Philosophie Platons*, Berlin.

Ehrenberg, V. (1947) '*Polypragmosyne*: A Study in Greek Politics', *Journal of Hellenic Studies* 67: 46–67.

Eisenstadt, M. (1981) 'A Note on *Charmides* 168e9–169a1', *Hermes* 109: 126–8.

Faraone, C. (2009) 'A Socratic Leaf-Charm for Headache (*Charmides* 155b–157c), Orphic Gold Leaves and the Ancient Greek Tradition of Leaf Amulets', in J. Dijkstra, J. Kroesen, and Y. Kuiper (eds.), *Myths, Martyrs, and Modernity: Studies in the History of Religion in Honour of Jan N. Bremmer*, Leiden: 145–66.

Fine, G. (1983) 'Relational Entities', *Archiv für Geschichte der Philosophie* 65/3: 225–49.

Fine, K. (2000) 'Neutral Relations', *The Philosophical Review* 109/1: 1–33.

Frede, M. (1987a) 'Philosophy and Medicine in Antiquity', in *Essays in Ancient Philosophy*, Oxford: 225–43.

(1987b) 'The Ancient Empiricists', in *Essays in Ancient Philosophy*, Oxford: 243–61.

(1992) 'Plato's Arguments and the Dialogue Form', in J. C. Klagge and N. D. Smith (eds.), *Methods of Interpreting Plato and His Dialogues*, Oxford: 201–20.

Gaiser, K. (1959) *Protreptik und Paränese bei Platon. Untersuchungen zu Form des platonischen Dialogs*, Stuttgart.

Garver, E. (2018) 'Charmides and the Virtue of Opacity: An Early Chapter in the History of the Individual', *Review of Metaphysics* 71: 469–500.

Gentzler, J. (1995) 'How to Discriminate between Experts and Frauds: Some Problems for Socratic Peirastic', *History of Philosophy Quarterly* 12: 227–46.

Gill, M.-L. (2003) 'Plato's *Phaedrus* and the Method of Hippocrates', *Modern Schoolman* 80: 295–314.

Gocer, A. (1999) '*Hesuchia*, a Metaphysical Principle in Plato's Moral Psychology', *Apeiron* 32: 17–36.

Goldschmidt, V. (1947) *Les dialogues de Platon. Structure et méthode dialectique*, Paris.

Gosling, J. C. (1968) 'Δόξα and Δύναμις in Plato's "Republic"', *Phronesis* 13/2: 119–30.

Gotshalk, R. (2001) *The Temporality of Human Excellence: A Reading of Five Dialogues of Plato*, Lanham, MD.

Gottlieb, P. (1993) 'Aristotle Versus Protagoras on Relatives and the Objects of Perception', *Oxford Studies in Ancient Philosophy* 11: 101–19.

Gould, J. (1955) *The Development of Plato's Ethics*, New York.

Griswold, C. (1986) *Self-Knowledge in Plato's Phaedrus*, New Haven, CT.

Gros, P. (1994) 'Le visage de Charmide', in M.-C. Amouretti and P. Villard (eds.), *Eukrata. Mélanges offerts à Claude Vatin*, Aix-en-Provence: 15–20.

Grote, G. (1865) *Plato and the Other Companions of Socrates*, 3 vols., London.

Guthrie, W. K. C. (1975) *A History of Greek Philosophy vol. IV. Plato: The Man and His Dialogues – Earlier Period*, Cambridge.

Halper, E. (2000) 'Is Knowledge of Knowledge Possible? Charmides 167a–169d', in T. M. Robinson and L. Brisson (eds.), *Plato: Euthydemus, Lysis, Charmides: Proceedings of the V Symposium Platonicum, Selected Papers*, IPS Series vol. 13, Sankt Augustin: 309–16.

Halperin, D. (1986) 'Plato and Erotic Reciprocity', *Classical Antiquity* 5: 60–80.

Harte, V. (2002) *Plato on Parts and Wholes: The Metaphysics of Structure*, Oxford.

(2017) 'Knowing and Believing in *Republic* 5', in V. Harte and R. Woolf (eds.), *Rereading Ancient Philosophy: Old Chestnuts and Sacred Cows*, Cambridge: 141–62.

Harte, V. and Lane, M. (eds.) (2013) *Politeia in Greek and Roman Philosophy*, Cambridge.

Hazebroucq, M.-F. (1997) *La folie humaine et ses remèdes. Platon. Charmide ou de la modération*, Paris.

Heitsch, E. and von Kutschera, F. (2000) *Zu Platons Charmides*, Stuttgart.

Hermann, K. F. (1850) 'Das Bruchstück des Kydias in Platons *Charmides*', *Philologus* 5: 737–9.

Herrmann, F.-G. (2018) 'Plato and Critias', in J. Yvonneau (ed.), *La Muse au long couteau. Critias, de la création littéraire au terrorisme de l'État*, Bordeaux: 83–116.

Hogan, R. A. (1976) 'Soul in the *Charmides*: An Examination of T.M. Robinson's Interpretation', *Philosophy Research Archives* 2: 635–45.

Hulme Kozey, E. (2018) *Philosophia and Philotechnia: The Technê Theme in the Platonic Dialogues*, PhD Dissertation, Princeton University.

(unpublished) 'The Interchangeability of Τέχνη and Ἐπιστήμη: Reflections on John Lyons' *Structural Semantics* Fifty Years Later'.

Hyland, D. A. (1981) *The Virtue of Philosophy: An Interpretation of Plato's Charmides*, Athens, OH.

Irwin, T. H. (1977) *Plato's Moral Theory: The Early and Middle Dialogues*, Oxford.

(1995) *Plato's Ethics*, Oxford.

Isnardi-Parente, M. (1966) *Techne: momenti del pensiero greco da Platone ad Epicuro*, Florence.

Jenks, R. (2008) *Plato on Moral Expertise*, Lanham, MD.

Joesse, A. (2018) '*Sôphrosunê* and the Poets: Rival Interpretations in Plato's *Charmides*', *Mnemosyne* 71: 574–92.

Johansen, T. K. (1997) *Aristotle on the Sense-Organs*, Cambridge.

(2005) 'In Defense of Inner Sense: Aristotle on Perceiving That One Sees', *Proceedings of the Boston Area Colloquium in Ancient Philosophy* 21: 235–76.

(2012) *The Powers of Aristotle's Soul*, Oxford.

(2021) *Productive Knowledge in Ancient Philosophy: The Concept of Technê*, Cambridge.

Jones, R. (2013) 'Wisdom and Happiness in *Euthydemus* 278–282', *Philosophers' Imprint* 13/14: 1–21.

Jowett, B. (transl.) (1961) '*Charmides*', in E. Hamilton and H. Cairns (eds.), *The Collected Dialogues of Plato*, Princeton, NJ: 99–122.

Kahn, C. (1966) 'Sensation and Consciousness in Aristotle's Psychology', *Archiv für Geschichte der Philosophie* 48: 43–81.

(1988) 'Plato's Charmides and the Proleptic Reading of Socratic Dialogues', *The Journal of Philosophy* 85/10: 541–9.

(1996) *Plato and the Socratic Dialogue: The Philosophical Use of a Literary Form*, Cambridge.

Kamtekar, R. (2017) 'Self-Knowledge in Plato', in U. Rentz (ed.), *Self-Knowledge: A History*, Oxford: 25–43.

Ketchum, R. J. (1991) 'Plato on the Uselessness of Epistemology: *Charmides* 166e–172a', *Apeiron* 24: 81–98.

Kirk, G. (2016) 'Self-Knowledge and Ignorance in Plato's *Charmides*', *Ancient Philosophy* 36: 303–20.

Kirwan, C. (1974) 'Plato and Relativity', *Phronesis* 19: 112–29.

Korobili, G. and Stefou, K. (in press) 'Plato's *Charmides* on Philosophy as Holistic Medical Practice', in Ch. Thumiger (ed.), *Ancient Holisms*, Leiden.

Kosman, A. (1975) 'Perceiving That We Perceive: *On the Soul* III.2', *Philosophical Review* 84: 499–519.

(1983) 'Charmides' First Definition: *Sophrosyne* as Quietness', in J. P. Anton and A. Preus (eds.), *Essays in Ancient Greek Philosophy*, Albany, NY: 203–16.

(2010) 'Beauty and the Good: Situating the *Kalon*', *Classical Philology* 105: 341–57.

(2014) 'Self-Knowledge and Self-Control in the *Charmides*', in *Virtues of Thought: Essays on Plato and Aristotle*, Cambridge, MA: 227–45.

Krentz, P. (1982) *The Thirty at Athens*, Ithaca, NY.

LaBarge, S. (1997) 'Socrates and the Recognition of Experts', *Apeiron* 30: 51–62.

Laín Entralgo, P. (1970) *The Therapy of the Word in Classical Antiquity*, edited and translated by L. J. Rather and J. M. Sharp, New Haven, CT and London.

Lamb, W. R. M. (1927) (Revised and reprinted 1955) *Plato: Charmides, Alcibiades I and II, Hipparchus, The Lovers. Theages, Minos, Epinomis*, Loeb Classical Library, vol. XII, Cambridge, MA.

(1955) *Plato: Charmides*. Loeb Classical Library, vol. XII, Cambridge, MA.

Lampert, L. (2010) *How Philosophy Became Socratic: A Study of Plato's Protagoras, Charmides, and Republic*, Chicago, IL.

Landy, T. (1998) 'Limitations of Political Philosophy: An Interpretation of Plato's *Charmides*', *Interpretation: A Journal of Political Philosophy* 26/2: 183–99.

Lane, M. S. (1998) *Method and Politics in Plato's Statesman*, Oxford.

Leigh, M. (2013) *From Polypragmon to Curiosus: Ancient Concepts of Curious and Meddlesome Behaviour*, Oxford.

Lesher, J. H. (1987) 'Socrates' Disavowal of Knowledge', *Journal of the History of Philosophy* 25: 275–88.

Levin, S. B. (2014) *Plato's Rivalry with Medicine: A Struggle and its Dissolution*, Oxford.

Levine, D. L. (1976) *Plato's Charmides*. PhD Dissertation, Pennsylvania State University.

(1984) 'The Tyranny of Scholarship', *Ancient Philosophy* 4: 65–72.

(2016) *Profound Ignorance: Plato's Charmides and the Saving of Wisdom*, Lanham, MD.

Lewis, S. (ed.) (2006) *Ancient Tyranny*, Edinburgh.

Linforth, I. M. (1918) 'ΟΊ ΑΘΑΝΑΤΊΖΟΝΤΕΣ', *Classical Philology* 13: 23–33.

Lloyd, G. E. R. (1987) *The Revolutions of Wisdom: Studies in the Claims and Practice of Ancient Greek Science*, Berkeley, CA.

Luckhurst, K. W. (1934) 'Note on Plato's *Charmides* 153b', *Classical Review* 48: 207–8.

Lutoslawski, W. (1897) *The Origin and Growth of Plato's Logic, with an Account of Plato's Style and of the Chronology of His Writings*, London/New York/Bombay.

Mahoney, T. A. (1996) 'The *Charmides*: Socratic *Sôphrosynê*, Human *Sôphrosynê*', *The Southern Journal of Philosophy* 34: 183–99.

Mansfeld, J. (1980) 'Plato and the Method of Hippocrates', *Greek, Roman and Byzantine Studies* 21: 341–62.

Marmodoro, A. and Yates, D. (2016) 'The Metaphysics of Relations', in A. Marmodoro and D. Yates (eds.), *The Metaphysics of Relations*, Oxford: 1–18.

Martens, E. (1973) *Das selbstbezügliche Wissen in Platons Charmides*, Munich.

Matthen, M. (1982) 'Plato's Treatment of Relational Statements in the *Phaedo*', *Phronesis* 27: 90–100.

(1984) 'Relationality in Plato's Metaphysics: Reply to McPherran', *Phronesis* 29/3: 304–12.

Matthews, G. B. (1999) *Socratic Perplexity and the Nature of Philosophy*, Oxford.

McAvoy, M. (1996) 'Carnal Knowledge in the *Charmides*', *Apeiron* 24: 63–103.

McCabe, M. M. (2000) *Plato and His Predecessors: The Dramatization of Reason*, Cambridge.

(2007a) 'Looking Inside Charmides' Cloak: Seeing Others and Oneself in Plato's *Charmides*', in D. Scott (ed.), *Maieusis: Essays in Ancient Philosophy in Honour of Myles Burnyeat*, Oxford: 1–19.

(2007b) 'Perceiving That We See and Hear: Aristotle on Plato on Judgement and Reflection', in M. M. McCabe and M. Textor (eds.), *Perspectives on Perception: Philosophische Forschung*, Frankfurt am Main: 143–77.

(2011) '"It Goes Deep with Me"? Plato's *Charmides* on Knowledge, Self-Knowledge, and Integrity', in C. Cordner and R. Gaita (eds.), *Philosophy, Ethics, and a Common Humanity: Essays in Honour of Raimond Gaita*, London/New York: 161–80.

McCoy, M. B. (2005) 'Philosophy, Elenchus, and Charmides' Definitions of σωφροσύνη', *Arethusa* 35: 133–59.

McKim, R. (1985) 'Socratic Self-Knowledge and "Knowledge of Knowledge" in Plato's *Charmides*', *Transactions of the American Philological Association* 115: 59–77.

McPherran, M. (2002) 'Elenctic Interpretation and the Delphic Oracle', in G. A. Scott (ed.), *Does Socrates Have a Method?*, University Park, PA: 114–44.

(2004) 'Socrates and Zalmoxis on Drugs, Charms, and Purification', *Apeiron* 37: 11–33.

Mignucci, M. (1986) 'Aristotle's Definitions of Relatives in *Cat. 7*.' *Phronesis* 31/2: 101–27.

(1988a) 'Platone e Relativi', *Elenchos* 9: 259–94.

(1988b) 'The Stoic Notion of Relatives', in J. Barnes and M. Mignucci, *Matter and Metaphysics: Proceedings of the Fourth Symposium Hellenisticum*, Naples: 129–221.

Moore, C. (2015) *Socrates and Self-Knowledge*, Cambridge.

Moore, C. and Raymond, C. C. (2019) *Plato: Charmides. Translated with Introduction, Notes, and Analysis*, Indianapolis, IN.

Morris, T. F. (1989) 'Knowledge of Knowledge and of the Lack of Knowledge in the *Charmides*', *International Studies in Philosophy* 21: 49–61.

Murphy, D. J. (1990) 'The Manuscripts of Plato's *Charmides*', *Mnemosyne* 43: 316–40.

(2000) 'Doctors of Zalmoxis and Immortality in the *Charmides*', in T. M. Robinson and L. Brisson (eds.), *Plato: Euthydemus, Lysis, Charmides: Proceedings of the V Symposium Platonicum, Selected Papers*, IPS Series vol. 13, Sankt Augustin: 287–95.

(2002) 'The Basis of the Text of Plato's *Charmides*', *Mnemosyne* 55: 131–58.

(2007) 'Critical Notes on Plato's *Charmides*', *Mnemosyne* 60: 213–34.

(2014) 'More Critical Notes on Plato's *Charmides*', *Mnemosyne* 67: 999–1007.

Nails, D. (2002) *The People of Plato: A Prosopography of Plato and the Other Socratics*, Indianapolis, IN.

Nehamas, A. (1975) 'Confusing Universals and Particulars in Plato's Early Dialogues', *The Review of Metaphysics* 29/2: 287–306.

(1984) '*Epistême* and *Logos* in Plato's Later Thought', *Archiv für Geschichte der Philosophie* 66/1: 11–36.

(1986) 'Socratic Intellectualism', *Proceedings of the Boston Area Colloquium in Ancient Philosophy* 2: 274–316.

(2007) 'Beauty of Body, Nobility of Soul: The Pursuit of Love in Plato's Symposium', in D. Scott (ed.), *Maieusis: Essays in Ancient Philosophy in Honour of Myles Burnyeat*, Oxford: 97–135.

Nehamas, A. and Woodruff, P. (trans.) (1989) *Plato's Symposium*, Indianapolis, IN.

North, H. (1966) *Sophrosyne: Self-Knowledge and Self-Restraint in Greek Literature*, Ithaca, NY.

Notomi, N. (2000) 'Critias and the Origin of Plato's Political Philosophy', in T. M. Robinson and L. Brisson (eds.), *Plato: Euthydemus, Lysis, Charmides: Proceedings of the V Symposium Platonicum, Selected Papers*, IPS Series vol. 13, Sankt Augustin: 237–50.

(2003) 'Ethical Examination in Context: The Criticism of Critias in Plato's *Charmides*', in M. Migliori and L. M. Napolitano Valditara (eds.), *Plato Ethicus: Philosophy Is Life, Proceedings of the International Colloquium*, Piacenza: 245–54.

Nussbaum, M. (1986) *The Fragility of Goodness: Luck and Ethics in Greek Tragedy and Philosophy*, Cambridge.

Obbink, D. (1996) *Philodemus on Piety. Part 1: Critical Text with Commentary*, Oxford.

Osborne, C. (1983) 'Aristotle, *De anima* 3.2: How Do We Perceive That We See and Hear?', *Classical Quarterly* 33: 401–11.

Papamanoli, K. (unpublished) '*Charmides* 154c–157d'.

Penner, T. (1992) 'Socrates and the Early Dialogues', in R. Kraut (ed.), *The Cambridge Companion to Plato*, Cambridge: 121–69.

Pichanick, A. (2005) 'Two Rival Conceptions of *Sôphrosunê*', *Polis* 22/2: 249–64.

Planeaux, C. (1999) 'Socrates, Alcibiades, and Plato's τὰ Ποτειδεατικά: Does the *Charmides* Have a Historical Setting?', *Mnemosyne* 52: 72–7.

Politis, V. (2006) '*Aporia* and Searching in the Early Plato', in L. Judson and V. Karasmanis (eds.), *Remembering Socrates: Philosophical Essays*, Oxford: 88–109.

(2007) 'The Aporia in the *Charmides* about Reflexive Knowledge and the Contribution to Its Solution in the Sun Analogy of the *Republic*', in D. Cairns, F.-G. Herrmann, and T. Penner (eds.), *Pursuing the Good: Ethics and Metaphysics in Plato's Republic*, Edinburgh: 231–50.

(2008) 'The Place of *Aporia* in Plato's *Charmides*', *Phronesis* 53: 1–34.

Press, G. A. (2002) 'The *Elenchos* in the *Charmides*, 162–175', in G. A. Scott (ed.), *Does Socrates Have a Method? Rethinking the Elenchus in Plato's Dialogues and Beyond*, University Park, PA: 252–65.

Rademaker, A. (2005) *Sophrosyne and the Rhetoric of Self-Restraint: Polysemy and Persuasive Use of an Ancient Value Term*, Leiden.

Rangos, S. I. (2019) Θαυμάζειν, Ἀπορεῖν, Φιλοσοφεῖν. Η αρχή της φιλοσοφίας και η φιλοσοφία ως αρχή στην κλασική εποχή, Athens (Greece).

Raymond, C. (2018) 'Αἰδώς in Plato's *Charmides*', *Ancient Philosophy* 38: 23–46.

Reale, G. (2015) *Platone. Carmide, sulla temperanza*, Milan.

Redfield, J. (2011) 'Socrates' Thracian Incantation', in Y. Volokhine and F. Prescendi Morresi (eds.), *Dans le laboratoire de l'historien des religions. Mélanges offerts à Philippe Borgeaud*, Geneva: 358–74.

Reece, A. (1998) 'Drama, Narrative, and Socratic Eros in Plato's *Charmides*', *Interpretation: A Journal of Political Philosophy* 26/1: 65–76.

Robinson, R. (1962) *Plato's Earlier Dialectic*, 2nd ed., Oxford.

Robinson, T. M. (1970) *Plato's Psychology*, Toronto.

Robinson, T. M. and Brisson, L. (eds.) (2000) *Plato: Euthydemus, Lysis, Charmides: Proceedings of the V Symposium Platonicum, Selected Papers*, IPS Series vol. 13, Sankt Augustin.

Roochnik, D. L. (1986) 'Socrates' Use of the *Technê* Analogy', *Journal of the History of Philosophy* 24: 295–310.

(1996) *Of Art and Wisdom: Plato's Understanding of Technê*, University Park, PA.

Rosenmayer, T. G. (1957) 'Plato on Mass Words', *Transactions of the American Philological Association* 88: 88–102.

Rotondaro, S. (1998) *Il sogno in Platone: fisiologia di una metafora*, Naples.

(2000) 'Strutture narrative e argomentative del *Carmide*', in G. Casertano (ed.), *La struttura del dialogo platonico*, Naples: 213–24.

Rowe, C. J. (1998) 'Review of M.-F. Hazebroucq 1997', *Phronesis* 43: 87–8.

(2007) *Plato and the Art of Philosophical Writing*, Cambridge.

(in press) 'Knowledge and Power in Plato's *Charmides*', in Yasunori Kasai and Noburu Notomi (eds.), *Essays in Honour of Masaaki Kubo*.

Russell, B. (1938) *The Principles of Mathematics*, 2nd ed., New York.

(1946) *History of Western Philosophy*, London.

Rutherford, R. (1995) *The Art of Plato: Ten Essays in Platonic Interpretation*, Cambridge, MA.

Santas, J. (1973) 'Socrates at Work on Virtue and Knowledge in Plato's *Charmides*', in E. N. Lee, A. P. D. Mourelatos, and R. M. Rorty (eds.), *Exegesis and Argument*, New York: 105–32.

Saunders, T. J. (ed.) (1987) *Early Socratic Dialogues: Ion, Laches, Lysis, Charmides, Hippias Major, Hippias Minor, with Some Fragments of Aeschines of Sphettus*, Harmondsworth.

Scaltsas, Th. (2016) 'Relations as Plural Predications in Plato', in A. Marmodoro and D. Yates (eds.), *The Metaphysics of Relations*, Oxford: 19–34.

Schaffer, J. (2010) 'The Internal Relatedness of All Things', *Mind* 119/474: 341–76.

Schamp, J. (2000) 'L'homme sans visage: pour une lecture politique du *Charmide*', *L'Antiquité Classique* 69: 103–16.

Scheibe, E. (1967) 'Über Relativbegriffe in der Philosophie Platons', *Phronesis* 12: 28–49.

Schirlitz, C. (1897) 'Der Begriff des Wissens vom Wissen in Platons *Charmides* und seine Bedeutung für das Ergebnis des Dialogs', *Jahrbücher für classische Philologie* 43: 513–37.

Schleiermacher, F. (1818) *Platons Werke*, Berlin.

Schmid, W. T. (1998) *Plato's Charmides and the Socratic Ideal of Rationality*, Albany, NY.

Schnieder, B., Steinberg, A. and Hoeltje, M. (eds.) (2013) *Varieties of Dependence: Ontological Dependence, Supervenience, and Response-Dependence*, Munich.

Schofield, M. (1973) 'Socrates on Conversing with Doctors', *Classical Review* 23: 121–3.

(2006) *Plato: Political Philosophy*, Oxford.

Scott, D. (ed.) (2007) *Maieusis: Essays in Ancient Philosophy in Honour of Myles Burnyeat*, Oxford.

Searle, J. (1982) *Intentionality*, Cambridge.

Sedley, D. (2002) 'Aristotelian Relativities', in M. Canto-Sperber and P. Pellegrin (eds.), *Le Style de La Pensée: Receuil de Textes En Hommage à Jacques Brunschwig*, Paris: 324–52.

(2003) *Plato's Cratylus*, Cambridge.

(2004) *The Midwife of Platonism: Text and Subtext in Plato's Theaetetus*, Oxford.

(2013) 'The Atheist Underground', in V. Harte and M. Lane (eds.), *Politeia in Greek and Roman Philosophy*, Cambridge: 329–48.

(2019) 'The *Timaeus* as Vehicle for Platonic Doctrine', *Oxford Studies in Ancient Philosophy* 56: 45–72.

(2020) 'Plato's Self-References', in B. Bossi and T. M. Robinson (eds.), *Plato's Theaetetus Revisited*, Berlin/Boston, MA: 3–9.

Shapiro, H. A. (1986) 'The Attic Deity Basile', *Zeitschrift für Papyrologie und Epigraphik* 63: 134–6.

Shorey, P. (1903) *The Unity of Plato's Thought*, Chicago, IL.

(1907) 'Emendation of *Charmides* 168b', *Classical Philology* 2/3: 340.

(1933) *What Plato Said*, Chicago, IL. (7th impression: 1968.)

Sisko, J. E. (2004) 'Reflexive Awareness Does Belong to the Main Function of Perception: Reply to Caston', *Mind* 113: 513–22.

Slings, S. R. (1988) 'Review of Van der Ben 1985', *Mnemosyne* 41: 409–14.

Solère-Queval, S. (1993) 'Lecture du *Charmide*', *Revue de Philosophie Ancienne* 11: 3–65.

Sprague, R. K. (1973) *Plato: Laches and Charmides*, New York.

(1993) *Plato: Laches and Charmides*, Indianapolis, IN.

(1997), 'Charmides', in J. M. Cooper (ed.), *Plato: Complete Works*, Indianapolis, IN: 639–63.

Stallbaum, G. (1834) *Platonis Opera*, vol. 5, sect. 1, Leipzig.

Stalley, R. F. (2000) '*Sôphrosynê* in the *Charmides*', in T. M. Robinson and L. Brisson (eds.), *Plato: Euthydemus, Lysis, Charmides: Proceedings of the V Symposium Platonicum, Selected Papers*, IPS Series vol. 13, Sankt Augustin: 265–77.

Steiner, P. M. (1992) *Psyche bei Platon*, Göttingen.

Stenzel, J. (1917) *Studien zur Entwicklung der Platonischen Dialektik von Sokrates zu Aristoteles*, Breslau.

(1940) *Plato's Method of Dialectic*, New York.

Stern, P. (1999) 'Tyranny and Self-Knowledge: Critias and Socrates in Plato's *Charmides*', *American Political Science Review* 93: 399–412.

Sue, Y.-S. (2006) *Selbsterkenntnis im Charmides*, Würzburg.

Sutton, D. (1981) 'Critias and Atheism', *Classical Quarterly* 31: 33–8.

Tarrant, H. (2000) 'Naming Socratic Interrogation in the *Charmides*', in T. M. Robinson and L. Brisson (eds.), *Plato: Euthydemus, Lysis, Charmides: Proceedings of the V Symposium Platonicum, Selected Papers*, IPS Series vol. 13, Sankt Augustin: 251–8.

Tarski, A. (1941) 'On the Calculus of Relations', *The Journal of Symbolic Logic* 6/3: 73–89.

Taylor, A. E. (1926) *Plato: The Man and His Work*, London.

Taylor, C. C. W. (1972) 'Review of Witte 1970', *The Classical Review* NS 22/2: 196–8.

Thesleff, H. (1993) 'Looking for Clues: An Interpretation of Some Literary Aspects of Plato's Two-Level Model', in G. Press (ed.), *Plato's Dialogues*, Lanham, MD: 17–45.

Thom, P. (1977) '*Termini Obliqui* and the Logic of Relations', *Archiv für Geschichte der Philosophie* 59/2: 143–55.

Tigner, S. S. (1970) 'Plato's Philosophical Uses of the Dream Metaphor', *American Journal of Philology* 91: 204–12.

Tsouna, V. (1998) 'Socrates' Attack on Intellectualism in the *Charmides*', *Apeiron* 30: 63–78.

(2000) 'Interprétations socratiques de la connaissance de soi', *Philosophie antique* 1: 37–64.

(2012) 'Is There an Answer to Socrates' Puzzle? Individuality, Universality, and the Self in Plato's *Phaedrus*', *Philosophie antique* 13: 199–235.

(2015) 'Plato's Representations of the "Socratics"', in U. Zilioli (ed.), *From Socrates to the Socratic Schools*, New York/London: 1–25.

(2017) 'What Is the Subject of Plato's *Charmides*?', in Y. Z. Liebersohn, L. Ludlam, and A. Edelheit (eds.), *For A Skeptical Peripatetic: Studies in Honour of John Glucker*, Sankt Augustin: 33–62.

(in press) 'Aristotle and Plato on Reflexivity in Perception'.

Tuckey, T. G. (1951) *Plato's Charmides*, Cambridge.

Tulli, M. (2000) 'Carmide fra poesia e ricerca', in T. M. Robinson and L. Brisson (eds.), *Plato: Euthydemus, Lysis, Charmides: Proceedings of the V Symposium Platonicum, Selected Papers*, IPS Series vol. 13, Sankt Augustin: 259–64.

Tuozzo, T. M. (2000) 'Greetings from Apollo: *Charmides* 164c–165b, *Epistle* III, and the Structure of the *Charmides*', in T. M. Robinson and L. Brisson (eds.), *Plato: Euthydemus, Lysis, Charmides: Proceedings of the V Symposium Platonicum, Selected Papers*, IPS Series vol. 13, Sankt Augustin: 295–305.

(2001) 'What's Wrong with these Cities? The Social Dimension of *Sophrosyne* in Plato's *Charmides*', *Journal of the History of Philosophy* 39: 321–50.

(2011) *Plato's Charmides: Positive Elenchus in a 'Socratic' Dialogue*, Cambridge.

Van der Ben, N. (1985) *The Charmides of Plato: Problems and Interpretations*, Amsterdam.

Vlastos, G. (1978) 'The Virtuous and the Happy', *Times Literary Supplement*, 24 February: 230–3.

(1983) 'The Socratic Elenchus', *Oxford Studies in Ancient Philosophy* 1: 27–58.

(1991) *Socrates: Ironist and Moral Philosopher*, Ithaca, NY.

(1994) 'The Socratic Elenchus: Method Is All', in G. Vlastos, *Socratic Studies*, edited by M. F. Burnyeat, Cambridge: 1–37.

Vorwerk, M. (2001) 'Plato on Virtue: Definitions of *Sôphrosynê* in Plato's *Charmides* and in Plotinus *Enneads* 1.2', *American Journal of Philology* 122/1: 29–47.

Wallace, J. (1972) 'Positive, Comparative, Superlative', *The Journal of Philosophy* 69: 773–82.

Wallace, R. W. (1992) 'Charmides, Agariste and Damon: Andokides 1.16', *Classical Quarterly* NS 42: 328–35.

Wellman, R. (1964) 'The Question Posed in *Charmides* 165a–166c', *Phronesis* 9: 107–13.

Williams, B. A. O. (1993) *Shame and Necessity*, Sather Classical Lectures, Berkeley / Los Angeles / London.

Williamson, T. (1985) 'Converse Relations', *The Philosophical Review* 94/2: 249–62.

Witte, B. (1970) *Die Wissenschaft vom Guten und Bösen. Interpretationen zu Platons Charmides*, Berlin.

Wolfsdorf, D. (2004) 'Interpreting Plato's Early Dialogues', *Oxford Studies in Ancient Philosophy* 27: 15–41.

(2008) *Trials of Reason: Plato and the Crafting of Philosophy*, Oxford.

Woodruff, P. (1987) 'Expert Knowledge in the *Apology* and the *Laches*: What a General Should Know', *Proceedings of the Boston Area Colloquium in Ancient Philosophy* 3: 79–115.

(1992) 'Plato's Early Theory of Knowledge', in H. Benson (ed.), *Essays on the Philosophy of Socrates*, Oxford: 86–106.

Woolf, R. (unpublished) 'Where Did the Love Go? Eros in Plato's *Charmides*'.

Index

For EU product safety concerns, contact us at Calle de José Abascal, 56–1°, 28003 Madrid, Spain or eugpsr@cambridge.org.

www.ingramcontent.com/pod-product-compliance
Ingram Content Group UK Ltd.
Pitfield, Milton Keynes, MK11 3LW, UK
UKHW020401140625
459647UK00020B/2589